OTHER TITLES BY ALICE C. FLETCHER
AVAILABLE IN BISON BOOKS EDITIONS

Indian Games and Dances with Native Songs
Arranged from American Indian Ceremonies and Sports

Indian Story and Song from North America

The Omaha Tribe (with Francis La Flesche)

A Study of Omaha Indian Music (with Francis La Flesche)

THE HAKO

Song, Pipe, and Unity
in a Pawnee Calumet Ceremony

ALICE C. FLETCHER

ASSISTED BY JAMES R. MURIE

MUSIC TRANSCRIBED BY EDWIN S. TRACY

Introduction to the Bison Books Edition
by Helen Myers

University of Nebraska Press
Lincoln and London

Introduction to the Bison Books Edition © 1996 by the University of
Nebraska Press
Manufactured in the United States of America

⊗ The paper in this book meets the minimum requirements of American
National Standard for Information Sciences—Permanence of Paper for
Printed Library Materials, ANSI Z39.48-1984.

First Bison Books printing: 1996
Most recent printing indicated by the last digit below:
10   9   8   7   6   5   4   3   2   1

Library of Congress Cataloging-in-Publication Data
Fletcher, Alice C. (Alice Cunningham), 1838–1923.
The hako: song, pipe, and unity in a Pawnee Calumet ceremony / Alice C.
Fletcher assisted by James R. Murie; music transcribed by Edwin S.
Tracy; introduction to the Bison books edition by Helen Myers.
p.   cm.
"Reprinted from the Twenty-second annual report of the Bureau of
American Ethnology . . . published by the Government Printing Office,
Washington, D.C., 1904"—T.p. verso.
Includes bibliographical references and index.
ISBN 0-8032-6889-0 (pbk.: alk. paper)
1. Hako (Pawnee rite)   2. Pawnee Indians—Rites and ceremonies.
3. Pawnee Indians—Religion.   4. Pawnee Indians—Music.   5. Calu-
mets—Nebraska.   I. Murie, James R.
E99.P3F6   1997
299'.74—dc20
96-34257   CIP

Reprinted from the Twenty-second Annual Report of the Bureau of
American Ethnology to the Secretary of the Smithsonian Institution
published by the Government Printing Office, Washington, D.C., 1904.
Originally published as *The Hako: A Pawnee Ceremony*.

CONTENTS

ILLUSTRATIONS

INTRODUCTION TO THE BISON BOOKS EDITION

Helen Myers
aided by Elsie Myers-Stainton

The great changes in practically every phase of the Indian's life that have taken place, especially within recent years, have been such that had the time for collecting much of the material . . . herein recorded, been delayed, it would have been lost forever. The passing of every old man or woman means the passing of some tradition, some knowledge of sacred rites possessed by no other; consequently the information that is to be gathered, for the benefit of future generations, respecting the mode of life of one of the great races of mankind, must be collected at once or the opportunity will be lost for all time.

Edward S. Curtis, *The North American Indian*, 1907

Tahirŭssawichi remembered well the sacred ceremony. Tahirŭssawichi fiercely cherished his memory of the ancient rites, for during many years of his long life he had been guardian of the sacred articles: the eagle feathers and buffalo robe; the sticks, the corn, the gourds, and wildcat skin; the pipes.

The Indian Priest

A suitable way of life was required of such a guardian, not by any means for his comfort or pleasure. He had said: "I can not live in a white man's house of any kind. The sacred articles committed to my care must be kept in an earth lodge, and in order that I may fulfill my duties toward them and my people, I must live there also, so that as I sit I can stretch out my hand and lay it on Mother Earth" (see p. 14).

Yet he grew old, his earth home crumbled, and venerable tribal customs continued to vanish as an increasingly restrictive U.S. government encroached upon the traditional Native American ways.

But when the opportunity came to preserve the rites for perhaps all time, Tahirŭssawichi hesitated, as tradition had required that the secrets of ancient ceremonies be passed only to his own people. Should he reveal these mysteries, even for their preservation and continuance, to a white person, to a white woman?

The Ethnologist

Alice Cunningham Fletcher, during her researches among the Omahas, had observed some parts of the Calumet, or Peace Pipe, or as the Pawnees called it, the Hako ceremony. But after the death of the only Omaha who knew the formulas, she searched for fifteen years before hearing about an elderly Pawnee, highly regarded in his tribe as guardian of the sacred articles and leader of the rites. He had served in an official capacity when his people took the Hako ceremony to the Omahas, and he thus became acquainted with the very Omaha leaders who, along with Fletcher's friend and collaborator, the Omaha Francis La Flesche, were able to vouch for her sincerity, knowledge, and trustworthiness.

James R. Murie, an educated Pawnee and long-time friend of La Flesche, also helped to reassure the Pawnee priest and the elders of his tribe. Murie then became Fletcher's collaborator on the project of recording and preserving the Hako ceremony. His ease in the language and culture of his ancestors made possible the elaborate translation, transcription, and analysis as it was spelled out by Tahirŭssawichi.

Fletcher found her Pawnee informant to be "possessed of a tenacious memory" (p. 14), and through four years of work together in Washington at the Pawnee Reservation, and with Murie as go-between, produced the present book, here reprinted. It is surely the most detailed and authoritative record of a Native American Indian ceremony ever presented.

Fletcher provides the words as sung, translations of the words and some comments on the euphony of the syllables, musical transcriptions, explanations of the powers evoked along with the expected blessings, and a guide to the elaborate symbolism embodied in all the objects, sound, and movement of the ceremony.

As the sequences of the ritual unfold and the actors and objects take their places, there is revealed on this stage a drama of heroic dimensions, teaching the young and reminding the old of a time-honored perspective—how American Indians perceived their place on the earth, their relation to their fellows and to the powers of the universe.

To break with tradition in order to preserve tradition was the old priest's dilemma. To present in a book the living spirit of an oral tradition was Alice Fletcher's task. In order to accomplish this, she endeavored to catch every nuance of gesture and voice in 372 pages. *The Hako*, published in 1904 as part 2 of the Twenty-second Annual Report of the Bureau of American Ethnology to the Secretary of the Smithsonian Institution, is her legacy.

Purpose of the Hako Ceremony

The Pawnee priest explained the overarching purpose of the ritual as follows: "The ceremony of the Hako is a prayer for children, in order that the tribe may increase and be strong; and also that the people may have long life, enjoy plenty, and be happy and at peace" (p. 26). But in time, the purpose expanded from the welfare of children to establishing a bond of friendship between groups or tribes to bring peace between them, "from the simple longing for offspring to the larger desire of establishing intertribal relationships" and "an appreciation of the benefits to be derived from peace and security" (p. 280).

Children took part in the ceremony, and at certain points a particular child might become the focus of the blessing.

The timing of the Hako was to reflect its purpose: "We take up the Hako in the spring when the birds are mating, or in the summer when the birds are nesting and caring for their young, or in the fall when the birds are flocking, but not in the winter when all things are asleep. With the Hako we are praying for the gift of life, of strength, of plenty, and of peace, so we must pray when life is stirring everywhere" (pp. 23–24). Natural phenomena reinforce the power and solemnity of the ceremony: dawn, sunset, stars, a ray of the sun, are significant.

The full ceremony took as many as five days. Sometimes travel of the Hako party from tribe to tribe became part of the ritual. Some of the songs originally were sung on the journey from tribe to tribe— songs mentioning buffalo, the mountains, or the mesas—but in the old priest's time they were sung mainly in the lodge.

The Sacred Articles

The articles used in the ceremony were renewed as necessary. They were always revered and handled carefully as they were passed from person to person in the ceremony or from tribe to tribe on tour. Fletcher says: "During the entire time that I was engaged with Tahirŭssawichi on this ceremony he never allowed the feathered stems to be placed on the floor or laid on a chair; they were always carefully deposited on the wildcat skin with a decorum that was not once abated" (p. 21).

Since two pipes are essential features of the Hako, they are minutely prepared. First two pipestems are made from ash sticks cut to the length of "four spans from the thumb to the third finger." The pith is removed; "the boring used to be done with a reed, but now the pith is burned out with a wire" (p. 35). After much other preparation, a woodpecker's head is attached near the mouthpiece and the other end of the stick thrust through a duck's body with just enough stem protruding for the bowl of a pipe to be attached. About the middle of the stem are attached feathers from an owl. "All the birds on the stems are leaders," the Pawnee said; "the eagle is chief of the day; the owl is chief of the night; the woodpecker is chief of the trees; the duck is chief of the water" (p. 40).

Then ten feathers from the tail of a brown eagle are fastened to one of the stems, and to two thongs "are fastened little balls of white down, taken from inside the thigh of the white male eagle. These balls of down represent the reproductive power," so Tahirŭssawichi explained (p. 41), and this pipe stands for the female. During the ceremony, the feathers swing as the stem is waved to simulate the movements of an eagle. To the other stem are attached seven tail feathers from what the priest calls a male white eagle, actually, Fletcher says, a young brown eagle. This pipe stands for the male, which must protect the female.

Symbolism

Powerful symbolism accrues to each item used in preparing the pipes. The priest tells that the singers during the decoration request that "life be breathed into the symbol, that it may have power as we use these sacred articles" (p. 40).

Fletcher says that the offering of smoke was considered "the closest and most sacred form of direct communication with the great unseen power" (p. 336). The Pawnee said: "In old times men did not smoke for pleasure as they do now, but only in religious ceremonies. The white people have taught the Pawnees to profane the use of tobacco" (p. 48).

Elements in the Hako ceremony underscore the Pawnee view that unseen powers rested in natural objects, and humankind's dependence on the supernatural was obvious.

Instruments

The Pawnees used only three instruments to accompany their singing, but these rattles, drums, and whistles could produce powerful sound. Two large gourds filled with stones as rattles were decorated during part of the ceremony. Their peculiar drums, Fletcher says, "are made of the section of a tree hollowed out by fire, over the open end of which a skin has been stretched and securely tied" (p. 247). A realistic whistle made from the wing bone of the eagle was used to accompany songs that mentioned the screams of the eagle.

The Transcriptions

Fletcher made graphophone cylinder recordings of all the songs, the transcriptions of 102 of which are included here. Her early collaborator, John Comfort Fillmore, who had transcribed and harmonized for piano her earlier notations (See *A Study of Omaha Indian Music*), died in 1898. In the present book on the Hako ceremony, Fletcher abandoned Fillmore's ill-starred effort at harmonization and concentrated on the word syllables and the vocal line. The musical scores are presented as "transcribed by Edwin S. Tracy," a task that proved more reasonable and successful.

Tracy (1875–1961), a pianist, composer, and arranger, was musical director of the Morris High School in New York City when he worked on the transcriptions for *The Hako*. Fletcher says he was well acquainted with Native American songs after several years of first-hand research.

Whereas Fillmore had distrusted the phonograph, Tracy transcribed all the Hako songs from cylinder recordings. And whereas Fillmore had taken liberties with the Omaha music in attempting to impose a "harmony" upon the Indian songs, Tracy permitted the simple vocal line to assert itself. And while Fillmore had tried to assign rigid meter signatures to the Indian rhythms, regardless of distortion, Tracy used mixed meters to represent the asymmetrical rhythms he heard in these songs.

When, in 1893, Fletcher permitted her Omaha notations to be transcribed (and "harmonized") for piano, she remarked that Indian singing did not lend itself to any scale and that a violin could better have sounded the chromatics, tremulo, and slurs of the Indian voices. In 1900 she again used transcriptions for piano in *Indian Story and Song from North America*. By 1904, when *The Hako* appeared, she had abandoned piano harmonizations, and with Tracy's help gave just the simple vocal line. So also in 1915, she used just the vocal line in *Indian Games and Dances with Native Songs*, subtitled *Arranged from American Indian Ceremonials and Sports*. Thus in her later writings Fletcher abandoned the idea that Indian melodies implied harmonies that could be supplied by musically trained Westerners, along with this idea's evolutionistic implications that Indian music was a simple precursor to a more sophisticated Western system of harmony. She made a silent but significant retreat from the theory of latent harmony.

Tracy used the conventional five-line treble-clef staff with key and time signatures and metronome markings. He introduced dots below notes to indicate "pulsation of the voice."

He called for instrumentation as follows: "Drum" or "No drum"; "Rattles"; "Drum" and "Rattles"; or "Drum," "Rattles," and "Whistle."

Notes are given for the drumbeats with the accents indicated, and quavers for the rattles and whistles. Different time signatures and tempos are indicated for the vocal and instrumental parts.

Fletcher says that, although Tracy was knowledgeable about the songs he was transcribing, "the exactions of Mr. Tracy's professional work in the field of music make it impossible for him to prepare an essay upon the character of these songs" (p. 16). Like Fletcher, we regret this loss, and wonder why Tracy declined to reveal his thoughts. Was he aiming to avoid controversy at a time when conflicting theories were being put forward about Native American music? Franz Boas had praised Fillmore's work, while Benjamin Ives Gilman was ridiculing Fillmore's use of Western notation.

Ethomusicologists today could feel more comfortable with Tracy's than with Fillmore's transcriptions, but if we add normal accents on beat 1 in 2/4 or 3/4 time and one beats 1 and 3 in 4/4 time, these transcriptions would sound more like piano accompaniment for silent western films than Indian ceremonial songs. Despite his efforts there is still an implication of Western tonality in Tracy's transcriptions: for example a key signature of B♭ (F major or D minor) in a song that has no B.

In her "Analytical Recapitulation," which comprises the last sections of *The Hako*, Fletcher breaks with traditional transcription. She provides numerous "Diagrams of Time." These time lines, a sensational departure from conventional notation, give a convenient assist to the reader.

Vocal Technique

Vocal technique among the Pawnees followed the Plains Indian style, characterized by considerable tension in the vocal organs and sustained throughout. The singers used strong accents, glissandos, and ornamentation, as well as pulsation of the voice on longer tones.

Fletcher's Final Word

Fletcher outlines an Omaha ceremony of the Pipes, or Wa-wan as they call it, in *A Study of Omaha Indian Music*. She says of this tribe's ritual that the two pipes, "ceremonially made, with secret ritual, are not used for smoking, have no bowl" (p. 35). But other features are similar to those described in *The Hako* (eagle feathers, wildcat skin, gourd rattles, and whistle), and the symbolism points to an identical message—reverence and hope for peace and fellowship. In her Omaha account she comments about the Pawnee music for their ceremony: "The Wa-wan music of this tribe is good and often quite spirited" (p. 40); she adds: "Among the Pawnees it is the custom to explain many of the songs, that they may be more heartily enjoyed" (p. 38). In *The Hako* she explains in detail—for our heartfelt enjoyment.

Fletcher sums up: "The Hako ceremony seems to have been peculiarly adapted to impress the mind of the people and to win their confidence and affection. It was picturesque, varied in movement, and communal in feeling. Its songs were rhythmic and attractive, and frequently choral in form, particularly those belonging to the public ceremony, where all, young and old, joined in the melody as feathered stems were swayed over their heads" (p. 362).

The Pawnee Priest's Credo

Tahirŭssawichi reflects upon his role: "I think over my long life with its many experiences; of the great number of Pawnees who have been with me in war, nearly all of whom have been killed in battle. . . . I was with those who went to the Rocky Mountains to the Cheyennes, when so many soldiers were slain that their dead bodies lying there looked like a great blue blanket spread over the ground. When I think of all the people of my own tribe who have died during my lifetime and then of those in other tribes that have fallen by our hands, they are so many they make a vast cover over Mother Earth. I once walked with these prostrate forms. I did not fall but I passed on, wounded sometimes but not to death, until I am here to-day doing this thing, singing these sacred songs into that great pipe (the graphophone) and telling you of these ancient rites of my people. It must be that I have been preserved for this purpose, otherwise I should be lying back there among the dead" (p. 278).

The Life of Alice Fletcher

Alice Cunningham Fletcher was born in 1838 in Cuba, where her parents had gone in hope of benefiting her father's health. The young Miss Fletcher attended exclusive schools, traveled in Europe, and taught at several private schools. With a pleasing voice and attractive manner, she became successful on the lecture circuits and thereby supported herself. While preparing lectures on ancient Americans, she met Frederick W. Putnam, director of the Peabody Museum at Harvard, who encouraged her to continue anthropological study and stressed a scientific approach to her work. For a time she was an assistant at the Museum.

Fletcher was one of the first American anthropologists to pay attention to Native American music. And she learned to listen with a

sympathetic ear to what many people called wild, aboriginal, un-
pleasant sounds. Her rapport with the American Indian psyche and
stance in the world was all the more remarkable in a woman of her
conventional and, in many ways, Victorian background.

Fletcher met Francis la Flesche (1857–1932), who became her life-
long friend and collaborator, at a Boston fund-raising event in 1879.
He was a son of Omaha Chief Joseph La Flesche. Susette, Francis's
sister, was interpreter for Standing Bear, the Ponca chief. Along with
Thomas Henry Tibbles, a Nebraska journalist who later married
Susette, they were touring the East to protest removal of the Poncas
from the Dakota Territory. Having lectured briefly on material gathered in libraries, Fletcher now wished for first-hand information. She
contacted Susette and Tibbles early in 1881, and during the summer,
they arranged for her to return with them that fall. They traveled, in
a wooden wagon, to the Omaha reservation in Nebraska and then on
into Sioux territory. This was the beginning. The result is described
by her mentor, Frederick Putnam, in his "Editorial Note" to A Study
of Omaha Indian Music: "Her long residence among the Indians and
her success in winning their love and perfect confidence have enabled her to penetrate the meaning of many things which to an ordinary observer of Indian life are incomprehensible" (p. 1).

Again early in 1882, while working for the Omahas in Washington, she frequently sought Francis La Flesche's help. They helped
each other thereafter for more than forty years. An important col-
laboration was The Omaha Tribe, published in 1911. In a volume
dedicated to the youth of America she endeavored to promote a better understanding of the Native American consciousness of oneness
with nature (Indian Games and Dances with Native Songs). With
another book she hoped to reach a wider audience by presenting in a
more popular form material hitherto appearing only in scientific
publications (Indian Story and Song from North America). She also
was pleased that some of her transcriptions of Indian songs had been
used by American composers as inspiration in their work.

While Francis was engaged in research for the Bureau of American Ethnology, Fletcher herself was involved in many important
projects. She became an intermediary between government agencies
and Indian tribes. She was asked to administer settlements of con-
troversial land allotments. She sponsored educational projects for
Indians. She was a vice president of the American Association for the
Advancement of Science (1896), a founding member of the American
Anthropological Association (1902), president of the American Floklore
Society (1905), and served on the editorial board of the American
Anthropologist (1899–1916).

In 1892 she moved into a house that had been bought for her at
214 First Street SE in Washington, D.C. This home became a gather-

ing place for intellectuals, among them Ainsworth Spofford, once President Lincoln's secretary and later Librarian of Congress. Fletcher lived there, with La Flesche, until her death in 1923.

Her Contributions

Walter Haugh's obituary for Alice Fletcher in *American Anthropologist* noted that she "made unusually important contributions to our knowledge of the inner spirit and beauty of the Indian's concepts. . . . Her collection of data was expedited by the simplicity of her dealings with the Indians and her entire sympathy with them. She was a friend among friends, and all her inquiries were answered freely and with confidence as one of the family. Such conditions are not often granted to anthropological investigators and for this reason much information on various lines of Indian life are irreparably lost. . . . As an interpreter of the Indian Miss Fletcher ranks among the highest. Mildly, peaceably, yet with great fortitude, she did what she could to advance the cause of science and science is her debtor."

At her death at age eighty-five, Alice Fletcher had been in the public eye for more than forty years—as lecturer, author, government official, anthropologist, and musicologist. She worked hard and welcomed the rewards. She was brave, determined, resourceful, and most important of all, she left a legacy of some forty-six writings on aspects of Indian life and music.

Fletcher had hoped for continued interest in Indian traditions. There is no lessening of that pursuit. Joseph Epes Brown writes, "The current renaissance of interest in the American Indian is in large measure related to our own critical concerns. In our search for ourselves we are beginning to look to the American Indian in a manner never attempted before. We wish to know who the Indian was and is, by what values he lived, and the nature of his special relationship with his natural environment. . . . If the search is sincere, it is possible that men may learn from the Indian's legacy and example."

For present-day Americans, *The Hako* is one of Alice Fletcher's finest contributions—detailed, keenly observed, sympathetically presented, with impeccable scholarship and love.

Bibliography

Brady, Erika, Maria La Vigna, Dorothy Sara Lee and Thomas Vennum Jr. *The Federal Cylinder Project: A Guide to Field Cylinder Collections in Federal Agencies.* Vol. I: *Introduction and Inventory. Studies in American Folklife,* no. 3, vol. 1. Washington, D.C.: Library of Congress, 1984.

Brown, Joseph Epes. *The North American Indians*. New York: Aperture Foundation, 1972.

Curtis, Edward S., and Joseph Epes Brown. *The North American Indians*. New York: Aperture Foundation, 1972.

———. *Visions of a Vanishing Race*. Text by Florence Curtis Graybill and Victor Boesen, Introduction by Harold Curtis. New York: Promontory Press, 1994.

Densmore, Frances. "The Study of Indian Music in the Nineteenth Century." *American Anthropologist* 29 (1927), 77–86.

Ellingson, Ter. "Transcription." In *Ethnomusicology: An Introduction*, ed. Helen Myers. London: Macmillan Press, 1992, 110–52.

Fillmore, John Comfort. "The Harmonic Structure of Indian Music." *American Anthropologist* no. 1 (1899), 297–318.

———. "Primitive Scales and Rhythms." In *Memoirs of the International Congress of Anthropologists*, ed. C. S. Wake. Chicago: Schulte, 1894, 158–75.

———. "Scales and Harmonies of Indian Music." *Music* 4 (1893), 478–89.

———. "A Study of Indian Music." *Century Magazine* 47 (1894), 616–23.

———. "What Do Indians Mean to Do When They Sing, and How Far Do They Succeed?" *Journal of American Folklore* 8, no. 29 (1895), 138.

———. "The Zuñi Music as Translated by Mr. Benjamin Ives Gilman." *Music* 5 (1893), 39–42.

Fletcher, Alice. "Historical Sketch of the Omaha Tribe of Indians in Nebraska." Washington, D.C.: Bureau of Indian Affairs, 1885.

———. "Leaves from My Omaha Note-book." *Journal of American Folk-Lore* 2 (1889), 219–26.

———. "Indian Songs: Personal Studies of Indian Life." *Century Magazine* 47 (January 1894), 421–31.

———. *The Omaha Tribe*. With Francis La Flesche. Smithsonian Institution, Bureau of American Ethnology, 27th Annual Report, 1905–1906. Washington, D.C., 1911. 2 vols. 672 pp. Reprinted by University of Nebraska Press with a new introduction by Robin Ridington, 1992.

———. *Indian Games and Dances with Native Songs: Arranged from American Indian Ceremonials and Sports*. Boston: C. C. Birchard, 1915; reprinted by the University of Nebraska Press with a new introduction by Helen Myers, 1994.

———. *A Study of Omaha Indian Music*. Aided by Francis La Flesche and John C. Fillmore. *Archaeological and Ethnological Papers*, Peabody Museum of Archaeology and Ethnology 1 (1893); reprinted by the University of Nebraska Press with a new introduction by Helen Myers, 1994.

Gilman, Benjamin Ives. "Hopi Songs." *Journal of American Archaeology and Ethnology* 5 (1908), 1–26.

———. "Zuñi Melodies." *Journal of American Ethnology and Archaeology* 1 (1891), 65–91.

Hough, Walter. "Alice Cunningham Fletcher." *American Anthropologist* 25 (1923), 254–58.

Lee, Dorothy Sara. "North America 1. Native American." In *Ethnomusicology: Historical and Regional Studies*, ed. Helen Myers. London: Macmillan Press, 1993, 19–36.

Lee, Dorothy Sara, and Maria La Vigna, eds. *Omaha Indian Music: Historical Recordings from the Fletcher/La Flesche Collection*. (Booklet accompanying Disk AFC L71) Washington, D.C.: Library of Congress, 1985.

Lummis, Charles F. "In Memoriam: Alice C. Fletcher." *Art and Archaeology* 16 (1923), 75–76.

McNutt, J. C. "John Comfort Fillmore: A Student of Indian Music Reconsidered." *American Music* 2 (1984), 61.

Mark, Joan. *Four Anthropologists*. New York: Science History Publications, 1981.

———. *A Stranger in her Native Land: Alice Fletcher and the American Indians*. Lincoln and London: University of Nebraska Press, 1988.

Miller, Terry E. *Folk Music in America: A Reference Guide*. New York and London, Garland Publishing, Inc., 1986.

Myers, Helen, ed. *Ethnomusicology: An Introduction*. London: Macmillan Press, 1992.

———. *Ethnomusicology: Historical and Regional Studies*. London: Macmillan Press, 1993.

Nettl, Bruno. *North American Indian Musical Styles*. Philadelphia: American Folklore Society, 1954.

Pantaleoni, Hewitt. "A Reconsideration of Fillmore Reconsidered." *American Music* 3 (1985), 217–28.

Welch, Rebecca Hancock. "Alice Cunningham Fletcher, Anthropologist and Indian Rights Reformer." Ph.D. diss., George Washington University, 1980.

Wilkins, Thurman. "Alice Cunningham Fletcher." In *Notable American Women*, ed. Edward T. James, Janet Wilson James, and Paul Boyer. Cambridge: Harvard University Press, 1971.

THE HAKO: A PAWNEE CEREMONY

By ALICE C. FLETCHER

PREFACE

In the early eighties of the last century, while pursuing my study of the Omaha tribe, I several times witnessed the ceremony described in the following pages. Owing to the death of the only man who knew all the rituals, it became impossible to secure a complete record, but as the ceremony was an intertribal one I hoped to make good the loss in some other tribe. From statements made by the Omahas, the Ponkas, and the Dakotas I was led to believe that among the Pawnees this ceremony could be found still preserved in its entirety. I need not recount the failure of efforts made during some fifteen years to gain the desired information, since at last, in 1898, I found the long-sought opportunity. After four years of work, I am able to present the entire ceremony, as observed in the Chaui band of the Pawnee tribe.

The difficulty of obtaining accurate first-hand information in regard to religious rites and beliefs is so well known that it seems proper to state briefly how I came by my opportunities. An extended and intimate acquaintance in one tribe opens the way in another. The warm friendship of old and leading men of the Omahas became my credentials to other tribes where these leaders were influential; and with the further assistance of Mr Francis LaFlesche, the son of the former head chief of the Omahas, I was able to establish relations of confidence with some of the old and prominent men of the Pawnees.

My experience has shown that no linguistic training will enable a student by himself to accomplish successfully the difficult task of recording and interpreting the rituals of a religious ceremony. He must have a native collaborator, one with a good knowledge of English and well versed in the intricacies of his own tongue, able to explain its "sacred language" and possessing those gifts of mind and character which fit him not only to grasp the ideals of his race but to commend himself to the keepers of the ancient rites. Such a collaborator makes a clear vision of the native mind possible to a student of another race.

My collaborator in the present work has been Mr James R. Murie, an educated Pawnee whom I have known since he was a schoolboy, twenty years ago. Mr Murie has taken up the task of preserving the ancient lore of his people, and he has not spared himself in his labor. How difficult his undertaking has been, and still is, can only be appreciated by those who have attempted to accomplish a similar work. His patience, tact, and unfailing courtesy and kindness have soothed the prejudice and allayed the fears of the old men who hold fast to the faith of their fathers and are the repositories of all that remains of the ancient rites of the tribe.

Tahirŭssawichi, a full-blood Pawnee, who is the authority for the text and explanation of the ceremony which forms the subject of this paper, officially accompanied the Hako when it was carried by his people to the Omahas. He thus became acquainted with the leading men of that tribe, who were my friends, and this circumstance has favored the successful prosecution of this work. During the fall of 1898 and again in 1900 he and Mr Murie were my guests in Washington; then, and also during my visits to the Pawnees in 1899 and 1901, we were engaged upon the rituals of this ceremony. A final review of the manuscript was made with Mr Murie in the spring of 1902.

Tahirŭssawichi is a member of the Chaui band of the Pawnee tribe and about 70 years of age. He is tall and well made, and preserves much of the vigor of his earlier days. He is mentally alert, quick to observe, possessed of a tenacious memory, and gifted with a genial nature. He enjoys a joke and is always ready with good-fellowship, but he never forgets the dignity of his calling, or fails to observe the conduct befitting his position as the guardian of sacred rites. Although he is childlike and trusting, he has a keen discernment of character and a shrewd common-sense way of looking at men and things. While he is not indifferent to the great changes which have overtaken his people, new conditions have failed to disturb in any way the convictions of his early religious training.

He has struggled to avoid living in a house, and has held to an earth lodge until it has dropped to pieces about him. He said:[a] "I can not live in a white man's house of any kind. The sacred articles committed to my care must be kept in an earth lodge, and in order that I may fulfill my duties toward them and my people, I must live there also, so that as I sit I can stretch out my hand and lay it on Mother Earth." Last fall (1901) I saw how he had propped up a part of the ruins of his lodge so that he might still keep the sacred objects in a primitive dwelling.

When he was in Washington in 1898 he was taken to the Capitol and the Library of Congress. While the vastness and beauty of these structures gave him pleasure, they did not appeal to him, for such

---

[a] See A Pawnee Ritual Used When Changing a Man's Name, American Anthropologist, n. s., v. 1, January, 1899.

JAMES R. MURIE

buildings he said were unfitted to contain the sacred symbols of the religion of his ancestors, in the service of which he had spent his long life. He admired at a distance the Washington Monument, and when he visited it he measured the base, pacing and counting his steps. Then he stood close to the white shaft and looked up, noting its great height. After going inside, he was asked which he would take, the elevator or the stairs, and replied: "I will not go up. The white man likes to pile up stones, and he may go to the top of them; I will not. I have ascended the mountains made by Tira'wa." Equally characteristic was his interview with the Commissioner of Indian Affairs. When introduced, he said: "I am glad to see you and to take you by the hand. Many chiefs of my tribe have done so. I never expected to do it. I came here to talk of the religion of my fathers, which I follow. You can ask my sister (referring to me) what I have said."

Tahirŭssawichi had never been east of the Mississippi river until he came to Washington to engage in the preservation of this rite. Of the genuineness of his statements there can be no doubt. His position in the Pawnee tribe is that of a man worthy of respect—one versed in a knowledge of serious things, whose life has been devoted to the acquisition and maintenance of certain sacred rites. He is esteemed as a man of truth—one who has the favor of Tira'wa. He possesses a knowledge of curative roots, and often attends the sick, using herbs as medicine. He is the keeper of certain old and sacred objects, and leads in their attendant ceremonies. His great care in observing all the details of the intricate ceremony of the Hako is well known in the tribe, and much good fortune is believed to follow his leadership in this ceremony. His title is Ku'rahus. This term is applied to a man of years who has been instructed in the meaning and use of sacred objects as well as their ceremonies. The word is sometimes employed as a synonym for a venerable man, one who commands respect, but throughout this paper it is used in its official sense—the leader of the ceremony.

It has taken four years of close friendly relations with my kind old friend to obtain this ceremony in its entirety. Many of its rituals deal with very sacred subjects, and it has required much patience in the presentation of reasons why they should be explained to overcome the scruples born of the early training of the Ku'rahus. That he has finally made this record complete, so that the ceremony as known among his people can be preserved, is worthy of commendation. His work as it now stands shows Tahirŭssawichi to be broadminded as well as thoughtful, reverent, and sincere.

Graphophone records were taken of all the songs belonging to this ceremony. The music as here printed has been transcribed from the cylinders by Mr Edwin S. Tracy and each transcription has been verified by him from the singing of the Ku'rahus. It is to be regretted that the exactions of Mr Tracy's professional work in the field of music make it impossible for him to prepare an essay upon the character of these songs and the light they throw upon the evolution of musical expression. His familiarity with native songs, growing out of several years of first-hand research, would render him peculiarly fitted to speak concerning them.

The songs are commended to the general student of music and particularly to the young composers of our country as offering native themes worthy of musical treatment.

In arranging the material for this paper it has seemed best to group it into two parts. The first contains such introductory explanations as are essential to the understanding of the ceremony, which is given without comment in the words of the Ku'rahus, together with his interpretation of the songs and accompanying rites. The second part consists of an analysis of the ceremony and treats of its structure, purpose, and teaching. The translations of the songs aim to convey to the English reader something of their native spirit and meaning.

As the purpose of this record is not primarily linguistic, it has been judged best not to observe the finer phonetic distinctions in recording native words. The vowels have their continental values, as in *a*re, th*ey*, p*i*que, g*o*, r*u*le; ow is used as in how; and ŭ represents oo in good. The consonants p, b, t, d, k, g (always hard), j, s, z, f, v, m, l, r, w, y, h are used approximately as in English, but k and t have been allowed to represent the semisonants (medial between k and g, t and d) as well, and the r has a slight trill. Dh represents th in the, ḫ a guttural breathing (German ch, Spanish j) and ḫr a surd or breathed r; th is used as in thorn, wh and ch as in which, x as in box, sh as in shall; n indicates that the preceding vowel is nasalized; and h at the end of a syllable indicates that the breath must be heard. When a consonant is doubled it is heard twice or distinctly prolonged. An accent mark is used to indicate stress where it seems necessary.

INTRODUCTION

Name of the Ceremony

The ceremony is called Skari by the Ku'rahus and by all who have been taught its rites and sacred songs. This word is from ska, hand, ri, many, and refers not merely to the many hands required for the preparation of the sacred articles used in the rites, but also to the culminating ceremony of touching the little child with the hand, which occurs on the morning of the fifth day (sixteenth and seventeenth rituals).

A peculiar expression is used to characterize the consultation which a man who desires to inaugurate this ceremony has with his kindred in reference to their assistance in the undertaking. This consultation is called "touching them." The Ku'rahus explained this expression as being connected with the meaning of the word Skari, many hands, in its double significance already noted.

Although the term Skari is said to be old, its descriptive character seems to be against its acceptance as the original name of the ceremony.

Among the people at large of the Pawnee tribe the ceremony is spoken of as Ruktaraiwariŭs. This composite word can be analyzed as follows: ruk, from rukkis, wood, or a stick of wood; ta, from tita, hung upon; ra, coming; iwariŭs, shaking or waving. This descriptive term refers to the two objects peculiar to this ceremony, the two feathered stems which are waved to the rhythm of the songs. The Pawnees who receive those who bring the sacred articles call the ceremony Haktara. The word is composed of hak, from hakkow, translated below; ta, have; ra, coming: haktara, they who have the breathing mouth of wood are coming. The Osages speak of it as "Bringing the drum," and the Omahas as "To sing with."

Hako is a comprehensive term used to designate all the articles which belong to the ceremony. The term is derived from the composite word hakkowpirus, meaning drum. Hakkow is from akow, mouth, with the aspirate prefix h, signifying breath, and the k added to the first syllable represents the word rukkis, wood. Hakkow may then be said to mean a breathing mouth of wood. Pirus means to whip or beat.

Three customs among the Indians can be traced in the composition of this word: first, the peculiarity of pulsating the voice on a note that is sustained over more than one count of the measure, by which a beating effect is produced; second, the custom of waving the hand to and from the mouth or beating the lips, so as to break a continuous note or call into a series of sounds or beats; third, the making of the drum from a section of a tree, hollowed out, with a skin stretched over the open end.   From this analysis of the word hakkowpirus we discern that the pulsating voice and the beaten lips were the first means employed to produce an effect which was afterward emphasized in an instrument, the drum (hakkowpirus, the breathing mouth of wood), which was made to give forth a series of sounds by the same device of whipping by the hand.

In Indian music the rhythm of the drum always follows closely the emotion expressed in the song; it is like a great pulsating voice.

In the term Hako the k of the first syllable in hakkow is dropped for the sake of euphony, and for the same reason the rough sound ow is changed to o.   The word Hako carries the idea of the breathing, vibrating tones from the wooden mouth.   It is applied to all the articles used in the ceremony, because, according to the explanations of the Ku'rahus, "everything speaks; the eagle, Kawas, speaks; the corn speaks; so we say Hako—the voice of all these things."

In the preparation of the record of the different rites, rituals, and songs of this ceremony it became necessary to adopt a convenient term which should apply to the ceremony as a whole, including the party inaugurating the ceremony, the rites, the rituals, and the articles used.   The term "Hako" has been chosen as best fitted for the purpose.   Three considerations influenced the choice: first, the fact that Hako is the native name by which the articles used in the ceremony are spoken of collectively; second, the meaning of the term Hako, as revealed by an analysis of the word and by the explanation given by the Ku'rahus; third, the ease with which this word can be spoken and remembered by the English reader.

PERSONNEL OF THE CEREMONY

Two distinct groups of persons were essential to the performance of this ceremony.   These two groups could not belong to the same clan or gens of a tribe, and they were often of different tribes.   One group, called the Fathers, was composed of the kindred of the man who had taken the initiative in organizing a party for the performance of the ceremony.   This man was called the Father.   His party comprised from 20 to 100 persons, and represented the well-to-do class in the tribe, the requisites for the ceremony being of such a character that only skillful hunters and thrifty households could supply them.   The second group, called the Children, was made up of the relatives of the man chosen by the Father to receive the visiting party of the Fathers. The leader of this group of Children was called the Son.   Each of the two groups, as well as the leaders of each group, had peculiar duties throughout the ceremony. Each had a special place in the lodge, and was the recipient of peculiar benefits supposed to be derived from the ceremony.

The Father was usually a chief, or a man prominent in the tribe, who not only had accumulated property, but had a large following of relatives who could contribute to the store of articles required for these rites. The tribal standing of the Son was always equal to that of the Father.

The Father selected a man from among those who had been taught the rites and ritual songs to take charge of the ceremony from beginning to end. Such a man was called Ku'rahus, and to him the entire party was required to yield obedience in every particular. The Ku'rahus chose an assistant, and also took with him a third person, a sort of acolyte, to whom he was teaching the rites.

If the Father was a chief, then he had to invite one other chief to be of his party, to act as substitute whenever he was obliged to be absent from his post of duty. If, however, the Father was not himself a chief, then it became necessary for him to secure the attendance of two chiefs, one to act as substitute for the other, as the constant presence of a chief was required throughout the ceremony.

The priest who had charge of the shrine sacred to rain was also of the Father's party. It was his duty to furnish the pipe and conduct the ceremony of offering smoke to Tira'wa. The Father's party also included two doctors, men who had received a knowledge of healing plants, either directly through visions or by initiation into certain rites by which this knowledge was communicated. Each was required to bring an eagle's wing, one the right wing and the other the left. The wing of the eagle is the official mark of a doctor. The Father must also secure a number of singers, whose duty it was to carry the drum and act as a choir to accompany the Ku'rahus, who always led the singing. The rest of the party of the Father was made up of his kindred, with such of his friends as might desire to contribute to the required food and gifts and thus to become entitled to share in the return gifts made to the Fathers by the Children.

The preliminary ceremonies (the first three rituals) took place at the lodge of the Father, and from it the party of the Fathers started on its journey.

Requisites of the Ceremony and their Symbolism

The objects peculiar to this ceremony were two feathered stems about a meter in length, made of ash wood. They were rounded and smoothed, and the pith was burned out to leave an opening for the breath to pass, as through a pipestem. One of these stems was named Raha'katittu, from ra, the, this one; ha=hak, a part of the word hakkow, breathing mouth of wood, the k being dropped for euphony (see translation of hawkowpirus, drum, page 17); katit, dark, brown, or black; tu=ruru, moving, the change of the r to t being for euphony. The translation of the whole word would be, the breathing mouth of wood with the dark moving feathers. The other stem was named Rahak'takaru, from ra, the, this one; hak, from hakkow, breathing mouth of wood; taka, white; ru, from ruru, moving or swaying. The translation of the whole word would be, the breathing mouth of wood with the white moving or waving feathers.

Associated with these two feathered stems, and sharing with them the prominent place in the rites, was an ear of white corn. In addition there were required two small, round, straight sticks from the plum tree; a crotched stick, also of the plum tree; feathers from the tail of an owl and from the wings and tail of an eagle; two entire wings of an eagle; the heads of two woodpeckers; the head, neck, and breast of two ducks; a wildcat skin; a shell; two wooden bowls; a braid of buffalo hair; a braid of sweet grass; blue, green, and red clay; fat from a deer or buffalo, the animal having been consecrated; the nest of an oriole.

The clays, the fat, and the oriole's nest were furnished by the Ku'rahus. The nest was kept in secret and not allowed to be seen. All the articles except those furnished by the Ku'rahus were provided by the Father. Besides these he had to secure robes, ornamented garments, and regalia for the ceremonial clothing of the Son, his messenger, and his little child; also gifts to be bestowed on the entire party of the Children. He was assisted by contributions from the relatives and friends who had agreed to share with him the responsibilities and the rewards attending this ceremony. Food for the entertainment of the Children as well as for the maintenance of the Fathers during their absence from home had also to be provided.

It was the duty of the Son, the leader of the group called the Children, to provide a spacious lodge wherein the ceremony could take place, and also a proper camping site for all who accompanied the Fathers. He had also to secure the requisite return gifts to be made to the Fathers.

Each of the articles used in the ceremony had a general symbolism well known to the people, but their special significance was peculiar to these rites.

The feathered stem Raha'katittu (plate LXXXVI, page 38) was painted blue to symbolize the sky, the abode of Tira'wahut, the circle of the lesser powers. A long straight groove running its length was painted red, the symbol of life. The red groove was the path along which the spirits of the various birds traveled on their way to bring help.

Three split feathers from an eagle's wing were fastened to the stem as to an arrow, to give sure flight to the symbol-freighted stem. On it was tied the fan-shaped pendant of ten feathers from the mature brown or golden eagle. This eagle was called Kawas in the Hako ceremony. It represented the mother and led in certain of the rites. It is this feathered stem that was carried by the Ku'rahus. This eagle is consecrated to the powers; it soars near their abode and is a medium of communication between them and man.

The woodpecker's head was fastened near the mouthpiece end of the feathered stem, the upper mandible turned back over the red crest and painted blue: This treatment of the upper mandible had a double significance. The red crest, which rises when the bird is angry, was here held down; it must not rise. The blue paint represented the clear, cloudless sky. The woodpecker has the favor of the storm gods and can avert from man the disaster of tempest and of lightning. The owl feathers were tied near the middle of the feathered stem. This bird has power to help and protect during the night. Soft blue feathers were fastened around the mouthpiece end. These blue feathers symbolized the clear sky, and it is this end which was always upward toward the abode of the powers.

The other end of the stem was thrust through the breast, neck, and mandibles of the duck. It was by this end that the feathered stem was held. The duck is familiar with the pathless air and water and is also at home on the land, knowing its streams and springs. It is the unerring guide.

The red and white streamers represented the sun and the moon, day and night. These were made of red cloth and dyed horsehair and white cotton cord, but it is said that formerly soft deerskin strips painted red and twisted hair from the white rabbit were used.

The other feathered stem, Rahak'takaru (plate LXXXVII, page 40), differed from the first feathered stem already described in two particulars, namely, it was painted green, to symbolize the earth, and the fan-shaped pendant was made of seven tail feathers from the white eagle (the young brown or golden eagle; see page 288). This eagle was not consecrated. It represented the male, the father, the warrior, and the defender. This feathered stem was carried by the Ku'rahus's assistant, and it was never allowed to be next to the Children; its place was always on the outside. There, it was explained, it could do no harm, could rouse no contention, but would serve to protect and defend.

I have many times remarked the reverence felt toward the feathered stems. Their sacred character seemed always to be remembered and they were never handled carelessly. During the entire time that I was engaged with Tahirŭssawichi on this ceremony he never allowed the feathered stems to be placed on the floor or laid on a chair; they were always carefully deposited on the wildcat skin with a decorum that was not once abated. I have seen manifested among the tribes not only reverence toward these sacred symbols, but an affection that was not displayed toward any other objects. Few persons ever spoke to me of them without a brightening of the eyes. "They make us happy," was a common saying.

They were preserved intact and passed from tribe to tribe as long as they held together, and they were sometimes freshened and repaired. This transfer of the feathered stems from tribe to tribe tended to preserve the model unchanged. Sometimes the Son did not care to part with the feathered stems left with him, so when he inaugurated a party and was to be the Father he had a new set made. It was a matter of pride with some not to use again feathered stems that had once seen service.

The ear of white corn (plate LXXXVIII, page 44), called Atira, Mother,[a] represented the fruitfulness of the earth. The tip end was painted blue to represent the dome of the sky, the dwelling place of the powers, and four blue equidistant lines, running halfway down the ear, were the four paths along which the powers descended to minister to man.

The two straight sticks cut from the plum tree were bound to the ear of corn by a braid of buffalo hair. One stick projected above the tip of the ear about a hand's breadth, and the other extended about the same length below the butt; the lower end of this stick was pointed so that it could be thrust into the ground to hold the ear of corn in an upright position. To the other stick was tied a white, downy eagle feather. This feather had a double significance: It represented the high, white clouds that float near the dome of the sky where the powers dwell, thus indicating their presence with the corn. It also stood for the tassel of the cornstalk. The feather here refers to the male principle, the corn to the female. The plum-tree wood was chosen for the sticks because the tree is prolific of fruit. It symbolized a prayer for abundance.

The braid of buffalo hair represented the animal which supplied food and clothing for the people.

The two gourd rattles (plate LXXXIX, page 46) represented the gift of the squash to man and the breast of the mother. Around the middle of each a blue circle was painted from which depended four equidistant lines of the same color. The circle represented the base of the dome of the sky, and the four lines the four paths descending therefrom to earth.

The crotched stick (plate XC, page 48) used to support one end of the feathered stems when they were laid at ceremonial rest was significant of the fork in the tree where the eagle builds its nest. The use of the plum tree for this crotched stick expressed the desire for many young in the nest.

The sacred ointment with which the plum-tree sticks were anointed was made from the fat of the deer or buffalo mixed with red clay. The fat was taken from an animal that had been consecrated through certain prescribed rites which recognized man's dependence upon the powers for the gift of food. Fat symbolized plenty. Ritual songs speak of paths dropping fatness, referring to the trails made by those who carried the dressed meat from the hunting fields to the camp; such

---

[a] The common term for corn, naksu, was not used in the ceremony.

a path would be strewn with drops of fat.   Red is the color typical of life.   The ointment signified a prayer for abundance and life.

The wildcat skin (plate XC, page 48) served as a covering for these objects when they were to be wrapped up and it was always spread on the ground for them to rest on.

The significance of the wildcat in this ceremony is of peculiar interest.   This animal, we are told, never misses his prey, never fails to attain the object of his pursuit, and accomplishes this end quietly, tactfully, without arousing antagonism.   From conversations with the Ku'rahus it became clear that it was these qualities and not the savageness and stealthly cruelty of the animal that were to be kept in mind.   To be able to accomplish a purpose without offending, without raising opposition, seems to have been regarded as the special attribute vouchsafed by Tira'wa to the wildcat.   It is because of this attribute that it was chosen to be always with the sacred objects during this ceremony.   The sacred objects symbolized not only an appeal from man to certain powers, but the presence of the powers themselves, while the nature of the appeal, a desire for children, long life, and plenty, was such that the enjoyment of the benefits craved must depend largely on the successful exercise by man of those qualities which were regarded as characteristic of the wildcat.   So the skin of the wildcat was the cover of the sacred objects when they were wrapped up; it was spread on the ground as their guard and support when they were laid at ceremonial rest, and when they were carried about the lodge during the ceremony it was borne by the chief, who walked between the Kurahus and his assistant, each of whom held a feathered stem.

Only a chief could carry the wildcat skin and the ear of corn.   Therefore, if the Father was not himself a chief he had to secure the service of one in order that the wildcat could be borne by a man possessing the authority of a ruler in the tribe.   As the wildcat stood for the ability to accomplish a purpose with tact and without exciting opposition, qualities essential to the successful ruler, it would seem that the imperative association of the wildcat with a chief was intended to convey the idea that only under the administration of such a man could the tribe have internal peace and enjoy the abundance and prosperity represented by Mother Corn.

As every article belonging to the ceremony and the position and movements of those who conducted the rites had a special significance, the position given to the wildcat, as explained by the Kurahus, reveals the mind of the native in regard to this animal, which figures conspicuously in other rites and ceremonies, and which controls one of the sacred shrines of the Chaui band of the Pawnee tribe.

TIME OF THE CEREMONY

There was no stated time for the performance of the Hako ceremony. It was not connected with planting or harvesting, hunting, or war, or any tribal festival.   The Ku'rahus said, "We take up the Hako in the spring when the birds are mating, or in the summer when the birds are nesting and caring for their young, or in the fall when the birds are flocking, but not in the winter when all things are asleep. With the Hako we are praying for the gift of life, of strength, of plenty, and of peace, so we must pray when life is stirring everywhere."

SCHEME OF THE CEREMONY

According to the Ku'rahus, no change in the order of rites or songs was permitted. The reason for this requirement becomes clear when we study the ceremony itself. Its fundamental ideas and teachings, which are among the most important for the welfare of the people, are steadily unfolded from the initial rite to the final act through a long series of observances which are replete with detail and accompanied by nearly one hundred songs, yet all these different parts are so closely articulated that any variation of relationship or any omission would be disastrous to the structure.

The Hako consists of the Preparation and the Ceremony.

The Preparation

First division. Initial rites.
    First ritual. Making the Hako:
        Part I. Invoking the powers.
        Part II. Preparing the feathered stems.
        Part III. Painting the ear of corn and preparing the other sacred objects.
        Part IV. Offering of smoke.
    Second ritual. Prefiguring the journey to the Son.
    Third ritual. Sending the messengers.
    Fourth ritual:
        Part I. Vivifying the sacred objects.
        Part II. Mother Corn assumes leadership.
        Part III. The Hako party presented to the Powers.
Second division. The journey.
    Fifth ritual:
        Part I. Mother Corn asserts authority.
        Part II. Songs and ceremonies of the way.
        Part III. Mother Corn reasserts leadership.
Third division. Entering the village of the Son and consecrating his lodge.
    Sixth ritual:
        Part I. The Son's messenger received.
        Part II. The Hako party enter the village.
    Seventh ritual:
        Part I. Touching and crossing the threshold.
        Part II. Consecrating the lodge.
        Part III. Clothing the Son and offering smoke.

The Ceremony

First division. The public ceremony.
    Eighth ritual (first day). The Fathers feed the Children.
    Ninth ritual (first night). Invoking the visions.
    Tenth ritual. The Dawn:
        Part I. The birth of Dawn.
        Part II. The Morning Star and the new-born Dawn.

First division—continued.
    Tenth ritual.   The Dawn— continued.
        Part III. Daylight.
        Part IV. The Children behold the day.
    Eleventh ritual (second day).   The male element invoked:
        Part I. Chant to the Sun.
        Part II. Day songs.
    Twelfth ritual (second night).   The rites came by a vision.
    (Tenth ritual.   The Dawn.   Repeated.)
    Thirteenth ritual (third day).   The female element invoked:
        Part I. The sacred feast of Corn.
        Part II. Song to the Earth.
        Part III. Offering of smoke.
        Part IV. Songs of the birds.
    Fourteenth ritual (third night).   Invoking the visions of the ancients.
Second division.   The secret ceremonies.
    Fifteenth ritual (fourth night):
        Part I. The flocking of the birds.
        Part II. The sixteen circuits of the lodge.
    Sixteenth ritual (fifth day, dawn):
        Part I. Seeking the child.
        Part II. Symbolic inception.
        Part III. Action symbolizing life.
    Seventeenth ritual:
        Part I. Touching the child.
        Part II. Anointing the child.
        Part III. Painting the child.
        Part IV. Putting on the symbols.
    Eighteenth ritual.   Fulfilment prefigured.
        Part I. Making the nest.
        Part II. Symbolic fulfilment.
        Part III. Thank offering.
Third division.   The dance of thanks.
    Nineteenth ritual:
        Part I. The call to the Children.
        Part II. The dance and reception of gifts.
Fourth division.   The presentation of the Hako.
    Twentieth ritual:
        Part I. Blessing the child.
        Part II. Presenting the Hako to the Son and thanks to the Children.

There are four rituals which can be interpolated during the progress of the public ceremony, namely:

Incidental Rituals

Comforting the child.
Prayer to avert storms.
Prayer for the gift of children.
Changing a man's name.

In the following pages the rituals and the explanations are presented as they were given by Tahirŭssawichi.   His descriptions are full of detail, with frequent repetitions, but as every article is symbolic and every movement has a meaning, this repetition is essential to an understanding of the ceremony as it appeals to the Pawnee, and it has been deemed best not to change his method or introduce comments.

THE HAKO

THE PREPARATION

Explanation by the Ku'rahus

The ceremony of the Hako is a prayer for children, in order that the tribe may increase and be strong; and also that the people may have long life, enjoy plenty, and be happy and at peace.

The articles that are used in the ceremony can be prepared only under the direction and supervision of a man who has been taught the sacred songs in their sequence and instructed as to their meaning. Such a man is called Ku'rahus, which means a man of years, venerated for his knowledge and experience.

When a man intends to inaugurate a party for the performance of this ceremony, he selects a Ku'rahus to have complete charge of it, and fixes a day when the preliminary rites are to be performed. On that day the Ku'rahus goes into the sweat lodge and there purifies himself. When he has come out of the sweat bath and has cooled off a little, he places sweet grass on a small pile of coals. Then he sits down (on his heels) and draws a robe about himself and the coals, so that the smoke of the sweet grass may reach every part of his body. He then takes a bit of fat which has been preserved from a deer or buffalo consecrated to Tira'wa, and mixes it with red paint and anoints himself. Then he puts on his leggings and moccasins, and a buffalo robe, with the hair outside, tying it about the waist with a rope made of buffalo hair. He fastens a white, downy eagle feather in his scalp lock and goes to the lodge of the man who has inaugurated the party. He takes with him a man as assistant; he is also accompanied by another man, who is learning the songs and the details of the ceremony, preparatory to becoming himself able to conduct this rite, but whose present duty is to minister to the wants of the Ku'rahus.

At the lodge the chiefs and leading men of the village have been assembled, with those who have agreed to be of the party and have contributed the requisite gifts. This lodge has been swept clean and put in order for the occasion. The Ku'rahus takes his seat at the west end of the lodge, facing the east, and before him, spread out on a mat, are the materials for the preparation of the ceremonial articles.

After the Ku'rahus has begun to sing the songs belonging to the act of preparing these articles there must be no coming in or going out of the lodge, and no one can move from his place until this (the first ritual) has been completed   An exception is made in the case of two men who are sent out by the Ku'rahus to cut and bring in two sticks of ash. They go out during the singing of a certain stanza of the first song and must return while another particular stanza of the same song is being sung.

THE KURAHUS IN CEREMONIAL DRESS

(TO ILLUSTRATE "HAKO, A PAWNEE CEREMONY," BY A.C.FLETCHER)

THE KURAHUS IN CEREMONIAL DRESS

(TO ILLUSTRATE "HAKO, A PAWNEE CEREMONY," BY A.C. FLETCHER)

FIRST DIVISION. INITIAL RITES

FIRST RITUAL. MAKING THE HAKO

PART I. INVOKING THE POWERS

Explanation by the Ku'rahus

At the creation of the world it was arranged that there should be lesser powers. Tira'wa atius, the mighty power, could not come near to man, could not be seen or felt by him, therefore lesser powers were permitted. They were to mediate between man and Tira'wa. The first song mentions some of these lesser powers in the order in which they come near to man, in the order of their creation.

SONG

Words and Music

M. M. ♪ = 126.
· = Pulsation of the voice.   Transcribed by Edwin S. Tracy.

I		IV	
1	Ho-o-o!	16	Ho-o-o!
2	I'hare, 'hare, 'ahe!	17	I'hare, 'hare, 'ahe!
3	I'hare, 'hare, 'ahe!	18	I'hare, 'hare, 'ahe!
4	Heru! Awahokshu. He!	19	Heru! H'Uraru. He!
5	I'hare, 'hare, 'ahe!	20	I'hare, 'hare, 'ahe!

II		V	
6	Ho-o-o!	21	Ho-o-o!
7	I'hare, 'hare, 'ahe!	22	I'hare, 'hare, 'ahe!
8	I'hare, 'hare, 'ahe!	23	I'hare, 'hare, 'ahe!
9	Heru! Hotoru. He!	24	Heru! Toharu. He!
10	I'hare, 'hare, 'ahe!	25	I'hare, 'hare, 'ahe!

III		VI	
11	Ho-o-o!	26	Ho-o-o!
12	I'hare, 'hare, 'ahe!	27	I'hare, 'hare, 'ahe!
13	I'hare, 'hare, 'ahe!	28	I'hare, 'hare, 'ahe!
14	Heru! Shakuru. He!	29	Heru! Chaharu. He!
15	I'hare, 'hare, 'ahe!	30	I'hare, 'hare, 'ahe!

VII

31   Ho-o-o!
32   I'hare, 'hare, 'ahe!
33   I'hare, 'hare, 'ahe!
34   Heru! Kusharu. He!
35   I'hare, 'hare, 'ahe!

VIII

36   Ho-o-o!
37   I'hare, 'hare, 'ahe!
38   I'hare, 'hare, 'ahe!
39   Heru! H'Akaru. He!
40   I'hare, 'hare, 'ahe!

IX

41   Ho-o-o!
42   I'hare, 'hare, 'ahe!
43   I'hare, 'hare, 'ahe!
44   Heru! Keharu. He!
45   I'hare, 'hare, 'ahe!

X

46   Ho-o-o!
47   I'hare, 'hare, 'ahe!
48   I'hare, 'hare, 'ahe!
49   Heru! Kataharu. He!
50   I'hare, 'hare, 'ahe!

XI

51   Ho-o-o!
52   I'hare, 'hare, 'ahe!
53   I'hare, 'hare, 'ahe!
54   Heru! Kekaru. He!
55   I'hare, 'hare, 'ahe!

XII

56   Ho-o-o!
57   I'hare, 'hare, 'ahe!
58   I'hare, 'hare, 'ahe!
59   Heru! Koritu. He!
60   I'hare, 'hare, 'ahe!

XIII

61   Ho-o-o!
62   I'hare, 'hare, 'ahe!
63   I'hare, 'hare, 'ahe!
64   Heru! Hiwaturu. He!
65   I'hare, 'hare, 'ahe!

Translation of First Stanza

1   Ho-o-o!   An exclamation introductory to the song.
2   I'hare, 'hare, 'ahe!

    i'hare! an exclamation that conveys the intimation that some-
thing is presented to the mind on which one must reflect,
must consider its significance and its teaching.

    'hare! an abbreviation of the word i'hare.

    'ahe! an abbreviation of the word i'hare. The change of the r
to h is for greater ease in singing.

3   See line 2.
4   Heru! Awahokshu. He!

    heru! an exclamation of reverent feeling, as when one is
approaching something sacred.

    Awahokshu, a composite word; awa is a part of Tira'wa, the
supernatural powers, and hokshu means sacred, holy; thus
the word Awahokshu means the abode of the supernatural
powers, the holy place where they dwell.

    he! a part of the exclamation i'hare, the change of the r to an h
being for the same reason as the similar change in 'ahe.
See line 2.

5   See line 2.

Explanation by the Ku'rahus

I'hare is an exclamation, as when one suddenly remembers something of which he has been unmindful, because other things demanded his attention. The mind having been recalled to the subject, now appreciates its importance, gives it complete attention, and becomes absorbed by it. The word means, I remember, I perceive, I give heed.

The repetition of the word as we sing "I'hare, 'hare, 'ahe!" indicates that our minds are dwelling upon the subject brought to our attention.

Heru is an exclamation of reverence, in recognition of a place where prayers can be sent and whence help can come to us.

Awahokshu is that place—the place where Tira'wa atius, the mighty power, dwells. Below are the lesser powers, to whom man can appeal directly, whom he can see and hear and feel, and who can come near him. Tira'wahut is the great circle in the sky where these lesser powers dwell. They are like deputies or attributes of Tira'wa atius. The North Star and the Brown Eagle are among these lesser powers. A number of them are mentioned in this song and in the order in which they come near to man. We begin by calling upon Tira'wa atius, the father of all, but we do not address the power directly; we mention the holy place where the power dwells, Awahokshu, and send our thoughts and our voice there, that our cry may reach those who have the ability to come to us and to help us.

I'hare, 'hare, 'ahe means that our minds are dwelling on our appeal to the powers.

Translation of Second Stanza

6, 7, 8　See the first stanza, lines 1, 2, 3.
9　Heru! Hotoru. He!
　　heru! an exclamation of reverence. See the first stanza, line 4.
　　Hotoru, the Winds, those that stand at the four cardinal points. This term is not used in ordinary speech. It refers to the supernatural powers, the Winds. The common word for wind is utawiu; windy, tihota.
　　he! part of i'hare! give heed! See the first stanza, line 4.
10　See the first stanza, line 2.

Explanation by the Ku'rahus

I'hare I have explained already. It always means the same, the arresting and fixing of the mind upon a subject of importance.

Heru! Hoturu. He! we exclaim, as we call on Hotoru. Hotoru, the Winds, were the first of the lesser powers to come near to man, so they are the first to be mentioned in this appeal. They are invisible, but they are very strong (efficient); they are from the breath of Tira'wa and they give life to man. They stand at the four directions (cardinal points) and guard the paths that are there, the paths down which the lesser powers must travel when they descend to bring help to man.

In this stanza, we remember the power given by Tira'wa to the Winds, and we cry to Hotoru to come and give their help to us at this time, to give life to the sacred articles about to be prepared for the ceremony of the Hako.

I'hare, 'hare 'ahe means, as we sing it this time, that we are reflecting upon Hotoru, we are thinking of all that they bring to man, the breath by which he lives.

The Winds are always near us by night and by day.

Translation of Third Stanza

11, 12, 13   See the first stanza, lines 1, 2, 3.
14   Heru! Shakuru. He!
    heru! an exclamation of reverence.   See the first stanza, line 4.
    Shakuru, the Sun.   This word is not used in ordinary speech; it refers to the supernatural power, the Sun, in its relation to man.   The common term for sun is ti'rasakariki, sun standing.
    he! part of i'hare! give heed!   See the first stanza, line 4.
15   See the first stanza, line 2.   The words in this line have special reference to the mind dwelling seriously upon Shakuru.

Explanation by the Ku'rahus

Shakuru, the Sun, is the first of the visible powers to be mentioned. It is very potent; it gives man health, vitality, and strength.   Because of its power to make things grow, Shakuru is sometimes spoken of as atius, father.   The Sun comes direct from the mighty power above; that gives it its great potency.

As we sing this stanza, we think of all that the Sun can do for us and we cry to it, to come now and give potentiality to the sacred articles about to be made ready for use in this ceremony.

Translation of Fourth Stanza

16, 17, 18   See the first stanza, lines 1, 2, 3.
19   Heru! H'Uraru. He!
    heru! an exclamation of reverence.   See the first stanza, line 4.
    h', the sign of breath; "breathing life."
    Uraru, the Earth.   This term is not used in ordinary speech; the common name for the earth is kahoraru.   H'Uraru refers to the supernatural power that belongs to the earth, the power to bring forth.
    he! part of i'hare! give heed!   See the first stanza, line 4.
20   See the first stanza, line 2.   In the last line of the stanza the word i'hare implies reflection: " We reflect on H'Uraru! "

Explanation by the Ku'rahus

H'Uraru, the Earth, is the lesser power we cry to next. The Earth is very near to man; we speak of her as Atira, Mother, because she brings forth. From the Earth we get our food; we lie down on her; we live and walk on her; we could not exist without her, as we could not breathe without Hotoru (the Winds) or grow without Shakuru (the Sun).

Mother Earth is very potent to help man and now we cry to her to come near and give potentiality to the sacred articles we are about to prepare.

We reverently reflect upon all that Mother Earth does for us.

Translation of Fifth Stanza

21, 22, 23   See the first stanza, lines 1, 2, 3.
24   Heru! Toharu. He!
     heru! an exclamation of reverence. See the first stanza, line 4.
     Toharu, the living covering of the earth, no special form being
        indicated; a general term for vegetation, but implying the
        supernatural power manifested therein. Katoha'ru, trees.
     he! part of i'hare! give heed! See the first stanza, line 4.
25   See lines 2 and 20. " We reflect on Toharu! "

Explanation by the Ku'rahus

Toharu means all the things that Mother Earth brings forth (all forms of vegetation); these are many. They are very necessary to man and they bring him much help. They too are lesser powers, though not so potent as some of the others. From them we get our food; from them comes the grass upon which the animals feed—the animals which supply clothing and food; from them come the trees which are very necessary to us. They have a part in this ceremony.

As we sing we think upon all that Toharu gives us and we cry to this power to come near, for without the help of Toharu some of the sacred articles required for this ceremony could not be obtained.

At this stanza the two men who have been selected to cut the two sticks of ash arise and go out of the lodge to perform this duty. The ash tree has been chosen beforehand, but the two men must cut the sticks when they go out at this time.

We stop between the stanzas of the song that this act may be performed.

Translation of Sixth Stanza

26, 27, 28   See lines 1, 2, 3.
29   Heru! Chaharu. He!
      heru! an exclamation of reverence. See line 4.
      Chaharu, Water. This term applies to the supernatural power
         of the water; it is not used in ordinary speech; the common
         word for water is kii'tzu.
      he! part of i'hare! give heed! See line 4.
30   See lines 2 and 20. "We reflect on Chaharu."

Explanation by the Ku'rahus

Chaharu, Water, is one of the lesser powers. Water is very necessary to the life of man and all living things. The Winds, the Sun,
the Earth, the Vegetation, and the Water are the five lesser powers
through which the life of our bodies is maintained. We cry to Chaharu to come near and give life to the sacred articles about to be
prepared.

I told you that these stanzas are in the order of creation. The
powers are mentioned in the order in which they come near to man
and enable him to live and to keep alive. As we sing we reflect upon
our dependence on these lesser powers.

Water is employed only for sacred purposes in this ceremony. It
can not be used in any ordinary way from the time we begin the
singing of these songs to the end of the entire ceremony. A man can
drink water to sustain his life, but he can not touch it for any other
purpose. He can not go swimming, nor can he step into water without first performing certain rites. It is difficult to abstain so long
from the use of water, but it must be done or we shall suffer punishment for our profanation. We shall have storms, the sky will be
filled with clouds, there will be obstructions between us and the
place where the powers above dwell—those whom we invoke in this
ceremony.

I have known of instances where some of the men of the party
sneaked out of the camp during this ceremony, went to a stream and
washed, or jumped in and took a swim, and the result was a storm
that brought great distress upon the people.

Translation of Seventh Stanza

31, 32, 33   See lines 1, 2, 3.
34   Heru! Kusharu. He!
      heru! an exclamation of reverence. See line 4.
      Kusharu, a place set apart for sacred purposes and made holy.
      he! part of i'hare! give heed! See line 4.
35   See lines 2 and 20. "We reflect on Kusharu!"

Explanation by the Ku'rahus

The first act of a man must be to set apart a place that can be made sacred and holy, that can be consecrated to Tira'wa; a place where a man can be quiet and think—think about the mighty power and the place where the lesser powers dwell; a place where a man can put his sacred articles, those objects which enable him to approach the powers. Kusharu means such a place.

In this stanza we are taught that before a man can build a dwelling he must select a spot and make it sacred and then, about that consecrated spot, he can erect a dwelling where his family can live peaceably. Kusharu represents the place where a man can seek the powers and where the powers can come near to man. Such a place is necessary for all ceremonies.

We are now to set aside a place where we shall put the sacred articles we are to prepare and make it holy. We are not only thinking of the holy place where we shall lay the sacred articles, but we think of all that holy place will mean. It will represent the place where new life will be given.

Translation of Eighth Stanza

36, 37, 38 See lines 1, 2, 3.
39 Heru! H' Akaru. He!
　　　heru! an exclamation of reverence. See line 4.
　　　h', the sign of breath, the giving of life.
　　　Akaru, a modified form of akaro, a dwelling place; the earth lodge
　　　　　with its dome-shaped roof is likened to the stretch of land
　　　　　bounded by the horizon and roofed by the dome of the sky.
　　　he! part of i'hare! give heed! See line 4.
40 See lines 2 and 20. "We reflect on H' Akaru!"

Explanation by the Ku'rahus

In this stanza we are told to think of the dwelling place Tira'wa has given to man. Upon this place man must build a lodge in accordance with the rites given to our fathers. It is by the observance of these rites in the building of a lodge that life is given to the dwelling and it is made a place where the lesser powers can come to those who dwell therein. H' Akaru means the giving of life to the dwelling place.

Translation of Ninth Stanza

41, 42, 43 See lines 1, 2, 3.
44 Heru! Keharu. He!
　　　heru! an exclamation of reverence. See line 4.
　　　Keharu, an enclosure, as a room, having walls and roof, like
　　　　　an earth lodge. The word does not refer to any enclosure
　　　　　or lodge, but is typical in its meaning.
　　　he! part of i'hare! give heed! See line 4.
45 See lines 2 and 20. "We reflect on Keharu!"

Explanation by the Ku'rahus

As we sing this stanza we think of the lodge erected about the holy place in accordance with the rites given to our fathers upon the earth, which Tirawa made to be our dwelling place.

In such a lodge this ceremony must take place, and as we sing we ask that the lodge in which we are assembled to prepare the sacred articles may be kept free from all hurtful influences and that the lesser powers which bring life and strength may come near us as we sit within.

We also think of the lodge to which we will go for the further performance of this ceremony, for we desire that the presence of the lesser powers may be there also.

In this ceremony the lodge represents the nest, the place where the young are enclosed. They are protected by the male; the male eagle guards his nest; within its walls there is safety.

Translation of Tenth Stanza

46, 47, 48   See lines 1, 2, 3.
49   Heru! Kataharu. He!
    heru! an exclamation of reverence.   See line 4.
    Kataharu, part of the word itkataharu, fireplace.   The dropping
        of the initial syllable, it, changes the meaning; the word here
        refers to the place where fire is to be kindled in the sacred
        manner for the performance of sacred rites.
    he! part of i'hare! give heed!   See line 4.
50   See lines 2 and 20.   "We reflect on Kataharu!"

Explanation by the Ku'rahus

As we sing this stanza we think of the place set apart for the kindling of fire after the manner taught our fathers, by rubbing two sticks together. Fire kindled in this way is sacred; it comes direct from the power granted to Toharu (Vegetation), in answer to man's appeal as he rubs the sticks. The sticks used to make this fire are kept in a shrine.

The sacred fire must come in a place set apart for it. All sacred things must have their place. Kataharu is the place set apart for the sacred fire, where it can come and bring good to man; without it he could hardly live. We make the fire in the center of the lodge, where all within can share in its benefits.

As I told you, the lodge in this ceremony represents the nest where the young are cared for and protected. The male eagle protects the nest, the female eagle broods over it, and there she nourishes her young. As we are asking for the gift of children to bind the people together as one family, so we sing about the fireplace, that fire may come as we prepare the sacred articles.

When we sing this stanza, the two men who were sent out to cut the sticks of ash must return. After they enter they are told to sit on the east side of the fireplace. There they must sit, each man holding his stick.

Translation of Eleventh Stanza

51, 52, 53   See lines 1, 2, 3.
54   Heru! Kekaru. He!

> heru! an exclamation of reverence. See line 4.
> Kekaru, glowing coals; that is, the glow of the igniting wood
> before it bursts into flames.
> he! part of i'hare! give heed! See line 4.

55   See lines 2 and 20. "We reflect on Keharu!"

Explanation by the Ku'rahus

As we sing this stanza we rub the sticks to make the sacred fire come, and we think of the lesser power that is making itself seen in the glowing wood.

Translation of Twelfth Stanza

56, 57, 58   See lines 1, 2, 3.
59   Heru! Koritu. He!

> heru! an exclamation of reverence. See line 4.
> Koritu, flames.
> he! part of i'hare! give heed! See line 4.

60   See lines 2 and 20. "We reflect on Koritu!"

Explanation by the Ku'rahus

When the flame leaps from the glowing wood it is the word of the fire. The power has come near.

As we sing we think upon Koritu, the word of the fire, and we ask it to enter into and remain with the sacred articles we are about to prepare, for they are to speak.

While we are singing the two men with the two ash sticks hold them over the fire, to warm and straighten them. Then they cut them to the required length, four spans from the thumb to the third finger. Next they peel and scrape the sticks, and remove the pith by boring them through from end to end, so that the breath can pass unobstructed (the boring used to be done with a reed, but now the pith is burned out with a wire). The men next cut a straight groove the entire length of each stick. When all this has been done, the scrapings and every particle of the ash wood are carefully placed on the fire, and as the flames arise the two sticks are passed through the blaze, that the word of the fire may enter and be with them.

The two men, each with a stick, pass from the east, where they have been standing, and take their places one on the north and the other on the south of the Ku'rahus, where he sits in the west, and there these stems are decorated in the manner taught by our fathers (figure 171).

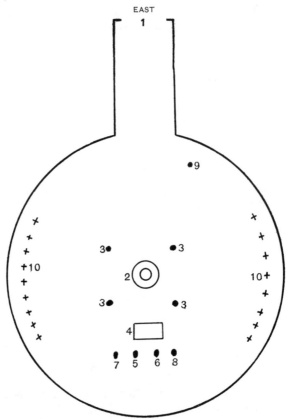

FIG. 171. Diagram of the Father's lodge during the decoration of the feathered stems.

1, the entrance to the lodge; 2, the fireplace; 3, inner posts supporting the dome-shaped roof; 4, the holy place; 5, the Ku'rahus; 6, his assistant; 7, the man with the blue feathered stem; 8, the man with the green feathered stem; 9, the server; 10, members of the Hako party.

Translation of Thirteenth Stanza

61, 62, 63   See lines 1, 2, 3.

64   Heru! Hiwaturu. He!

> heru! an exclamation of reverence. See line 4.
>
> Hiwaturu, the entranceway to the lodge. Hiwaturu is composed of a part of the words hutturaru, a road, and hiwa, a hollow or depression. The word hiwaturu implies a sunken pathway.
>
> he! part of i'hare! give heed! See line 4.

65   See lines 2 and 20. "We reflect on Hiwaturu."

Explanation by the Ku'rahus

We sing of the entranceway of the lodge because it is through this way that man goes to and fro. It is the place made for all to enter into the lodge; through it come those powers which are represented on the sacred articles about to be prepared for the ceremony of the Hako. Through it come the promises of the Hako, and through it the visions come.

The long passageway represents the days of man's life.

Part II. Preparing the Feathered Stems

Explanation by the Ku'rahus

Before the next song is sung the Ku'rahus prepares the blue paint which is to be put on one of the sticks of ash. The water with which the blue clay is mixed must be taken from a running stream. Water from a spring or well can not be used. Running water represents the continuity of life from one generation to another.

The paint is mixed in a white shell. The shell must be white; it is used because it was once a living thing. It lived in the water; it had no disease or sickness. As we use the shell we ask that disease and sickness may be kept from us and that our life may be long.

Before the people knew anything about vessels they used shells as spoons and to put their food in. Tira'wa gave us the shells and gave them long life and the power to keep away disease and sickness.

When the Ku'rahus has mixed the blue paint in the shell, he hands it to the man at his left, who is sitting toward the north. This man applies the mixture with his finger to the stick of ash, spreading the paint over its entire length, but being very particular not to let any of 'it get into the straight groove that runs from one end of the stick to the other, while the following song is sung.

FIRST SONG

Words and Music

M. M. ♪ = 126.
• = Pulsation of the voice.   Transcribed by Edwin S. Tracy.

Ho-o-o-o! H'a-re-ri, h'a-re-ri. He! H'a-re-ri, h'a-re-ri, h'a-re-
Drum.

ri, 're-ri, h'a-re-ri. He! H'a-re-ri, h'a-re-ri. He! ..... 'Re-ri, h'a-

re-ri, h'a-re-ri,'re-ri, h'a-re-ri. He! H'a-re-ri, h'a-re-ri. He!

66 Ho-o-o-o!
67 H'areri, h'areri. He!
68 H'areri, h'areri, h'areri, 'reri, h'areri. He!
69 H'areri, h'areri. He!
70 'Reri, h'areri, h'areri, 'reri, h'areri. He!
71 H'areri, h'areri. He!

Translation

66 Ho-o-o-o! An introductory exclamation.
67 H'areri, h'areri. He!
   h', an aspiration, symbolic of a breathing forth, as the giving
      of breath so that a thing may live.
   areri, a part of the word irarihi, a particular place. The
      change of the h in the final syllable of the word to r when
      the abbreviation areri is sung is for ease of utterance and
      euphony.
   h'areri. Translated above.
   he! a part of the exclamation i'hare! meaning I think upon, I
      give heed to the significance of the act which accompanies
      this song. The change of the initial r in the last syllable
      of the word to an h, making it he, is for euphony.
68 H'areri, h'areri, h'areri, 'reri, h'areri. He!
   H'areri, h'areri, h'areri. See line 67.
   'reri, a part of the abbreviation areri, translated above.
   h'areri. He! See line 67.
69 See line 67.
70 'Reri, h'areri, h'areri, 'reri, h'areri. He! See lines 67 and 68.
71 See line 67.

Explanation by the Ku'rahus

Blue is the color of the sky, the dwelling place of Tira'wahut, that
great circle of the powers which watch over man. As the man paints
the stick blue we sing. We ask as we sing that life be given to this
symbol of the dwelling place of Tira'wa.

When the man has completed the painting of the stick he hands it
to the Ku'rahus, who has already mixed red clay with water from a
running stream in a shell, and he paints the straight groove red.
This groove is the path along which the spirits of all the things that
are to be put upon this stick of ash may travel as they go forth to
give their help during this ceremony. "H'areri" is a prayer that the
symbol may have life.

We paint the groove red because the passageway is red through
which man's breath comes and goes to give him life. The sun, too, is
red, and the groove represents the straight path whereon the sun
shines, the path which man must travel if he would live in peace and
prosper. The teachings of this ceremony make a straight path along
which if a man walks he will receive help from the powers.

KAWAS, THE BROWN FEATHERED STEM (FEMALE)

(TO ILLUSTRATE "HAKO, A PAWNEE CEREMONY," BY A.C.FLETCHER)

When the Ku'rahus has finished painting the groove, he hands the blue stem back to the man on his left, toward the north, who holds it.

Before singing the second song the Ku'rahus prepares the green paint to be used on the other stick of ash by the man on his right, toward the south. The clay is mixed in a shell with water taken from a running stream. When it is ready for use the Ku'rahus hands it to the man on his right, who, with his finger, rubs the paint over the ash stick, being very careful not to get any of the green color into the groove that runs the length of the stick.

When the man begins to paint the stick green this song is sung.

SECOND SONG

Words and Music

M. M. ♩ = 126.
• = Pulsation of the voice.   Transcribed by Edwin S. Tracy.

72 H'areri, h'areri;
73 H'areri, 'hare! I'hare re!
74 H'areri, 'hare! I'hare re! H'areri;
75 Hure-e!
76 H'areri, 'hare! I'hare re! H'areri;
77 Hure-e!

Translation

72 H'areri, h'areri.

 h', an aspiration, a breathing forth. See the second song, line 67.

 areri, an abbreviation of the word irarihi, a particular or special place. The change in the last syllable from hi to ri is for euphony.

73 H'areri, 'hare! I'hare re!

 h'areri. See lines 72 and 67.

 'hare, a part of the word i'hare; an exclamation used to indicate that something of serious import has been presented to the mind and is being reflected upon. See line 2.

 i'hare re. Translated above. The doubling of the last syllable is to meet the requirements of the rhythm of the music.

74 H'areri, 'hare! I'hare re! H'areri. All the words are translated above. See lines 72 and 73.
75 Hure-e! An abbreviation of the word haurae, coming from above.
The vowel changes and prolongation are for greater ease in
singing and also for euphony.
76, 77 See lines 74, 75.

Explanation by the Ku'rahus

The color green represents Toharu (Vegetation), the covering of
H'Uraru, Mother Earth. As we sing, we ask that life be breathed
into the symbol, that it may have power as we use these sacred articles. "H'areri" is a prayer that living power may be where we place
this symbol of the covering of Mother Earth. We remember as we
sing that the power of Mother Earth to bring forth comes from above,
"Hure-e."

The Ku'rahus paints the groove red in the same way, for the same
reason as on the other ash stick, and when he has finished he hands
the green stem back to the man on his right, toward the south, who
holds it.

The Ku'rahus rubs upon his hands the sacred ointment which has
been made by mixing red clay with fat from a deer or buffalo that
has been consecrated to Tira'wa. He is now ready to tie the symbolic
articles upon the two painted stems.

He splits long feathers, taken from the wings of an eagle, and glues
them to each stem as feathers are glued upon the shaft of an arrow.
He uses for this purpose pitch from the pine tree. These wing feathers are to remind us that the eagle flies near to Tira'wa.

About one end of the stem (the mouthpiece) he fastens soft blue
feathers, in color like the sky where the powers dwell. He ties a
woodpecker's head on the stem near the mouthpiece and turns the
upper mandible back upon the red crest. The mandible covers the red
crest and keeps it from rising. This shows that the bird may not be
angry. The inner side of the mandible, which is exposed by being
turned back upon the crest, is painted blue, to show that Tirawa is
looking down upon the open bill as the spirit of the bird travels along
the red groove to reach the people.

About the middle of the stem the Ku'rahus binds feathers from the
owl. The other end of the stem he thrusts through the breast, neck,
and mandibles of the duck, the breast reaching to the owl feathers.
The end of the stem protrudes a very little through the bill of the
duck, so that the bowl of a pipe could be fitted to it. The duck's
head, therefore, is always downward, looking toward the earth and
the water.

All the birds on the stems are leaders: the eagle is chief of the day;
the owl is chief of the night; the woodpecker is chief of the trees;
the duck is chief of the water.

THE WHITE FEATHERED STEM (MALE)

(TO ILLUSTRATE "HAKO, A PAWNEE CEREMONY," BY A.C.FLETCHER)

The Ku'rahus takes ten feathers from the tail of the brown eagle and prepares them so that they can be tied upon one of the stems. A buckskin thong is run through a hole punctured near the end of the quills and another is threaded through the quills, about the middle of their length, so that upon these two thongs the feathers can be spread like a fan. To the end of the thongs are fastened little balls of white down, taken from inside the thigh of the white male eagle. These balls of down represent the reproductive power. When the fan-like appendage is completed it is tied to the side of the blue-painted stem, so that it can swing when the stem is waved, to simulate the movements of an eagle.

When the Ku'rahus takes from the man on his left, toward the north, the blue-painted stem and attaches to it the fan-like pendant made of the feathers of the brown eagle, we give thanks in our hearts as the following song is sung.

THIRD SONG

Words and Music

M. M. ♪ = 126.
• = Pulsation of the voice.   Transcribed by Edwin S. Tracy.

Ha-a-a-a! Ka - was we-rit - ta we - re rit- ta we - re; Ka - was we- ritta we- re rit- ta we- re; Ka - was we -rit - ta we - re rit - ta we - re.

78   Ha-a-a-a-a!
79   Kawas weritta were ritta were;
80   Kawas weritta were ritta were;
81   Kawas weritta were ritta were.

Translation

78   Ha-a-a-a-a! An introductory exclamation to the song.
79   Kawas weritta were ritta were.
  Kawas, the name given to the brown eagle in this ceremony. The
     common name for this bird is letahkots katit; letahkots,
     eagle; katit, dark or brown.
  weritta, now hung.
  were, at this or that particular time.
  ritta, an abbreviated form of weritta, now hung.
  were, at this time.
80, 81   See line 79.

Explanation by the Ku'rahus

In this ceremony the brown eagle is called Kawas. This eagle has been made holy by being sacrificed to Tira'wa. Its feathers are tied upon the stem that has been painted blue to represent the sky.

This stem was the first one painted and decorated, because it is female and the leader. It represents the night, the moon, the north, and stands for kindness and helpfulness. It will take care of the people. It is the mother.

Throughout the ceremony the Ku'rahus carries this feathered stem.

After the Kawas stem is prepared the Ku'rahus hands it back to the man on his left, toward the north, to hold while he prepares a pendant of seven tail feathers from the white eagle. Then he takes from the man on his right, toward the south, the stem which had been painted green and ties on it this white-eagle pendant.

No song is sung while this is being done. The white eagle is not holy; it has not been sacrificed to Tira'wa. It has less power than Kawas; it is inclined to war, to hurt some one. It can not lead; it must follow. So the green stem is painted last, and all the decorations are put upon it after the other stem is completed.

This feathered green stem represents the male, the day, the sun, and the south. During the ceremony it is carried by the assistant of the Ku'rahus, whose place is on the right of the Ku'rahus, toward the south.

When we move about the lodge waving the two feathered stems to the rhythm of the song we are singing, Kawas, the brown eagle, is carried next the people, and the white-eagle stem on the farther side, away from the people, where it can do good by defending them and keeping away all harm. If it were carried next the Children it would bring them war and trouble. It is the brown eagle that is always kept near the people and is waved over their heads to bring them the gifts of plenty and of peace.

The red and white streamers tied upon the two stems represent the sun and the moon.

While the Ku'rahus still has the sacred ointment upon his hands he anoints a crotched stick and two straight sticks, all three of which have been carefully scraped and smoothed. These sticks were cut from a plum tree, because this tree is prolific in bearing fruit.

PART III. PAINTING THE EAR OF CORN AND PREPARING THE OTHER SACRED OBJECTS

Explanation by the Ku'rahus

The Ku'rahus now mixes in a round wooden bowl blue clay with water taken from a running stream and paints with it an ear of white corn, in the way our fathers were taught to do. During this act the following song is sung.

SONG

Words and Music

M. M. ♪ = 138.
• = Pulsation of the voice.   Transcribed by Edwin S. Tracy.

Ha - a-a - a-a! H'A - ti - ra,   we - ri hra ri - ki;   H'A - ti - ra,...   we - ri

Drum.

hra   ri - ki;   H'A - ti - ra, . we - ri hra   ri - ki;   H'A - ti - ra,   hra

ri - ki   re;   We - ri hra ri - ki; H'A -   ti - ra,   we - ri hra ri - ki.

	I		IV
82	Ha-a-a-a-a!	103	Ha-a-a-a-a!
83	H'Atira, weri hra riki;	104	H'Atira, weri taiwa;
84	H'Atira, weri hra riki;	105	H'Atira, weri taiwa;
85	H'Atira, weri hra riki;	106	H'Atira, weri taiwa;
86	H'Atira, hra riki re;	107	H'Atira, taiwa re;
87	Weri hra riki;	108	Weri taiwa;
88	H'Atira, weri hra riki.	109	H'Atira, weri tiawa.

	II		V
89	Ha-a-a-a-a!	110	Ha-a-a-a-a!
90	H'Atira, weri ruata;	111	H'Atira, weri tawawe;
91	H'Atira, weri ruata;	112	H'Atira, weri tawawe;
92	H'Atira, weri ruata;	113	H'Atira, weri tawawe;
93	H'Atira, ruata re;	114	H'Atira, tawawe re;
94	Weri ruata;	115	Weri tawawe;
95	H'Atira, weri ruata.	116	H'Atira, weri tawawe.

	III		VI
96	Ha-a-a-a-a!	117	Ha-a-a-a-a!
97	H'Atira, weri tukuka;	118	H'Atira, weri tawitshpa;
98	H'Atira, weri tukuka;	119	H'Atira, weri tawitshpa;
99	H'Atira, weri tukuka;	120	H'Atira, weri tawitshpa;
100	H'Atira, tukuka re;	121	H'Atira, tawitshpa re;
101	Weri tukuka;	122	Weri tawitshpa;
102	H'Atira, weri tukuka.	123	H'Atira, weri tawitshpa.

Translation of First Stanza

82 Ha-a-a-a-a! Introduction. An exclamation.
83 H'Atira, weri hra riki.

> h', an aspiration, a breathing forth, as the giving of life.
> atira, mother.
> weri, I am. The singular pronoun refers to the party which is taking the initiative in this ceremony and not merely to the Ku'rahus.
> hra, an abbreviated form of the word rararit, to hold.
> riki, standing. This word not only refers to the position of the person who holds the ear of corn and to the position of the corn itself, but it indicates the present time, now.

84, 85 See line 83.
86 H'Atira, hra riki re.

> h'Atira, hra riki. See line 83.
> re, a sign of the plural. This plural sign indicates the impersonation of the ear of corn; h'Atira and Ku'rahus are standing as two persons.

87 Weri hra riki. See line 83.
88 See line 83.

Explanation by the Ku'rahus

The ear of corn represents the supernatural power that dwells in H'Uraru, the earth which brings forth the food that sustains life; so we speak of the ear of corn as h'Atira, mother breathing forth life.

The power in the earth which enables it to bring forth comes from above; for that reason we paint the ear of corn with blue. Blue is the color of the sky, the dwelling place of Tira'wahut.

The running water with which the blue clay is mixed is put into a round, wooden bowl, not in a shell, as when we painted the stems. The bowl is of wood, taken from the trees, a part of the living covering of Mother Earth, representing the power of Toharu (see explanation of line 24).

The bowl is round, like the dome shape of the sky, and holds the blue paint, which also represents the sky. The bowl is a vessel from which we eat when we have the sacred feast of the corn. Tira'wa taught us how to get the corn.

As we sing the first stanza the Ku'rahus stands in front of the bowl containing the blue paint and holds in his hand, by the butt, h'Atira, the ear of corn.

Translation of Second Stanza

89 Ha-a-a-a-a! An introductory exclamation.
90 H'Atira, weri ruata.

> h'Atira, weri. See line 83.
> ruata, flying. Ruata indicates that the ear of corn is moving through the air, not touching the ground; the fact that the ear is in the hand of the Ku'rahus is ignored. Throughout this ceremony the ear of corn is a person.

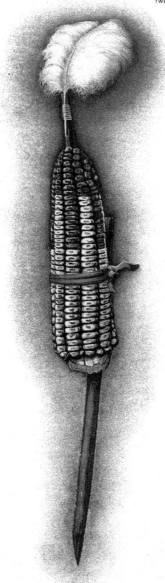

"MOTHER CORN"

(TO ILLUSTRATE "HAKO, A PAWNEE CEREMONY," BY A.C.FLETCHER)

91, 92 See line 90.

93 H'Atira ruata re. All the words have been translated. See lines
     83, 86, and 90.

94 Weri ruata. See lines 83 and 90.

95 See line 90.

Explanation by the Ku'rahus

As we sing this stanza the Ku'rahus, holding the ear of corn in
his hand by the butt, moves it slowly toward the bowl containing the
blue paint.

The bowl and the blue paint represent the blue sky, where the powers
above dwell, so we sing that the mother is flying (ruata) toward the
heavens to reach these powers.

The spirit of the corn and the spirit of the Ku'rahus are now flying
together (see line 86 for translation of the plural sign, re, and its
significance).

Translation of Third Stanza

96 See line 82.

97 H'Atira, weri tukuka.

     h'Atira, weri. See line 83.

     tukuka, now touches, or touching.

98, 99 See line 97.

100 H'Atira, tukuka re. See lines 83, 86, and 97.

101 Weri tukuka. See lines 83 and 97.

102 See line 97.

Explanation by the Ku'rahus

As this stanza is sung the Ku'rahus dips his finger in the blue paint
and touches (tukuka) the ear of corn with it.

This act means that Mother Corn in her flight toward the sky now
touches the place where the sky begins.

Translation of Fourth Stanza

103 See line 82.

104 H'Atira, weri taiwa.

     h'Atira, weri. See line 83.

     taiwa, to rub downward or mark.

105, 106 See line 104.

107 H'Atira taiwa re. See lines 83, 86, and 104.

108 Weri taiwa. See lines 83 and 104.

109 See line 104.

Explanation by the Ku'rahus

As we sing this stanza the Ku'rahus marks with his finger four
equidistant lines of blue paint on the ear of corn. He begins at the
tip of the ear and rubs his finger down (taiwa) about halfway to the
butt on the four sides of the ear.

The four blue lines represent the four paths at the four directions (cardinal points), near which the winds stand as guards. Down these paths the powers descend to bring help to man.

The blue paint came down one of these paths, but I was not taught which one.

Translation of Fifth Stanza

110 Ha-a-a-a-a! An introductory exclamation.
111 H'Atira, weri tawawe.
     h'Atira, weri. See line 83.
     tawawe, to spread.
112, 113 See line 111.
114 H'Atira tawawe re. See lines 83, 86, and 111.
115 Weri tawawe. See lines 83 and 111.
116 See line 111.

Explanation by the Ku'rahus

As we sing this stanza the Ku'rahus spreads (tawawe) with his finger the blue paint over the tip of the ear of corn, to represent the blue dome of the sky, where the powers dwell, above whom is the mighty Tira'wa atius, the father of all.

This act signifies that Mother Corn has reached the abode of Tira'wahut, where she will receive authority to lead in this ceremony.

Translation of Sixth Stanza

117 Ha-a-a-a-a! An introductory exclamation.
118 H'Atira, weri tawitshpa.
     h'Atira, weri. See line 83.
     tawitshpa, the attainment of an object; the completion of an
          undertaking; the end reached.
119, 120 See line 118.
121 H'Atira tawitshpa re. See lines 83, 86, and 118.
122 Weri tawitshpa. See lines 83 and 118.
123 See line 118.

Explanation by the Ku'rahus

Mother Corn having reached the blue dome where dwells the great circle of powers, Tira'wahut, and having gained what she went for, tawitshpa, authority to lead in the ceremony, she descends to earth by the four paths.

The blue paint having now been put on the ear of corn, this part of the ceremony is completed.

In all that is to follow h'Atira, Mother Corn breathing forth life, is to lead. She came forth from Mother Earth, who knows all places and all that happens among men, so she knows all places and all men, and can direct us where to go when we carry the sacred articles which give plenty and peace.

THE RATTLES

(TO ILLUSTRATE "HAKO, A PAWNEE CEREMONY," BY A.C. FLETCHER)

When we have finished singing this song the Ku'rahus takes one of the plum-tree sticks, which has been anointed with red clay mixed with fat, and ties on it with a thread of sinew a downy eagle feather. This stick is bound to the ear of corn so as to project a hand's breadth above the tip end, letting the downy feather wave above Mother Corn. This feather represents Tira'wa. It is always moving as if breathing.

The Ku'rahus then binds the other plum-tree stick to the corn so that it extends below the butt. When the corn is placed in ceremonial position this end of the stick is thrust in the ground so that the ear will stand upright without touching the earth. Both sticks are bound to the ear of corn by a braided band of hair taken from the head of a buffalo. The braided band signifies the gift of animal food and the provision of skin clothing. (The Skidi band of the Pawnees tie a bit of buffalo wool, such as is shed by the animal in the spring, together with a braid of sweet grass, to the ear of corn.)

The two gourd rattles, which represent the squash given us by Tira'wa, and also the breasts of the mother, are each painted with a blue circle about the middle, with four equidistant lines from the circle to the bottom of the gourd. The circle represents the wall or boundary of the dome of the sky; the four lines are for the four paths at the four directions down which the powers descend. No song is sung while this painting is being done.

All the sacred articles are laid at rest on a wildcat skin when they are not being used ceremonially, and it is a cover for them in which they are all wrapped together at the close of the ceremony. The skin is never tanned, and the ears of the animal, the skin of the head, the feet, and the claws must all be intact.

Tira'wa made the wildcat to live in the forest. He has much skill and ingenuity. The wildcat shows us that we must think, we must use tact, and be shrewd when we set out to do anything. If we wish to approach a person we should not do it bluntly; we should not rush at him; that might offend him so that he would not receive us or the gifts we desired to offer him. The wildcat does not make enemies by rash action. He is observant, quiet, and tactful, and he always gains his end.

In this ceremony we are to carry the sacred articles to one not of our kindred in order to bind him to us by a sacred and strong tie; we are to ask for him many good gifts, long life, health, and children, and we should receive gifts from him in return. If we would succeed we must learn of the wildcat, and be wise as he is wise.

The wildcat is one of the sacred animals. A man who killed a wildcat could sacrifice it to Tira'wahut. The man who brought such an offering had the right to ask the priest to teach him some of the mysteries that belong to the sacred shrine.

Many years ago two men took the Hako to the Omaha tribe. On the journey one of them killed a wildcat. I said to the man: "I am glad Mother Corn is here leading us, and the wildcat goes with the Hako." But the man who killed it said: "No, this skin will not go with the Hako! I am going to take it to the priest for sacrifice that I may learn some of the mysteries." But he did wrong and suffered for it, because that wildcat belonged with the Hako, for it was killed while we were being led by Mother Corn.

The sacred articles having been completed are now laid at ceremonial rest. The wildcat skin is spread upon the earth in the holy place, which is in the west part of the lodge opposite the entrance, a little way back from the fireplace. The head of the skin is placed toward the east; the crotched plum-tree stick is thrust into the ground close to the head; the two feathered stems are laid in the crotch, the brown-eagle stem first, then the white-eagle stem on the top or outside. The eagle builds its nest in the crotch of a tree, so these eagle-feathered stems are laid in the crotch of the plum-tree stick. The ends which are thrust through the duck's head rest upon the wildcat, and under the wing-like pendants the gourd rattles are placed. Directly in front of the crotched stick stands Mother Corn.

Part IV. Offering of Smoke

Explanation by the Ku'rahus

The time has now come for the offering of smoke to Tira'wa.

The priest of the Rain shrine must be present with the pipe belonging to that shrine and he must conduct the ceremony. After he has filled the pipe with native tobacco the Ku'rahus tells the people that the time has come to offer smoke to Tira'wa, the father and the giver of all things. He selects from the company a man to act as pipe bearer during the ceremony of offering smoke. The pipe bearer must be one who has made sacrifices at the sacred tents where the shrines are kept and has been annointed, and who in consequence has been prospered in his undertakings. The prayers of such a man are thought to be more acceptable to the powers than those of a man who has never made sacrifices.

In old times men did not smoke for pleasure as they do now, but only in religious ceremonies. The white people have taught the Pawnees to profane the use of tobacco.

Each of the sacred shrines of the tribe has a pipe, and its priest knows the proper order in which the pipe should be offered to Tira'-wahut. I am not a priest, so I do not know the order in which the Rain pipe is offered, nor can I tell you the ceremony; the knowledge of that belongs to its priest and not to me.

Up to this point (the conclusion of the ceremony of smoking) all the people present have been obliged to remain quiet in their places; now they are at liberty to move about or to leave the lodge.

THE WILDCAT SKIN AND CROTCHED STICK ON WHICH
THE TWO FEATHERED STEMS ARE PLACED
WHEN AT CEREMONIAL REST
(TO ILLUSTRATE "HAKO, A PAWNEE CEREMONY," BY A.C.FLETCHER)

SECOND RITUAL. PREFIGURING THE JOURNEY TO THE SON

Explanation by the Ku'rahus

Honor is conferred upon a man who leads a Hako party to a distant tribe and there makes a Son, while to the Son help is given from all the powers represented by the sacred objects.   Between the Father

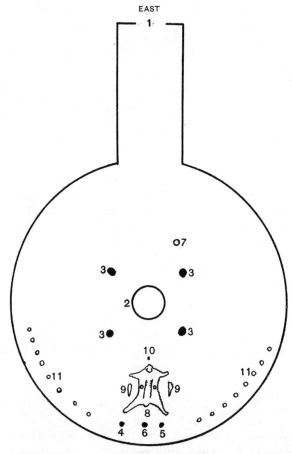

FIG. 172. Diagram of the Father's lodge during the second ritual.

1, the entrance to the lodge; 2, the fireplace; 3, inner posts supporting the dome-shaped roof; 4, the Ku'rahus; 5, his assistant; 6, the Father (a chief); 7, the server; 8, the wildcat skin, on which are the feathered stems and rattles; 9, the eagle wings; 10, the ear of corn; 11, members of the Hako party.

and the Son and their immediate families a relationship similar to that which exists between kindred is established through this ceremony.   It is a sacred relationship, for it is made by the supernatural powers that are with the Hako.

22 ETH—PT 2—04——4

Because of the sacred and binding character of this relationship, and the gifts brought by it to the Son, namely, long life and many children to make his family strong, the selection of a man to be made a Son is regarded as a serious and important act, one in which the chiefs and the leading men of the Father's tribe must have a voice.

The Son should be a chief or a man who has the respect of the leading men of his tribe, and whom the Father's tribe would be glad to have bound to them by the tie of Son.

While the Father has been gathering the materials necessary for this ceremony, which may have taken him a year or more, he has had some particular person in his mind whom he desired to make a Son. When everything is ready he mentions this particular person to the chiefs and leading men, and when we are gathered together to sing this song we think of this chosen man and we ask the assistance of Mother Corn, and if he is the right person she will lead us to him.

The selection of the Son takes place soon after the preparation of the sacred objects, frequently on the night of the same day. It must always be in the night time, because the spirits can travel best at night. The spirit of the corn and the spirits of the people present in the lodge at this time are to decide who shall be the Son, and Mother Corn is to lead us to him. The same persons are present at this ceremony that were present at the preparation of the Hako.

In the west of the lodge, facing the east, sit the Ku'rahus, his assistant, and the Father. Before them are the sacred objects arranged as at ceremonial rest. A little way in front of the crotched stick stands the ear of corn which has been painted in the sacred manner (see figure 172). It is held in position by one of the sticks to which it is tied being thrust into the ground. This ear of corn is the mother, and upon her everyone present must fix his mind.

The singing of the following stanzas occupies most of the night; they do not follow each other quickly, for we must pause after each one.

SONG

Words and Music

M. M. ♪ = 132.
· = Pulsation of the voice.   Transcribed by Edwin S. Tracy.

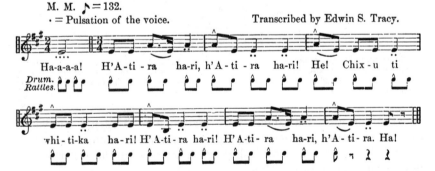

Ha-a-a-a! H'A-ti - ra ha-ri, h'A - ti - ra ha-ri! He! Chix -u ti
Drum.
Rattles.

vhi - ti-ka ha-ri! H'A-ti - ra ha-ri! H'A-ti - ra ha-ri, h'A-ti - ra. Ha!

I

124 Ha-a-a-a!
125 H'Atira hari, h'Atira hari!
126 He! Chixu ti whitika hari!
127 H'Atira hari!
128 H'Atira hari, h'Atira. Ha!

II

129 Ha-a-a-a!
130 H'Atira hari, h'Atira hari!
131 He! Chixu ti uchitika hari!
132 H'Atira hari!
133 H'Atira hari, h'Atira. Ha!

III

134 Ha-a-a-a!
135 H'Atira hari, h'Atira hari!
136 He! Chixu uti hiata hari!
137 H'Atira hari!
138 H'Atira hari, h'Atira. Ha!

IV

139 Ha-a-a-a!
140 H'Atira hari, h'Atira hari!
141 He! Chixu tih whichuru hari!
142 H'Atira hari!
143 H'Atira hari, h'Atira. Ha!

V

144 Ha-a-a-a!
145 H'Atira hari, h'Atira hari!
146 He! Chixu ti whichata hari!
147 H'Atira hari!
148 H'Atira hari, h'Atira. Ha!

VI

149 Ha-a-a-a!
150 H'Atira hari, h'Atira hari!
151 He! Chixu tih itchahka wara hari!
152 H'Atira hari!
153 H'Atira hari. h'Atira. Ha!

VII

154 Ha-a-a-a!
153 H'Atira hari, h'Atira hari!
156 He! Chixu ti itwhichata hari!
157 H'Atira hari!
158 H'Atira hari, h'Atira. Ha!

VIII

159 Ha-a-a-a!
160 H'Atira hari, h'Atira hari!
161 He! Chixu ti tokoka hari!
162 H'Atira hari!
163 H'Atira hari, h'Atira. Ha!

Translation of First Stanza

124 Ha-a-a-a! An introductory exclamation.
125 H'Atira hari, h'Atira hari.

 h', the sign of an inspiration, a breath, the symbol of giving forth life.

 atira, mother. The term is here applied to the ear of corn, the life-giving product of h'Uraru, the Earth.

 hari, a part of the word iha'ri, young, the young of animals; also a general term for children.

126 He! Chixu ti whitika hari.

 he! an exclamation, as when bidding one to look at something.

 chixu, the spirit or mind of a person or thing.

 ti, have, in the sense of having done something, accomplished a purpose or carried out a plan.

 whitika, converged, come together and united for a given purpose.

 hari, part of the word iha'ri, offspring. The word here refers to the Son.

127 H'Atira hari! The words have been translated. See line 125.
128 H'Atira hari, h'Atira. Ha!

 h'Atira hari. See line 125.

 ha! an exclamation, calling attention.

Explanation by the Ku'rahus

As we sing this stanza everyone bends his mind toward the ear of
corn, for our spirits (chixu) and the spirit (chixu) of the corn must
converge (whitika), must come together and unite for the purpose of
finding the Son. The ear of corn is a part of h'Uraru (see line 19),
Mother Earth, the mother of all things, so we call the ear of corn
Mother Corn; and because she supports our life through food, we
speak of her as h'Atira, mother giving forth life.

All things live on the earth, Mother Corn knows and can reach all
things, can reach all men, so her spirit is to lead our spirits in this
search over the earth. When Mother Corn went up to Tira'wahut at
the time she was painted (see lines 82 to 123), power was given her to
lead the spirits of all things in the air and to command the birds and
the animals connected with the Hako. Endowed with power from
Tira'wahut above and from h'Uraru (Mother Earth) below, Mother
Corn leads and we must follow her, our spirits must follow her spirit.
We must fix our minds upon Mother Corn and upon the Son, who is
the object of our search. It is a very difficult thing to do. All our
spirits must become united as one spirit, and as one spirit we must
approach the spirit of Mother Corn. This is a very hard thing to do.

Translation of Second Stanza

129 Ha-a-a-a! An introductory exclamation.
130 H'Atira hari, h'Atira hari.
       h'Atira, Mother breathing forth life. See line 125.
       hari, part of the word iha'ri, offspring, children.
131 He! Chixu ti uchitika hari.
       he! look! behold!
       chixu, spirit of a person or thing.
       ti, have. See line 126.
       uchitika, meditating on; turning over a subject in one's
            mind and considering it in all its aspects.
       hari, part of iha'ri, young; refers to the Son.
132 H'Atira hari! See line 130.
133 H'Atira hari, h'Atira. Ha! See lines 128, 130.

Explanation by the Ku'rahus

When we sing this stanza our spirits and the spirit of Mother Corn
have come together. Now we are all to meditate. We sit with bowed
heads, and Mother Corn sits with bowed head. We are all to think
over and consider (uchitika) who shall be the Son.

We must all agree upon the choice, Mother Corn and all.

It is very difficult for all to unite, but we must do so before we can
follow Mother Corn where she determines to lead us. It often takes
a long time.

Translation of Third Stanza

134   Ha-a-a-a! An introductory exclamation.
135   H'Atira hari, h'Atira hari.
     H'Atira, mother breathing forth life. See line 125.
     hari, part of the word iha'ri, young; refers to the Son.
136   He! Chixu uti hiata hari.
     he! look! behold!
     chixu, the spirit. See line 126.
     uti, moving.
     hiata, the air. Uti hiata refers to the spirits moving
       through the air.
     hari, part of iha'ri, young; refers to the Son.
137   H'Atira hari! See line 135.
138   H'Atira hari, h'Atira. Ha! See lines 135, 128.

Explanation by the Ku'rahus

When we sing this stanza the decision has been made. Mother
Corn lifts her head and stands erect. Then she moves through the
air (uti hiata), flying on her journey to the Son, and we follow.

It is not the ear of corn that travels through the air, nor do our
bodies follow, it is the spirit (chixu) of the corn that moves, and it is
our spirits (chixu) that follow, that travel with her to the land of the
Son.

The path now opened by the spirit of Mother Corn we, the Fathers,
will take, when we in our bodies journey to the Son, but the way must
first be opened and the path prepared by the spirit of Mother Corn.
This she is about to do.

Translation of Fourth Stanza

139, 140   See lines 134, 135.
141   He! Chixu tih̲ whichuru hari;
     he! look! behold!
     chixu, the spirit of a person or a thing.
     tih̲, are in the act of.
     whichuru, approaching, drawing near to a place.
     hari, part of iha'ri, children.
142, 143   See lines 127, 128.

Explanation by the Ku'rahus

As we sit and sing this stanza our spirits follow the spirit of Mother
Corn, and now we are approaching (tih̲ whichuru), drawing near to
the village where the Son lives. We see it all (in the spirit) as with
Mother Corn we approach the place where the Son dwells.

Translation of Fifth Stanza

144, 145   See lines 124, 125.

146   He! Chixu ti whichata hari.

       he! look! behold!

       chixu, the spirit of a person or thing.

       ti, have, in the sense of having accomplished a purpose or carried out a plan.

       whichata, reached one's destination, the end of one's journey.

       hari, part of iha'ri, young, children.

147, 148   See lines 127, 128.

Explanation by the Ku'rahus

As we sing this stanza Mother Corn reaches her destination (ti whichata). The journey across the country is now at an end. Mother Corn has opened the way from the tribe of the Fathers to the tribe of the Children. We shall now be able to travel safely along that path, for she has made it straight, she has removed all evil influences from it, so that we shall be happy when we pass over this path she has made.

Here Mother Corn pauses, and we shall pause when we arrive at this place, for it will be here that we shall stop and await the messenger from the Son. He will bring words of welcome and precede us to the lodge set apart for us by the Son.

After a pause we shall follow the spirit of Mother Corn when she enters the village of the Son.

Translation of Sixth Stanza

149, 150   See lines 124, 125.

151   He! Chixu tih itchahka wara hari.

       he! look! behold!

       chixu, the spirit of a person or thing.

       tih, are, are in the act of.

       itchahka; it, a prefix, indicating desire; chahka, a part of the word chahkahawe, village: itchahka, the village one has desired to reach.

       wara, walking.

       hari, part of iha'ri, children.

152, 153   See lines 127, 128.

Explanation by the Ku'rahus

As we sing this stanza the spirit of Mother Corn walks through the village she has desired to reach (tih itchahka wara). She opens the way for us through the village to the door of the lodge of the Son. Our spirits, as one spirit, follow hers as she walks among the lodges, seeking the one in which the Son dwells.

As we follow we keep our minds fixed upon Mother Corn and upon the Son to whom we are now drawing near.

Translation of Seventh Stanza

154, 155　See lines 124, 125.

156　He! Chixu ti itwhichata hari.

　　he! look! behold!

　　chixu, the spirit of a person or thing.

　　ti, have, in the sense of having accomplished a purpose.

　　itwhichata; it, a prefix indicating desire; whichata, reached one's destination: itwhichata, reached the desired end or object of one's journey.

　　hari; part of the word iha'ri, young; refers here to the Son.

157, 158　See lines 127, 128.

Explanation by the Ku'rahus

As we sing this stanza the spirit of Mother Corn arrives at the lodge of the Son and enters. Our spirits follow her spirit. We have now reached the object of our search and the end of our journey (ti itwhichata hari). The Son does not see us as we stand there; he is sleeping. We fix our minds upon Mother Corn and upon him; we think of the gifts we are to bring him when we come to him with the Hako, the gifts that the birds and the animals that attend these sacred objects will surely bestow upon him—long life, children, and plenty. These gifts will be his, and we shall share in them, for all these good things go with this ceremony.

Translation of Eighth Stanza

159, 160　See lines 124, 125.

161　He! Chixu ti tokoka hari.

　　he! look! behold!

　　chixu, the spirit of a person or thing.

　　ti, have, in the sense of having accomplished.

　　tokoka, touched, made itself felt.

　　hari, part of iha'ri, young.

162, 163　See lines 127, 128.

Explanation by the Ku'rahus

While we sing this stanza the spirit of Mother Corn touches the Son (ti tokoka hari).

We fix our minds upon Mother Corn and upon the Son; if we are in earnest he will respond to her touch. He will not waken, he will not see her, but he will see in a dream that which her touch will bring to him, one of the birds that attend the Hako, for all the spirits of those birds are with Mother Corn and they do her bidding, and he may hear the bird call to him. Then, when he awakens, he will remember his dream, and as he thinks upon it, he will know that he has been chosen to be a Son, and that all the good things that come with the ceremony which will make him a Son are now promised to him.

By touching the Son Mother Corn opened his mind, and prepared the way for our messengers to him, so that he would be willing to receive them, and later to receive us.

Mother Corn has now found the Son; she has made straight and safe the path from our country to his land, and she has made his mind ready to receive us and to carry out his part of this ceremony of the Hako.

THIRD RITUAL. SENDING THE MESSENGERS

Explanation by the Ku'rahus

On the day following the night when Mother Corn selected the Son the members of the Father's party brought to his lodge the gifts which they were to take to the Children.

Four men were chosen to carry the message of the Ku'rahus to the Son. They were clothed by the Father with the buffalo robe in the ceremonial manner, and led by him to a place near the entrance of the lodge.

The Ku'rahus gave a little of the sacred native tobacco to the Father, who tied it in a small piece of bladder and returned it to the Ku'rahus, who then addressed to the messengers the first stanza of the following song.

SONG

Words and Music

M. M. ♩ = 112.

• = Pulsation of the voice.   Transcribed by Edwin S. Tracy.

Slow and heavy.

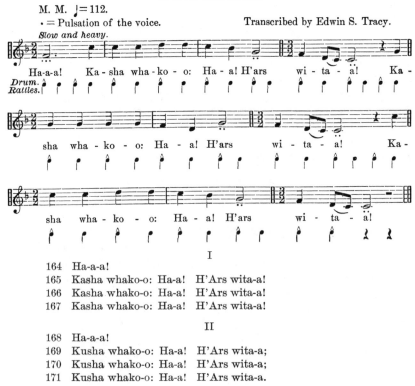

I

164   Ha-a-a!
165   Kasha whako-o: Ha-a! H'Ars wita-a!
166   Kasha whako-o: Ha-a! H'Ars wita-a!
167   Kasha whako-o: Ha-a! H'Ars wita-a!

II

168   Ha-a-a!
169   Kusha whako-o: Ha-a! H'Ars wita-a;
170   Kusha whako-o: Ha-a! H'Ars wita-a;
171   Kusha whako-o: Ha-a! H'Ars wita-a.

Translation of First Stanza

164 Ha-a-a! An introductory exclamation.
165 Kasha whako-o: Ha-a! H'ars wita-a!
> kasha, a form of command, referring to an act to be performed
>> at a future time.
> whako-o; whako, tell or say; o, vowel prolongation.
> ha-a! ha! behold! a, vowel prolongation.
> h', a contraction of ha, your.
> ars, a contraction of atius, father.
> wita-a! wita, he coming; a, vowel prolongation.
166, 167 See line 165.

Explanation by the Ku'rahus

This stanza is a command to the messengers to say, when they hand
the tobacco to the Son, "Behold! Your father is coming!" ("Ha!
H'ars wita!")

The stanza is sung four times. At the fourth time the Ku'rahus
puts the tobacco into the hand of the leader of the four messengers,
who at once leave the lodge and start upon their journey.

Translation of Second Stanza

168 See line 164.
169 Kusha whako-o: Ha-a! H'ars wita-a.
> kusha, they will; that is, those that have been commanded
>> will do as they have been directed.
> whako-o; whako, tell, say; o, vowel prolongation.
> ha-a! ha! behold! a, vowel prolongation.
> h', a contraction of ha, your.
> ars, a contraction of atius, father.
> wita-a, wita, he coming; a, vowel prolongation.
170, 171 See line 169.

Explanation by the Ku'rahus

When the messengers are out of sight of the village the Ku'rahus
sings the second stanza. It is addressed to the members of the
Father's party, who are still sitting in his lodge. It is an authoritative
assurance that the messengers will (kusha) fulfil their mission and
deliver to the Son the message, "Behold! Your father is coming!"

After the Ku'rahus has sung this second stanza four times, the
people disperse to await the return of the messengers, while he and
his assistant, or two persons designated by him, must sit with the
sacred objects until the four men come back from the Son.

As the Son hears the words of the messengers he will be reminded
of his dream, in which Mother Corn touched him. And as he looks
at the men he will recognize the tribe from which they have come and
will know who has chosen him to be the Son. Then he will call
together his relatives and they will talk over the matter. If it is
decided to accept the ceremony they will keep the little bundle of

tobacco and the messengers will be told to return and say to the Father, "I am ready!"

The messengers start back immediately, and when they are in sight of their village the news of their arrival is proclaimed. Then all the men of the Father's party hasten to his lodge. The Ku'rahus, his assistant, and the Father put on their buffalo robes in the ceremonial manner, with the hair outside, and take their places back of the Hako. The other members of the party range themselves against the wall of the lodge, on either side, and all await the coming of the messengers.

As the four men enter the lodge the people cry, "Nawairi!" ("Thanks!") while the Ku'rahus lifts his hands, palms upward, and then brings them down slowly. This movement means thanks, and the calling down of help from above.

The leader of the messengers, addressing the Ku'rahus, delivers the words sent by the Son, "I am ready!" This closes the ceremony.

FOURTH RITUAL

PART I.   VIVIFYING THE SACRED OBJECTS

Explanation by the Ku'rahus

When the messengers return from the Son with the words, "I am ready," there is rejoicing in the lodge.

The young men of the Father's party rise and dance. From these dancers two are selected, by the Ku'rahus and the chief, to perform the final dance, which takes place on the morning of the fifth day of the ceremony. The choice of these two dancers is signified by tying on their hair a downy white eagle's feather (see plate XLI). Meanwhile the other members of the party are busy with their final preparations. They tie in packs, ready for transportation, the gifts they are to carry to the Children. The singers make ready the drum, while outside the women are engaged preparing food and other necessaries for the long journey.

The Ku'rahus orders a straight tent pole to be selected and brought to the lodge of the Father.

On the morning of the day the journey is to begin the Ku'rahus rises from his place in the lodge behind the Hako and goes outside. There he ties the sacred objects on the selected tent pole. He puts the two feathered stems near the top—the brown eagle toward the north and the white eagle toward the south—and he spreads out their feather pendants. Below these he fastens the ear of corn, and underneath it the two rattles and, lastly, the wildcat skin. These objects must face the east when the pole is raised. Behind them, so as to face the west, the right and left wing of an eagle are fastened and spread out.

The rope of buffalo hair is used to tie these sacred objects to the pole, which is then set up at the entrance of the lodge. Here it stands where the wind of the dawn may breathe upon the Hako and the first rays of the sun strike the sacred objects and give them life.

THE FEATHER SYMBOL OF TIRAWA

(TO ILLUSTRATE "HAKO, A PAWNEE CEREMONY," BY A.C.FLETCHER)

We do this that Tira'wa and all the lesser powers—the Winds, the Sun, the Earth, and the four at the west which control the storm—may see that all is complete and ready for the ceremony.

It is all done in silence before the day dawns. No song is sung when we put the objects on the pole and raise it nor when we take it down and remove them. We must let them stay up there for some time in order that all the powers may surely see that everything is correct, so the sun is well up when the Ku'rahus goes out to the pole, lowers it, and removes the sacred objects and carries them into the lodge and puts them on the holy place.

PART II. MOTHER CORN ASSUMES LEADERSHIP

Explanation by the Ku'rahus

As I told you before, the Ku'rahus at the beginning of the ceremony anointed himself with the sacred ointment and fastened upon his head

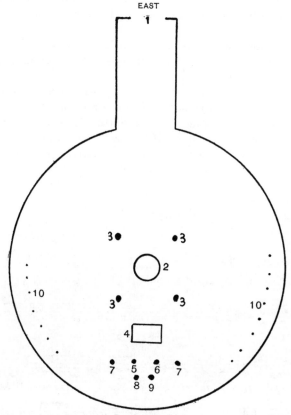

FIG. 173. Diagram of the Father's lodge during the singing of the first stanza of the song of the fourth ritual, part II.

1, the entrance to the lodge; 2, the fireplace; 3, inner posts supporting the dome-shaped roof; 4, the holy place; 5, the Ku'rahus; 6, his assistant; 7, the bearers of the eagle wings; 8, the Father (a chief); 9, the second chief; 10, members of the Hako party.

the downy eagle feather (see plate XCI).   Now he takes the rope of
buffalo hair with which the sacred objects have been bound to the
pole, and with it ties his buffalo robe around his waist.   He is now
fully dressed for the ceremony, and he stands at the west, back of the
holy place.

He anoints with the sacred ointment the face, arms, and body of
his assistant, ties a downy eagle feather on his scalp lock, puts a
buffalo robe on him in the ceremonial manner and hands him the
feathered stem with the white-eagle pendant; then the assistant
takes his position behind the holy place, toward the south.

The Ku'rahus next annoints the face of the chief and fastens on
his head a small tuft of down taken from under the wing of an eagle.
The chief wears his buffalo robe in the ceremonial manner.   The Ku'-
rahus hands the wildcat skin to the chief, who folds its head about
the crotched stick and the butt of the ear of corn, so that the tip to
which the downy eagle feather is fastened is well in sight above the
head of the cat.   The skin hangs down in front of the chief as he
holds it with both hands by the neck.   He takes his place back of the
Ku'rahus.

The second chief, who is to assist the first, is now given the sacred
pipe and tobacco bag of the Rain shrine and told to stand behind the
Ku'rahus's assistant.

The Ku'rahus hands the eagle wings to the doctors; the one with
the left wing stands to the north of the Ku'rahus, and the one with
the right wing takes his place to the south of the assistant.   Lastly
the Ku'rahus takes up for himself the feathered stem with the brown-
eagle pendant and then, with the six men all in position (see figure
173), they sing the first stanza of the following song.

SONG

Words and Music

I	II
172 H'Atira hu weta ariso!	178 H'Atira hu weti arisut!
173 H'Atira hu weta ariso!	179 H'Atira hu weti arisut!
174 H'Atira hu weta ariso!	180 H'Atira hu weti arisut!
175 H'Atira hu weta ariso!	181 H'Atira hu weti arisut!
176 H'Atira hu weta ariso!	182 H'Atira hu weti arisut!
177 H'Atira hu weta ariso!	183 H'Atira hu weti arisut!

Translation of First Stanza

172   H'Atira hu weta ariso!

> h', the sign of an aspiration; a breath; the symbol of giving life.
>
> atira, mother. The term is here applied to the ear of corn, the representative of Mother Earth.
>
> hu, the same as ha, yonder. The vowel is changed from a to u to give greater euphony in singing by avoiding the repetition of the sound a.
>
> weta, coming toward one, so as to overtake one.
>
> ariso, a living thing that has come from a great distance in time or space.

173–177   See line 172.

Explanation by the Ku'rahus

This stanza is sung four times. As we sing it the first time the principal chief takes a step with his right foot, which brings him on a line with the Ku'rahus and his assistant. When we sing it a second time he takes a step with his left foot, which leaves him in advance of the line of the Ku'rahus and his assistant. As we sing it a third time he takes a step with his right foot and turns toward the north. When we sing it the fourth time he advances a step with his left foot. He has now passed in front of the Ku'rahus as leader, and faces the north.

As we sing this song we remember that Mother Earth is very old. She is everywhere, she knows all men, she gave (supported) life to our fathers, she gives (supports) life to us, and she will give life to our children.

The ear of corn represents venerable Mother Earth, and also the authority given by the powers above; so, as the chief, holding the ear of corn, takes the four steps that bring him in advance of the Ku'rahus, we sing that Mother breathing forth life and bearing the sign of the powers above is now coming from the far distant past to go before us.

At the close of the fourth repeat the Ku'rahus tells the assistant chief to pass in front and stand at the right hand of the principal

chief.   When this is done, the Ku′rahus and his assistant and the two
doctors form a line behind the two chiefs; then we sing the following
stanza (see figure 174).

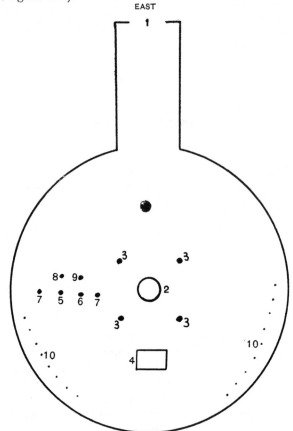

FIG. 174. Diagram of the Father's lodge during the singing of the second stanza of the song of
the fourth ritual, part II.

1, the entrance to the lodge; 2, the fireplace; 3, inner posts supporting the dome-shaped roof;
4, the holy place; 5, the Ku′rahus; 6, his assistant; 7, the bearers of the eagle wings; 8, the Father
(a chief); 9, the second chief; 10, members of the Hako party.

Translation of Second Stanza

178   H′Atira hu weti arisut!
> h′, the sign of breath, of giving forth life.
> atira, mother; the term applied to the ear of corn.
> hu; ha, yonder; the vowel is changed for euphony.
> weti, starting forward.   The object which was coming toward
>   one has overtaken the speaker and has started onward
>   before him.
> arisut, a living thing that is starting or has started to go a long
>   distance, as into future time or on a long journey.

179–183   See line 178.

Explanation by the Ku'rahus

We sing this stanza four times, taking a step at each repeat, the two chiefs leading with Mother Corn and the sacred pipe.

As we sing we think that Mother breathing forth life, who has come out of the past, has now started to lead us on the journey we are to take and to the fulfilment of our desire that children may be given us, that generations may not fail in the future, and that the tie may be made strong between the Father and the Son.

After this song the six men walk slowly toward the entrance to the lodge, going by the north, and all the others follow.

PART III. THE HAKO PARTY PRESENTED TO THE POWERS

Explanation by the Ku'rahus

When the Hako party are all outside of the door of the lodge, the six men stand abreast, the doctor with the left wing of the eagle to the north, on his right the Ku'rahus, then the principal chief, then the second chief, then the Ku'rahus's assistant, and the doctor with the right wing of the eagle at the end of the line toward the south.

At the word of the Ku'rahus the six men bearing the sacred objects advance abreast toward the east. The men of the Hako party fall in behind and are followed by the women. When all have walked forward a little way, the six men halt and sing the following song.

As the party sings the Ku'rahus lifts and points his feathered stem toward the east; the assistant does the same with his feathered stem; the chief makes the same movement with the wildcat skin, from the head of which protrudes the ear of corn; the second chief offers the stem of the pipe, and the two doctors hold up their eagle wings.

FIRST SONG

Words and Music

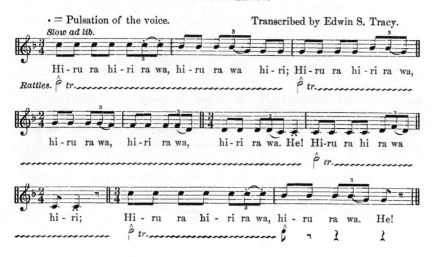

• = Pulsation of the voice. Transcribed by Edwin S. Tracy.
Slow ad lib.

Hi - ru ra hi - ri ra wa, hi - ru ra wa hi - ri; Hi - ru ra hi - ri ra wa,
Rattles. tr.

hi - ru ra wa, hi - ri ra wa, hi - ri ra wa. He! Hi - ru ra hi ra wa

hi - ri; Hi - ru ra hi - ri ra wa, hi - ru ra wa. He!

184 Hiru ra hiri ra wa, hiru ra wa hiri;
185 Hiru ra hiri ra wa, hiru ra wa, hiri ra wa. hiri ra wa. He!
186 Hiru ra hi ra wa hiri;
187 Hiru ra hiri ra wa, hiru ra wa. He!

Translation

184 Hiru ra hiri ra wa, hiru ra wa hiri.
    hiru; iru, they yonder; the h is prefixed for euphony and to
       give ease in singing.
    ra, coming.
    hiri; iri, they who are far away; the h is prefixed for euphony.
    ra, moving, moving this way.
    wa, part of the word teware, passing through the air.
    hiru, they yonder; the h is for euphony.
    ra, coming.
    wa, from teware, darting through the air.
    hiri, they who are far away; the h is used for euphony.
185 Hiru ra hiri ra wa, hiru ra wa, hiri ra wa, hiri ra wa. He!
    hiru ra hiri ra wa, hiru ra wa, hiri ra wa. See line 184.
    he! a part of the exclamation i'hare! meaning I think upon
       and consider the significance of (the act which accompanies
       the song); the change of the r to h is for euphony.
186 Hiru ra hi ra wa hiri.
    hiru ra. See line 184.
    hi, part of the word hiri, translated above.
    ra wa hiri. See line 184.
187 Hiru ra hiri ra wa, hiru ra wa. He! All the words are trans-
    lated above. See lines 184 and 185.

Explanation by the Ku'rahus

This song is addressed to Tira'wa atius. He is the father of all and
all things come from him. We pray in our hearts as we sing. We
ask Tira'wa to watch over the Ku'rahus, to guide his acts and to guard
his words so that he may make no mistake and the ceremony may be
complete. From the east the flashes of the eyes of Tira'wa come darting through the air upon us and upon the sacred objects.

We sing this song four times and then take sixteen steps to the
east; there we turn and face the west, the people all behind us.

As we stand and look toward the west we remember that it is there
that the four lesser powers dwell who were permitted by Tira'wa atius
to bring life to man. These powers also control the thunder, the
lightning, the storm, and death.

We sing the first stanza of the following song to them eight times.

Words and Music

M. M. ♩ = 42.
• = Pulsation of the voice.   Transcribed by Edwin S. Tracy.

A! Hi - ri, ra ri - hi - u!   A! Hi - ri, ra ri - hi - u!   A!

Rattles.

Hi - ri, ra ri - hi - u!   A! Hi - ri, ra ri - hi - u!   A! Hi - ri, ra ri - hi - u!   A!

Hi - ri, ra ri - hi - u!   A! Hi - ri, ra ri - hi - u!   A! Hi - ri, ra ri - hi - u!

I

188 A! Hiri, ra rihiu!   A! Hiri, ra rihiu!
189 A! Hiri, ra rihiu!   A! Hiri, ra rihiu!
190 A! Hiri, ra rihiu!
191 A! Hiri, ra rihiu!
192 A! Hiri, ra rihiu!
193 A! Hiri, ra rihiu!

II

194 H'Uraru ha! Hiri re! H'Uraru ha! Hiri re!
195 H'Uraru ha! Hiri re! H'Uraru ha! Hiri re!
196 H'Uraru ha! Hiri re!
197 H'Uraru ha! Hiri re!
198 H'Uraru ha! Hiri re!
199 H'Uraru ha! Hiri re!

III

200 H'Uraru riri wari!   H'Uraru riri wari!
201 H'Uraru riri wari!   H'Uraru riri wari!
202 H'Uraru riri wari!
203 H'Uraru riri wari!
204 H'Uraru riri wari!
205 H'Uraru riri wari!

Translation of First Stanza

188 A! Hiri, ra rihiu! A! Hiri, ra rihiu!

  a! a part of ha! behold! The exclamation nas here a double
    meaning; the people are to look toward the powers and the
    powers are called upon to behold the people.

  hiri, they far away; an address to the powers. The h is pre-
    fixed for euphony.

  ra, come.

  rihiu; rihi, is the place; u, a vocable to fill out the measure.

189–193. See line 188.

Explanation by the Ku'rahus

When we have finished singing the six men take sixteen steps back to the place where the first song was sung as we faced the east. Then they take eight steps toward the south, where they stand facing the south and sing the following stanza, the people being all behind them.

Translation of Second Stanza

194   H'Uraru ha!   Hiri re!   H'Uraru ha!   Hiri re!
  H'Uraru, the earth.
  ha! behold!
  hiri, they far away; an address to the powers of the south.
  re, are, in the sense of being, living.
195–199   See line 194.

Explanation by the Ku'rahus

When we sing this stanza we are standing and looking toward the south. That is the place where the sun travels, where the light comes, and the brightness of day.

As we look we ask the powers of the south to give life and increase to us, as well as to the seeds within Mother Earth.

After we have sung this stanza eight times to the powers of the south, we turn and take eight steps toward the entrance of the lodge, to a place just back of where we sang the first song to the east; then eight steps toward the north, all the people following. Here, facing the north, we sing the next stanza.

Translation of Third Stanza

200   H'Uraru riri wari!   H'Uraru riri wari!
  H'Uraru, the earth.
  riri, on.
  wari, walking.
201–205   See line 200.

Explanation by the Ku'rahus

The people are now looking toward the north, the moon, the night, the mother of the day.

We ask the powers of the north, they who can see the path of life, to lead us and make us able to walk, us and our children.

We sing this song eight times to the powers of the north.

Then the six men turn south and take eight steps toward the entrance of the lodge, to a point before the place where we sang the first song to the east; there they turn and face east and walk to the place where they sang to the powers of the west, and there they halt.

To all the powers of the east, west, south, and north we have sung and have presented ourselves. As we walked, we have traced upon

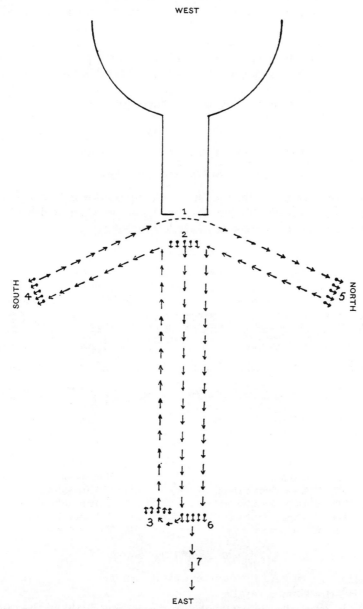

FIG. 175. Diagram showing the movements of the principal members of the Father's party during the presentation to the powers.

1, entrance to the lodge; 2, place where the first song is sung; 3, place where the first stanza of the second song is sung; 4, place where the second stanza of the second song is sung; 5, place where the third stanza of the second song is sung; 6, place where the halt is made after the last sixteen steps; 7, the four steps taken in the presence of the powers.

The dots represent the following persons, beginning at the left: the doctor with the left wing of the eagle, the Ku'rahus, the principal chief (the Father, if he is a chief), the second chief, the Ku'rahus's assistant, and the doctor with the right wing of an eagle. The arrows attached to the dots show the direction in which the persons are facing. (By an error, but five dots were drawn, instead of six.) Each of the other arrows represents a step taken by the group, and points in the direction in which it is taken.

the earth the figure of a man. This image that we have traced is from Tira'wa. It has gone around with us, and its feet are where we now stand; its feet are with our feet and will move with them as we now take four steps, bearing the sacred objects, in the presence of all the powers and begin our journey to the land of the Son (see figure 175).

SECOND DIVISION. THE JOURNEY

FIFTH RITUAL

PART I. MOTHER CORN ASSERTS AUTHORITY

Explanation by the Ku'rahus

After we have taken the four steps in the presence of all the powers we are ready to begin our journey, but before we start, and while we stand facing the east, we sing the following song:

FIRST SONG

Words and Music

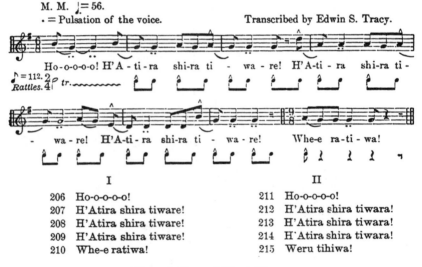

I

206   Ho-o-o-o-o!
207   H'Atira shira tiware!
208   H'Atira shira tiware!
209   H'Atira shira tiware!
210   Whe-e ratiwa!

II

211   Ho-o-o-o-o!
212   H'Atira shira tiwara!
213   H'Atira shira tiwara!
214   H'Atira shira tiwara!
215   Weru tihiwa!

Translation of First Stanza

206   Ho-o-o-o-o!   An introductory exclamation.
207   H'Atira shira tiware!

> h', an aspiration, symbolic of a breathing forth, as the giving of breath so that a thing may live.

> atira, mother. The term is here applied to the ear of corn.

> shira, it and me; it refers to the ear of corn, Mother Corn; me refers to the Father's party spoken of or speaking in the singular, as one person.

> tiware, walking in a devious or a winding course.

208–209   See line 207.

210　Whe-e ratiwa!

　　　whe, now, at this time.

　　　e, prolongation of the final e in whe.

　　　ratiwa, walking, plural form; that is, Mother Corn and the
　　　　　Father's party are walking as two persons. See the trans-
　　　　　lation of shira (line 207).

Explanation by the Ku'rahus

Mother Corn, who led our spirits over the path we are now to travel,
leads us again as we walk, in our bodies, over the land.

When we were selecting the Son (second ritual) we had to fix our
minds on Mother Corn and make our spirits as one spirit with her.
We must do so now, as we are about to start on this journey; we must
be as one mind, one person, with Mother Corn (h'Atira shira); we,
as one person, must walk with her over the devious, winding path
(tiware) which leads to the land of the Son.

We speak of this path as devious, not merely because we must go
over hills and through valleys and wind around gulches to reach the
land of the Son, but because we are thinking of the way by which,
through the Hako, we can make a man who is not of our blood a Son;
a way which has come down to us from our far-away ancestors like a
winding path.

Translation of Second Stanza

211　Ho-o-o-o-o! An introductory exclamation.

212　H'Atira shira tiwara.

　　　h', symbolic of breathing forth.

　　　atira, mother; the term refers to the corn.

　　　shira, it and me; the ear of corn and the party of the Father.

　　　tiwara, walking in a definite path, a straight path.

213, 214　See line 212.

215　Weru tihiwa.

　　　weru, by or according to, indicating order or arrangement.

　　　tihiwa, equal stages; divided into equal lengths, as when mark-
　　　　　ing a line of travel by a number of camps.

Explanation by the Ku'rahus

This stanza means that Mother Corn will lead us in the path she
opened and made safe for us when she went in search of the Son.
The path is definite to her, like a straight path, in which we are to
journey by equal stages (weru tihiwa). First we are to travel, then
we are to camp, then travel, and again camp. This is the way our
fathers did, and the knowledge has come down to us from father to
son, from father to son, by generations, in equal stages all the way.

After singing the stanza the six men with the Hako move forward
and all follow; Mother Corn is leading and breathing forth life.

After we have moved on a little distance, and have left the village behind us so that we can no longer see our homes, we halt and sing the first stanza of the following song.

SECOND SONG

Words and Music

M. M. ♪=112.
• = Pulsation of the voice.   Transcribed by Edwin S. Tracy.

I

216 Ho-o-o-o!
217 Kara haturu ta? Kara haturu ta?
218 H'Atira kuhra haturu e?
219 Kara haturu ta? H'Atira kuhra haturu e?

II

220 Ho-o-o-o!
221 Wiri haturu ta, wiri haturu ta;
222 H'Atira kuhra haturu e;
223 Wiri haturu ta, h'Atira kuhra haturu e.

Translation of First Stanza

216 Ho-o-o-o! An introductory exclamation.
217 Kara haturu ta? Kara haturu ta?
    kara, is there? An inquiry.
    haturu, path, road, way.
    ta, a part of the word ruta, a long stretch, as a long stretch
        of road or of country. In order to make the words con-
        form to the rhythm of the music the final syllable of
        haturu is made to serve as the first syllable of the next
        word (ruta), so only the last syllable, ta, is given.
218 H'Atira kuhra haturu e?
    h', symbolic of the breath; a breathing forth.
    atira, mother. The term applies to Mother Corn.
    kuhra, hers; the owner of.
    haturu, path, road, way.
    e, the equivalent of ta, a part of ruta. The change from ta to
        e is for euphony.
219 Kara haturu ta? H'Atira kuhra haturu e? All the words are
        translated above. See lines 217 and 218.

Explanation by the Ku'rahus

Before us lies a wide pathless stretch of country. We are standing alone and unarmed, facing a land of strangers, and we call upon

Mother Corn and we ask her: "Is there a path through this long stretch of country before us where we can see nothing? Does your path, the one which you opened for us, wherein is safety, lie here?"

Translation of Second Stanza

220 Ho-o-o-o! An introductory exclamation.
221 Wiri haturu ta, wiri haturu ta.
    wiri; here, at this place; right before one.
    haturu, path, road, way.
    ta, part of the word ruta, a long stretch.
222 See line 218.
223 Wiri haturu ta, h'Atira kuhra haturu e. All the words are translated above. See lines 221 and 218.

Explanation by the Ku'rahus

As we stand and sing the second stanza, Mother Corn speaks to us and we are assured in our spirits. She answers our appeal; she says that here, right before us, stretches out the path she has made straight. Then our eyes are opened and we see the way we are to go.

But although we see our way we are not to take the path by ourselves; we must follow Mother Corn; she must lead us, must direct and guide our steps. The next song is to enforce obedience to Mother Corn.

THIRD SONG

Words and Music

M. M. ♪ = 112.
• = Pulsation of the voice.   Transcribed by Edwin S. Tracy.

I	II
224 Ho-o-o-o!	230 Ho-o-o-o!
225 Ra rihi u hawa ratira e;	231 Ti rihi u hawa ratira e;
226 Ra rihi u hawa ratira e;	232 Ti rihi u hawa ratira e;
227 Hawa-a ra rihi u hawa ratira e;	233 Hawa-a ti rihi u hawa ratira e;
228 Ra rihi u hawa ratira e;	234 Ti rihi u hawa ratira e;
229 Ra rihi u hawa ratira e.	235 Ti rihi u hawa ratira e.

Translation of First Stanza

224   Ho-o-o-o!   An introductory exclamation.
225   Ra rihi u hawa ratira e.
        ra, at a distance; yonder.
        rihi, a place; a locality.
        u, a particular place.
        hawa, whence; from where.
        ratira, I came.
        e, vowel prolongation to meet the rhymth of the music.
226   See line 225.
227   Hawa-a ra rihi u hawa ratira e.
        hawa, whence; from where.
        a, vowel prolongation.
        ra rihi u hawa ratira e.   See line 225.
228, 229   See line 225.

Explanation by the Ku'rahus

When this song is to be sung, the Ku'rahus bids all the people go in front of him, then he and they all turn and face the west, and look toward the lodge of the Father within which the preliminary ceremonies have been performed, and before the entrance of which the powers have looked on the elevated sacred objects and upon all the people.

In this song Mother Corn is speaking of the place whence she came when she was consecrated according to the rites given to our fathers. She led our fathers and she leads us now, because she was born of Mother Earth and knows all places and all people, and because she has on her the sign (the blue-paint symbol) of having been up to Tira'wahut, where power was given her over all creatures. She also is speaking of the path over which her spirit led our spirits when we were traveling in search of the Son.[a]

Translation of Second Stanza

330   Ho-o-o-o!   An introductory exclamation.
331   Ti rihi u hawa ratira e;
        ti, this.
        rihi u hawa ratira e.   See line 225.
332   See line 331.
333   Hawa-a ti rihi u hawa ratira e.   See lines 225, 227, and 331.
334, 335   See line 331.

Explanation by the Ku'rahus

As we sing the second stanza, the Ku'rahus points along the path we have already traveled under the leadership of Mother Corn.

This act and the song are to impress upon the people that they

---

[a] See first ritual, second ritual, and fourth ritual.

are not moving at random, but in a prescribed manner, which the Ku'rahus has been taught and directed to follow; that they are led by Mother Corn authorized by the powers, and to her they must give unquestioning obedience throughout the ceremony.

After this song the Ku'rahus and the other bearers of the sacred objects turn, and facing the east, pass on in front of the people, who also turn and follow as they go forth on the journey.

The three songs we have just sung are in sequence. Their order can not be changed; they belong to the beginning of the journey, and teach us to obey Mother Corn.

PART II. SONGS AND CEREMONIES OF THE WAY

Explanation by the Ku'rahus

The journey we are taking is for a sacred purpose, and as we are led by the supernatural power in Mother Corn we must address with song every object we meet, because Tira'wa is in all things. Everything we come to as we travel can give us help, and send help by us to the Children.

Trees are among the lesser powers, and they are represented on the Hako which we carry, so when we see trees we must sing to them.

Trees grow along the banks of the streams; we can see them at a distance, like a long line, and we can see the river glistening in the sunlight in its length. We sing to the river, and when we come nearer and see the water and hear it rippling, then we sing to the water, the water that ripples as it runs.

SONG TO THE TREES AND STREAMS

Words and Music

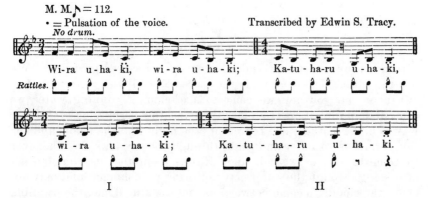

M. M. ♪ = 112.
• = Pulsation of the voice.   Transcribed by Edwin S. Tracy.
No drum.

Wi-ra u-ha-ki, wi-ra u-ha-ki; Ka-tu-ha-ru u-ha-ki,

Rattles.

wi-ra u-ha-ki; Ka-tu-ha-ru u-ha-ki.

I	II
236 Wira uhaki, wira uhaki;	239 Wira uhaki, wira uhaki;
237 Katuharu uhaki, wira uhaki;	240 Kichaharu uhaki, wira uhaki;
238 Katuharu uhaki.	241 Kichaharu uhaki.

III

242 Wira wihaku, wira wihaku;
243 Kichaharu wihaku, wira wihaku;
244 Kichaharu wihaku.

Translation

I

236 Wira uhaki, wira uhaki.
    wira; wi, a qualifying word meaning that an object is long or
        stretched out; ra, at a distance, yonder.
    uhaki, something that is in a line, a stretch.
237 Katuharu uhaki, wira uhaki.
    katuharu, trees, timber, woods.
    uhaki, a long line, a stretch.
    wira uhaki. See line 236.
238 Katuharu uhaki. See line 237.

II

239 See line 236.
240 Kichaharu uhaki, wira uhaki.
    kichaharu, a stream, a river.
    uhaki, a long stretch.
    wira uhaki. See line 236.
241 Kichaharu uhaki. See line 240.

III

242 Wira wihaku, wira wihaku.
    wira, something that is long seen at a distance.
    wihaku, rippling.
243 Kichaharu wihaku; wira wiharu.
    kichaharu, a stream, a river.
    wihaku, rippling.
    wira wihaku. See line 242.
244 Kichaharu wihaku. See line 243.

Explanation by the Ku'rahus

In this ceremony water is not used except for sacred purposes. We
mix the paint that we use upon the sacred objects with running water.
When on our journey we come to a stream of running water we
can not step into it to cross it without asking permission of Kawas.
Kawas is the mother; she represents the night and the moon, and she
can permit us to enter and wade through the stream. So, whenever
we come to a river we call upon Kawas to protect us, that our act
of passing through the water may not bring punishment, and may not
cause the clouds to come between us and the blue dome, the dwelling
place of Tira'wa, or break the continuity of life from one generation
to another.

The following song is our appeal to Kawas. When we sing the
first stanza we enter the stream, the water touches our feet.

SONG WHEN CROSSING THE STREAMS

Words and Music

M. M. ♪ = 116.

• = Pulsation of the voice.   Transcribed by Edwin S. Tracy.

No drum.

Ho-o-o! He! Ka-was si-re te-wi   hu-ku-ka, Te-wi hu-ku-ka. He! Ka-was si-re a he!

Ka-was si-re   te-wi   hu-ku-ka. He! Ka-was si-re   te-wi   hu-ku-ka.

I

245 Ho-o-o!
246 He! Kawas sire tewi hukuka,
247 Tewi hukuka.
248 He! Kawas sire a he! Kawas sire tewi hukuka.
249 He! Kawas sire tewi hukuka.

II

250 Ho-o-o!
251 He! Kawas sire tewi hariki,
252 Tewi hariki.
253 He! Kawas sire a he! Kawas sire tewi hariki.
254 He! Kawas sire tewi hariki.

III

255 Ho-o-o!
256 He! Kawas sire tewi haiwa,
257 Tewi haiwa.
258 He! Kawas sire a he! Kawas sire tewi haiwa.
259 He! Kawas sire tewi haiwa.

IV

260 Ho-o-o!
261 He! Kawas sire tewi hawitshpa,
262 Tewi hawitshpa.
263 He! Kawas sire a he! Kawas seri tewi hawitshpa.
264 He! Kawas sire tewi hawitshpa.

Translation

I

245 Ho-o-o! An introductory exclamation.

246 He! Kawas sire tewi hukuka.

he! a part of the exclamation hiri! give heed! harken!

Kawas; the brown eagle, which in this ceremony represents the feminine principle, the night, the moon.

sire, its; a possessive pronoun referring to Kawas.

tewi, it has; refers to the water.

hukuka, a composite word; hu, from chaharu, water; kuka, to step into, as to put one's feet in the water, to wade.

247 Tewi hukuka.

tewi, it has; the water has touched the feet.

hukuka, step into the water. The feet have stepped into the water.

248 He! Kawas sire a he! Kawas sire tewi hukuka.
  he! give heed! harken!
  Kawas, the mother, the brown eagle.
  sire, its; refers to the control of the water by Kawas.
  a, a vocable used to fill out the measure of the music.
  he! Kawas sire tewi hukuka. See line 246.
249 See line 246.

II

250 Ho-o-o! An introductory exclamation.
251 He! Kawas sire tewi hariki.
  he! part of the exclamation hiri! harken! give heed!
  Kawas, the brown eagle, representing the female principle.
  sire, its.
  tewi, it has.
  hariki, a composite word; ha, a part of chaharu, water; riki,
   standing.
252 Tewi hariki.
  tewi, it has.
  hariki, water standing. Our feet are standing in the water.
253 He! Kawas sire a he! Kawas sire tewi hariki. See lines 248
  and 251.
254 See line 251.

III

255 Ho-o-o! An introductory exclamation.
256 He! Kawas sire tewi haiwa.
  he! part of the word hiri! harken! give heed!
  Kawas, the brown eagle; the mother, the female principle.
  sire, its; refers to Kawas.
  tewi, it has.
  haiwa, a composite word; ha, part of chaharu, water; iwa,
   moving in: haiwa, moving in the water.
257 Tewi haiwa. See line 256.
258 He! Kawas sire a he! Kawas sire tewi haiwa. See lines 248
  and 256.
259 See line 256.

IV.

260 Ho-o-o! An introductory exclamation.
261 He! Kawas sire tewi hawitshpa.
  he! harken! give heed!
  Kawas, the brown eagle; the mother, the female principle.
  sire, its; refers to Kawas.
  tewi, it has; refers to the water.
  hawitshpa, a composite word; ha, part of chaharu, water;
   witshpa, completed, accomplished a purpose, reached an
   end. The meaning of the word is that the water has covered the feet.

262   Tewi hawitshpa.   See line 261.

263   He! Kawas sire a he! Kawas sire tewi hawitshpa.   See lines
            248 and 261.

264   See line 261.

Explanation by the Ku'rahus

When we sing the second stanza, our feet are standing in the water.
When the third stanza is sung, our feet are moving in the water.   At
the fourth stanza the water covers our feet.   So as we sing this song we
enter the stream and, under the protection of Kawas, we pass through
to the other side.

Every time we come to a stream across which our path lies we must
sing this song.

After we have forded the stream we pause at the bank.   We are
wet with water through which we have just passed, but we must not
touch our bodies where we are wet to dry ourselves, for the running
water is sacred.

So, we sing the first stanza of the following song and call on the
Wind, Hotoru, to come and touch us that we may become dry.

SONG TO THE WIND

Words and Music

M. M. ♪ = 132.
• = Pulsation of the voice.   Transcribed by Edwin S. Tracy.

I		III
265 Ho-o-o-o !	273 Ho-o-o-o !
266 Tukuka, tukuka ha Hotoru,	274 Tawawe, tawawe he Hotoru,
267 Tukuka ha Hotoru,	275 Tawawe he Hotoru,
268 Tukuka ha !	276 Tawawe he !

II		IV
269 Ho-o-o-o !	277 Ho-o-o-o !
270 Taiwa, taiwa ha Hotoru,	278 Tawitshpa, tawitshpa ha Hotoru,
271 Taiwa ha Hotoru,	279 Tawitshpa ha Hotoru,
272 Taiwa ha !	280 Tawitshpa ha !

Translation

I

265 Ho-o-o-o! An introductory exclamation.
266 Tukuka, tukuka ha Hotoru.
    tukuka, touch or touched.
    ha, a syllable added to meet the rhythm of the music.
    Hotoru, the Wind, the supernatural power.
267 Tukuka ha Hotoru. See line 266.
268 Tukuka ha! See line 266.

II

269 Ho-o-o-o! An introductory exclamation.
270 Taiwa, taiwa ha Hotoru.
    taiwa, to touch lightly or brush on the sides of anything.
    ha, a syllable added for the sake of rhythm.
    Hotoru, the Wind, one of the lesser power.
271 Taiwa ha Hotoru. See line 270.
272 Taiwa ha! See line 270.

III

273 Ho-o-o-o! An introductory exclamation.
274 Tawawe, tawawe he Hotoru.
    tawawe, a creeping touch, felt now here and now there.
    he, a syllable added to keep the rhythm of the music.
    Hotoru, the Wind, one of the lesser powers.
275 Tawawe he Hotoru. See line 274.
276 Tawawe he! See line 274.

IV

277 See line 265.
278 Tawitshpa, tawitshpa ha Hotoru.
    tawitshpa, the completion of an act, the accomplishment of
      a purpose. Hotoru has completely touched all parts of
      the body.
    ha, a syllable added to fill out the rhythm of the music.
    Hoturu, the Wind; one of the lesser powers.
279 Tawitshpa ha Hotoru. See line 278.
280 Tawitshpa ha! See line 278.

Explanation by the Ku'rahus

As we sing the second stanza the Wind brushes lightly the sides of our bodies and our wet legs and feet. With the third stanza the Wind circles about, touching us here and there. When we sing the fourth stanza the Wind completely envelops us, touching all parts of our bodies. Now, we are ready to move forward in safety. No harm will follow our passage of the river and we can pursue our journey.

Whenever, as we travel, we have to cross a river we must sing this song to the Wind to come and dry our bodies before we can continue our journey.

When the spirit of Mother Corn was traveling in search of the Son (second ritual) she saw buffalo; the first stanza of the following song refers to that time (ira saka riki, an indefinite time in the past). So, when on our journey we come to buffalo trails, or see the herds at a distance, we know that they have been seen before, at this place, by the spirit of Mother Corn, and we sing this song.

SONG TO THE BUFFALO

Words and Music

M. M. ♩ = 120.
• = Pulsation of the voice.   Transcribed by Edwin S. Tracy.

Ha a-a a!   Ha! I-ra sa-ka ri-ki;   Ha! I - ra   ri-ki;   Ha! I-ra sa-ka ri- ki;

Drum.
Rattles.

Ha! I - ra   ri-ki; Ha! I-ra sa-ka ri - ki;   Ha! I - ra   ri-ki.

I

281 Ha-a-a-a!
282 Ha! Ira saka riki; Ha! Ira riki;
283 Ha! Ira saka riki; Ha! Ira riki;
284 Ha! Ira saka riki; Ha! Ira riki.

II

285 Ha-a-a-a!
286 Ha! Tira saka riki; Ha! Ire wawa;
287 Ha! Tira saka riki; Ha! Ire wawa;
288 Ha! Tira saka riki; Ha! Ire wawa.

Translation

I

281   Ha-a-a-a! An introductory exclamation.
282   Ha! Ira saka riki; Ha! Ira riki.
  ha! behold!
  ira, a single object in the distance; ra, distant, also means in
    the past, distant as to time.
  saka, part of the word tarasaka, sun.
  riki, standing. Saka riki means present time; but, as the
    words follow ira, the phrase ira saka riki means an indefi-
    nite time in the past.
  ha! behold! see!
  ira, the object seen at an indefinite time in the past.
  riki, standing; referring to the object that was seen. Al-
    though the object seen is not mentioned by name, it was
    known to be buffalo.
283, 284 See line 282.

II

285 Ha-a-a-a! An introductory exclamation.
286 Ha! Tira saka riki; Ha! Ire wawa.

> ha! behold!
> tira, this.
> saka, part of the word tarasaka, sun.
> riki, standing. Saka riki means present time. The phrase tira saka riki means a definite time, at this time or moment.
> ha! behold! see! look!
> ire, many objects at a distance, as many trails with buffalo.
> wawa, many walking. The phrase "Ha! Ire wawa" means "Look, where many buffalo walk in many different trails!" This refers to different herds seen at a distance.

287, 288 See line 286.

Explanation by the Ku'rahus

The second stanza refers to our seeing with our own eyes the buffalo herds walking in many different trails. We sing of this sight and we carry its promise of plenty to the Children.

These stanzas are not now sung upon the journey with the Hako, because the buffalo herds are all gone; but we sing them in the lodge of the Son, in remembrance of the buffalo, the animal Tira′wa gave us for food.

SONG OF THE PROMISE OF THF BUFFALO

Words and Music

M. M. ♩ = 120.
• = Pulsation of the voice.   Transcribed by Edwin S. Tracy.

He-e-e-e! We-re ru-wa-wa, we-re ru-wa-wa, Si-ra rit-ka

Drum. Rattles.

ru-wa-wa, We-re ru-wa-wa, Si-ra rit-ka ru-wa-wa-a ra.

I

289 He-e-e-e!
290 Were ruwawa, were ruwawa,
291 Sira ritka ruwawa,
292 Were ruwawa,
293 Sira ritka ruwawa-a ra.

II

294 He-e-e-e!
295 Wera hara-a, wera hara-a.
296 Taraha-a rahara,
297 Wera hara-a,
298 Taraha-a rahara-a ra.

Translation

I

289 He-e-e-e! An introductory exclamation.
290 Were ruwawa, were ruwawa.
  were, they; a number of persons or animals.
  ruwawa, running from, as from the place where one is standing or where one is walking.
291 Sira ritka ruwawa.
  sira, their.
  ritka, dust; the soil raised by the feet in running.
  ruwawa, running away from.
292 Were ruwawa. See line 290.
293 Sira ritka ruwawa-a ra.
  sira ritka ruwawa. See lines 290, 291.
  a ra, vocables used to fill out the rhythm of the music.

II

294 He-e-e-e! An introductory exclamation.
295 Wera hara-a, wera hara-a.
  wera, one coming; we, one, it, singular number; ra, coming.
  hara-a, a composite word made up of the syllable ha, from the
   word iha're, the young of animals (the word is also used
   for offspring, children) and ra, coming. The final a is a
   vowel prolongation to fill the rhythm of the music.
296 Taraha-a rahara.
  taraha, the female buffalo.
  a, vowel prolongation because of the rhythm of the music.
  rahara, a composite word; ra, from wera, one coming; ha, from
   iha're, young; ra, coming. The line "Taraha-a rahara"
   means that the female buffalo and her calf are coming.
297 Wera hara-a. See line 295.
298 Taraha-a rahara-a ra. See lines 293, 296.

Explanation by the Ku'rahus

While we were traveling we sometimes saw a great cloud of dust
rising in the distance. When we saw this cloud rolling up from the
earth we knew it was caused by a herd of buffalo running away from
us toward the land of the Children.

Sometimes a cow and her calf would separate from the herd and
come nearer us. We were taught to be mindful of all that we saw
upon the journey, for these sights meant the promise of plenty of food
for the Children.

We do not sing this song any more as we travel, for now there are
no buffalo herds to be seen sending the dust up to the sky as they
run. We sing the song in the lodge of the Son, that we may remember the buffalo, and that our children may hear of them.

When as we travel we come to mountains or hills we sing the following song.

Hills were made by Tira'wa. We ascend hills when we go away alone to pray. From the top of a hill we can look over the country to see if there are enemies in sight or if any danger is near us; we can see if we are to meet friends. The hills help man, so we sing to them.

SONG TO THE MOUNTAINS

Words and Music

M. M. ♪ = 168.

• = Pulsation of the voice.   Transcribed by Edwin S. Tracy.

I

299   Ha-a-a-a-a!
300   Ira whaku werechih whara;
301   Ira whaku werechih whara.
302   Ha! Chih whaku werechih whara.
303   Ha! Whaku werechih whara.

II

304   Ha-a-a-a-a!
305   Ira whaku werechih katawara;
306   Ira whaku werechih katawara.
307   Ha! Chih katawara chih wara.
308   Ha! Whaku werechih katawara.

III

309   Ha-a-a-a-a!
310   Ira whaku werechih kitta hra;
311   Ira whaku werechih kitta hra.
312   Ha! Chih e werechih kitta hra.
313   Ha! Whaku werechih kitta hra.

IV

314   Ha-a-a-a-a!
315   Ira whaku werechih kitta witit;
316   Ira whaku werechih kitta witit.
317   Ha! Chih werechih kitta witit.
318   Ha! Whaku werechih kitta witit.

Translation

I

299   Ha-a-a-a-a! An introductory exclamation.
300   Ira whaku werechih whara.
    ira, yonder particular and single object.
    whaku, an elevation, a mountain, a hill.
    werechih, a party, a number of persons.
    whara, walking, traveling on foot.
301   See line 300.
302   Ha! Chih whaku werechih whara.
    ha! behold!
    chih, the last syllable of the word werechih, a party.
    whaku werechih whara. See line 300.
303   Ha! Whaku werechih whara. See lines 300, 302.

II

304 Ha-a-a-a-a! An introductory exclamation.
305 Ira whaku werechiḫ katawara.
    ira, a particular and a single object at a distance.
    whaku, a mountain, a hill.
    werechiḫ, a group of persons making an organized party.
    katawara, climbing as they walk.
306 See line 305.
307 Ha! Chiḫ katawara chiḫ wara.
    ha! behold!
    chiḫ, the last syllable of the word werechiḫ, a company of
        persons, a party having a common purpose.
    katawara, climbing, ascending a mountain or a hill.
    chiḫ, part of the word werechiḫ, party.
    wara, a part of the word katawara, ascending, climbing.
308 Ha! Whaku werechiḫ katawara. See lines 305, 307.

III

309 Ha-a-a-a-a! An introductory exclamation.
310 Ira whaku werechiḫ kitta hra.
    ira, a particular and single object at a distance.
    whaku, a mountain or a hill.
    werechiḫ, a party.
    kitta, top, as the top of a mountain or hill.
    hra, from whara, walking.
311 See line 310.
312 Ha! Chiḫ e werechiḫ kitta hra.
    ha! behold!
    chiḫ, the last syllable of werechiḫ, party.
    e, a vocable used to fill out the measure of the music.
    werechiḫ, a party, a company of people.
    kitta, top; the summit of a mountain or a hill.
    hra, from whara, traveling on foot.
313 Ha! Whaku werechiḫ kitta hra. See lines 310, 312.

IV

314 Ha-a-a-a-a! An introductory exclamation.
315 Ira whaku werechiḫ kitta witit.
    ira, yonder particular object.
    whaku, mountain or hill.
    werechiḫ, an organized group of persons, a party.
    kitta, summit, top.
    witit, sitting down.
316 See line 315.

317 Ha! Chih werechih kitta witit.

    ha! behold!

    chih, the last syllable of werechih, a party.

    verechih, an organized group of persons, a party.

    kitta, summit of a mountain or hill.

    witit, to sit down, to rest.

318 Ha! Whaku werechih kitta witit. See lines 315, 317.

Explanation by the Ku'rahus

The first stanza is sung when we who are traveling see in the distance the top of a mountain or hill rising above the horizon. The Ku'rahus calls the attention of the people and bids them look at the mountain that lies in the path before them. We sing the next stanza as we are about to climb the mountain. The third stanza is sung when the party reaches the top of the mountain. While the people are sitting down to rest on the summit we sing the fourth stanza.

As a Hako party does not now go in a direction where there are mountains and hills, they do not sing these songs on the journey. They are generally sung in the lodge of the Son.

SONG TO THE MESAS

Words and Music

M. M. Melody. ♩ = 58.
M. M. Drum. ♪ = 116.
• = Pulsation of the voice.

Transcribed by Edwin S. Tracy.

Ho- o-o-o-o! Ha-re wi - tu; ha-re wi-tu; ha-re wi - tu; ha-

Drum. ⅔
Rattles. ⅝

re wi - tu; Ha-re wi-tu; ha-re wi - tu; ha-re wi - tu.

I

319 Ho-o-o-o-o!

320 Hare witu; hare witu; hare witu; hare witu;

321 Hare witu; hare witu; hare witu.

II

322 Ho-o-o-o-o!

323 Ha rha witu; ha rha witu; ha rha witu; ha rha witu;

324 Ha rha witu; ha rha witu; ha rha witu.

III

325 Ho-o-o-o-o!

326 Hare wawe; hare wawe; hare wawe; hare wawe;

327 Hare wawe; hare wawe; hare wawe.

IV

328 Ho-o-o-o-o!

329 Ha rha wawe; ha rha wawe; ha rha wawe; ha rha wawe;

330 Ha rha wawe; ha rha wawe; ha rha wawe.

Translation

I

319 Ho-o-o-o-o! An introductory exclamation.
320 Hare witu; hare witu; hare witu; hare witu.
  hare, yonder, at a short distance.
  witu, a mesa, an elevation or hill with a flat top.
321 See line 320.

II

322 Ho-o-o-o-o! An introductory exclamation.
323 Ha rha witu; ha rha witu; ha rha witu; ha rha witu.
  ha, yonder.
  rha, beyond this one; meaning that another mesa is seen
    beyond the one in the foreground.
  witu, a mesa.
324 See line 323.

III

325 Ho-o-o-o-o! An introductory exclamation.
326 Hare wawe; hare wawe; hare wawe.
  hare, yonder, at a short distance.
  wawe, the ridge or rim of the mesa.
327 See line 326.

IV

328 Ho-o-o-o-o! An introductory exclamation.
329 Ha rha wawe; ha rha wawe; ha rha wawe; ha rha wawe.
  ha, yonder.
  rha, beyond this one; that is, the one in the foreground just
    spoken of.
  wawe, the rim or sharp ridge of the mesa.
330 See line 329.

Explanation by the Ku'rahus

We are told that long ago our fathers used to see the mesas; that
on their journeys with the Hako they passed by or over these flat-
topped mountains. This song has come down to us from that time.
As we have never seen mesas, we do not sing the song on the journey;
we sing it in the lodge of the Son, that we may not forget what our
fathers saw when they traveled far from where we now dwell.

PART III. MOTHER CORN REASSERTS LEADERSHIP

Explanation by the Ku'rahus

The next two songs are in sequence.

When we have reached the borders of the country where the Children dwell we sing the first song. We give an exclamation of thankfulness (Iri!) that we behold the land where they dwell. Mother Corn
had passed here when she was seeking the Son (second ritual), and
now she has led us to this place.

FIRST SONG

Words and Music

M. M. ♩ = 60.

♩ = Pulsation of the voice.   Transcribed by Edwin S. Tracy.

Ha-a-a-a! I - ri! Ho-ra - ro. I - ri! Ho - ra-ro. Ho-ra - ro e pi-ra-o
Drum.
Rattles.

ku - re ho-ra - ro. I - ri! Ho - ra - ro; ho-ra - ro e.

I	II
331 Ha-a-a-a!	335 Ha-a-a-a!
332 Iri! Horaro. Iri! Horaro.	336 Weri shu riwa, weri shu riwa wi;
333 Horaro e pirao kure horaro.	337 Shu riwa wi pirao, shu riwa wi;
334 Iri! Horaro; horaro e.	338 Weri shu riwa, shu weri wi.

III

339 Ha-a-a-a!
340 Weri huriwa, weri huriwa wi;
341 Huriwa wi pirao, huriwa wi;
342 Weri huriwa, huriwa wi.

Translation

I

331 Ha-a-a-a! An introductory exclamation.
332 Iri! Horaro. Iri! Horaro.
    iri! a part of nawairi! an exclamation of thankfulness.
    horaro, land, country.
333 Horaro e pirao kure horaro.
    horaro, land, country.
    e, a vocable used to fill out the measure.
    pirao, children; a general term.
    kure, their.
    horaro, country.
334 Iri! Horaro; horaro e. See lines 332, 333.

II

335 Ha-a-a-a! An introductory exclamation.
336 Weri shu riwa, weri shu riwa wi.
    weri, here, at this place.
    shu, a part of the word ashuro, moccasin.
    riwa, an impress, as an imprint made by moccasins on the soft
        ground.
    wi, many.

337 Shu riwa wi pirao, shu riwa wi.
    shu riwa wi. See line 336.
    pirɛ o, children; not necessarily one's offspring.
    shu riwa wi. See line 336.
338 Weri shu riwa, shu weri wi. See line 336.

III

339 Ha-a-a-a! An introductory exclamation.
340 Weri huriwa, weri huriwa wi.
    weri, here.
    huriwa, walking.
    wi, many.
341 Huriwa wi pirao, huriwa wi. See lines 337, 340.
342 Weri huriwa, huriwa wi. See line 340.

Explanation by the Ku'rahus

As we move on and enter the land of the Children we sing, in the second stanza, about their footprints, the marks of their moccasins where they have walked to and fro on the ground.

We may not actually see these marks, but the song represents us as seeing them; Mother Corn has seen them, and she is leading us.

Farther on we sing in the third stanza that we see the Children themselves walking over their land. Mother Corn can see them if we do not; she has been here before; she knows all the people and can reach them all, so she leads us where we can see them walking.

This song represents the Fathers coming to the country where the Son lives. They first see his footprints; then they see him and his kindred, the Children, walking about where they live. So the way is made plain for us and we go forward.

When the village of the Children is in sight the following song is sung. Mother Corn speaks in the first stanza and tells us she has come again to this place. Her spirit had been here before when she came seeking the Son. To-day we have arrived with her at this her destination, and we give thanks to Mother Corn.

SECOND SONG

Words and Music

M. M. ♪ = 112.
ᵕ= Pulsation of the voice.   Transcribed by Edwin S. Tracy.

A ti-ra sa-ka ri-ki   a-wa ra-ti whi-cha;   A ti-ra sa-ka ri-ki

Drum.
Rattles.

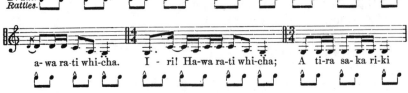

a-wa ra-ti whi-cha.   I - ri! Ha-wa ra-ti whi-cha;   A ti-ra sa-ka ri-ki

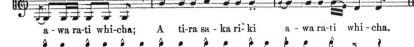

a-wa ra-ti whi-cha;   A ti-ra sa - ka ri-ki   a - wa ra-ti whi-cha.

I

343 A tira saka riki awa rati whicha;
344 A tira saka riki awa rati whicha.
345 Iri! Hawa rati whicha;
346 A tira saka riki awa rati whicha;
347 A tira saka riki awa rati whicha.

II

348 A tira saka riki awa rashihri whicha;
349 A tira saka riki awa rashihri whicha.
350 Iri! Hawa rashihri whicha;
351 A tira saka riki awa rashihri whicha;
352 A tira saka riki awa rashihri whicha.

Translation

I

343 A tira saka riki awa rati whicha.
    a, a vowel sound introduced for euphony·
    tira, this.
    saka, part of the word tarasaka, sun.
    riki, standing; tira saka riki means this present time, to-day.
    awa, again.
    rati, a modification of the word itira, I coming.
    whicha, arrived.
344 See line 343.
345 Iri! Hawa rati whicha.
    iri! thanks! a part of the word na'wairi, thanks, thankful.
    hawa, again.
    rati, I coming; refers to Mother Corn.
    whicha, arrived, reached the point of destination.
346, 347 See line 343.

II

348   A tira saka riki awa rashihri whicha.
        a, a vowel sound used for euphony.
        tira, this.
        saka, sun; part of the word tara saka, sun.
        riki, standing.   tira saka riki, to-day, this present time.
        awa, again.
        rashihri, you have brought.
        whicha, arrived, come.
349   See line 348.
350   Iri! Hawa rashihri whicha.
        iri! an exclamation of thanks or thankfulness. A part of
            the word na'wairi, thanks, it is good.
        hawa, again.
        rashihri, you have brought.
        whicha, arrived.
351, 352   See line 348.

Explanation by the Ku'rahus

The second stanza says that Mother Corn has arrived, bringing
gifts for the Children. These gifts are not only the things in our
packs; but they are the promise of long life, of children, of plenty,
and of peace. It is for these that the Children will give thanks, and
we sing their thanks in this song.

THIRD DIVISION. ENTERING THE VILLAGE OF THE SON AND CONSE-
CRATING HIS LODGE

SIXTH RITUAL

PART I. THE SON'S MESSENGERS RECEIVED

Explanation by the Ku'rahus

When the messengers sent by the Fathers (third ritual) turned
homeward the Son began his preparations to receive the Hako party.
Each of his relatives selected from among his ponies those which he
desired to present to the Fathers. The Son chose a messenger as his
representative to go out and receive the Hako party when it should
arrive within sight of the village. He also selected the little child
necessary to the performance of certain rites belonging to the fifth
morning of the ceremony. It could be one of his own children or the
child of a near relative. Finally, an earth lodge of suitable size was
secured, the occupants with all their belongings moving out for the
occasion.

In this vacated lodge the ceremony was to be performed and the
Fathers were to live day and night, for no member of the Hako party
ever separated himself from the sacred objects from the time of starting on the journey until the close of the entire ceremony.

Every Pawnee village keeps certain men on the lookout to give notice of the approach of strangers. As soon as the Hako party was recognized one of these men ran with the news to the village. The Son at once dispatched his messenger, bidding him go to the Fathers and say, "I am ready."

As soon as the Fathers discerned the messenger hastening toward them, the Ku'rahus sent two men to meet him and conduct him to the Hako party.

A cushion was placed for him to sit upon and a bowl of buffalo meat was given him. While he ate, the Ku'rahus, his assistant, and the chief, holding the sacred objects, sang the first stanza of this song.

SONG

Words and Music

I

353	Ho-o-o-o!
354	Tiwe rakushe ti hao;
355	Tiwe rakushe ti hao;
356	Tiwe rakushe hawa ti hao;
357	Tiwe rakushe ti hao;
358	Tiwe rakushe.

II

359	Ho-o-o-o!
360	Tiwe riata ti hao;
361	Tiwe riata ti hao;
362	Tiwe riata hawa ti hao;
363	Tiwe riata ti hao;
364	Tiwe riata.

Translation of First Stanza

353   Ho-o-o-o!   An introductory exclamation.
354   Tiwe rakushe ti hao.
        tiwe, here.
        rakushe, he sitting.
        ti, my.
        hao, my own child; my offspring.
355   See line 354.
356   Tiwe rakushe hawa ti hao.
        tiwe, here.
        rakushe, he sitting.
        hawa, again.
        ti, my.
        hao, my own child.
357   See line 354.
358   Tiwe rakushe.   See line 354.

Explanation by the Ku'rahus

In this stanza we speak of the messenger as "my own child" (ti hao), because he represents the Son, to whom we are being led by Mother Corn. Although the man who is the Son is not and can not be of any blood kinship to us, yet by the power of the sacred objects in this ceremony he is to be made as our own child, as our offspring, we are to be bound to him by a tie as unalterable as that which exists between father and son. So we sing, "My own child, my offspring, is sitting here."

When we sing "Tiwe rakushe hawa ti hao," we are thinking that our child has again said "I am ready."

Translation of Second Stanza

359 Ho-o-o-o! An introductory exclamation.
360 Tiwe riata ti hao.
     tiwe, here.
     riata, he walking.
     ti, my.
     hao, my own child.
361 See line 360.
362 Tiwe riata hawa ti hao.
     tiwe, here.
     riata, he walking.
     hawa, again.
     ti, my.
     hao, my own child.
363 See line 360.
364 Tiwe riata. See line 360.

Explanation by the Ku'rahus

The pack containing the clothing provided for this representative of the Son is now opened. After the messenger has finished eating he is dressed in the new clothing.

We clothe him because that is an act which marks the care of a father for his child. The garments we put upon him are fine and embroidered; these fine and carefully made garments show that we have been thinking of him, that we regard him highly and wish to do him honor.

After the messenger is clothed he walks toward the village; we follow, walking slowly and singing the second stanza. The words tell that the Son is walking before us and that we again are walking toward the lodge of the Son.

Just before we reach the village we halt and sing the next song.

PART II. THE HAKO PARTY ENTER THE VILLAGE

SONG

Words and Music

M. M. ♪ = 116.
• = Pulsation of the voice.

Transcribed by Edwin S. Tracy.

Ho-o-o-o!   Ki - ru ra - ka wi?   Ki-ru ra-ka   wi,   ti ha - o?
Drum.
Rattles.

Ki - ru ra - ka wi,   ti ha - o?   Ki-ru ra-ka, ki - ru ra - ka wi?

I	II
365 Ho-o-o-o!	370 Ho-o-o-o!
366 Kiru raka wi?	371 Tiwi reka wi!
367 Kiru raka wi, ti hao?	372 Tiwi reka wi, ti hao!
368 Kiru raka wi, ti hao?	373 Tiwi reka wi, ti hao!
369 Kiru raka, kiru raka wi?	374 Tiwi reka, tiwi reka wi!

Translation

I

365 Ho-o-o-o! An introductory exclamation.
366 Kiru raka wi?
        kiru? where?
        raka, a composite word; ra, where; ka, part of akaro, a lodge.
        wi, is.
367 Kiru raka wi, ti hao?
        kiru raka wi? See line 366.
        ti, my.
        hao, my own child, my offspring.
368 See line 367.
369 Kiru raka, kiru raka wi? See line 366.

II

370 Ho-o-o-o! An introductory exclamation.
371 Tiwi reka wi!
        tiwi, here.
        reka, a composite word; re, here; ka, part of akaro, lodge.
        wi, is.
372 Tiwi reka wi, ti hao!
        tiwi reka wi. See line 371.
        ti, my.
        hao, my own child, my offspring.
373 See line 372.
374 Tiwi reka, tiwi reka wi! See line 371.

Explanation by the Ku'rahus

When Mother Corn went in search of the Son (second ritual) she halted at the edge of the village where he lived. As we follow in the path that she opened for us, we must do as she did. So, when we are just outside the village, we halt and sing the first stanza. The words mean, ''Where is the lodge of my Son wherein he sits waiting for me?''

By the time we have finished singing, the messenger, who has walked on in advance, has reached and entered the lodge set apart for the ceremony.

When Mother Corn had decided which was the lodge of the Son she made ready to enter the village and go to that lodge (second ritual). Now, we follow her again and sing, as we walk, the second stanza: ''Here is the lodge of my Son wherein he sits waiting for me.''

When we arrive at the lodge we halt, for we must enter ceremonially.

SEVENTH RITUAL

PART I. TOUCHING AND CROSSING THE THRESHOLD

Explanation by the Ku'rahus

When the Son has dispatched his messenger to the Hako party, he, with a few of his near relatives, enters the lodge set apart for the ceremony, there to await the return of his messenger and the coming of the Fathers.

He seats himself at the south side of the lodge near the door. This is the humblest place, and he takes it to show that he is not seeking his own honor. By the choice of him as the Son a very high honor has been bestowed upon him, and his appreciation of this is shown by his taking the seat of the lowliest and not assuming prominence before the people.

When the Hako party arrive at the door of the lodge they halt and await the ceremony of touching and crossing the threshold, for no one can pass into the lodge until this has been performed.

At the doorway the three men stand abreast—the chief with the ear of corn and the wildcat skin between the Ku'rahus and his assistant, each bearing a feathered stem—and behind these stand the two doctors, each with his eagle wing.

The Ku'rahus directs the chief to advance one step and to stand upon the threshold while the first stanza of the next song is sung.

SONG

Words and Music

M. M. ♩= 58.

• = Pulsation of the voice.   Transcribed by Edwin S. Tracy.

Ho-o-o! H'A - ti-ra ra ko-ka,   ri! H'A - ti-ra ra ko-ka,   ri! H'A -

Drum
Rattles. tr.   tr.   tr.

ti-ra ra ko-ka,   ri! Wi ra ko-ka, ri! H'A - ti-ra ra ko ka,   ri!

tr.   tr.

I	III
375 Ho-o-o!	387 Ho-o-o!
376 H'Atira ra koka, ri!	388 Kawas i ra koka, ri!
377 H'Atira ra koka, ri!	389 Kawas i ra koka, ri!
378 H'Atira ra koka, ri!	390 Kawas i ra koka, ri!
379 Wi ra koka, ri!	391 Wi ra koka, ri!
380 H'Atira ra koka, ri!	392 Kawas i ra koka, ri!

II	IV
381 Ho-o-o!	393 Ho-o-o!
382 H'Atira ra koka, ri!	394 Kawas i ra koka, ri!
383 H'Atira ra koka, ri!	395 Kawas i ra koka, ri!
384 H'Atira ra koka, ri!	396 Kawas i ra koka, ri!
385 We ra koka, ri!	397 We ra koka, ri!
386 H'Atira ra koka, ri!	398 Kawas i ra koka, ri!

Translation of First Stanza

375 Ho-o-o! An introductory exclamation.

376 H'Atira ra koka, ri!

    h', a symbol of breath; "breathing forth life."

    atira, mother. The term is applied to the ear of corn.

    ra, moving, walking.

    koka, enter.

    ri, part of the word nawairi, an expression of thankfulness, of
        confidence that all is well.

377, 378 See line 376.

379 Wi ra koka, ri!

    wi, now.

    ra koka, ri. See line 376.

380 See line 376.

Explanation by the Ku'rahus

The words of this stanza mean that Mother Corn, breathing life,
has come to the entrance. She is now moving there, bringing the
promise of life, a promise that makes the heart of man glad, so we
give the cry of thankfulness as we sing: "Nawairi!"

This stanza is sung four times, for we are thinking that this promise of life given by Mother Corn is known to the powers of the four
directions.   These powers give strength and make the promise sure.

When we have finished singing, the Ku'rahus tells the chief to take
four steps beyond the threshold within the entrance way.   These
four steps are in recognition of the same powers.

While the chief stands there we sing the second stanza.

Translation of Second Stanza

381   Ho-o-o!   An introductory exclamation.
382   H'Atira ra kokạ, ri!
      h', a symbol of breath; "breathing forth life."
      atira, mother; the term is applied to the ear of corn.
      ra, moving, walking.
      koka, entered.
      ri, part of nawairi, an expression of thankfulness.
383, 384.   See line 382.
385   We ra koka, ri!
      we, it has.
      ra koka, ri.   See line 382.
386   See line 382.

Explanation by the Ku'rahus

The words of this stanza mean that Mother Corn has entered the
doorway of the lodge, she has walked within the entranceway with
her promise of life which makes the heart of man thankful.

Mother Corn has now opened the door of the lodge for the entrance
of life, so we give the cry of thankfulness, "Nawairi!"

This stanza is sung four times, and then the Ku'rahus tells the
chief to step backward out of the entrance way and to stand two
steps behind the Ku'rahus and his assistant, who now advance and
stand upon the threshold while the third stanza is sung.

Translation of Third Stanza

387   Ho-o-o!   An introductory exclamation.
388   Kawas i ra koka, ri!
      Kawas, the name used in this ceremony to designate the brown
         eagle.
      i, it.
      ra, moving.
      koka, enter.
      ri, part of nawairi, an exclamation of thankfulness.
389, 390   See line 388.
391   Wi ra koka, ri!
      wi, now.
      ra koka, ri.   See line 388.
392   See line 388.

Explanation by the Ku'rahus

The words of this stanza mean that Kawas is now moving at the entrance way and is about to enter, carrying the promise of the powers above, a promise which makes the heart of man thankful.

We sing this stanza four times, remembering the powers of the four directions.

Then the Ku'rahus and his assistant advance four steps into the entranceway and pause while the fourth stanza is sung.

Translation of Fourth Stanza

393 Ho-o-o! An introductory exclamation.
394 Kawas i ra koka, ri!
    Kawas, the name given to the brown eagle in this ceremony.
    i, it.
    ra, moving.
    koka, entered.
    ri, part of nawairi, an expression of thankfulness.
395, 396 See line 394.
397 We ra koka, ri!
    we, it has.
    ra koka, ri. See line 394.
398 See line 394.

Explanation by the Ku'rahus

The words of this stanza mean that Kawas has entered the passage. way of the lodge bearing the promise that makes the heart thankful—the promise of life from the powers above.

After singing this stanza four times, the Ku'rahus and his assistant step back outside the lodge door and take their places at either side of the chief bearing the ear of corn.

The three together now advance to the threshold, and the Ku'rahus tells the chief to go forward and keep a step in advance. The Ku'rahus and his assistant carrying the feathered stems follow the chief, and behind them walk the two doctors with the eagle wings.

The five men walk slowly and silently down the long entrance way. When the chief reaches the ridge at the inner door of the passageway, he steps over it into the lodge and pauses. Mother Corn is the first to enter the lodge. The Ku'rahus and his assistant follow and take their places, the Ku'rahus on the left of the chief, the assistant on the right. Next the doctors step in; the one with the left wing goes to the left of the Ku'rahus, and the other with the right wing to the right hand of the assistant. The five men, now abreast, walk slowly around the lodge, going by the south, west, and north to the east, while they sing the first stanza of the following song four times. They move in step, keeping close together, the chief with the ear of corn just a little forward of the line. As they sing they sway the feathered stems, the ear of corn, and the eagle wings.

PART II. CONSECRATING THE LODGE

FIRST SONG

Words and Music

M. M. ♪ = 120.
• = Pulsation of the voice.   Transcribed by Edwin S. Tracy.

I	II
399 A-a-a!	404 A-a-a!
400 H'Atira we rika wara;	405 H'Atira wetih ka wara;
401 H'Atira we rika wara;	406 H'Atira wetih ka wara;
402 We rika wara;	407 Wetih ka wara;
403 H'Atira we rika wara.	408 H'Atira wetih ka wara.

Translation

I

399   A-a-a!   An introduction to the song.
400   H'Atira we rika wara.
    h', a symbol of breath, a breathing forth.
    atira, mother; the term refers to the ear of corn.
    we, his; refers to the owner of the lodge, the Son.
    rika, a composite word, ri, this; ka, part of the word akaro,
        lodge.
    wara, walking.
401   See line 400.
402   We rika wara.   See line 400.
403   See line 400.

II

404   A-a-a!   An introductory exclamation.
405   H'Atira wetih ka wara.
    h', a symbol of breath, a breathing forth.
    atira, mother; the term is here applied to the ear of corn.
    wetih, it has; an act accomplished.
    ka, part of the word akaro, lodge.
    wara, walked.
406   See line 405.
407   Wetih ka wara.   See line 405.
408   See line 405.

Explanation by the Ku'rahus

The words of the first stanza mean that Mother Corn breathing life is now walking in the lodge. We sing this stanza four times, remembering the four directions where the paths are down which the powers descend to man.

When we have passed entirely around the lodge and reached the east, we begin the second stanza and sing it four times as we make the second circuit around the lodge.

The words tell that Mother Corn has walked within the lodge, bringing the promise of life.

After a short pause at the east the five men turn again toward the south and begin a third circuit of the lodge. This time the chief with the ear of corn falls back into line with the Ku'rahus and his assistant, who bear the feathered stems, and, as they walk, sing the following song:

SECOND SONG

Words and Music

M. M. ♪ = 126.
• = Pulsation of the voice.   Transcribed by Edwin S. Tracy.

I	II
409 Ho-o-o!	413 Ho-o-o!
410 Kawas tewi kawe hera ti rao;	414 Kawas tewi kire hera ti rao;
411 Kawas tewi kawe hera ti rao;	415 Kawas tewi kire hera ti rao;
412 Kawas tewi kawe hera ti rao.	416 Kawas tewi kire hera ti rao.

Translation of First Stanza

409 Ho-o-o! An introductory exclamation.
410 Kawas tewi kawe hera ti rao.
    Kawas, the name given to the brown eagle in this ceremony.
        Kawas represents the female and the beneficent powers.
    tewi, hovering, with a slow circling movement.
    kawe, a composite word, meaning within the lodge.
    hera, my.
    ti, possessive pronoun.
    rao, part of the word pirao, child.
411, 412 See line 410.

Explanation by the Ku'rahus

The words of the first stanza tell us that Kawas is now hovering overhead in the lodge.

The eagle soars in the skies and can communicate with the powers that are above; so the eagle represents these powers. As we stand facing the east the white-eagle feathered stem, on the right, toward the south, represents brightness, the light, the day, the sun, and it is the male. It is for defense and is carried on the side farthest from the people. The brown-eagle feathered stem, Kawas, is to the left, toward the north; it represents darkness, the night, the moon, and is the female. Kawas is carried nearest the people. Kawas has the right to make the nest and to seek help from Tira'wa for the Children.

Kawas leads in this ceremony, which is to ask for the gift of children, not only that children may be born to us, but that the tie of parent and child may be established between us and those to whom we are bringing these sacred objects, that peace may be between the tribes, and plenty and long life and prosperity. So we sing that Kawas is hovering in the lodge, as an eagle hovers over her nest.

This stanza is sung slowly, for the eagle as it hovers is slow in its movements.

Translation of Second Stanza

413   Ho-o-o! An introductory exclamation.
414   Kawas tewi kire hera ti rao.
      Kawas, the brown eagle, representing the beneficent powers.
      tewi, hovering, moving with a slow, circling movement.
      kire, starting to fly.
      hera, my.
      ti, possessive pronoun.
      rao, part of the word pirao, child.
415, 416   See line 414.

Explanation by the Ku'rahus

We sing the second stanza faster, for now Kawas has stretched her mighty wings and is flying within the lodge, driving away all harmful influences and making the place ready for all the good that is promised to us through this ceremony.

When, on the fourth circuit, the west is reached, we pause and face the east, but we continue to sing until we have repeated this second stanza four times.

As soon as we have reached the west the two doctors with the eagle wings move away, the one with the left wing going by the north and the one with the right wing going toward the south. They raise and lower the wings to simulate the eagle cleaning its nest, flapping and blowing out all impurities. When the doctors meet at the east they face the open entrance way and flirt the wings toward the opening, as though brushing out something from the lodge. These motions mean that Kawas has now cleared the lodge of all that is bad, of all disease and trouble, and made the place ready for the coming ceremony.

Then the doctors join the Ku'rahus, his assistant, and the chief.

At the west, back of the fire, a space is now set apart and made sacred. Here the wildcat skin is spread and at its head the crotched stick is thrust into the ground; one end of the feathered stems is laid against the crotch, the other upon the skin, and the rattles are placed under the eagle pendants. The wings are laid on the edge of the skin. In front of the wildcat the ear of corn is held in an upright position by one of the sticks to which it is tied being thrust into the ground. The sacred objects are always laid at rest in this position, and are never left alone or unguarded.

The members of the Hako party now enter and place the packs containing the ceremonial gifts at the north side of the lodge. Meanwhile the women of the party are busy pitching tents, for, as only a few of the Hako party remain and live within the lodge, all the other men must camp with their families in a place set apart for them.

The Ku'rahus at this time appoints certain men to attend to special duties.

Some are to bring wood and water and attend to the cooking. They divide themselves into different groups, one for each day of the ceremony, so that the work will be evenly distributed and there will be no confusion or delays.

Others are appointed to fill the pipes for the Children to smoke. To attend to this duty they are required to be always present in the lodge.

Some eight or ten men are chosen to be in readiness to do any work that may be demanded of them. For instance, if the crops of the Children are being planted or gathered, these men are to attend to this work, so that the Children can at all times be present at the ceremony and suffer no loss.

A man is selected to notch a stick as a record of the number of ponies presented to the Fathers and to whom each pony is given.

In this way the labor attendant upon the long ceremony is planned and divided so that nothing will be neglected and there will be no dispute or confusion.

While these appointments are being made the Son dispatches runners to notify the people that the Hako party has arrived and to bid his relatives come to the lodge.

PART III. CLOTHING THE SON AND OFFERING SMOKE

Explanation by the Ku'rahus

The Ku'rahus orders that the pack containing the new garments brought for the Son be opened, and he directs the chief to clothe the Son. The embroidered shirt, leggings, and moccasins are then put upon him and he is wrapped in a fine robe.

The Ku'rahus asks the priest of the shrine which controls the rain to take its sacred pipe and direct the Son how to offer tobacco and smoke to Tira'wa.

The priest fills the sacred pipe and carries it toward the south, where he sits down beside the Son and instructs him what to do.

The Ku'rahus, his assistant, and the chief, bearing the sacred objects, follow the priest and halt before the Son.

The priest puts the sacred pipe in the hand of the Son, and the first stanza of the following song is sung.

FIRST SONG

Words and Music

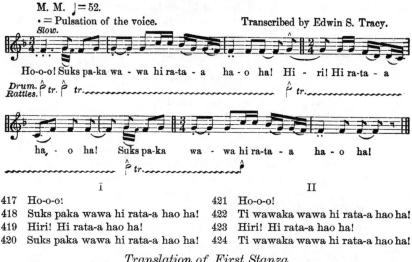

M. M. ♩ = 52.
• = Pulsation of the voice.
Slow.   Transcribed by Edwin S. Tracy.

Ho-o-o! Suks pa-ka wa - wa hi ra-ta - a   ha - o ha! Hi - ri! Hi ra-ta - a

ha, - o ha! Suks pa-ka   wa - wa hi ra-ta - a   ha - o ha!

I	II
417 Ho-o-o!	421 Ho-o-o!
418 Suks paka wawa hi rata-a hao ha!	422 Ti wawaka wawa hi rata-a hao ha!
419 Hiri! Hi rata-a hao ha!	423 Hiri! Hi rata-a hao ha!
420 Suks paka wawa hi rata-a hao ha!	424 Ti wawaka wawa hi rata-a hao ha!

Translation of First Stanza

417 Ho-o-o! An introductory exclamation.

418 Suks paka wawa hi rata-a hao ha!

    suks, a command; you must.

    paka, pako, speak.   The change in the last vowel is for euphony.

    wawa, part of rawawa, to send something; in this instance, to send the words or thoughts of the prayer.

    hi, that person.

    rata, my or mine.

    a, vowel prolongation.

    hao, child; offspring.

    ha, a musical vocable used to fill out the measure.

419   Hiri! Hi rata-a hao ha!
          hiri! an exclamation meaning give heed! harken!
          hi rata-a hao ha!   See line 418.
420   See line 418.

Explanation by the Ku'rahus

The words of this stanza are a command to the Son. They are,
"Give heed, my child; you must now send your prayers to the powers
which dwell above."

This stanza is sung four times.

Then the Son takes a pinch of tobacco from the bowl of the pipe
and passes it along the stem and offers it as the priest directs.

There is a certain order to be observed in the offering of tobacco
and smoke to the powers above peculiar to each of the sacred shrines,
and only the priest or keeper of a shrine knows the order in which
the powers which preside over his shrine should be approached. The
sacred pipe belonging to the Rain shrine is used in this ceremony, and
its priest must direct the Son how to make the offering. I do not
know this order; it does not belong to me to know it.

When the pinch of tobacco has been presented to the powers above
it is placed upon the earth.

After this act the second stanza is sung.

Translation of Second Stanza

421   Ho-o-o! An introductory exclamation.
422   Ti wawaka wawa hi rata-a hao ha!
          ti, he.
          wawaka; wako, spoken; the added wa indicates that he has
              spoken to those who are at a great distance.
          wawa, part of tiwari, traveling from one, and towawa, travel-
              ing in many ways, to many different places.
          hi, that person.
          rata, my or mine.
          a, vowel prolongation.
          hao, child.
          ha, a musical vocable.
423   See line 419.
424   See line 422.

Explanation by the Ku'rahus

As the Son offers tobacco in the directions indicated by the priest,
he prays to the powers that dwell in these directions. What he says
is not audible to us, for it is not intended for us to hear.

The words of this stanza refer to the prayers of the Son.

We are bidden to take heed that the prayers of the Son, who is as
our child, have been spoken and have traveled far, going on and on
to the different distant places where the great powers abide which
watch over the rain.

This stanza is sung four times.

The priest now lights the pipe and the Son smokes, sending little puffs in the directions indicated by the priest. As he smokes we sing the first stanza of the following song.

SECOND SONG

Words and Music

M. M. ♩= 56.
• = Pulsation of the voice.   Transcribed by Edwin S. Tracy.

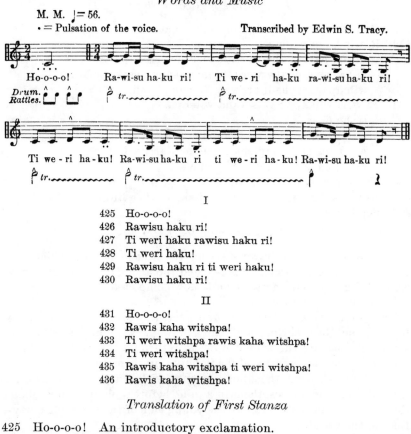

I

425   Ho-o-o-o!
426   Rawisu haku ri!
427   Ti weri haku rawisu haku ri!
428   Ti weri haku!
429   Rawisu haku ri ti weri haku!
430   Rawisu haku ri!

II

431   Ho-o-o-o!
432   Rawis kaha witshpa!
433   Ti weri witshpa rawis kaha witshpa!
434   Ti weri witshpa!
435   Rawis kaha witshpa ti weri witshpa!
436   Rawis kaha witshpa!

Translation of First Stanza

425   Ho-o-o-o!   An introductory exclamation.
426   Rawisu haku ri.
    rawisu, smoke.
    haku, passes by.
    ri, present time.
427   Ti weri haku rawisu haku ri.
    ti, it.
    weri; we, now; ri, present time.
    haku, passes by.
    rawisu haku ri.   See line 426.
428   Ti weri haku.   See line 427.
429   Rawisu haku ri ti weri haku.   See lines 426, 427.
430   See line 426.

Explanation by the Ku'rahus

The words tell us that the smoke offered by the Son is now passing by, leaving us and going on its way to the different places where the powers dwell that guard the rain.

We sing this stanza four times as the smoke passes by us.

Translation of Second Stanza

431   Ho-o-o-o! An introductory exclamation.
432   Rawis kaha witshpa.
    rawis, part of the word rawisu, smoke.
    kaha, part of the word kaharu, smell, savor, odor.
    witshpa, reached, arrived at, completed.
433   Ti weri witshpa rawis kaha witshpa.
    ti, he or it.
    weri; we, now; ri, is; denotes present time.
    witshpa, has completed, reached, arrived.
    rawis kaha witshpa. See line 432.
434   Ti weri witshpa. See line 433.
435   Rawis kaha witshpa ti weri witshpa. See lines 432, 433.
436   See line 432.

Explanation by the Ku'rahus

As the smoke disappears we sing the second stanza, which tells that the odor of the smoke has reached the abode of the mighty powers and that our offering to them is now completed.

We sing this song four times.

The ceremony of offering smoke over, the priest with the sacred pipe of the Rain shrine, and the Ku'rahus with his assistant and the chief, bearing the sacred objects, return to the west and there, upon the space set apart and made holy, lay them down.

The Son takes off the fine garments with which the Father has clothed him and places them in a pile before a chief of his village, that they may be distributed to the young men of the receiving party—that is, the Children.

The lodge has now been opened by Mother Corn and cleansed of all bad influences by Kawas; the Son, clothed as a child by the Father, has offered prayer and smoke to the powers above; the garments worn during this act have been removed and given away; and now everything is ready for the public ceremony to begin.

THE CEREMONY

First Division. The Public Ceremony

EIGHTH RITUAL (FIRST DAY). THE FATHERS FEED THE CHILDREN

Explanation by the Ku'rahus

The runners dispatched by the Son deliver their message, and soon men, women, and children, dressed in their best attire, can be seen

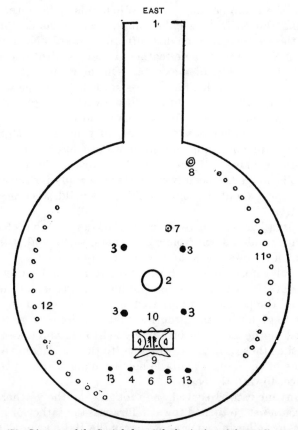

FIG. 176.   Diagram of the Son's lodge at the beginning of the public ceremony.

1, the entrance to the lodge; 2, the fireplace; 3, inner posts supporting the dome-shaped roof; 4, the Ku'rahus; 5, his assistant; 6, the Father (a chief); 7, the server; 8, the Son; 9, the Hako at rest upon the holy place; 10, the ear of corn (should be represented by a dot just below the number); 11, members of the Son's party; 12, members of the Hako party; 13, the bearers of the eagle wings.

walking through the village toward the lodge set apart for the ceremony (figure 176).

As they pass into the lodge they see the Ku'rahus and his assistant with the chief between them sitting behind the Hako at the west, facing the entrance at the east. They who have brought gifts to the Fathers go around to the sacred place and lay them down upon the ground between the central fire and the Hako. All gifts are received silently unless someone brings a present of food; for such an offering the Ku'rahus gives thanks.

In old days it was not unusual for the Children to bring packs filled with dried buffalo meat; sometimes the packs contained the entire product of a hunt.

When all the Children are gathered within the lodge the Ku'rahus directs that the Hako be taken up. When this is done, the five men stand facing the east. The chief, in the center, holds the wildcat skin and the ear of corn; on his left and toward the north is the Ku'rahus with the brown-eagle feathered stem, and at his left is the doctor with the left wing of the eagle. On the right of the chief and toward the south is the Ku'rahus's assistant holding the white-eagle feathered stem, and at his right the doctor with the right wing of the eagle. The Ku'rahus now addresses the Children:

"Mother Corn has led us to the border of your land. Mother Corn has brought us to your village. Mother Corn has guided us to the entrance of this lodge. Mother Corn has crossed the threshold and entered. The lodge has been swept and made ready for the ceremony. Kawas has flown about the lodge seeking its child, and here he has been found.

" You must all help me by reverent conduct as I try to perform faithfully the rite handed down from our fathers, so that all the promise of good which follows the Hako may come to us here."

No particular form of speech was taught me to be used on this occasion. Every Ku'rahus can choose his own words, but he must at this time tell the people of the sacredness of this ceremony and call upon them to give reverent attention that the rite may go forward to the end and be the means of bringing good to all who take part in it.

By this time those appointed to attend to the cooking have prepared food outside of the lodge. This is now brought in and placed near the fireplace, toward the east.

Before anyone can be served the thoughts of the Fathers and of the Children must be turned toward Tira'wa, the father of all things, so we sing the following song as we carry the Hako around the lodge and wave the feathered stems over the heads of the people.

FIRST SONG

Words and Music

M. M. ♩= 126.

• = Pulsation of the voice. Transcribed by Edwin S. Tracy.

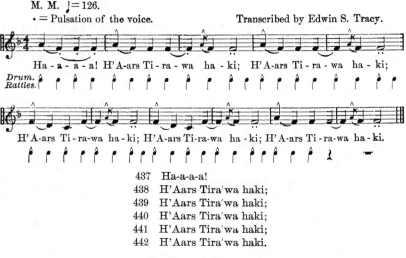

Ha - a - a - a! H'A-ars Ti - ra - wa ha - ki; H'A-ars Ti - ra - wa ha - ki;

Drum.
Rattles.

H'A-ars Ti - ra-wa ha - ki; H'A-ars Ti - ra-wa ha - ki; H'A-ars Ti - ra-wa ha - ki.

437 Ha-a-a-a!
438 H'Aars Tira'wa haki;
439 H'Aars Tira'wa haki;
440 H'Aars Tira'wa haki;
441 H'Aars Tira'wa haki;
442 H'Aars Tira'wa haki.

Translation

437 Ha-a-a-a! An introductory exclamation.
438 H'Aars Tira'wa haki.

> h', a part of the word ha, your.
> aars, a contraction of the word atius, father.
> Tira'wa, the designation of the great power Tira'wa atius, thought to be above all other powers.
> haki, many.

439–442 See line 438.

Explanation by the Ku'rahus

When the Ku'rahus begins to sing this song he must think what this ceremony is for and be mindful that all the powers that the heavens contain and all the powers that are felt over the earth are now coming near and bending over the Hako.

All the powers that are in the heavens and all those that are upon the earth are derived from the mighty power, Tira'wa atius. He[a] is the father of all things visible and invisible. He is the father of all the powers represented by the Hako. He is the father of all the lesser powers, those which can approach man. He is the father of all the people, and perpetuates the life of the tribe through the gift of children. So we sing, your father, meaning the father of all people everywhere, the father of all things that we see and hear and feel.

As we sing the words over and over we think about Tira'wa atius being the father of all things. This and all stanzas are sung four times.

When we have gone entirely around the lodge and have returned

---

[a]The Pawnee pronoun here translated "he" does not in the original indicate sex, nor is it equivalent to "it," as the word relates to a person.

to the west we pause, and start again to make the second circuit, always going by the north, the east, the south, to the west. On this second circuit we sing this song, which must always follow the one we have just sung. Both songs are about Tira'wa atius, the father of all.

These two songs belong to the first two of the first four circuits of the lodge, which are made in the presence of all the Children. We shall sing these same songs twice again; the first time, after the sacred feast of corn and, the second time, when we are beginning the last four circuits of the lodge on the fourth and last night of the ceremony.

SECOND SONG

Words and Music

M. M. ♩ = 126.
• = Pulsation of the voice.   Transcribed by Edwin S. Tracy.

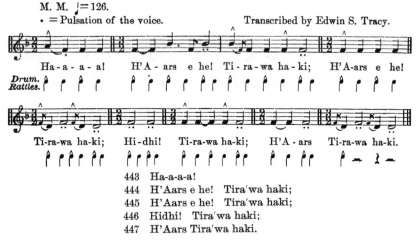

Ha-a-a-a!   H'A - ars e he! Ti - ra - wa ha - ki;   H'A-ars e he!
Drum.
Rattles.

Ti-ra-wa ha-ki;   Hi-dhi!   Ti-ra-wa ha-ki;   H'A - ars   Ti-ra-wa ha-ki.

443   Ha-a-a-a!
444   H'Aars e he! Tira'wa haki;
445   H'Aars e he! Tira'wa haki;
446   Hidhi! Tira'wa haki;
447   H'Aars Tira'wa haki.

Translation

443   Ha-a-a-a! An introductory exclamation.
444   H'Aars e he! Tira'wa haki.
    h', a part of the word "ha", your.
    aars, an abbreviation of atius, father.
    e, a vocable used to fill out the rhythm.
    he! an exclamation indicating that something is brought to
      one's attention which demands thoughtful consideration.
    Tira'wa, a part of Tira'wahut, the dwelling place of the lesser
      powers, those which can come near to man.
    haki, many.
445   See line 444.
446   Hidhi! Tira'wa haki.
    hidhi, on high; above, as when one points upward.
    Tira'wa, a part of Tira'wahut, the dwelling place of the lesser
      powers. The word Tira'wa is not the same as in the pre-
      ceding song and therefore has not the same meaning.
    haki, many. The phrase Tira'wa haki in this song refers to
      the many lesser powers which dwell above.
447   H'Aars Tira'wa haki. See line 444.

Explanation by the Ku'rahus

When we begin this song and sing "H'Aars" (your father), we think of what we have been told in the first song, that Tira'wa atius is the father of all things; that he is the father of all those lesser powers which come to us in our visions and dreams. These lesser powers are many, but Tira'wa atius is the father of them all.

When we sing, "Hidhi!" we think that all these powers have their dwelling place on high, Tira'wahut, and that above them all is the abode of Tira'wa atius, their father. It is he who sends help to us by these lesser powers, because they alone can come to us so that we can see and feel them.

When we have reached the west we pause and then begin the third circuit of the lodge. On this round we sing of Mother Corn, she who has led us on our journey, who has entered the lodge of the Son, and is now to walk before the Children with the promise of plenty.

THIRD SONG

Words and Music

M. M. ♪ = 126.
· = Pulsation of the voice.   Transcribed by Edwin S. Tracy.

Ho-o! Ho-o! Nawa 'Ti - ra,   na - wa 'Ti - ra,   na 'Ti - ra   we-ri-ra! Na 'Ti-ra
Drum.
Rattles.

we-ri-ra! Na-wa 'Ti - ra,   na - wa 'Ti - ra,   na - wa.   Ha! We-ri-ra!

I

448   Ho-o! Ho-o!
449   Nawa 'Tira, nawa 'Tira, na 'Tira werira!
450   Na 'Tira werira!
451   Nawa 'Tira, nawa 'Tira, nawa. Ha! Werira!

II

452   Ho-o! Ho-o!
453   Ha wa 'Tira, ha wa 'Tira, ha 'Tira werai!
454   Ha 'Tira werai!
455   Ha wa 'Tira, ha wa 'Tira, ha 'Tira werai!

Translation of First Stanza

448   Ho-o! Ho-o! Introductory exclamations.
449   Nawa 'Tira, nawa 'Tira, na 'Tira werira!
      nawa, now.
      'tira, part of the word atira, mother. The term refers to the
          ear of corn.
      na, part of nawa, now.
      'tira, atira, mother.
      werira, she comes.

450   Na 'tira werira!   See line 449.
451   Nawa 'tira, nawa 'tira, nawa.   Ha!   Werira!
          ha!   behold!   look!   For the other words, see line 449.

Explanation by the Ku'rahus

In the first stanza the Fathers speak; they tell the Children to behold Mother Corn, who comes bringing the promise of good gifts. They must fix their eyes and thought upon Mother Corn, who now comes hither.   They must give her thanks for all she is bringing to make their hearts glad.

We sing this stanza four times as we go around the lodge.

When we reach the west we pause and then start on the fourth circuit singing the second stanza.

Translation of Second Stanza

452   Ho-o!   Ho-o!   Introductory exclamations.
453   Ha wa 'Tira, ha wa 'Tira, ha 'Tira werai!
          ha, yonder.
          wa, part of nawa, now.
          'tira, part of atira, mother.   Refers to the corn.
          ha, yonder.
          'tira, atira, mother.
          werai, she is coming.
454   Ha 'Tira werai!   See line 453.
455   See line 453.

Explanation by the Ku'rahus

In this stanza the Children speak.   Yonder Mother Corn is coming. She is bringing good gifts of peace and plenty to make glad our hearts.

The Fathers, they who are carrying the sacred objects, are singing, but if the Children choose they can join in the song as the waving feathered stems are passing by.

When we have sung this stanza four times and have reached the west we have completed the fourth circuit of the lodge.

We sing each stanza four times during one circuit and we must make four circuits of the lodge after we have taken up the Hako and before we can lay them down.

The four circuits of the lodge are made in recognition of the four directions, the four powers at the west and the four sacred objects, the two eagles, the ear of corn, and the wildcat skin.

Up to this time the feathered stems have been simply laid down upon the wildcat skin without ceremony, but now and hereafter during the ceremony, whenever we complete a fourth circuit of the lodge and return to the west, they are laid to rest upon the skin with certain peculiar movements made to the rhythm of song.[a]   The songs which belong to this act explain its meaning.

---

[a] In the following pages the places will be indicated where these songs must be sung, but to avoid unnecessary repetition the songs themselves will be omitted.

The feathered stems represent the eagle; the holy place, where the stems are laid to rest, represents the eagle's nest.   A nest is made for the young; the making of a nest in the lodge of the Son by Ka-was presages the fulfilment of the promise of children to the Son, as well as the establishment of a close bond, like that of father and son, between the members of two unrelated clans or tribes.

The cat skin lies next to the ground on the holy place; it protects by its skill the nest and all that the nest represents.

Whenever we lay the feathered stems down, after they have been carried four times around the lodge and waved over the heads of the people, they are moved in a way to represent the eagle hovering over her nest and then alighting on her young.   These songs and these movements are a prayer for the gift of children, and that the bond between the Father and the Son may be true and strong.

There are four songs for the ceremony of laying down the feathered stems.   Each song has two stanzas.   We sing two of these songs every time we lay these objects to rest.   We sway the stems over the cat skin, dropping them lower and lower, then suddenly we raise them again and finally let them gently down on the nest.   The eagle acts in this manner when going to her nest.   She does not at once settle down; she flies over it, sweeping lower and lower, then rises to see if all is well, and slowly descends to drop lightly on the nest.

When the young eagles see the mother coming and hear her call, they answer back, they are glad.   We are like the young birds in the nest, so we cry "Hiri!" expressing our gratitude to Kawas, who is making her nest with us.   We pray in our hearts as we sing.

SONGS FOR LAYING DOWN THE FEATHERED STEMS

SONG

Words and Music

M. M. ♩. = 69.
• = Pulsation of the voice.   Transcribed by Edwin S. Tracy.

I

456 He-e-e-e!
457 Whe ria-a; whe ria-a; whe ria. Hiri!
458 Whe ria. Hiri!
459 Whe ria. Hiri!
460 Whe ria. Hiri!
461 Whe ria-a; whe ria-a; whe ria. Hiri!

II

462 He-e-e-e!
463 Whe ria-a; whe ria-a; whe ria. Hiri!
464 Whe ria. Hiri!
465 Whe ria. Hiri!
466 Whe ria. Hiri!
467 Whe ria-a; whe ria-a; whe ria. Shpetit!

Translation

I

456 He-e-e-e! An introductory exclamation.
457 Whe ria-a; whe ria-a; whe ria-a. Hiri!
whe, now.
ria, flying and circling over something, as a nest.
a, vowel prolongation.
hiri! part of nawairi! thanks! The initial h is added for
euphony.
458, 459, 460 Whe ria. Hiri! See line 457.
461 See line 457.

II

462 He-e-e-e! An introductory exclamation.
463 See line 457.
464, 465, 466 See line 458.
467 Whe ria-a, whe ria-a, whe ria. Shpetit!
whe ria-a, whe ria-a, whe ria. See line 457.
shpetit, to light upon, as on a nest, and sit down upon it.

SONG

Words and Music

M. M. ♩= 108.
•= Pulsation of the voice.   Transcribed by Edwin S. Tracy.

Hi - ri! Hawa ra-ti - ra. Hi - ri! Hawa ra-ti - ra! Hi   tu-ka i ra - ra - spi!

Drum.
Rattles.   ♩ tr. ⁓⁓⁓⁓⁓⁓   ♩ tr. ⁓⁓⁓⁓⁓   ♩ tr. ⁓⁓⁓⁓⁓

Hi - ri! Hawa ra-ti - ra. Hi - ri! Hawa ra-ti - ra! Hi   tu-ka i ra - ra - spi.

♩ tr. ⁓⁓⁓⁓⁓   ♩ tr. ⁓⁓⁓⁓⁓   ♩ tr. ⁓⁓⁓⁓⁓

I

468   Hiri! Hawa ratira.   Hiri!   Hawa ratira!
469   Hi tuka i raraspi!
470   Hiri! Hawa ratira.   Hiri!   Hawa ratira!
471   Hi tuka i raraspi!

II

472   Hiri! Hawa rassira.   Hiri!   Hawa rassira!
473   Hi tuka i rarispi!
474   Hiri! Hawa rassira.   Hiri!   Hawa rassira!
475   Hi tuka i rarispi!

Translation

I

468   Hiri!   Hawa ratira.   Hiri!   Hawa ratira.
 hiri! part of nawairi! an exclamation of thanks, gratitude, of
 confidence that all is well. The initial h is added to iri
 for euphony and ease in singing.
 hawa, again.
 ratira, coming.
469   Hi tuka i raraspi.
 hi, it; refers to the eagle.
 tuka, slantwise.
 i, vocable to fill out the measure.
 raraspi, very near to alighting, referring to the movements of
 the eagle, which makes feints of descending upon her nest
 and then rises again.
470   See line 468.
471   See line 469.

II

472   Hiri! Hawa rassira. Hiri! Hawa rassira!
    hiri! an exclamation of thankfulness. See explanation in
      line 468.
    hawa, again.
    rassira, you coming, or returning. Refers to the movements
      of the eagle. After the feint of alighting she rises and
      then she returns again preparatory to settling on her nest.
473   Hi tuka i rarispi.
    hi, it; refers to the eagle.
    tuka, slantwise.
    i, vocable used to fill out the measure of the music.
    rarispi, has alighted.
474   See line 472.
475   See line 473.

SONG

Words and Music

M. M. ♩= 56.
• = Pulsation of the voice.   Transcribed by Edwin S. Tracy.

I

476   Ha-a-a!
477   Era hera iruwa. Ha! Ti wi ruwa, ti wi ruwa, kara witika?
478   Kawas ti wi ruwa, ti wi ruwa, kara witika?
479   Era hera iruwa. Ha! Ti wi ruwa, ti wi ruwa, kara witika?

II

480   Ha-a-a!
481   Era hera eria. Ha! Ti wi ria, ti wi ria, hara witika;
482   Kawas ti wi ria, ti wi ria, hara witika.
483   Era hera eria. Ha! Ti wi ria, ti wi ria, hara witika.

Translation

I

476   Ha-a-a!   An introductory exclamation.
477   Era hera iruwa.   Ha!   Ti wi ruwa, ti wi ruwa, kara witika?
      era, it coming; refers to the eagle.
      hera; era, it coming; the h is added for euphony.
      iruwa, one flying this way, toward us one (singular) is flying.
      ha! look! behold!
      ti, here.
      wi, is.
      ruwa, flying this way.
      kara? has it? a question.
      witika, sat down within, or alighted and settled on, its nest.
478   Kawas ti wi ruwa, ti wi ruwa, kara witika?
      Kawas, the brown eagle, the leading bird in the ceremony.
      ti wi ruwa.   See line 477.
      kara witika? has it alighted and sat down within its nest?
479   See line 477.

II

480   Ha-a-a!   An introductory exclamation.
481   Era hera eria.   Ha!   Ti wi ria, ti wi ria, hara witika.
      era, it coming.
      hera, a repetition of era, the h being added for euphony.
      eria, circling overhead; refers to the movements of the eagle.
      ha! look! behold!
      ti, here.
      wi, is.
      ria, a part of the word eria, circling over.
      hara, it has.
      witika, sat down within, or settled on, its nest.
482   Kawas ti wi ria, ti wi ria, hara witika.
      Kawas, the brown eagle, the leading symbolic bird in the cere-
         mony.
      ti wi ria, hara witika.   See line 481.
483   See line 481.

SONG

Words and Music

M. M. ♩= 58.
• = Pulsation of the voice.   Transcribed by Edwin S. Tracy.

Ha-a-a-a! Ka-ra wi-tit? Ka-ra wi-tit? Ka-ra wi-tit? Ka-ra wi-tit? Ka-ra wi-tit?

Drum.
Rattles.

Ka-ra   e?   Ka-ra wi-tit? Ka-ra wi-tit? Ka-ra wi-tit? Ka-ra   e?

484 Ha-a-a-a!
485 Kara witit? Kara witit? Kara witit? Kara witit? Kara witit? Kara e?
486 Kara witit? Kara witit? Kara witit? Kara e?

487 Ha-a-a-a!
488 Hara witit; hara witit; hara witit; hara witit; hara witit; hara e!
489 Hara witit; hara witit; hara witit; hara e!

Translation

I

484 Ha-a-a-a! An introductory exclamation.
485 Kara witit? Kara witit? Kara witit? Kara witit? Kara witit?
     Kara e?
     kara? has it? a question.
     witit, sat down or lit upon (its nest). The iteration of the
         words follow the picture made by the movements of the
         feathered stems as they are waved now lower and now
         higher over the cat skin, simulating the eagle as she pre-
         pares to alight on her nest.
     e, a vocable to fill out the measure of the music.
486 Kara witit? Kara witit? Kara witit? Kara e? See line 485.

II

487 Ha-a-a-a! An introductory exclamation.
488 Hara witit; hara witit; hara witit; hara witit; hara witit; hara e!
     hara, it has.
     witit, sat down or alighted and settled upon (its nest). The
         repetition of the words accompanies the movements of the
         feathered stems as they are waved lower and lower toward
         the cat skin.
     e, a vocable to fill out the measure of the music.
489 Hara witit; hara witit; hara witit; hara e! See line 488.

Explanation by the Ku'rahus

When the Hako are at rest, the food which has been standing beside the fire is served by the Fathers to the Children. Certain men are appointed for this task.

It is the duty of a father to provide food for his child, and not to partake himself until the child is satisfied. As we are to simulate the relation of father to child, we prepare a meal for the Children twice and sometimes thrice a day during the continuance of this ceremony. We are obliged to bring much food for this purpose, as the Children are sometimes many, and we have also ourselves to feed.

Where we must travel far to reach the tribe of the Son, the burden of carrying so much food is hard upon our ponies. So much cooking for the Children keeps the women very busy, but they are willing, for the ceremony brings good to them.

After the Children have eaten they rest a while and then go home, returning to the lodge when the sun has set. Before they go they generally make gifts of ponies to the Fathers.

When the Fathers are left alone in the lodge they eat their evening meal.

The Hako throughout this ceremony are never left unattended by night or day. When the Ku'rahus, or his assistant, or the chief needs to leave the lodge, someone is requested to take his place during his absence.

NINTH RITUAL (FIRST NIGHT). INVOKING THE VISIONS

Explanation by the Ku'rahus

When the sun has set and it is dark and the stars are shining, then the Children gather in the lodge. Some, as they come in, will advance to the holy place and there drop a stick; this means the gift of a pony. For every such gift the Ku'rahus returns thanks to the giver.

After all are seated, wood is piled upon the fire, and when the flames leap high the Ku'rahus rises, then his assistant and the chief rise and the Hako are taken up.

The singers carrying the drum follow the Hako bearers as they move slowly around the lodge, singing the following song.

SONG

Words and Music

M. M. ♪ = 132.

. = Pulsation of the voice.   Transcribed by Edwin S. Tracy.

Ho-o-o-o! Hit-ka-sha-ru! Ru-hu - ri-hi   hit-ka-sha-ru!

Ru-hu - ri-hi! Ru-hu - ri-hi , hit-ka-sha-ru! Ru-hu - ri-hi!

I

490 Ho-o-o-o!
491 Hitkasharu!
492 Ruhurihi hitkasharu!
493 Ruhurihi!
494 Ruhurihi hitkasharu!
495 Ruhurihi!

II

496 Ho-o-o-o!
497 Hitkasharu!
498 Weri rawha hitkasharu!
499 Weri rawha!
500 Weri rawha hitkasharu!
501 Weri rawha!

III

502 Ho-o-o-o!
503 Hitkasharu!
504 Weri whicha hitkasharu!
505 Weri whicha!
506 Weri whicha hitkasharu!
507 Weri whicha!

IV

508 Ho-o-o-o!
509 Hitkasharu!
510 We rahruka hitkasharu!
511 We rahruka!
512 We rahruka hitkasharu!
513 We rahruka! *a*

V

514 Ho-o-o-o!
515 Hitkasharu!
516 We rakawa hitkasharu!
517 We rakawa!
518 We rakawa hitkasharu!
519 We rakawa!

VI

520 Ho-o-o-o!
521 Hitkasharu!
522 We riteri hitkasharu!
523 We riteri!
524 We riteri hitkasharu!
525 We riteri!

VII

526 Ho-o-o-o!
527 Hitkasharu!
528 We rahwara hitkasharu!
529 We rahwara!
530 We rahwara hitkasharu!
531 We rahwara!

VIII

532 Ho-o-o-o!
533 Hitkasharu!
534 Wera rawhishpa hitkasharu!
535 Wera rawhishpa!
536 Wera rawhishpa hitkasharu!
537 Wera rawhishpa! *a*

Translation of First Stanza

490   Ho-o-o-o!   An exclamation introductory to the song.

491   Hitkasharu!   A composite term; hit, from hittu, feather; ka, from rotkaharu, night; sharu, visions, dreams.   Hittu, feather, refers to the birds represented upon the feathered stems.   The term indicates the night visions which attend or belong to these symbolic objects, the feathered stems.

a Here the Hako are laid at ceremonial rest.   See pages 111–116.

492   Ruhurihi hitkasharu!
    ruhurihi, a command, a call; "let it be so!"
    hitkasharu.   See line 491.
493   Ruhurihi!   See line 492.
494   See line 492.
495   See line 493.

Explanation by the Ku'rahus

We sing about the visions which the birds on the feathered stems are to bring to the Children.

Visions come from above, they are sent by Tira'wa atius.   The lesser powers come to us in visions.   We receive help through the visions.   All the promises which attend the Hako will be made good to us in this way.

Visions can come most readily at night; spirits travel better at that time.   Now when we are met together we, the Fathers, call upon the visions to come to the Children.

The spirits of the birds upon the feathered stems join our spirits in this call to the visions.   That is what the words of this stanza mean.   We sing it four times as we make the first circuit of the lodge.

When we reach the west we pause.

Translation of Second Stanza

496   Ho-o-o-o!   An introductory exclamation.
497   Hitkasharu!   The visions that attend the Hako.   See line 491.
498   Weri rawha hitkasharu!
    weri, they.
    rawha, are coming.
    hitkasharu, the visions which attend the Hako.
499   Weri rawha!   See line 498.
500   See line 498.
501   See line 499.

Explanation by the Ku'rahu

As we go around the lodge the second time we sing this stanza.

The visions have heard the call of the spirits of the birds upon the feathered stems, joined to the call of our spirits, and they are descending by the east from their dwelling place above, and are coming toward the lodge.

We sing "They are coming," and the Children join in the song, as we pass around and wave the feathered stems.

When we reach the west we pause.

Translation of Third Stanza

502 Ho-o-o-o! An introductory exclamation.
503 Hitkasharu! The visions that attend the Hako. See line 491.
504 Weri whicha hitkasharu!
       weri, they.
       whicha, a part of the word rawhicha, arrived, have arrived.
       hitkasharu, the visions which attend the Hako.
505 Weri whicha. See line 504.
506 See line 504.
507 See line 505.

Explanation by the Ku'rahus

We start on the third circuit of the lodge, singing this stanza. We sing it four times.

The visions have been traveling from the east, whence they descended; they have been passing over the quiet earth, coming nearer and nearer in answer to our call, and at last they reach the door of the lodge. There they pause.

When we reach the west we pause. We are waiting, all the Children are waiting. We are thinking of these visions, of the place where they dwell, of their coming at our call, of all they are to bring to us. They are holy visions.

Translation of Fourth Stanza

508 Ho-o-o-o! An introductory exclamation.
509 Hitkasharu! The visions that attend the Hako. See line 491.
510 We rahruka hitkasharu!
       we, a part of the word weri, they.
       rahruka, a composite word; rahru, to go through or enter; ka, a part of the word akaro, lodge; the word means entered and passed through the long passageway that leads into the earth lodge.
       hitkasharu, the visions that attend the Hako.
511 We rahruka! See line 510.
512 See line 510.
513 See line 511.

Explanation by the Ku'rahus

We turn toward the north to make the fourth circuit of the lodge, singing this stanza. We sing it four times.

As we sing the visions touch and cross the threshold and then pass down the long passageway leading into the lodge. As we reach the west they have entered the lodge.

Kawas and all the birds have called these visions to bless the Children. The visions have heard, they have traveled far, they have reached the lodge, and now they have entered and are in the presence of the Children.

Kawas now goes to her nest, so we lay the Hako down with the movements and songs which belong to this act,[a] and then we sit down behind the Hako and are quiet.

Perhaps some one of the Children may rise and come to the holy place and there lay down a stick, signifying the gift of a horse to the Fathers in recognition of their having called the visions which are now present.

Translation of Fifth Stanza

514 Ho-o-o-o! An introductory exclamation.
515 Hitkasharu! The visions that attend the Hako. See line 491.
516 We rakawa hitkasharu!
    we, part of weri, they.
    rakawa, walking, moving; conveys the idea of spreading
        through, pervading the space within the lodge.
    hitkasharu, the visions that attend the Hako.
517 We rakawa! See line 516.
518 See line 516.
519 See line 517.

Explanation by the Ku'rahus

Near midnight the Ku'rahus, his assistant, and the chief rise and take up the Hako, and we go around the lodge again and sing this stanza four times.

As we walk, the visions walk; they fill all the space within the lodge; they are everywhere, all about us.

When we reach the west we pause.

Translation of Sixth Stanza

520 Ho-o-o-o! An introductory exclamation.
521 Hitkasharu! The visions that attend the Hako. See line 491.
522 We riteri hitkasharu!
    we, a part of the word weri, they.
    riteri, touching in different places, touching here and there.
    hitkasharu, the visions that attend the Hako.
523 We riteri! See line 522.
524 See line 522.
525 See line 523.

Explanation by the Ku'rahus

As we go around the second time we sing the next stanza four times.

The visions which attend the Hako are now touching the Children, touching them here and there and by their touch giving them dreams, which will bring them health, strength, happiness, and all good things.

---

[a] See pages 111–116.

The visions touch all who are in the lodge, so it is a good thing to be there, to be touched by the visions.

At the west we pause.

Translation of Seventh Stanza

526 Ho-o-o-o! An introductory exclamation.
527 Hitkasharu! The visions that attend the Hako. See line 491.
528 We rahwara hitkasharu!
       we, a part of the word weri, they.
       rahwara, walking away, departing.
       hitkasharu, the visions that attend the Hako.
529 We rahwara! See line 528.
530 See line 528.
531 See line 529.

Explanation by the Ku'rahus

We go around the lodge for the third time and sing this stanza four times.

As we sing, the visions are walking away; they have done what they came to do; they are now leaving the lodge, and when we reach the west the space they had filled is empty.

We pause and we think of the visions going away over the silent earth to ascend to their dwelling place.

Translation of Eighth Stanza

532 Ho-o-o-o! An introductory exclamation.
533 Hitkasharu! The visions that attend the Hako. See line 491.
534 Wera rawhishpa hitkasharu!
       wera, they have.
       rawhishpa, arrived at the place from which the start was
         made.
       hitkasharu, the visions that attend the Hako.
535 Wera rawhishpa! See line 534.
536 See line 534.
537 See line 535.

Explanation by the Ku'rahus

Once more, for the fourth time, we go around the lodge singing this stanza four times.

As we sing, the visions ascend to their dwelling place; they have returned whence they came, to their abode in the sky.

When we reach the west we lay the Hako down with the songs and movements which accompany the act.[a] Kawas rests in her nest.

One by one the Children go to their homes, and the dreams brought by the visions which attend the Hako go with them to make their hearts glad.

---

[a] See pages 111-116.

TENTH RITUAL. THE DAWN

PART I. THE BIRTH OF DAWN

Explanation by the Ku'rahus

As the night draws to a close, the Ku'rahus orders the server to lift the skins which hang at the outer and inner doors of the long passageway of the lodge, and to go outside and watch for the first glimmer of light.

The Ku'rahus, his assistant, and the chief, sitting behind the Hako, where they lie at rest, look toward the east through the open doorway and watch for the first signs of the dawn.

At the first indication of a change, when the air begins to stir, the server comes in with the tidings, and we rise, take up the Hako, and stand at the west, behind the holy place; there, looking toward the east, we sing this song. We sing it slowly and with reverent feeling, for it speaks of the mysterious and powerful act of Tira'wa atius in the birth of Dawn.

SONG

Words and Music

M. M. ♪ = 116.
• = Pulsation of the voice.

Transcribed by Edwin S. Tracy.

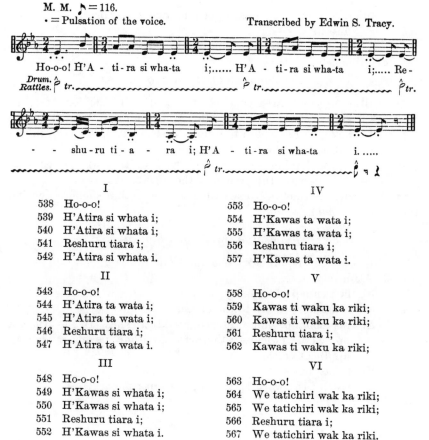

	I		IV
538	Ho-o-o!	553	Ho-o-o!
539	H'Atira si whata i;	554	H'Kawas ta wata i;
540	H'Atira si whata i;	555	H'Kawas ta wata i;
541	Reshuru tiara i;	556	Reshuru tiara i;
542	H'Atira si whata i.	557	H'Kawas ta wata i.
	II		**V**
543	Ho-o-o!	558	Ho-o-o!
544	H'Atira ta wata i;	559	Kawas ti waku ka riki;
545	H'Atira ta wata i;	560	Kawas ti waku ka riki;
546	Reshuru tiara i;	561	Reshuru tiara i;
547	H'Atira ta wata i.	562	Kawas ti waku ka riki;
	III		**VI**
548	Ho-o-o!	563	Ho-o-o!
549	H'Kawas si whata i;	564	We tatichiri wak ka riki;
550	H'Kawas si whata i;	565	We tatichiri wak ka riki;
551	Reshuru tiara i;	566	Reshuru tiara i;
552	H'Kawas si whata i.	567	We tatichiri wak ka riki.

VII

568   Ho-o-o!
569   Pirau si whata i;
570   Pirau si whata i;
571   Reshuru tiara i;
572   Pirau si whata i.

VIII

573   Ho-o-o!
574   Pirau ta wata i;
575   Pirau ta wata i;
576   Reshuru tiara i;
577   Pirau ta wata i.

Translation of First Stanza

538   Ho-o-o!   An introductory exclamation.
539   H'Atira si whata i.
    h', the sign of breath, of breathing forth life.
    atira, mother. The term here refers to Mother Earth, repre-
        sented by the ear of corn.
    si, you; singular number, used in addressing a person.
    whata, arise, move, stir about. The word is used when mak-
        ing a request or a suggestion, not a command.
    i, a part of the word riki, now, the present time.
540   See line 539.
541   Reshuru tiara i.
    Reshuru, the Dawn.
    tiara, a birth, a transformation, one form proceeding from
        another.
    i, part of the word riki, now, the present time.
542   See line 539.

Explanation by the Ku'rahus

We call to Mother Earth, who is represented by the ear of corn.
She has been asleep and resting during the night. We ask her to
awake, to move, to arise, for the signs of the dawn are seen in the
east and the breath of the new life is here.

H'Atira means Mother breathing forth life; this life is received
from Tira'wa atius with the breath of the new-born Dawn.

Mother Earth is the first to be called to awake, that she may receive
the breath of the new day.

Translation of Second Stanza

543   Ho-o-o!   An introductory exclamation.
544   H'Atira ta wata i.
    h', the symbol of breath, life.
    atira, mother; refers to the earth.
    ta, a personal pronoun referring to atira; she. In the original
        no sex is indicated; there are no pronouns he or she; ta
        applies to either sex.
    wata, has arisen.
    i, a part of the word riki, now, present time.
545   See line 544.

546   Reshuru tiara i.
      Reshuru, the Dawn.
      tiara, born.
      i, a part of riki, now, present time.
547   See line 544.

Explanation by the Ku'rahus

Mother Earth hears the call; she moves, she awakes, she arises, she feels the breath of the new-born Dawn. The leaves and the grass stir; all things move with the breath of the new day; everywhere life is renewed.

This is very mysterious; we are speaking of something very sacred, although it happens every day.

Translation of Third Stanza

548   Ho-o-o! An introductory exclamation.
549   H'Kawas si whata i.
      h', the symbol of breath, breathing forth life.
      Kawas, the brown eagle, representative of the lesser and
         beneficient powers above.
      si, you; a personal pronoun, singular number.
      whata, arise, stir, move about.
      i, a part of riki, now, the present time.
550   See line 549.
551   See line 546.
552   See line 549.

Explanation by the Ku'rahus

We call upon Kawas to awake, to move, to arise. Kawas had been sleeping and resting during the night.

Kawas represents the lesser powers which dwell above, those which are sent by Tira'wa atius to bring us help. All these powers must awake and arise, for the breath of the new life of the Dawn is upon them.

The eagle soars where these powers dwell and can communicate with them. The new life of the new day is felt by these powers above as well as by Mother Earth below.

Translation of Fourth Stanza

553   Ho-o-o! An introductory exclamation.
554   H'Kawas ta wata i.
      h', the symbol of breath, life.
      Kawas, the brown eagle, representative of the lesser powers
         above.
      ta, a personal pronoun referring to Kawas.
      wata, has arisen.
      i, a part of the word riki, now, the present time.
555   See line 554.
556   See line 546.
557   See line 554.

Explanation by the Ku'rahus

H'Kawas hears the call and awakes. Now all the powers above
wake and stir, and all things below wake and stir; the breath of new
life is everywhere. With the signs in the east has come this new life.

Translation of Fifth Stanza

558   Ho-o-o! An introductory exclamation.
559   Kawas ti waku ka riki.
> Kawas, the brown eagle, the intermediary as well as the repre-
> sentative of the lesser and beneficent powers above.
> ti, a personal pronoun referring to Kawas, singular number,
> spoken of.
> waku, speaks.
> ka, a part of the word akaro, lodge; refers to the space
> within the lodge about the fire.   In this instance ka indi-
> cated the holy place set apart for the sacred objects.
> riki, standing; the word implies the present time.
560   See line 559.
561   Reshuru tiara i.   See line 546.
562   See line 559.

Explanation by the Ku'rahus

Kawas, the brown eagle, the messenger of the powers above, now
stands within the lodge and speaks. The Ku'rahus hears her voice
as she tells him what the signs in the east mean.

She tells him that Tira'wa atius there moves upon Darkness, the
Night, and causes her to bring forth the Dawn. It is the breath of the
new-born Dawn, the child of Night and Tira'wa atius, which is felt by
all the powers and all things above and below and which gives them
new life for the new day.

This is the meaning of this stanza. The words of the song do not
tell all that the song means; the meaning has been handed down
from our fathers and taught to the Ku'rahus, who may teach it to
anyone who is serious-minded and sincerely desires to learn these
sacred things.

Translation of Sixth Stanza

563   Ho-o-o! An introductory exclamation.
564   We tatichiri wak ka riki.
> we, I.
> tatichiri, understand, have knowledge of the meaning.
> wak, a part of the word waku, speech, to speak.
> ka, a part of akaro, lodge; within the lodge.   See line 559.
> riki, standing.
565   See line 564.
566   Reshuru tiara i.   See line 546.
567   See line 564.

Explanation by the Ku'rahus

In this stanza the Ku'rahus answers Kawas. He tells her that he understands the words she spoke to him when standing there in the lodge, that now he knows the meaning of the signs in the east; that night is the mother of the day, that it is by the power of Tira'wa atius moving on Darkness that she gives birth to the Dawn.

The Dawn is the child of Tira'wa atius. It gives the blessing of life; it comes to awaken man, to awake Mother Earth and all living things that they may receive the life, the breath of the Dawn which is born of the Night by the power of Tira'wa atius.

Our fathers were taught by Kawas and understood what she told them, and what they then learned has been handed down to us.

Translation of Seventh Stanza

568 Ho-o-o! An introductory exclamation.
569 Pirau si whata i.
    pirau, my son. The term refers to the Son, the person to whom the Father has brought the Hako to establish a bond between the two by means of this ceremony. The Son has remained in the lodge through the night.
    si, you.
    whata, arise. See line 539.
    i, a part of riki; now, present time.
570 See line 569.
571 See line 546.
572 See line 569.

Explanation by the Ku'rahus

We now call upon the Son, who has been asleep and resting in the lodge, to awake, to move, and to arise, for the east gives signs of the birth of the dawn, whose breath is on all things.

Translation of Eighth Stanza

573 Ho-o-o! An introductory exclamation.
574 Pirau ta wata i.
    pirau, my son; the term refers to the Son.
    ta, a personal pronoun referring to the Son.
    wata, has arisen.
    i, a part of riki; now.
575 See line 574.
576 See line 546.
577 See line 574.

Explanation of the Ku'rahus

The Son hears the call. He wakes, he moves, he rises, he looks to the east and sees the signs of the dawn.

PART II. THE MORNING STAR AND THE NEW-BORN DAWN

Explanation by the Ku'rahus

Now all have risen and have received the breath of the new life just born, all the powers above, all things below. Kawas has stood and spoken in the lodge; the Ku'rahus has heard and understood; the Son is awake and stands with the Ku'rahus awaiting the coming of dawn. The Ku'rahus has sent the server outside the lodge to watch for the morning star. We stand at the west and wait its coming. When it appears he sings the following song:

SONG

Words and Music

M. M. ♪ = 132.

• = Pulsation of the voice.   Transcribed by Edwin S. Tracy.

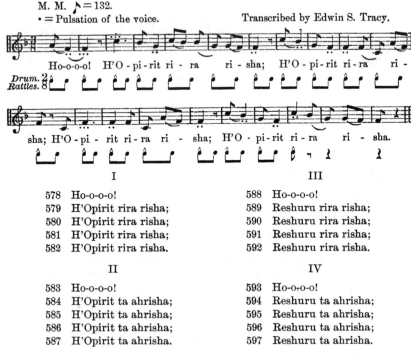

Ho-o-o-o! H'O - pi - rit ri - ra   ri - sha; H'O - pi - rit ri ra   ri -

Drum.
Rattles.

sha; H'O - pi - rit ri - ra ri - sha; H'O - pi - rit ri - ra   ri - sha.

	I		III
578	Ho-o-o-o!	588	Ho-o-o-o!
579	H'Opirit rira risha;	589	Reshuru rira risha;
580	H'Opirit rira risha;	590	Reshuru rira risha;
581	H'Opirit rira risha;	591	Reshuru rira risha;
582	H'Opirit rira risha.	592	Reshuru rira risha.
	II		**IV**
583	Ho-o-o-o!	593	Ho-o-o-o!
584	H'Opirit ta ahrisha;	594	Reshuru ta ahrisha;
585	H'Opirit ta ahrisha;	595	Reshuru ta ahrisha;
586	H'Opirit ta ahrisha;	596	Reshuru ta ahrisha;
587	H'Opirit ta ahrisha.	597	Reshuru ta ahrisha.

Translation of First Stanza

578   H-o-o-o! An introductory exclamation.
579   H'Opirit rira risha.
  h', the symbol of breath, breathing forth life.
  Opirit, the Morning Star.
  rira, coming; approaching toward one.
  risha, something seen at a great distance; it seems to appear and then to be lost, to disappear. The word conveys the picture of a gradual advance, as from a great distance, where the object was scarcely discernable, to a nearer point of view, but still distant.
580, 581, 582   See line 579.

Explanation by the Ku'rahus

We sing this song slowly with reverent feeling, for we are singing of very sacred things.

The Morning Star is one of the lesser powers. Life and strength, and fruitfulness are with the Morning Star. We are reverent toward it. Our fathers performed sacred ceremonies in its honor.

The Morning Star is like a man; he is painted red all over; that is the color of life. He is clad in leggings and a robe is wrapped about him. On his head is a soft downy eagle's feather, painted red. This feather represents the soft, light cloud that is high in the heavens, and the red is the touch of a ray of the coming sun. The soft, downy feather is the symbol of breath and life.

The star comes from a great distance, too far away for us to see the place where it starts. At first we can hardly see it; we lose sight of it, it is so far off; then we see it again, for it is coming steadily toward us all the time. We watch it approach; it comes nearer and nearer; its light grows brighter and brighter.

This is the meaning of this stanza, and the star comes as we sing it four times.

Translation of Second Stanza

583   H-o-o-o! An introductory exclamation.
584   H'Opirit ta ahrisha.
      h', the symbol of breath, life.
      Opirit, the Morning Star.
      ta, approaching.
      ahrisha, coming still nearer, but at the same time disappearing. The word conveys the picture of the morning star by its increased brilliancy coming nearer, and then fading, disappearing in the light of day.
585, 586, 587   See line 584.

Explanation by the Ku'rahus

As we sing this stanza the Morning Star comes still nearer and now we see him standing there in the heavens, a strong man shining brighter and brighter. The soft plume in his hair moves with the breath of the new day, and the ray of the sun touches it with color. As he stands there so bright, he is bringing us strength and new life.

As we look upon him he grows less bright, he is receding, going back to his dwelling place whence he came. We watch him vanishing, passing out of our sight. He has left with us the gift of life which Tira'wa atius sent him to bestow.

We sing this stanza four times.

Translation of Third Stanza

588   Ho-o-o-o!   An introductory exclamation.
589   Reshuru rira risha.

Reshuru, the Dawn.

rira, coming toward one.

risha, something scarcely to be seen because of its distance;
it eludes, seems to appear and then to disappear.

590, 591, 592   See line 589.

Explanation by the Ku'rahus

As we sing this stanza we are still standing at the west of the
lodge, looking through the long passageway toward the east.   Now
in the distance we see the Dawn approaching; it is coming, coming
along the path of the Morning Star.   It is a long path and as the
Dawn advances along this path sometimes we catch sight of it and
then again we lose it, but all the time it is coming nearer.

The Dawn is new born, its breath has sent new life everywhere, all
things stir with the life Tira'wa atius has given this child, his child,
whose mother is the Night.

We sing this stanza four times.

Translation of Fourth Stanza

593   Ho-o-o-o!   An introductory exclamation.
594   Reshuru ta ahrisha.

Reshuru, the Dawn.

ta, approaching, coming.

ahrisha, coming nearer but only to disappear.   The Dawn
comes nearer, grows brighter, but disappears in the
brighter light of day.

595, 596, 597   See line 594.

Explanation by the Ku'rahus

As we stand, looking through the long passageway of the lodge,
watching and singing, we see the Dawn come nearer and nearer; its
brightness fills the sky, the shadowy forms on the earth are becoming
visible.   As we watch, the Dawn, like the Morning Star, recedes.   It
is following the star, going back to the place whence it came, to its
birthplace.

The day is close behind, advancing along the path of the Morning
Star and the Dawn, and, as we watch, the Dawn vanishes from our
sight.

We sing this song four times.

PART III. DAYLIGHT

SONG

Words and Music

M. M. ♪ = 132.
• = Pulsation of the voice.   Transcribed by Edwin S. Tracy.

Ta-he-sha!   Ta-he - sha!..... Pi - ra - o rux ki-ri ka.   Ta-he - sha!........   Ta-he -

Drum.
Rattles.

sha!.....   Ta-he-sha!   Ta-he - sha!   Pi - ra - o rux ki-ri ka.   Ta-he-sha!..

....   Ta - he - sha!.........   Ta - he - sha!   Ta - he - sha!......

I

598 Tahesha! Tahesha!
599 Pirao rux kiri ka. Tahesha! Tahesha!
600 Tahesha! Tahesha!
601 Pirao rux kiri ka. Tahesha! Tahesha!
602 Tahesha! Tahesha!

II

603 Ta ira! Ta ira!
604 Ira, ta ira! Heru rera, ta ira!
605 Ta ira! Ta ira!
606 Ira, ta ira! Heru rera, ta ira!
607 Ta ira! Ta ira!

Translation of First Stanza

598 Tahesha! Tahesha!
    tahesha, daylight, the light of day, before the sun rises.
599 Pirao rux kiri ka. Tahesha! Tahesha!
    pirao, child, son.
    rux, let; a command or a bidding, as, let him, or, do this.
    kiri, a part of kiriku, eyes.
    ka, a part of taka, to come out, to be seen by coming out from
        under a covering. The meaning of these words becomes
        clear when the custom of sleeping with the robe over the
        head is remembered; the Son is bidden to throw the robe
        off his head and let his eyes be free to behold the day.
    tahesha, the light of day.
600 See line 598.
601 See line 599.
602 See line 598.

Explanation by the Ku'rahus

We sing this song with loud voices, we are glad. We shout, "Daylight has come! Day is here!" The light is over the earth. As we look out through the door of the lodge we can see the trees, and all things stand out clearly in the light.

We call to the Children, we bid them awake and throw off the robes that covered their heads as they slept and let their eyes look out and behold the light of day, the day that has come, that is here.

This stanza is sung four times.

Translation of Second Stanza

603 Ta ira! Ta ira!
     ta, deer, a general term.
     ira, coming into sight.
604 Ira, ta ira; heru rera, ta ira.
     ira, ta ira. See line 603.
     heru, there.
     rera, coming.
605 See line 603.
606 See line 604.
607 See line 603.

Explanation by the Ku'rahus

Still we sing and shout, "Day is here! Daylight has come!" We tell the Children that all the animals are awake. They come forth from the places where they have been sleeping. The deer leads them. She comes from her cover, bringing her young into the light of day. Our hearts are glad as we sing, "Daylight has come! The light of day is here!"

We sing this stanza four times.

PART IV. THE CHILDREN BEHOLD THE DAY

SONG

Words and Music

M. M. ♪ = 160.
• = Pulsation of the voice.   Transcribed by Edwin S. Tracy.

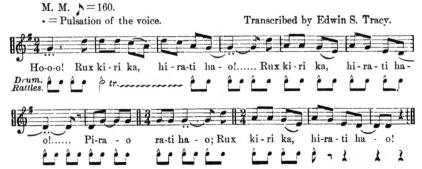

Ho-o-o! Rux ki-ri ka, hi-ra-ti ha-o!...... Rux ki-ri ka, hi-ra-ti ha-
Drum.
Rattles.

o!...... Pi-ra-o   ra-ti ha-o; Rux ki-ri ka, hi-ra-ti ha-o!

	I		II
608	Ho-o-o!	613	Ho-o-o!
609	Rux kiri ka, hirati hao!	614	Ti kiri ka, hirati hao!
610	Rux kiri ka, hirati hao!	615	Ti kiri ka, hirati hao!
611	Pirao rati hao;	616	Pirao rati hao;
612	Rux kiri ka, hirati hao!	617	Ti kiri ka. Ha! Wita hesha!

Translation of First Stanza

608   Ho-o-o! An introductory exclamation.

609   Rux kiri ka, hirati hao!

    rux, a command, let him now.

    kiri, a part of the word kiriku, eyes.

    ka, a part of the word taka, to become visible, to come out.

    hirati, my or mine. The common word is kurati; the ku is changed in this ceremony to the aspirate syllable hi, making the word hirati. The idea of breath, as significant of life, is united to desire in the change from ku to hi, in this word meaning my.

    hao, offspring, my own child.

610   See line 609.

611   Pirao rati hao.

    pirao, child, a general term.

    rati, my, mine.

    hao, offspring.

612   See line 609.

Explanation by the Ku'rahus

In this stanza the Son (pirao), the man who is not of our kindred, but who through this ceremony is made as our offspring, our own son (hao), is commanded by the Ku'rahus to go forth and arouse the Children, to bid them awake, and open their eyes to behold the light of day.

The Son, who with the Ku'rahus has been watching for the dawn, receives the order and sends his messengers to the lodges of his relatives to arouse them from sleep.

This is done that the Children may be in readiness to come to the lodge before the sun is above the horizon.

This stanza is sung four times.

Translation of Second Stanza

613   Ho-o-o! An introductory exclamation.

614   Ti kiri ka, hirati hao!

    ti, he.

    kiri, a part of the word kiriku, eyes.

    ka, a part of the word taka, to become visible, to be seen.

    hirati, my or mine. See explanation of the word in line 609.

    hao, offspring, my own child.

615   See line 614.

616   Pirao rati hao.
         pirao, child, a general term, anybody's child.
         rati, a part of the word hirati, my.
         hao, my own child.
617   Ti kiri ka.   Ha!   Wita hesha!
         ·ti kiri ka.   See line 614.
         ha! behold!
         wita, coming.
         hesha, a part of the word tahesha, daylight.

Explanation by the Ku'rahus

While the messengers are going from one lodge to another to awake
the people and bid them come to the lodge where the ceremony is
being performed, we sing this second stanza.

It tells that the Son, now become as our own offspring, has gone
forth to awake the Children, who have heard his call, and now, behold!
they come forth to look upon the light of day.

This stanza is sung four times.

ELEVENTH RITUAL (SECOND DAY).   THE MALE ELEMENT INVOKED

PART I.   CHANT TO THE SUN

Explanation by the Ku'rahus

On this, the second day of the ceremony, we remember our father
the Sun.   The sun comes directly from Tira'wa atius, and whoever is
touched by the first rays of the sun in the morning receives new life
and strength which have been brought straight from the power above.
The first rays of the sun are like a young man, they have not yet
spent their force or grown old, so, to be touched by them is to receive
an accession of strength.

The door of the lodge where the ceremony is performed must face
the east, so that the first rays of the sun can enter and reach the
Children.   I believe that as we sing this song and as the first rays
touch the Children they will receive help and strength.   I was told by
my predecessor that it would be so, and he was taught by those who
had received the knowledge from the fathers; therefore I tell the same
to the Children.   All the time I am singing this song I remember the
Sun, the Moon, the Stars, the Corn; all these were made by Tira wa
atius, and I ask them to give us success and plenty; success in hunting and in war; plenty of food, of children, and of health.   The Sun,
the Moon, the Stars, the Corn, are powerful.

The Children, who have been aroused by the messengers of the Son,
gather at the lodge before the sun is up.   They must be there when
the first ray appears if they would gain its blessing.

As soon as we who are standing at the west of the lodge, looking
through the doorway, catch sight of the first ray of the sun on the
horizon, we take up the Hako and move by the north to make a first
circuit of the lodge, and sing the first verse of this chant.

CHANT

Words and Music

M. M. ♪ = 120.
• = Pulsation of the voice.　　　　　Transcribed by Edwin S. Tracy.

Ho-o-o!　　Hi-ra　　h'A-ars i - ra - a,　we-re hu-ka-wi, hu-ru ka ha-a

hu - ka - wi,　hu - ru ka hu - ka - wi,　　hu - ka - wi　hu - ru　ka　ha.

I

618 Ho-o-o!
619 Hira h'Aars ira-a, were hukawi, huru ka ha-a hukawi, huru ka hukawi,
　　hukawi huru ka ha.

II

620 Ho-o-o!
621 Hira h'Aars ira-a, were hukawi, ta kusi hi-i hukawi, ta kusi hukawi,
　　hukawi ta kusi hi.

III

622 Ho-o-o!
623 Hira h'Aars ira-a, were hukawi, ta wira ka-a hukawi, ta wira hukawi,
　　hukawi ta wira ha.

IV

624 Ho-o-o!
625 Hira h'Aars ira-a, were hukawi, ka hakidhihi hukawi, ka hakidhihi
　　hukawi, hukawi ka hakidhihi.

V

626 Ho-o-o!
627 Hira h'Aars ira-a, were hukawi, ka waraha ha hukawi, ka waraha hukawi,
　　hukawi ka waraha.

VI

628 Ho-o-o!
629 Hira h'Aars ira-a, were hukawi, ta wara ka-a hukawi, ta wara hukawi,
　　hukawi ta wara ha.

VII

630 Ho-o-o!
631 Hira h'Aars ira-a, were hukawi, ta riki hi-i hukawi, ta riki hukawi, hukawi
　　ta riki hi.

VIII

632 Ho-o-o!
633 Hira h'Aars ira-a, were hukawi, ta witspa ha-a hukawi, ta witspa hukawi,
　　hukawi ta witspa ha.

Translation of First Verse

618   Ho-o-o! An introductory exclamation.
619   Hira H'Aars ira-a, were hukawi, huru ka ha-a hukawi, huru ka
          hukawi, hukawi huru ka ha.

hira, will come. The word is ira, the h is added for euphony
    and greater ease in singing.

h', the symbol of breath, life, breathing forth, giving life.

aars, a contraction of atius, father.

ira, will come.

a, a prolongation of the last syllable of ira.

were, at that time, when, or then.

hukawi, the ray or beam of the sun.

huru, entering.

ka, a part of akaro, lodge. Ka, however, refers to the open
    space within, around the fireplace, where the people
    gather, where they sit and pursue their avocations.

ha-a, a prolongation of ka.

hukawi, huru ka hukawi, hukawi huru ka ha. All the words
    are translated above.

Explanation by the Ku'rahus

We speak of the sun as Father breathing forth life (h'Aars), causing
the earth to bring forth, making all things to grow. We think of the
sun, which comes direct from Tira'wa atius, the father of life, and
his ray (hukawi) as the bearer of this life. (You have seen this ray
as it comes through a little hole or crack.) While we sing, this ray
enters the door of the lodge to bring strength and power to all within.

We sing this verse four times as we go around the lodge. When
we reach the west we pause.

Food, which has been prepared outside the lodge, is now brought in,
and the Children are given their morning meal. Then we sing the
second verse.

Translation of Second Verse

620   Ho-o-o! An introductory exclamation.
621   Hira h'Aars ira-a, were hukawi, ta kusi hi-i hukawi, ta kusi
          hukawi, hukawi ta kusi hi.

hira h'Aars ira-a, were hukawi. See line 619.

ta, a spot; the word refers to the place where the ray touches
    and makes a bright spot.

kusi, alights upon, rests upon.

hi, a part of hira, will come. See line 619.

i, a prolongation of the syllable hi.

hukawi, the ray or beam of the sun.

ta kusi hukawi, hukawi ta kusi hi. Translated above.

Explanation by the Ku'rahus

As the sun rises higher the ray, which is its messenger, alights upon the edge of the central opening in the roof of the lodge, right over the fireplace. We see the spot (ta), the sign of its touch, and we know that the ray is there.

The fire holds an important place in the lodge; you remember we sang about it when we were preparing the sacred objects (first ritual, first song, line 49). Father Sun is sending life by his messenger to this central place in the lodge.

As we sing we look at the bright spot where the ray has alighted, and we know that life from our father the Sun will come to us by the ray.

We sing this verse four times, and when we have completed the second circuit of the lodge and have reached the west we pause.

Translation of Third Verse

622 Ho-o-o! An introductory exclamation.
623 Hira h'Aars ira-a, were hukawi, ta wira ka-a hukawi, ta wira hukawi, hukawi ta wira ha.
    hira h'Aars ira-a, were hukawi. See line 619.
    ta, the spot, the place that is touched by the ray
    wira, climbing down, descending into.
    ka, a part of the word akaro, lodge.
    a, a vowel prolongation.
    hukawi, the ray or beam.
    ta wira hukawi, hukawi ta wira. Translated above.
    ha, a vocable to fill out the measure.

Explanation by the Ku'rahus

As the sun rises higher we turn toward the north and begin the third circuit of the lodge. The ray is now climbing down into the lodge. We watch the spot where it has alighted. It moves over the edge of the opening above the fireplace and descends into the lodge, and we sing that life from our father the Sun will come to us by his messenger, the ray, which is now climbing down into the space within the lodge where we are gathered together.

We sing this verse four times, and after the third circuit we pause at the west.

Translation of Fourth Verse

624 Ho-o-o! An introductory exclamation.
625 Hira h'Aars ira-a, were hukawi, ka hakidhihi hukawi, ka haki-dhiki hukawi, hukawi ka hakidhihi.
    hira h'Aars ira-a, were hukawi. See line 619.
    ka, a part of the word akaro, lodge, particularly the space within the lodge, about the fire.
    hakidhiki, walking, moving about the room, the open space within the lodge.
    hukawi, the ray.
    ka hakidhiki hukawi, hukawi ka hakidhiki. Translated above.

Explanation by the Ku'rahus

When the spot where the ray has alighted reaches the floor, we turn toward the north and begin the fourth circuit of the lodge.

Now the spot is walking here and there within the lodge, touching different places. We know that the ray will bring strength and power from our father the Sun as it walks within the lodge. Our hearts are glad and thankful as we sing.

When we reach the west the fourth circuit is completed. Then we lay the Hako down upon the holy place and sing the songs which tell what that act means.[a]

The first four verses of this chant are sung in the morning; they follow the movements of the ray. When the spot has reached the floor we stop singing and do not begin again until the afternoon, so that our song can accompany the ray as it leaves the lodge, touches the hills, and finally returns to the sun.

All through the ceremony we must be careful as to the time when we sing the songs, for each has its own time of day. If we do not observe this teaching of our fathers we shall fail to receive the benefits of the ceremony.

Between the two parts other songs can be sung; it will not interfere with this chant to the Sun.

Translation of Fifth Verse

626   Ho-o-o! An introductory exclamation.
627   Hira h'Aars ira-a, were hukawi, ka waraha ha hukawi, ka waraha hukawi, hukawi ka waraha.

hira h'Aars ira-a, were hukawi. See line 619.
ka, a part of the word akaro, lodge, the space within.
waraha, walked here and there, in different parts of the lodge.
ha, a repetition and prolongation of the last syllable of waraha.
hukawi, ka waraha hukawi, hukawi ka waraha. Translated above.

Explanation by the Ku'rahus

In the afternoon when we observe that the spot has moved around the lodge, as the sun has passed over the heavens, we sing the fifth verse. The ray has touched the Children and all of us as it has walked here and there in different parts of the lodge. It has brought strength to us from our father the Sun.

We sing the verse four times as we make the first circuit of the lodge, and we pause when the west is reached.

---

[a] See pages 111-116 for these songs.

Tranlation of Sixth Verse

628   Ho-o-o! An introductory exclamation.
629   Hira h'Aars ira-a, were hukawi, ta wara ka-a hukawi, ta wara
          hukawi, hukawi ta wara ha.
       hira h'Aars ira-a, were hukawi.   See line 619.
       ta, the spot, the place where the ray touches.
       wara, climbing up, ascending.
       ka, a part of akaro, lodge, the space within the lodge.
       a, a vowel prolongation.
       hukawi, ta wara hukawi, hukawi ta wara.   Translated above.
       ha, a vocable to fill out the measure.

Explanation by the Ku'rahus

   After a little time we see the spot leave the floor of the lodge and
climb up toward the opening over the fireplace, where it had entered
in the morning.   As we see it climbing up out of the lodge and leaving us we sing this verse four times.
   We reach the west at the completion of the second circuit of the
lodge, and there we pause.

Translation of Seventh Verse

630   Ho-o-o! An introductory exclamation.
631   Hira h'Aars ira-a, were hukawi, ta riki hi-i hukawi, ta riki
          hukawi, hukawi ta riki hi.
       hira h'Aars ira-a, were hukawi.   See line 619.
       ta, the spot, the place touched by the ray.
       riki, standing.
       hi, a part of hiri, will come.   See above.
       i, a vowel prolongation.
       hukawi, ta riki hukawi, hukawi ta riki hi.   Translated above.

Explanation by the Ku'rahus

   Later, when the sun is sinking in the west, the land is in shadow,
only on the top of the hills toward the east can the spot, the sign of
the ray's touch, be seen.   Then we sing this stanza as we go around
the lodge the third time.
   The ray of Father Sun, who breathes forth life, is standing on the
edge of the hills.   We remember that in the morning it had stood on
the edge of the opening in the roof of the lodge over the fireplace; now
it stands on the edge of the hills that, like the walls of a lodge, inclose
the land where the people dwell.
   When the third circuit of the lodge is completed we again pause at
the west.

Translation of Eighth Verse

632   Ho-o-o!   An introductory exclamation.
633   Hira h'Aars ira-a, were hukawi, ta witspa ha-a hukawi, ta witspa
        hukawi, hukawi ta witspa ha.

   hira h'Aars ira-a, were hukawi.   See line 619.
   ta, the spot, the place touched by the ray.
   witspa, destination, the end of a journey, a completion.
   ha-a, a prolongation of the last syllable of witspa.
   hukawi, ta witspa hukawi, hukawi ta witspa ha.   Translated
        above.

Explanation by the Ku'rahus

When the spot, the sign of the ray, the messenger of our father the
Sun, has left the tops of the hills and passed from our sight, we sing
this verse as we make the fourth circuit of the lodge.

We know that the ray which was sent to bring us strength has now
gone back to the place whence it came.   We are thankful to our father
the Sun for that which he has sent us by his ray.

At the west we lay the Hako down to rest and sing the songs which
belong to that action.[a]

PART II.   DAY SONGS

Explanation by the Ku'rahus

We sing each stanza of the two following songs four times, and we
make four circuits of the lodge, one stanza to a circuit; then we lay
the Hako down to rest with songs that belong to that act.[a]

SONG

Words and Music

M. M. ♪ = 112.
• = Pulsation of the voice.   Transcribed by Edwin S. Tracy.

Ha-a-a-a!   Ha! Re-ri-re-a-wa;   Ha! Re-ri-re-a-wa, pi-ras-ki   ka si - ri hu-ra!

Drum.
Rattles.

Ha! Re-ri - re-a-wa;   Ha! Re-ri - re-a-wa, pi-ras-ki   ka si - ri hu-ra!

I

634   Ha-a-a-a!
635   Ha! Rerireawa;   Ha! Rerireawa, piraski ka siri hura!
636   Ha! Rerireawa;   Ha! Rerireawa, piraski ka siri hura!

II

637   Ha-a-a-a!
638   Ha! Rerireawa;   Ha! Rerireawa, piraski kat tsiri huwa!
639   Ha! Rerireawa;   Ha! Rerireawa, piraski kat tsiri huwa!

[a] See pages 111-116 for these songs.

Translation of First Stanza

634 Ha-a-a-a! An introductory exclamation.
635 Ha! Rerireawa; Ha! Rerireawa, piraski ka siri hura.
    ha! an exclamation directing attention; in this instance, hark!
      listen!
    rerireawa, the sound made by the flapping of wings, as in the
      alighting of birds.
    piraski, boys.
    ka, now, a form of command.
    siri, you.
    hura, come.
636 See line 635.

Explanation by the Ku'rahus

This song likens the bustle and stir of the Hako party as it comes into the village to the flapping of the wings of a flock of birds as they come to a place and alight. It refers also to the birds represented on the feathered stems—the eagle, the duck, the woodpecker, and the owl. The noise of the wings of these birds is what is meant, for they are moving with the Fathers toward the Children.

In this stanza the Fathers speak: "Hark to the sound of wings! The Hako is here. Now, boys, you are to come forward!" That is, the Children are now to send their gifts of ponies to the Fathers as a return for the promised good brought to them by the Hako. The ponies are always led up to the Fathers by a small boy, the child of the man making the gift.

Translation of Second Stanza

637 Ha-a-a-a! An introductory exclamation.
638 Ha! Rerireawa; Ha! Rerireawa, piraski kat tsiri huwa.
    ha! hark! listen!
    rerireawa, the sound of the wings of birds as they alight.
    piraski, boys.
    kat, come, the response to the command ka, come.
    tsiri, we.
    huwa, go.
639 See line 638.

Explanation by the Ku'rahus

The second stanza is a response to the call made by the Fathers. The people in the camp say, "Hark! The Hako comes. Now we go to meet the Fathers with our gifts."

SONG

Words and Music

M. M. ♪ = 132.

• = Pulsation of the voice.   Transcribed by Edwin S. Tracy.

Ho-o-o-o! I-ri! Ha-ko ti-we ra-tu ri wi-cha; I-ri! Ha-ko ti-we ra-tu ri wi-cha;

Drum Rattles.

.... we ra-tu ri wi-cha; I - ri! Ha-ko ti - we ra-tu ri wi-cha.

I

640 Ho-o-o-o!
641 Iri! Hako tiwe ratu ri wicha;
642 Iri! Hako tiwe ratu ri wicha; we ratu ri wicha;
643 Iri! Hako tiwe ratu ri wicha.

II

644 Ho-o-o-o!
645 Iri! Hako tiwe rus kori wicha;
646 Iri! Hako tiwe rus kori wicha; we rus kori wicha;
647 Iri! Hako tiwe rus kori wicha.

Translation of First Stanza

640 Ho-o-o-o! An introductory exclamation.
641 Iri! Hako tiwe ratu ri wicha.
         iri! a part of nawairi! an exclamation of thankfulness, of grati-
             tude, of confidence.
         Hako, the general term for the symbolic objects peculiar to
             this ceremony.
         tiwe, have.
         ratu, to me;
         ri, modified from the word tara, to bring.
         wicha, reached a destination, arrived.
642 Iri! Hako tiwe ratu ri wicha; we ratu ri wicha.
         Iri! Hako tiwe ratu ri wicha. See line 641.
         we, a part of the word tiwe, have.
         ratu ri wicha. See line 641.
643 See line 641.

Explanation by the Ku'rahus

In the first stanza the Fathers speak. They tell the Children that with the Hako comes the promise of good. For this thanks are given to Mother Corn, who has led us to the Son, and also to the birds upon the Hako, which come from Tira'wa atius and make us father and son.

Translation of Second Stanza

644   Ho-o-o-o! An introductory exclamation.
645   Iri! Hako tiwe rus kori wicha.
     iri! a part of nawairi! an exclamation of thankfulness.
     Hako, the symbolic objects peculiar to this ceremony.
     tiwe, have.
     rus, a modified form of the word wasu, you.
     kori, you bring. The word implies that what you bring is
          something that is yours, or something over which you have
          control.
     wicha, reached a destination; arrived.
646   Iri! Hako tiwe rus kori wicha, we rus kori wicha.
     Iri! Hako tiwe rus kori wicha. See line 645.
     we, a part of the word tiwe, have.
     rus kori wicha. See line 645.
647   See line 645.

Explanation by the Ku'rahus

In the second stanza the Children respond. They thank the Fathers for bringing the Hako, and they thank all the powers represented on the Hako. Their hearts are glad, for they are to be as sons.

I have explained to you that there are certain songs to be sung at certain times and in a fixed order, but there are not enough of these songs to fill all the time of the ceremony.

It may be that the Children who wish to make presents will ask the Fathers to sing for them, and there are several songs that can be sung at such times.

All songs must be chosen in reference to the time. Songs of the visions can only be sung at night. Songs like the following one of Mother Corn can be sung in the daytime, and in the night after the day when we sing of the earth and have had the sacred corn ceremony, but can not be sung in any other night. None of these extra songs can interrupt those which have a fixed sequence.

Words and Music

M. M. ♩=116.
• = Pulsation of the voice.   Transcribed by Edwin S. Tracy.

Ho-o-o-o! H'A-ti - ra!...... H'A-ti - ra!...... H'A-ti - ra! Ki - ra   i - tsi.
Drum.
Rattles.

H'A -ti - ra!...... H'A-ti - ra! Ki-ra   i - tsi   wa - ña - ra.

I

648   Ho-o-o-o!
649   H'Atira! H'Atira! H'Atira! Kira itsi.
650   H'Atira! H'Atira! Kira itsi wahara.

II

651   Ho-o-o-o!
652   H'Atira! H'Atira! H'Atira! Kira tatsi.
653   H'Atira! H'Atira! Kira tatsi wahara.

III

654   Ho-o-o-o!
655   H'Atira! H'Atira! H'Atira! Kira itsi.
656   H'Atira! H'Atira! Kira itsi wehitshpa.

IV

657   Ho-o-o-o!
658   H'Atira! H'Atira! H'Atira! Kira tatsi.
659   H'Atira! H'Atira! Kira tatsi wehitshpa.

Translation

I

648   Ho-o-o-o!   An introductory exclamation.
649   H'Atira!   H'Atira!   H'Atira!   Kira itsi.
    h', the symbol of breath, life.
    atira, mother.   The term refers to the corn.
    kira, now, at this time, under these conditions.
    itsi, let us.
650   H'Atira!   H'Atira!   Kira itsi wahara.
    H'Atira!   H'Atira!   Kira itsi.   See line 649.
    wahara, go.

II

651　Ho-o-o-o!　An introductory exclamation.
652　H'Atira!　H'Atira!　H'Atira!　Kira tatsi.
　　　h'Atira.　See line 649.
　　　kira, now.
　　　tatsi, we are.
653　H'Atira!　H'Atira!　Kira tatsi wahara.
　　　H'Atira!　H'Atira!　Kira tatsi.　See lines 649, 652.
　　　wahara, go, going.

III

654　Ho-o-o-o!　An introductory exclamation.
655　See line 649.
656　H'Atira!　H'Atira!　Kira itsi wehitshpa.
　　　H'Atira!　H'Atira!　Kira itsi.　See line 649.
　　　wehitshpa, to approach one's destination, the object of one's
　　　　journey, or the end sought after.

IV

657　Ho-o-o-o!　An introductory exclamation.
658　See line 652.
659　H'Atira!　H'Atira!　Kira tatsi wehitshpa.
　　　H'Atira!　H'Atira!　Kira tatsi.　See lines 649, 652.
　　　wehitshpa, to approach one's destination.

Explanation by the Ku'rahus

This song is a prayer to Mother Corn to give life and plenty to us all, and to make strong the bond between the Fathers and the Children, by the power granted to her by Tira'wa atius.

In the first stanza we ask Mother Corn, who breaths forth life and gives food to her children, to lead us to the Son.

In the second stanza we sing that she consents, and we start upon our way with our mother.

In the third stanza we ask Mother Corn if we are drawing near to the Son.

In the fourth stanza we see our journey's end; we are approaching our destination, led by her who breathes forth life to her children.

We sing each stanza four times and make four circuits of the lodge as we sing this song; at the west we pause and there lay down the Hako upon the holy place, singing as we do so the songs which belong to that action.[a]

---

[a] See pages 111-116 for these songs.

EXTRA DAY SONG

Words and Music

M. M. ♪ = 116.

• = Pulsation of the voice.   Transcribed by Edwin S. Tracy.

Ho-o-o-o!   Ki ru - ra   hi?   Ki ru-ra - a, ki ru-ra - a,   ki ru - ra - a hi?

Drum. Rattles.

Ki ru - ra hi? Ki ru - ra - a,   ki ru - ra - a hi? A - ru - sha - ha?

I		II	
660	Ho-o-o-o!	666	Ho-o-o-o!
661	Ki rura hi?	667	Iru ra-a;
662	Ki rura-a, ki rura-a, ki rura-a hi?	668	Iru ra-a, iru ra-a, iru ra-a hi;
663	Ki rura hi?	669	Iru ra-a;
664	Ki rura-a, ki rura-a hi?	670	Iru ra-a, iru ra-a hi;
665	Arushaha?	671	Arushaha.

Translation

I

660 Ho-o-o-o!   An introductory exclamation.
661 Ki rura hi?
         ki? where? a question.
         rura, moving, traveling.
         hi, a part of the word arushahi, arushaha, horse.
662 Ki rura-a, ki rura-a, ki rura-a hi?
         ki rura.   See line 661.
         a, vowel prolongation.
         ki rura-a, ki rura-a hi.   See lines 661, 662.
663 See line 661.
664 Ki rura-a, ki rura-a hi?   See line 661.
665 Arushaha?   Horse.

Translation of Second Stanza

II

666 Ho-o-o-o!   An introductory exclamation.
667 Iru ra-a.
         iru, yonder moving.
         ra, coming this way.
         a, vowel prolongation.
668 Iru ra-a, iru ra-a, iru ra-a hi.
         Iru ra-a, iru ra-a, iru ra-a.   See line 667.
         hi, a part of the word arushahi, arushaha, horse.
669 See line 667.
670 Iru ra-a, iru ra-a hi.   See lines 667, 668.
671 Arushaha.   Horse.

Explanation by the Ku'rahus

It may happen during the ceremony that a young man of the village who is not a relative of the Son may desire to lay up for himself an honor which will help him to advance his social position in the tribe.　He mounts a horse, rides to the lodge, and there makes a gift of the animal to the Fathers.　On such an occasion this song is sung.

The words are few, but the meaning of the song has been handed down to the Ku'rahus.　It is not intended that everyone should know all that these songs imply.

The first stanza means:　Whence has he come?　Where does he go, he who rides his horse so fast?　Who is the man?

The second stanza means:　He is coming this way on his horse.　He is bringing it to the Fathers; he is in earnest to make them a gift.

TWELFTH RITUAL (SECOND NIGHT).　THE RITES CAME BY A VISION

FIRST SONG

Words and Music

M. M. ♪ = 126.

• = Pulsation of the voice.　　　　　Transcribed by Edwin S. Tracy.

I

672　Ho-o-o-o!
673　Whitit kasharu, ha! kira rehra wi;
674　Whitit kasharu, ha! kira rehra wi;
675　Ta hao!
676　Hiri!　Hako-o!
677　Whitit kasharu, ha! kira rehia wi;
678　Ta hao!

II

679　Ho-o-o-o!
680　Kutit kasharu, ha! kira rehra wi;
681　Kutit kasharu, ha! kira rehra wi;
682　Ta hao!
683　Hiri!　Hako-o!
684　Kutit kasharu, ha! kira rehra wi;
685　Ta hao!

Translation of First Stanza

672 Ho-o-o-o! An introductory exclamation.
673 Whitit kasharu, ha! kira rehra wi.

whitit, it is believed, it is supposed.   The word implies a question with the desire to know the truth of the belief.

kasharu, a composite word; ka, from rotkaharu, night; sharu, dreams, visions.

ha! behold!

kira, accomplished or brought to pass.

rehra, I hold standing; present tense.

wi, from wirit, an article swinging. The word tells that the article which the person stands holding is swinging in his hand; this refers to the rhythmic swaying of the feathered stems during the singing of the songs of the ceremony.

674 See line 673.
675 Ta hao!

ta, a part of kutati, my.

hao, offspring; my own child.   The term refers to the Son.

676 Hiri! Hako-o!

hiri! give heed; harken.

Hako-o; Hako, the sacred articles of the ceremony; o, vowel prolongation.

677 See line 673.
678 See line 675.

Explanation by the Ku'rahus

This stanza asks about the origin of the Hako, about the account which has come down to us that the Hako and its ceremonies were sent by the powers above to our fathers through a vision.

We have been taught that in a vision our fathers were told how to make the feathered stems, how to use them, how to sway them to the songs, so that they should move like the wings of a bird in its flight. It was in a vision that our fathers were told how they could cause a man who was not their bodily offspring to become a Son, to be bound to them by a tie as strong as the natural tie between father and son.

For this knowledge our fathers gave thanks and we give thanks, for by this ceremony peace and plenty, strength, and all good things come to the people.

Translation of Second Stanza

679 Ho-o-o-o! An introductory exclamation.
680 Kutit kasharu, ha! kira rehra wi.

kutit, it is; an assertion.   The word gives a definite answer to the implied question in the first word of the first stanza, whitit.   The belief, the supposition, is declared to be the truth.

kasharu, ha! kira rehra wi.   See line 673.

681　See line 680
682　See line 675.
683　Hiri!　Hako-o!　See line 676.
684　See line 680.
685　See line 675.

Explanation by the Ku'rahus

This stanza tells the Children that it is true that the knowledge of this ceremony was given to our fathers by the powers above through a vision. We speak of the vision as kasharu, because visions are apt to come in the night when all is still; they then descend, pass over the earth, and come to man.

This stanza also tells that the man to whom we have brought the Hako is to be made a Son in the way our fathers were directed in the vision.

None of the songs of this ceremony can be changed; they must be sung accurately, just as they have been handed down to us, for the words speak of the powers above and their gifts to us, and we must be careful of such words.

SECOND SONG

Words and Music

M. M. ♪ = 116.
• = Pulsation of the voice.　　　　　Transcribed by Edwin S. Tracy.

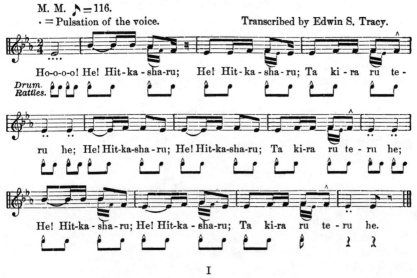

Ho-o-o-o! He! Hit-ka-sha-ru; He! Hit-ka-sha-ru; Ta ki-ra ru te-ru he; He! Hit-ka-sha-ru; He! Hit-ka-sha-ru; Ta ki-ra ru te-ru he; He! Hit-ka-sha-ru; He! Hit-ka-sha-ru; Ta ki-ra ru te-ru he.

I

686　Ho-o-o-o!
687　He! Hitkasharu; He! Hitkasharu;
688　Ta kira ru teru he;
689　He! Hitkasharu; He! Hitkasharu;
690　Ta kira ru teru he;
691　He! Hitkasharu; He! Hitkasharu;
692　Ta kira ru teru he.

II

693   Ho-o-o-o!
694   He! Hitkasharu; He! Hitkasharu;
695   Ta kira te ra-a he;
696   He! Hitkasharu; He! Hitkasharu;
697   Ta kira te ra-a he;
698   He! Hitkasharu; He! Hitkasharu;
699   Ta kira te ra-a he.

Translation

I

686   Ho-o-o-o! An introductory exclamation.
687   He! Hitkasharu; He! Hitkasharu.
    he, an exclamation calling attention to a subject or a teaching.
    hitkasharu; hit, from hittu, feather, referring to the birds that
        attend the Hako; ha, part of rotkaharu, night; sharu,
        dreams, visions.   This composite word refers to the visions
        or dreams brought by the birds that are associated with
        the Hako.
688   Ta kira ru teru he.
    ta, verily.
    kira, brought to pass.
    ru, it, the rite, or ceremony.
    teru, is; the entire ceremony with its promises
    he, vocable.
689   See line 687.
690   See line 688.
691   See line 687.
692   See line 688.

II

693   Ho-o-o-o! An introductory exclamation.
694   See the first stanza, line 687.
695   Ta kira te ra-a he.
    ta, verily.
    kira, brought to pass.
    te, it; the good promised through the ceremony.
    ra-a, is coming.
    he, vocable.
696   See line 687.
697   See line 695.
698   See line 687.
699   See line 695.

Explanation by the Ku'rahus

In this song we are told that verily it is a truth that everything pertaining to this ceremony came through a vision. All the good, all the happiness that comes to those who take part in these rites have been promised in a dream, and the dreams which brought this ceremony and its promises came from the east; they always descend from above by that path.

Were it not true that these dreams come to us and bring us all the good things promised our fathers, we should long ago have abandoned the Hako and its ceremony.

This song says to the Children: "As you listen you will have dreams brought you by the birds represented with the Hako. The visions will bring you help; they will bring you happiness. They are coming to you from the east."

SONG TO THE PLEIADES

Words and Music

M. M. ♪ = 116.
• = Pulsation of the voice.

Transcribed by Edwin S. Tracy.

Ho-o-o-o! We - ta ra-cha; ha! We - ta ra - cha; We - ta ra-cha,

Cha-ka - a! Ru - to chi - ra - o! Ha! Wi-ra; ha! Ha! We-ra; ha!

700   Weta racha; ha!
701   Weta racha; weta racha;
702   Chaka-a!
703   Ruto chirao! Ha! Wira; ha!
704   Weta racha; weta racha;
705   Chaka-a!
706   Ruto chirao! Ha! Wera; ha!

Translation

700   Weta racha, ha!
        weta, coming, advancing.
        racha, rising, moving upward.
        ha! look! behold!
701   Weta racha; weta racha;
        weta racha. See line 700.
702   Chaka-a! The name of the Pleiades.
703   Ruto chirao! Ha! Wira, ha!
        ruto, it is. "It" refers to the coming of the constellation.
        chirao, good, well.
        ha! behold!
        wira, wera, them coming.
        ha! behold!
704   Weta racha; weta racha; See line 700.
705   Chaka-a! See line 702.
706   Ha! Wera; ha! See line 703.

Explanation by the Ku'rahus

When, during the ceremony of the Hako, the Pleiades appear above the horizon, this song must be sung. If, when the coming of these stars is reported, we should be singing, we must break off at the third stanza and sing this song for the fourth circuit of the lodge.

This song to the Pleiades is to remind the people that Tira'wa has appointed the stars to guide their steps. It is very old and belongs to the time when this ceremony was being made. This is the story to explain its meaning which has been handed down from our fathers:

A man set out upon a journey; he traveled far; then he thought he would return to his own country, so he turned about. He traveled long, yet at night he was always in the same place. He lay down and slept and a vision came. A man spoke to him; he was the leader of the seven stars. He said: "Tira'wa made these seven stars to remain together, and he fixed a path from east to west for them to travel over. He named the seven stars Chaka. If the people will look at these stars they will be guided aright."

When the man awoke he saw the Pleiades rising; he was glad, and he watched the stars travel. Then he turned to the north and reached his own country.

The stars have many things to teach us, and the Pleiades can guide us and teach us how to keep together.

We sing this song four times as we make the circuit of the lodge; then we lay the Hako down to rest upon the holy place and sing the songs which belong to that action.

The following songs can be sung at night after the regular song has been completed, if the Children should call for them:

EXTRA NIGHT SONG

Words and Music

M. M. ♪ = 132.
• = Pulsation of the voice.

Transcribed by Edwin S. Tracy.

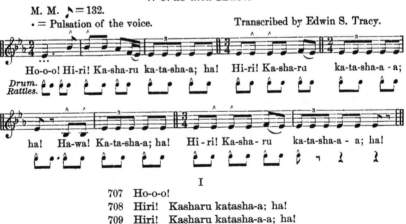

I

707 Ho-o-o!
708 Hiri! Kasharu katasha-a; ha!
709 Hiri! Kasharu katasha-a-a; ha!
710 Hawa! Katasha-a; ha!
711 Hiri! Kasharu katasha-a-a; ha!

II

712 Ho-o-o!
713 He! Hitkasharu shkatasha-a; ha!
714 He! Hitkasharu shkatasha-a-a; ha!
715 Hawa! Shkatasha-a; ha!
716 He! Hitkasharu shkatasha-a-a; ha!

III

717 Ho-o-o!
718 Hiri! Kasharu katata-a; ha!
719 Hiri! Kasharu katata-a-a; ha!
720 Hari! Katata-a; ha!
721 Hiri! Kasharu katata-a-a; ha!

IV

722 Ho-o-o!
723 He! Hitkasharu shkatata-a; ha!
724 He! Hitkasharu shkatata-a-a; ha!
725 Hari! Shkatata-a; ha!
726 He! Hitkasharu shkatata-a-a; ha!

V

727 Ho-o-o!
728 He! Hitshkasharu kitta sha-a; ha!
729 He! Hitshkasharu kitta sha-a-a; ha!
730 Hari! Kitta sha-a; ha!
731 He! Hitshkasharu kitta sha-a-a; ha!

VI

732 Ho-o-o!
733 He! Hitkasharu shkitta sha-a; ha!
734 He! Hitkasharu shkitta sha-a-a; ha!
735 Hari! Shkitta sha-a; ha!
736 He! Hitkasharu shkitta sha-a-a; ha!

Translation of

I

707 Ho-o-o! An introductory explanation.
708 Hiri! Kasharu katasha-a; ha!

hiri! an exclamation, give heed! harken! the word implies reverent feeling.

kasharu; ka, from rotkaharu, night; sharu, vision, dream.

Katasha, the place where the visions dwell.

a, vowel prolongation.

ha! behold!

709 See line 708.
710 Hawa! Katasha-a; ha!

hawa, truly; the word refers to something singular in number.

Katasha-a; ha! See line 708.

711 See line 708.

II

712   Ho-o-o! An introductory exclamation.
713   He! Hitkasharu shkatasha-a; ha!
    he! an exclamation calling attention to a subject or teaching.
    hitkasharu; hit, from hittu, feather; ka, from rotkaharu,
        night; sharu, dream, vision; the visions brought by the
        birds of the Hako.
    Shkatasha; sh, a prefix denoting feminine gender; Katasha,
        the place where the visions dwell when they are at rest.
    a, vowel prolongation.
    ha! behold!
714   See line 713.
715   Hawa! Shkatasha-a; ha!   See lines 710, 713.
716   See line 713.

III

717   Ho-o-o! An introductory exclamation.
718   Hiri! Kasharu katata-a; ha.
    hiri! harken! give heed!
    kasharu, night visions or dreams.   See line 708.
    katata, climbing.
    a, vowel prolongation.
    ha! behold!
719   See line 718.
720   Hari! Katata-a; ha!
    hari, truly.   The word refers to more than one; it is plural.
    katata-a; ha!   See line 718.
721   See line 718.

IV

722   Ho-o-o! An introductory exclamation.
723   He! Hitkasharu shkatata-a; ha!
    he! an exclamation calling attention to a teaching.
    hitkasharu, feather night dreams.   See line 713.
    shkatata; sh, feminine prefix; katata, climbing.   The word
        implies that the visions which were climbing were femi-
        nine, those which belonged to the brown eagle feathered
        stem.
    a, vowel prolongation.
    ha! behold!
724   See line 723.
725   Hari! Shkatata-a; ha!
    hari, truly.   The word is plural.
    shkatata-a; ha!   Translated above; see line 723.
726   See line 723.

V

727 Ho-o-o! An introductory exclamation.
728 He! Hitshkasharu kitta sha-a; ha!
      he! an exclamation calling attention to a teaching.
      hitshkasharu; hit, from hittu, feather; sh, feminine prefix;
          ka from rotkaharu, night; sharu, dreams, visions. The
          composite word refers to the visions which pertain to the
          promises of the Hako ceremony.
      kitta, the top; refers to the locality of Katasha, the dwelling
          place of the visions.
      sha, lying down, as to rest.
      a, vowel prolongation.
      ha! behold!
729 See line 728.
730 Hari! Kitta sha-a; ha!
      hari, truly; plural number.
      kitta sha-a; ha! See line 728.
731 See line 728.

VI

732 Ho-o-o! An introductory exclamation.
733 He! Hitkasharu shkitta sha-a; ha!
      he! an exclamation calling attention to a teaching.
      hitkasharu, feather night dreams. See line 713.
      shkitta, sh, feminine prefix; kitta, the top.
      sha, lying down, reposing.
      a, vowel prolongation.
      ha! behold!
734 See line 733.
735 Hari! Shkitta sha-a; ha! See lines 730, 733.
736 See line 733.

Explanation by the Ku'rahus

Visions come in the night, for spirits can travel better by night than by day. Visions come from Katasha, the place where they dwell. This place is up in the sky, just below where Tira'wa atius appointed the dwelling place of the lesser powers (eighth ritual, part I, second song). Katasha, the place where the visions dwell, is near the dwelling place of the lesser powers, so they can summon any vision they wish to send to us. When a vision is sent by the powers, it descends and goes to the person designated, who sees the vision and hears what it has to say; then, as day approaches, the vision ascends to its dwelling place, Katasha, and there it lies at rest until it is called again.

This song tells about Katasha, where the visions dwell. This is its story:

A holy man who lived long ago, no one knows how long, for there have been many generations since, had a dream. He was taken up to the place where all the visions dwell, those that belong to Kawas, the brown eagle, and those that belong to the white eagle, the male. While he was there the day began to dawn and he saw the visions that had been sent down to earth come climbing up, and he recognized among them some of the visions that had visited him in the past. Then he knew of a truth that all visions of every kind dwell above in Katasha, and that they descend thence to us in the night, and that as the day dawns they ascend, returning to rest in their dwelling place.

The holy man made this song about his dream and told its meaning, and the song and the story have been handed down to us that we might know where visions come from, where they dwell and where they go to when they depart from us.

Among the Pawnees there are shrines, in the keeping of certain men, which contain articles that are used in the sacred ceremonies of the different bands of the tribe. These shrines are very old, they were given by the lesser powers to our fathers with a knowledge of their contents and how to use them.

An ear of corn belongs to one of these shrines. It is a peculiar ear. It is white, with perfect and straight lines of kernels, and there is a tassel on its tip. In the fall the priest of the shrine tells the women to look carefully for such ears when they gather their corn, for Tira'wa causes such ears to grow in the fields for the purposes of this shrine and they belong to it. The little tassel on the tip of the ear of corn represents the feather worn on the head of the warrior. The sacred ear of corn is sometimes borrowed from the priest by the leader of a war party. The ear of corn is born of Mother Earth, she knows all places and the acts of all men who walk the earth, so she is a leader.

Sometimes a young man who proposed going to war would request the following song to be sung. He desired success and wished Mother Corn to lead him. After the Hako ceremony was over he would borrow a sacred ear of corn and put it in a pack which the leader of the war party would sling upon his back. When the party was successful, he would thrust into the ground the stick upon which the ear of corn was tied and as this ear stood before him he would give thanks to it for having led him in safety.

EXTRA NIGHT SONG

Words and Music

M. M. Melody. ♩= 60.
M. M. Drum. ♩= 120.
• = Pulsation of the voice.

Transcribed by Edwin S. Tracy.

Ha - a-a - a-a-a!   A - ti - ra!......   A - ti - ra   hi - ra   i;

Hi - ri! Hi - ri!   Ri whi - e   ri;   Sa - wi ra - re   ka wa - ra, sa - wi ra -

re   ka wa - ra;   A - ti - ra!.....   A - ti - ra   hi - ra - a.

I

737   Ha-a-a-a-a-a!
738   Atira!   Atira hira i;
739   Hiri!   Hiri!   Ri whie ri;
740   Sawi rare ka wara, sawi rare ka wara;
741   Atira!   Atira hira-a.

II

742   Ha-a-a-a-a-a!
743   Hitkasharu, hitkasharu, iri!
744   Hiri!   Hiri!   Ri rai i;
745   Sawi rare ka wara, sawi rare ka wara;
746   Hitkasharu, hitkasharu, iri!

Translation

I

737   Ha-a-a-a-a-a!   An introductory exclamation.

738   Atira!   Atira hira i.

atira, mother.   The term applied to the ear of corn.

hira, coming.

i, it; refers to the corn.

739   Hiri!   Hiri!   Ri whie ri.

hiri! harken! give heed!

ri, has, possesses.

whie, it, within itself.

ri, has.

740   Sawi rare ka wara, sawi rare ka wara.

sawi, part of asawiu, a trap or snare.

rare, it has a likeness to.

ka, part of akaro, the open space bounded by the horizon.

wara, walking.

741   Atira! Atira hira-a.
         Atira! Atira hira. See line 738.
         a, vowel prolongation.

II

742   Ha-a-a-a-a! An introductory exclamation.
743   Hitkasharu, Hitkasharu, iri!
         hitkasharu, a composite word; hit, from hittu, feather; ka,
         from rotkaharu, night; sharu, dream. The word refers
         to dreams brought by the birds that attend the Hako. As
         the song refers to war, the word refers to the white eagle
         stem, the male, the warrior, the dream that attends that
         eagle.
         iri! a part of the exclamation nawairi! expressing thankful-
         ness that all is well.
744   Hiri! Hiri! Ri rai i;
         hiri! harken! give heed!
         ri, has.
         rai, coming; in the future.
         i, it.
745   Sawi rare ka wara, sawi rare ka wara. See first stanza, line 740.
746   See line 743.

Explanation by the Ku'rahus

There are not many words to this song, but the meaning and the
story have been handed down from our fathers.

The first stanza tells of a war party which started out carrying
Mother Corn. As the warriors left the village the old men wished
them good luck, and said: "Mother Corn will be like a snare to
entangle the enemy, so that they will fall easily. Mother Corn will
be like a trap into which the enemy will fall and out of which there
will be no escape.'

The young men started and took a straight course for the enemy's
country; they knew the land and they went directly there, but they
found nothing. They went to the east, there was nothing. They
turned to the west, there was nothing. They traveled to the north,
there was nothing. They went to the south, there was nothing. Then
they made their way back to the point from which they had started
on the border of the enemy's land.

The leader said: "I am worn out, our moccasins are in holes, we
are without food, we must turn back. We will return to our home
tomorrow."

That night they lay down and slept. The leader placed the pack
with the ear of corn under his head, and with a heavy heart he fell
asleep.

The second stanza tells that in the night the ear of corn spoke to
the leader in a dream and said: "Tira'wa bade me test you, and I

have been putting you on trial. I am able to bring strength to the people, the gift of life, and good fortune and success in war. I caused all your misadventures that I might try your courage. Now, you shall not go home on the morrow. If you should, the people would say, 'Mother Corn is powerless.' In the morning you must do as I tell you. You must go toward the southeast; there you will come upon a village where the people have many ponies; these you shall capture and return safely and in triumph, and learn that I have power to lead to success."

The leader did as Mother Corn had directed, and everything came to pass as she had said.

This song has no fixed place in the ceremony but it must be sung at night, because the dream came at that time to the warrior.

The next song is about a man to whom Mother Corn came in a dream; it happened very long ago. The song and the story are very old and have come down to us from our fathers, who knew this ceremony.

Mother Corn spoke to this man in his dream. We are not told what she said to him, but when he awoke he started out to find the man in whose keeping was a shrine containing the ear of corn. As he walked he met a man and asked him, "Is it far to the lodge where the corn is?" The man pointed to a lodge some distance off and said, "It is within." Then the man who had had the dream walked toward the place. As he entered the lodge he saw a shrine hanging on one of the poles and he asked the keeper if it contained the sacred ear of corn, and he was told that it did. Then he took his pipe and offered smoke and prayer in the presence of the corn; because Mother Corn had appeared to him in a dream and had spoken to him he came to offer her reverence.

EXTRA NIGHT SONG

Words and Music

M. M. ♪ = 126.
• = Pulsation of the voice.   Transcribed by Edwin S. Tracy.

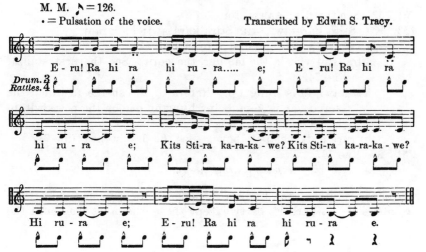

I

747 Eru! Ra hi ra hi rura e;
748 Eru! Ra hi ra hi rura e;
749 Kits Stira karakawe? Kits Stira karakawe? Hi rura e;
750 Eru! Ra hi ra hi rura e.

II

751 Eru! Ra hi ra hi rura e;
752 Eru! Ra hi ra hi rura e;
753 Kits Stira karatawi; kits Stira karatawi; hi rura e;
754 Eru! Ra hi ra hi rura e.

Translation

I

747 Eru! Ra hi ra hi rura e.
     eru! an exclamation of reverence.
     ra, part of rura, coming.
     hi, it.
     ra, coming.
     hi, it.
     rura, coming.
     e, vocable.
748 See line 747.
749 Kits Stira karakawe? Kits Stira karakawe? Hi rura e.
     kits, an abbreviation of kerits? is it?
     stira; s, feminine sign; tira, part of atira, mother; refers to
        the ear of corn.
     karakawe? is it inside?
     hi rura e. See line 747.
750 See line 747.

II

751, 752 See the first stanza, line 747.
753 Kits Stira karatawi; kits Stira karatawi; hi rura e.
     kits? is it? See the first stanza, line 749.
     stira, she who is the mother, the corn. See the first stanza,
        line 749.
     karatawi, it is hung up. Refers to the shrine in which the
        sacred. ear is kept being hung on one of the posts within
        the lodge of the priest.
     hi rura e, translated above. See the first stanza, line 747.
754 See line 747.

Explanation of Ku'rahus

About midnight the Children disperse to their homes and all the
members of the Father's party except those who must remain in the

lodge in charge of the Hako go to their tents. Soon all is quiet within the lodge, the fire burns down to coals and every one sleeps except the man on guard. He must watch through the night and give warning of the first sign of a change in the appearance of the east. As soon as this is seen the skins that hang over the doors of the lodge are lifted and the Ku'rahus makes ready to repeat the songs to the Dawn (tenth ritual). We sing these sacred songs at the dawn of the second day, the day when we chant to our father the Sun, and we sing them again at the dawn of the third day, when we sing to our mother the Earth.

THIRTEENTH RITUAL (THIRD DAY). THE FEMALE ELEMENT INVOKED

PART I. THE SACRED FEAST OF CORN

Explanation by the Ku'rahus

With the morning sun the Children gather at the lodge to receive their morning meal given them by the Fathers. Soon afterward the sacred feast of the Corn takes place. For this feast the Children prepare the food in the manner our fathers did. They pound the dried corn in a wooden mortar and boil the coarse meal until it is thoroughly cooked. They do this in their own homes and then carry the food in the kettles in which it has been cooked to the lodge where the ceremony is being performed, and set them near the fireplace toward the southeast, where wooden bowls and horn spoons have been provided for the occasion.

When all the company have been seated the Fathers ladle out the food into the bowls. The Ku'rahus takes up a little of the food on the tip of a spoon, offers it toward the east, flipping a particle toward the horizon line. He then passes to the north, drops a bit on the rim of the fireplace, and goes to the west, where, facing the east, he lifts the spoon toward the zenith, pauses, waves it to the four quarters and slowly lowers it to the earth and drops a bit on the rim of the fireplace. After this ceremony of offering thanks the filled bowls are placed before the people. Two or more persons take a few spoonfuls from the same bowl, then, hanging the spoons on the edge to prevent their falling into the food, they pass the bowl on to the next group at the left. In this way all the people partake of a common feast.

PART II. SONG TO THE EARTH

Explanation by the Ku'rahus

On the third day of the ceremony it is the duty of the Ku'rahus to teach the Children concerning h'Uraru, Mother Earth, and of those things which she brings forth to sustain the life of the people.   The Ku'rahus has received these teachings from older Ku'rahus, who also received them, and so on through generations back to the time when they were revealed to our fathers through a vision from the mysterious powers above.   A Ku'rahus must devote his life to learning these songs and their meaning and the ceremonies which accompany them.   He must spend much of his time in thinking of these things and in praying to the mighty powers above.

The Ku'rahus speaks to the Children and tells them that Tira'wa atius is the father of all things.   Then the feathered stems are taken up and we sing again the song which we sang the first day before the Children had partaken of the food prepared for them by the Fathers. We sang it then remembering Tira'wa atius, the father of all, of whose gift of food we were about to receive.   Now we sing it, remembering that he is the father of the sun which sends its ray, and of the earth which brings forth.

FIRST SONG

Words and Music

M. M. ♩ = 126.

• = Pulsation of the voice.   Transcribed by Edwin S. Tracy.

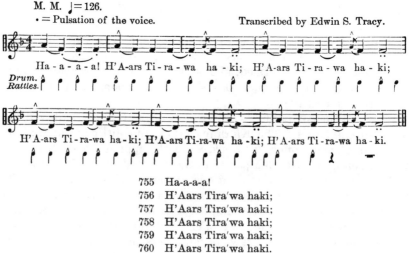

755	Ha-a-a-a!
756	H'Aars Tira'wa haki;
757	H'Aars Tira'wa haki;
758	H'Aars Tira'wa haki;
759	H'Aars Tira'wa haki;
760	H'Aars Tira'wa haki.

For translation, see eighth ritual, first song, page 107.

Explanation by the Ku'rahus

On the second circuit of the lodge we sing the song which follows the first.   It tells us that all the lesser powers are from Tira'wa atius, the father of all.   As we sing we remember the power given to Mother Earth.

SECOND SONG

M. M. ♩ = 126.

• = Pulsation of the voice.   Transcribed by Edwin S. Tracy.

Ha - a - a - a!   H'A - ars e he!   Ti - ra - wa ha - ki;   H'A - ars e he!

Ti - ra - wa ha - ki;   Hi - dhi!   Ti - ra - wa ha - ki;   H'A - ars   Ti - ra - wa ha - ki.

761   Ha-a-a-a!
762   H'Aars e he!   Tirawa haki;
763   H'Aars e he!   Tirawa haki;
764   Hidhi!   Tirawa haki;
765   H'Aars Tirawa haki.

For translation, see eighth ritual, second song, page 108.

Explanation by the Ku'rahus

Now we begin the song of Mother Earth, making a circuit of the lodge to each of the eight stanzas, but not laying down the Hako at the close of the fourth circuit, nor at the end of the song.

THIRD SONG

Words and Music.

M. M. ♪ = 126.

• = Pulsation of the voice.   Transcribed by Edwin S. Tracy.

Ho - o - o! I - ri! H'U - ra - ru   ti ra - sha - a; ha! I - ri! H'U - ra - ru ti ra - sha - a;

ha! A - wa!   Ti ra - sha - a; ha! I - ri! H'U - ra - ru   ti ra - sha - a; ha!

I	III
766 Ho-o-o!	776 Ho-o-o!
767 Iri! H'Uraru ti rasha-a; ha!	777 Ka-a kaharu ti rasha-a; ha!
768 Iri! H'Uraru ti rasha-a; ha!	778 Ka-a kaharu ti rasha-a; ha!
769 Awa! Ti rasha-a; ha!	779 Awa! Kaharu a; ha!
770 Iri! H'Uraru ti rasha-a; ha!	780 Ka-a kaharu ti rasha-a; ha!
II	IV
771 Ho-o-o!	781 Ho-o-o!
772 Iri! H'Uraru ko ti sha-a; ha!	782 Ka-a kaharu ko ti sha-a; ha!
773 Iri! H'Uraru ko ti sha-a; ha!	783 Ka-a kaharu ko ti sha-a; ha!
774 Awa! Ko ti sha-a; ha!	784 Awa! Ko ti sha-a; ha!
775 Iri! H'Uraru ko ti sha-a; ha!	785 Ka-a kaharu ko ti sha-a; ha!

	V		VII
786	Ho-o-o!	796	Ho-o-o!
787	Iri! Toharu ti rasha-a; ha!	797	Iri! Chaharu ti rasha-a; ha!
788	Iri! Toharu ti rasha-a; ha!	798	Iri! Chaharu ti rasha-a; ha!
789	Awa! Ti rasha-a; ha!	799	Awa! Ti rasha-a; ha!
790	Iri! Toharu ti rasha-a; ha!	800	Iri! Chaharu ti rasha-a; ha!

	VI		VIII
791	Ho-o-o!	801	Ho-o-o!
792	Iri! Toharu ko ti sha-a; ha!	802	Iri! Chaharu ko ti sha-a; ha!
793	Iri! Toharu ko ti sha-a; ha!	803	Iri! Chaharu ko ti sha-a; ha!
794	Awa! Ko ti sha-a; ha!	804	Awa! Ko ti sha-a; ha!
795	Iri! Toharu ko ti sha-a; ha!	805	Iri! Chaharu ko ti sha-a; ha!

Translation of First Stanza

766 Ho-o-o! An introductory exclamation.
767 Iri! H'Uraru ti rasha-a; ha!
    iri, a part of nawairi, an expression of thankfulness.
    h'Uraru, the Earth, the fruitful Earth.
    ti, this here.
    rasha, lying.
    a, vowel prolongation.
    ha! behold.
768 See line 767.
769 Awa! Ti rasha-a; ha!
    awa, true, verily.
    ti rasha-a; ha! See line 767.
770 See line 767.

Explanation by the Ku'rahus

In the first stanza we sing: "Behold! Here lies Mother Earth, for a truth she lies here to bring forth, and we give thanks that it is so."

Translation of Second Stanza

771 Ho-o-o! An introductory exclamation.
772 Iri! H'Uraru ko ti sha-a. Ha!
    iri, a part of nawairi, an expression of thankfulness.
    h'Uraru, Mother Earth.
    ko, I am reminded to think of.
    ti, here.
    sha, a part of rasha, to lie, lying.
    a, vowel prolongation.
    ha! behold!
773 See line 772.
774 Awa! Ko ti sha-a; ha!
    awa, true, verily.
    ko ti sha-a; ha! See line 772.
775 See line 772.

Explanation by the Ku'rahus

In the second stanza the Children respond. They say that now they know of a truth that Tira'wa atius causes Mother Earth to lie here and bring forth, and they give thanks that it is so.

Translation of Third Stanza

776 Ho-o-o! An introductory exclamation.
777 Ka-a kaharu ti rasha-a; ha!
     ka, part of akaro, the stretch of land between the horizons.
     a, vowel prolongation.
     kaharu, a cultivated patch, as an aboriginal field of maize.
     ti, here.
     rasha, lying, lies.
     a, vowel prolongation.
     ha! behold!
778 See line 777.
779 Awa! Kaharu a; ha!
     awa, true, verily.
     kaharu, cultivated patches.
     a, vowel prolongation.
     ha! behold!
780 See line 777.

Explanation by the Ku'rahus

There are patches here and there over the land which are cultivated by the different families, where seed is put in Mother Earth, and she brings forth corn. In the third stanza we sing of these fields that lie on Mother Earth, where she brings forth corn for food, and bid the Children behold these fields and remember the power of Tira'wa atius with Mother Earth.

Translation of Fourth Stanza

781 Ho-o-o! An introductory exclamation.
782 Ka-a kaharu ko ti sha-a; ha!
     ka, part of akaro, the stretch of land between the horizons.
     a, vowel prolongation.
     kaharu, cultivated patches, where the corn is planted.
     ko, I am reminded to think of.
     ti, here.
     sha, part of rasha, lies, lying.
     a, vowel prolongation.
     ha! behold!
783 See line 782.
784 Awa! Ko ti sha-a; ha!
     awa, true, verily.
     ko ti sha-a; ha! See line 782.
785 See line 782.

Explanation by the Ku'rahus

In the fourth stanza the Children answer that the fruitful fields are brought to mind, and now they are taught about the gifts of the corn from the powers above and Mother Earth.

Translation of Fifth Stanza

786   Ho-o-o!   An introductory exclamation.
787   Iri!   Toharu ti rasha-a; ha!
    iri, from nawairi, thankfulness.
    toharu, trees, forests.
    ti, this here.
    rasha, lying.
    a, vowel prolongation.
    ha! behold!
788   See line 787.
789   Awa!   Ti rasha-a; ha!
    awa, true, verily.
    ti rasha-a; ha!   See line 787.
790   See line 787.

Explanation by the Ku'rahus

In the fifth stanza the Fathers give thanks for the trees and forests which lie on Mother Earth, which Tira'wa caused her to bring forth, and tell the Children that truly it is so, and that we give thanks because it is so.   From the trees we gain shelter and fire and many other good things.

Translation of Sixth Stanza

791   Ho-o-o!   An introductory exclamation.
792   Iri!   Toharu ko ti sha-a; ha!
    iri, from nawairi, thankfulness.
    toharu, trees, forests.
    ko, I am reminded to think of.
    ti, here.
    sha, from rasha, lying.
    a, vowel prolongation.
    ha! behold!
793   See line 792.
794   Awa!   Ko ti sha-a; ha!
    awa, true, verily.
    ko ti sha-a; ha!   See line 792.
795   See line 792.

Explanation by the Ku'rahus

The Children respond in the sixth stanza, and give thanks for the forests that lie on Mother Earth.   They remember that Tira'wa atius caused Mother Earth to bring them forth, and they give thanks that it is so.

Translation of Seventh Stanza

796 Ho-o-o! An introductory exclamation.
797 Iri! Chaharu ti rasha-a; ha!
    iri, from nawairi, thankfulness.
    chaharu, rivers, streams, water.
    ti, here.
    rasha, lying.
    a, vowel prolongation.
    ha! behold!
798 See line 797.
799 Awa! Ti rasha-a; ha!
    awa, true, verily.
    ti rasha-a; ha! See line 797.
800 See line 797.

Explanation by the Ku'rahus

In the seventh stanza the Fathers give thanks for the water, the springs, streams, and rivers which flow over Mother Earth. Of a truth she brings them forth by the power of Tira'wa atius. I have told you of the meaning of running water. We give thanks for it and all it promises to us.

Translation of Eighth Stanza

801 Ho-o-o! An introductory exclamation.
802 Iri! Chaharu ko ti sha-a; ha!
    iri, from nawairi, thankfulness.
    chaharu, rivers, streams, springs, water.
    ko, I am reminded to think of.
    ti, here.
    sha, from rasha, lying.
    a, vowel prolongation.
    ha! behold!
803 See line 802.
804 Awa! Ko ti sha-a; ha!
    awa, true, verily.
    ko ti sha-a; ha! See line 802.
805 See line 802.

Explanation by the Ku'rahus

In the eighth stanza the Children answer, giving thanks for the water, the springs, the streams, and the rivers that flow over Mother Earth. Of a truth the Children now know that Mother Earth brings them forth by the power of Tira'wa atius. (I did not sing these last two stanzas loud, for if I had done so they would have brought rain. As it is I think it will rain soon.)

PART III. OFFERING OF SMOKE

At the close of the song to Mother Earth the chief spreads the wild-cat skin on the holy place and the assistant lays upon it the white feathered stem, resting one end on the crotched stick.

Then the Ku'rahus says: "My Children, your fathers are listening to what I have to say. Yesterday we remembered our father the Sun, today we remember our mother the Earth, and today Tira'wa has appointed that we should learn of those things which have been handed down to us. Tira'wa is now to smoke from the brown-eagle stem, Kawas, the mother, and you are to smoke from it also."

The bowl from the pipe belonging to the Rain shrine is put on the brown-eagle stem and the priest of the shrine fills it and calls on some one to light it. He also directs in what order the smoke shall be offered. I can not remember the order—if I said anything about it I might tell it wrong, for it is not my business to remember it, the priest alone knows it.

After the offering of smoke as directed by the priest, the feathered stem is taken to the Son, who sits near the door, and after he has smoked the pipe is offered to everyone; all the men, women, and children of the Son's party smoke. This is a holy act and gives long life to the people.

When the west is reached, the feathered stem is lifted four times and the ashes are emptied on the edge of the fireplace. The Ku'rahus then hands the feathered stem to his assistant and returns to his seat, where he takes the feathered stem from his assistant, removes the bowl and replaces it upon its own stem. Then he puts the feathered stem beside its mate on the wildcat skin, resting it against the crotched stick.

PART IV. SONGS OF THE BIRDS

Explanation by the Ku'rahus

The songs about the birds begin with the egg, so the song of the bird's nest where the eggs are lying is the first to be sung. Then comes the song about the wren, the smallest of birds. After that we sing about the birds that are with the Hako, from the smallest to the largest.

These songs are to teach the people to care for their children, even before they are born. They also teach the people to be happy and thankful. They also explain how the birds came to be upon the feathered stems and why they are able to help the people.

There is no fixed time for these songs to be sung, but they belong to the third day of the ceremony—the day when we sing the song to Mother Earth. Sometimes the songs of the nest and the wren are sung early in the day, as these songs were made in the morning. The song of the owl must be sung toward night.

The words of these songs are few, but the story of each has come down to us, so that we know what they mean.

THE SONG OF THE BIRD'S NEST

Words and Music

M. M. ♪ = 160.
Graphophone sound one fourth lower in pitch.
• = Pulsation of the voice.   Transcribed by Edwin S. Tracy.

No drum.

Ho - o-o - o-o!   'Ha - re, 'ha - re,   i - ha - re!   'Ha - re, 'ha - re,

i - ha - re!   Re   wha - ka, 'ha - re,   re   'ha - re,   Wha - ka

'ha - re,   re   'ha - re,   Re   wha - ka 'ha - re,   re   'ha - re.

806 Ho-o-o-o-o!	812 Ho-o-o-o-o!
807 'Hare, 'hare, iha're!	813 'Hare, 'hare, iha're!
808 'Hare, 'hare, iha're!	814 'Hare, 'hare, ira're!
809 Re whaka 'hare, re 'hare.	815 Re whari 'hare, re 'hare,
810 Whaka 'hare, re 'hare,	816 Whari 'hare, re 'hare,
811 Re whaka 'hare, re 'hare.	817 Re whari 'hare, re 'hare.

Translation

I

806   Ho-o-o-o-o!   An introductory exclamation.
807   'Hare, 'hare, iha're!
      'hare, a part of the word iha're, young, as the young of ani-
        mals.   The term is also applied to children.
      iha're, young.   The word in the song refers to the young
        birds as yet unhatched, still in the egg.
808   See line 807.
809   Re whaka 'hare, re 'hare!
      re, they.
      whaka, wha, part of whako, noise; ka, part of akaro, inclo-
        sure, dwelling place; ka refers to the shell of the egg and
        to the nest in which the eggs lay.
      'hare, young.
      re 'hare.   Translated above.
810   Whaka 'hare, re 'hare.   See line 809.
811   See line 809.

II

812 Ho-o-o-o o!   An introductory exclamation.
813 'Hare, 'hare, iha're!   See line 807.
814 See line 813.
815 Re whari 'hare, re 'hare.
    re, they.
    whari, moving, walking.
    'hare, part of iha're, young.
    re 'hare.   Translated above.
816 Whari 'hare, re 'hare.   See line 815.
817 See line 815.

Explanation by the Ku'rahus

One day a man whose mind was open to the teaching of the powers wandered on the prairie. As he walked, his eyes upon the ground, he spied a bird's nest hidden in the grass, and arrested his feet just in time to prevent stepping on it. He paused to look at the little nest tucked away so snug and warm, and noted that it held six eggs and that a peeping sound came from some of them. While he watched, one moved and soon a tiny bill pushed through the shell, uttering a shrill cry. At once the parent birds answered and he looked up to see where they were. They were not far off; they were flying about in search of food, chirping the while to each other and now and then calling to the little one in the nest.

The homely scene stirred the heart and the thoughts of the man as he stood there under the clear sky, glancing upward toward the old birds and then down to the helpless young in the nest at his feet. As he looked he thought of his people, who were so often careless and thoughtless of their children's needs, and his mind brooded over the matter. After many days he desired to see the nest again. So he went to the place where he had found it, and there it was as safe as when he left it. But a change had taken place. It was now full to overflowing with little birds, who were stretching their wings, balancing on their little legs and making ready to fly, while the parents with encouraging calls were coaxing the fledglings to venture forth.

"Ah!" said the man, "if my people would only learn of the birds, and, like them, care for their young and provide for their future, homes would be full and happy, and our tribe be strong and prosperous."

When this man became a priest, he told the story of the bird's nest and sang its song; and so it has come down to us from the days of our fathers.

THE SONG OF THE WREN

Words and Music

M. M. Melody. ♩.=54.
M. M. Drum. ♪=108.

Transcribed by Edwin S. Tracy.

818 Kichi ruku waku, Whe ke re re we chi;
819 Kichi ruku waku, Whe ke re re we chi;
820 Kichi ruku waku, Whe ke re re we chi;
821 Kichi ruku waku, Whe ke re re we chi;
822 Kichi ruku waku, Whe ke re re we chi;
823 Kichi ruku waku, Whe ke re re we chi.

Translation

818 Kichi ruku waku, Whe ke re re we chi.
      kichi, so it; but this one.
      ruku, sang.
      waku, sound from the mouth, speech.
      whe ke re re we chi, syllables imitative of the sound of the
           bird.
819–823 See line 818.

Explanation by the Ku'rahus

The wren is always spoken of as the laughing bird. It is a very happy little bird, and we have stories about it. Every one likes to hear the wren sing. This song is very old; I do not know how old, how many generations old. There are very few words in the song, but there is a story which has come down with it and which tells its meaning.

A priest went forth in the early dawn. The sky was clear. The grass and wild flowers waved in the breeze that rose as the sun threw its first beams over the earth. Birds of all kinds vied with one another as they sang their joy on that beautiful morning. The priest stood listening. Suddenly, off at one side, he heard a trill that rose higher and clearer than all the rest. He moved toward the place whence the song came that he might see what manner of bird it was that could send farther than all the others its happy, laughing notes. As he came near he beheld a tiny brown bird with open bill, the feathers on its throat rippling with the fervor of its song. It was the wren, the smallest, the least powerful of birds, that seemed to be most glad and to pour out in ringing melody to the rising sun its delight in life.

As the priest looked he thought: "Here is a teaching for my people. Everyone can be happy; even the most insignificant can have his song of thanks."

So he made the story of the wren and sang it; and it has been handed down from that day, a day so long ago that no man can remember the time.

THE SONG OF THE WOODPECKER AND THE TURKEY

Words and Music

M. M. ♪ = 108.
• = Pulsation of the voice.   Transcribed by Edwin S. Tracy.

Ho-o-o!   I - ra - ri ha-o ra;   i - ra - ri ha-o   ra;   i - ra-ri ha-o ra;
Drum.
Rattles.

Ka ko-ra-she ha-o? Re ku-ta-ti ha-o; I - ra-ri ha-o   ra;   i - ra-ri ha - o   i.

824   Ho-o-o!
825   Irari hao ra; irari hao ra; irari hao ra;
826   Ka korashe hao? Re kutati hao;
827   Irari hao ra; irari hao i.

Translation

824   Ho-o-o!   An introductory exclamation.
825   Irari hao ra; irari hao ra; irari hao ra.
    irari, brother.
    hao, offspring, child.
    ra, coming.
826   Ka korashe hao? Re kutati hao.
    ka? is? a question.
    korashe, your.
    hao, offspring.   Is it or are they your offspring?
    re, they.
    kutati, my or mine.
    hao, offspring.   They are my offspring.

827   Irari hao ra; irari hao i.

    Irari hao ra; irari hao.   See line 825.

    i, ——.

Explanation by the Ku'rahus

We are told that in old times, long, long ago, the feathers of the turkey were used where now the feathers of the brown eagle are placed on the blue feathered stem. In those days the turkey, not the brown eagle, was leader, but, through the mysterious power of the woodpecker, the turkey lost its position. This song refers to the dispute between the woodpecker and the turkey, which resulted in the supplanting of the turkey by the brown eagle.

The words of the song are few, but the story of their meaning has come down to us from the fathers.

Both the turkey and the woodpecker desired to be the protector of the children of the human race, and there was trouble between them on that account. One day the woodpecker was flying about looking for its nest when the turkey chanced that way and the woodpecker called out: "Brother, where are my eggs?"

The woodpecker talked of his eggs, but he meant the children of the people on the earth and the turkey knew that was what he was talking about.

"They are not your eggs (offspring); they are mine," said the woodpecker.

"They are mine to take care of," answered the turkey; "for in my division of life there is great power of productiveness. I have more tail feathers than any other bird and I have more eggs. Wherever I go my young cover the ground."

"True," replied the woodpecker, "but you build your nest on the ground, so that your eggs are in constant danger of being devoured by serpents, and when the eggs hatch the young become a prey to the wolves, the foxes, the weasels; therefore, your number is continually being reduced. Security is the only thing that can insure the continuation of life. I can, therefore, claim with good reason the right to care for the human race. I build my nest in the heart of the tall oak, where my eggs and my young are safe from the creatures that prey upon birds. While I have fewer eggs they hatch in security and the birds live until they die of old age. It is my place to be a protector of the life of men."

The woodpecker prevailed, and the turkey was deposed; for, although the turkey had more children, they did not live; they were killed.

Then the brown eagle was put in the turkey's place, because it was not quarrelsome, but gentle, and cared for its young, and was strong to protect them from harm.

The woodpecker was given an important place on the stem, where it presides over the path along which the help that comes from the

Hako travels—the red path. The woodpecker is wise and careful, and, that it may not get angry and be warlike on the Hako, its upper mandible is turned back over its red crest.

The Hako ceremony was given in a vision, and all these things, such as the dispute between the turkey and the woodpecker, were made known to our fathers in a vision.

THE SONG OF THE DUCK

Words and Music

M. M. ♩=104.
• = Pulsation of the voice.   Transcribed by Edwin S. Tracy.

828   H-o-o-o!
829   Huka ware, huka ware hora;
830   Ha! Wiri hukaharu we;
831   Hao e!
832   Huka ware, huka ware hora:
833   Ha! Wiri aha ha rawe we;
834   Hao e!

Translation

828   Ho-o-o-o! An introductory exclamation.
829   Huka ware, huka ware hora.
        huka, a part of the word hukaharu, valley, a valley through
            which a stream is flowing.
        ware, a part of teware, flying.
        hora, a part of the word horaro, the earth, the land.
830   Ha! Wiri hukaharu we.
        ha! behold!
        wiri, it is.
        hukaharu, a valley through which a stream flows.
        we, they; refers to the young of the duck.
831   Hao e!
        hao, offspring.
        e, vocable.
832   See line 829.

833   Ha! Wiri aha ha rawe we.

   ha! wiri; behold! it is.

   aha, a part of kiwaharu, a pond, a small body of water.

   ha, a part of iha're, young; refers to the young of the duck.

   rawe, living in.

   we, they.

834   See line 831.

Explanation by the Ku'rahus

The words of this song about the duck are few, and if the story had not come down to us from the fathers, we should not know all that the song means.

The duck has great power.   The story tells us about this power.

Long ago when the feathered stems were being made, the holy man who was preparing these sacred objects had a dream.   In his vision the duck with the green neck appeared and said to him:

"I desire to have a place upon the feathered stem, for I have power to help the Children.   This is my power: I lay my eggs near the water and, when the young are hatched, straightway they can swim; the water can not kill them.   When they are grown they can go, flying through the air, from one part of the earth to the other.   No place is strange to them; they never lose their way; they can travel over the water without harm and reach safely their destination.   They can walk upon the land and find the springs and streams.   I am an unerring guide.   I know all paths below on the earth, and on the water and above in the air.   Put me on the feathered stem where it is grasped by the hand, that the Children may take hold of me and not go astray."

When the holy man awoke, he did as the duck had told him, and so to this day we put the duck with the green neck on the feathered stem where it is held by the hand.

This is the meaning of the song.

THE SONG OF THE OWL

Words and Music

M. M.   ♪ = 168.

• = Pulsation of the voice.   Transcribed by Edwin S. Tracy.

835   He! Hiri wahoru! Hi, hiri wahoru!
836   He! Hiri wahoru! Hi, hiri wahoru!
837   He! Wahoru.

Translation

835   He!   Hiri wahoru!   Hi, hiri wahoru!

he! an exclamation signifying that something has been brought to one's mind that should be reflected on.

hiri; iri, a part of nawairi, an expression of thankfulness, of appreciation of good promised, or of some benefit to be derived; the initial letter h is added for euphony and ease in singing.

wahoru, owl.

hi, the same as hiri, translated above.

836   See line 835.
837   He! Wahoru! See line 835.

Explanation by the Ku'rahus

In this song we give thanks to the owl, for it gives us help in the night. We sing it twice; the first time it is sung very slowly; the second time it is sung very fast, as we sing a dance song.

The meaning of the song has come down to us from the fathers; the words tell very little about the song.

To the same holy man to whom the duck came in a vision, the owl spoke in a dream and said:

"Put me upon the feathered stem, for I have power to help the Children. The night season is mine. I wake when others sleep. I can see in the darkness and discern coming danger. The human race must be able to care for its young during the night. The warrior must be alert and ready to protect his home against prowlers in the dark. I have the power to help the people so that they may not forget their young in sleep. I have power to help the people to be watchful against enemies while darkness is on the earth. I have power to help the people to keep awake and perform these ceremonies in the night as well as in the day."

When the holy man awoke, he remembered all that the owl had said to him, and he put the owl's feathers upon the stem, next to the duck. So the people are guided by the duck and kept awake by the owl.

SONG OF THANKFULNESS

Words and Music

M. M. ♪ = 132.
• = Pulsation of the voice.　　　　　Transcribed by Edwin S. Tracy.

Ho-o-o-o!　I - ri!　Ha ko　ti re-hra　re-ki;　I - ri! Ha-ko　ti re-hra　re-ki;

Drum.
Rattles.

I - ri! Ha - ko　ti re - hra　re - ki;　I - ri! Ha ko　ti re - hra　re-ki.

I		II	
838	Ho-o-o-o!	843	Ho-o-o-o!
839	Iri! Hako ti rehra reki;	844	Iri! Hako ti resstah riki;
840	Iri! Hako ti rehra reki;	845	Iri! Hako ti resstah riki;
841	Iri! Hako ti rehra reki;	846	Iri! Hako ti resstah riki;
842	Iri! Hako ti rehra reki.	847	Iri! Hako ti resstah riki.

Translation of First Stanza

838　Ho-o-o-o!　An introductory exclamation.
839　Iri!　Hako ti rehra reki.

　　　iri! a part of the word nawairi, an expression of thankful-
　　　　ness; "It is well!"

　　　Hako, all the symbolic objects peculiar to this ceremony.

　　　ti, me (present time).

　　　rehra, a part of rehrara, I have.

　　　reki; re, pertaining or belonging to me; ki, a part of riki,
　　　　standing.

840–842　See line 839.

Explanation by the Ku'rahus

　This stanza means that it is well, a cause of thankfulness, that all
the birds and all the symbols are here with the Hako and able to
bring good.　The Fathers now stand with the complete Hako extend-
ing to the Children the promised blessings.　So we sing: "I stand
here before you with the Hako!"

Translation of Second Stanza

843　Ho-o-o-o!　An introductory exclamation.
844　Iri!　Hako ti resstah riki.

　　　iri! it is well!　An exclamation of thankfulness.

　　　Hako, all the symbolic articles belong to this ceremony.

　　　ti, me (present time).

　　　resstah, you hold.

　　　riki, standing.

845–847　See line 844.

22 ETH—PT 2—04——12

Explanation by the Ku'rahus

In this stanza the Children reply: "It is well for us that you are here with the complete Hako!"

The Fathers sing these words, but they are really from the Children.

FOURTEENTH RITUAL (THIRD NIGHT).   INVOKING THE VISIONS OF THE ANCIENTS

Explanation by the Ku'rahus

This ceremony was given to our fathers in a vision, and to our fathers the promise was made that dreams bringing happiness would be brought to the Children by the birds that are with the Hako. This promise given to our fathers is always fulfilled; happiness always comes with the Hako, and the Children have visions.

When the ceremony is near the end (the third night) we sing this song, for we remember the visions of our fathers, the holy men to whom was taught this ceremony. We ask that the visions which came to them may come again to us.

SONG

Words and Music

M. M. ♪ = 126.
• = Pulsation of the voice.   Transcribed by Edwin S. Tracy.

Ha-a-a! Ra - ra wha-ri; Hit - ka - sha-ru, ra - ra wha-ri; Hit-ka - sharu! Hi - ri! H'A-ti-a si...... ha-wa ra - ra wha-ri, Hit-ka - sha-ru.

I		III	
848	Ha-a-a!	860	Ha-a-a!
849	Rara whari;	861	Rara whicha;
850	Hitkasharu, rara whari;	862	Hitkasharu, rara whicha;
851	Hitkasharu!	863	Hitkasharu!
852	Hiri! H'Atia si hawa rara whari,	864	Hiri! H'Atia si hawa rara whicha,
853	Hitkasharu.	865	Hitkasharu.

II		IV	
854	Ha-a-a!	866	Ha-a-a!
855	Rara wha-a;	867	Rara ruka;
856	Hitkasharu, rara wha-a;	868	Hitkasharu, rara ruka;
857	Hitkasharu!	869	Hitkasharu!
858	Hiri! H'Atia si hawa rara wha-a,	870	Hiri! H'Atia si hawa rara ruka,
859	Hitkasharu.	871	Hitkasharu.

V

872 Ha-a-a!
873 Werih kawa;
874 Hitkasharu, werih kawa;
875 Hitkasharu!
876 Hiri! H'Atia si hawa werih kawa,
877 Hitkasharu.

VI

878 Ha-a-a!
879 Werih teri;
880 Hitkasharu, werih teri;
881 Hitkasharu!
882 Hiri! H'Atia si hawa werih teri,
883 Hitkasharu.

VII

884 Ha-a-a!
885 Rarah whara;
886 Hitkasharu, rarah whara;
887 Hitkasharu!
888 Hiri! H'Atia si hawa rarah whara.
889 Hitkasharu.

VIII

890 Ha-a-a!
891 Rarah whishpa;
892 Hitkasharu. rarah whishpa;
893 Hitkasharu;
894 Hiri! H'Atia si hawa rarah whi-
        shpa,
895 Hitkasharu.

Translation of First Stanza

848 Ha-a-a! An introductory exclamation.
849 Rara whari.
> rara, coming this way, approaching.
> whari, walking.

850 Hitkasharu, rara whari.
> hitkasharu, a composite word; hit, from hittu, feather; ka, from rotkaharu, night; sharu, dream, vision. The word feather refers to the birds that are with the Hako.
> rara whari. See line 849.

851 Hitkasharu. See line 850.
852 Hiri! H'Atia si hawa rara whari.
> hiri! an exclamation telling one to give heed, to harken, and also to be thankful.
> h', the sign of breath, breathing, giving life.
> atia, a modification of atius, father.
> si, part of sidhihi, you are the one.
> hawa, again.
> rara, coming this way, approaching.
> whari, walking.

853 Hitkasharu. See line 850.

Explanation by the Ku'rahus

As we sing this stanza we think of the visions which attend the Hako and we are thankful that these visions, which gave life, success, and plenty to our fathers, are again coming this way to us.

After we have sung this stanza four times and have passed around the lodge and reached the west we pause.

Translation of Second Stanza

854 Ha-a-a! An introductory exclamation.
855 Rara wha-a.
        rara, coming this way, approaching.
        wha-a, coming nearer.
856 Hitkasharu, rara wha-a.
        hitkasharu. See the first stanza, line 850.
        rara wha-a. See line 855.
857 Hitkasharu. See line 850.
858 Hiri! H'Atia si hawa rara wha-a. See lines 852 and 855.
859 Hitkasharu. See line 850.

Explanation by the Ku'rahus

On the second circuit of the lodge, as we wave the feathered stems, we sing that the visions granted to our fathers are coming nearer and nearer to us and to the Children. We are thankful as we sing.

Four times we repeat this stanza and when we reach the west we pause.

Translation of Third Stanza

860 Ha-a-a! An introductory exclamation.
861 Rara whicha.
        rara, coming this way, approaching.
        whicha, arrived, reached the destination.
862 Hitkasharu, rara whicha. See lines 850 and 861.
863 Hitkasharu. See line 850.
864 Hiri! H'Atia si hawa rara whicha. See lines 852 and 861.
865 Hitkasharu. See line 850.

Explanation by the Ku'rahus

The third time we go around the lodge we sing the third stanza four times. It tells that the visions of our fathers have arrived at the lodge door. At the west we pause.

Translation of Fourth Stanza

866 Ha-a-a! An introductory exclamation.
867 Rara ruka.
        rara, coming this way.
        ruka, entered the lodge.
868 Hitkasharu, rara ruka. See lines 850 and 867.
869 Hitkasharu. See line 850.
870 Hiri! H'Atia si hawa rara ruka. See lines 852 and line 867.
871 Hitkasharu. See line 850.

Explanation by the Ku'rahus

The visions of our fathers have entered the lodge as we sing the fourth stanza, and our hearts are thankful that they have come.

At the west we pause and lay the Hako down with ceremonial songs and movements. Then we rest a while and are quiet in the presence of the visions.

Translation of Fifth Stanza

872 Ha-a-a! An introductory exclamation.
873 Werih kawa.
    werih, the owner of the lodge. The Son is regarded as the owner of the lodge in which the ceremony takes place and the word refers to him.
    kawa, the open space within the lodge between the fireplace and the couches around the wall. In this space the ceremony takes place.
874 Hitkasharu werih kawa. See lines 850 and 873.
875 Hitkasharu. See line 850.
876 Hiri! H'Atia si hawa werih kawa. See lines 852 and 873.
877 Hitkasharu. See line 850.

Explanation by the Ku'rahus

After a time we take up the feathered stems and move around the lodge, singing the fifth stanza.

The Son, into whose lodge the visions of our fathers have now entered, gives thanks in his heart, for he knows that they have come in fulfilment of the promise given generations ago, and that he is recognized by them as a Son.

When we reach the west we pause.

Translation of Sixth Stanza

878 Ha-a-a! An introductory exclamation.
879 Werih teri.
    werih, the owner of the lodge, the Son.
    teri, hovering over.
880 Hitkasharu, werih teri. See lines 850 and 879.
881 Hitkasharu. See line 850.
882 Hiri! H'Atia si hawa werih teri. See lines 852 and 879.
883 Hitkasharu. See line 850.

Explanation by the Ku'rahus

Again we go around the lodge and sing the sixth stanza. The visions of our fathers, received from the birds of the Hako, are now hovering over the Children in the lodge of the Son. Everyone is thankful as we sing. At the west we pause.

Translation of Seventh Stanza

884   Ha-a-a! An introductory exclamation.
885   Rarah whara.
    rarah, walking from one.
    whara, going away, going from a person or place.
886   Hitkasharu rarah whara.   See lines 850 and 885.
887   Hitkasharu.   See line 850.
888   Hiri! H'Atia si hawa rarah whara.   See lines 852 and 885.
889   Hitkasharu.   See line 850.

Explanation by the Ku'rahus

The visions are walking away from us as we sing the seventh stanza.
We are thanking them in our hearts as we sing, and while they are
leaving the lodge. At the west we pause.

Translation of Eighth Stanza

890   Ha-a-a! An introductory exclamation.
891   Rarah whishpa.
    rarah, walking from one.
    whishpa, arrived at the place from which one started.
892   Hitkasharu rarah whishpa.   See lines 850 and 891.
893   Hitkasharu.   See line 850.
894   Hiri! H'Atia si hawa rarah whishpa.   See lines 852 and 891.
895   Hitkasharu.   See line 850.

Explanation by the Ku'rahus

In a little while we start and go again around the lodge and sing
the eighth stanza. The visions of our fathers have left the lodge;
they are walking away from us, passing over the sleeping earth, and
at last they reach their dwelling place, the place from which they
descended when they started to come to us. As we think of them we
again thank them for coming to us.

At the west we lay the Hako down to rest with the songs and movements belonging to that action.[a]

After singing this song the Children usually rise and go to their
homes and the Fathers take a rest during the remainder of the night.

There are no ceremonies at the dawn of the fourth day. During
the forenoon the Fathers are busy unpacking the various articles they
have brought for their final gifts to the Children. They place in a
pile the robes, embroidered shirts, leggings, and ornaments.

About noon the food is cooked for the last meal to be given by the
Fathers to the Children. After the Fathers have served the food,
they put the cooking utensils beside the pile of gifts and then present
the heap to the Children and walk out of the lodge, leaving the Children to distribute the gifts among themselves.

---

[a] See pages 111–116.

There is a very general scattering of the gifts, and songs of thanks are sung by those who receive them. When this ceremony of distribution and acknowledgment is over, the Children return to their several lodges. By this time the afternoon is well advanced.

The Fathers now enter the empty lodge and begin preparations for the last night of the ceremony and for the following morning. At this time they partake of their last meal before the close of the ceremony at about noon the next day.

The best dancers in the party are chosen to perform the final dance, which occurs on the morning of the fifth day. The songs which accompany this dance are rehearsed and everything necessary for the closing acts of the ceremony is put in readiness.

If a tent has been used for the ceremony, the Fathers on this afternoon must build around the tent at a little distance from it a wall of saplings and brush, to keep off outsiders and prevent anyone from looking in. If the ceremony takes place in an earth lodge, then both the outer and inner doors are closed, for on this last night no one is allowed to be present but the Fathers, the Son, and his near relatives.

On this night a sixth man is added to the five who carry the sacred objects—the two feathered stems, the ear of Corn wrapped in the wild cat skin, and the two eagle wings. The sixth man has a whistle, made from the wing bone of the eagle, which he blows in rhythm of the songs. The whistle imitates the scream of the eagle over its young.

SECOND DIVISION. THE SECRET CEREMONIES

FIFTEENTH RITUAL (FOURTH NIGHT)

PART I. THE FLOCKING OF THE BIRDS

Explanation by the Ku'rahus

At sunset the Fathers call the Children to the lodge. When all have been seated, the Children on the south side, the Fathers on the north, the Ku'rahus, who sits at the west, back of the holy place where the Hako are at rest, addresses the Children in the name of the Fathers. He explains the meaning of the ceremony about to take place, for on this last night and the following morning everything that is done refers to the nest and to the direct promise of Children to the Son, who is also to be bound by a symbolic tie to the Father.

When the talk is over the feathered stems are taken up and we sing the following song, which prefigures the joy that is coming to the people.

SONG

Words and Music

M. M. ♪ = 108.
• = Pulsation of the voice.

Transcribed by Edwin S. Tracy.

No drum.

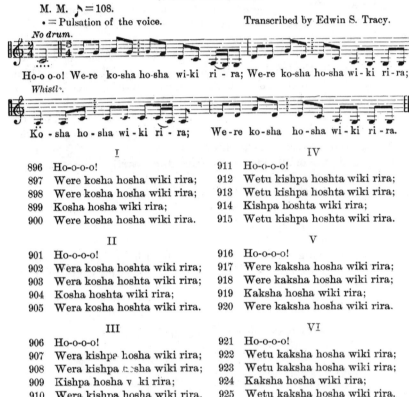

Ho-o o-o! We-re ko-sha ho-sha wi-ki ri - ra; We-re ko-sha ho-sha wi-ki ri-ra;

Whistl°.

Ko - sha ho - sha wi-ki ri - ra;   We-re ko-sha ho-sha wi-ki ri - ra.

I

896   Ho-o-o-o!
897   Were kosha hosha wiki rira;
898   Were kosha hosha wiki rira;
899   Kosha hosha wiki rira;
900   Were kosha hosha wiki rira.

II

901   Ho-o-o-o!
902   Wera kosha hoshta wiki rira;
903   Wera kosha hoshta wiki rira;
904   Kosha hoshta wiki rira;
905   Wera kosha hoshta wiki rira.

III

906   Ho-o-o-o!
907   Wera kishpa hosha wiki rira;
908   Wera kishpa cosha wiki rira;
909   Kishpa hosha v ki rira;
910   Wera kishpa hosha wiki rira.

IV

911   Ho-o-o-o!
912   Wetu kishpa hoshta wiki rira;
913   Wetu kishpa hoshta wiki rira;
914   Kishpa hoshta wiki rira;
915   Wetu kishpa hoshta wiki rira.

V

916   Ho-o-o-o!
917   Were kaksha hosha wiki rira;
918   Were kaksha hosha wiki rira;
919   Kaksha hosha wiki rira;
920   Were kaksha hosha wiki rira.

VI

921   Ho-o-o-o!
922   Wetu kaksha hosha wiki rira;
923   Wetu kaksha hosha wiki rira;
924   Kaksha hosha wiki rira;
925   Wetu kaksha hosha wiki rira.

Translation of First Stanza

896   Ho-o-o-o!   An introductory exclamation
897   Were kosha hosha wiki rira.

were, they.

kosha, a flock of birds.

hosha, a composite word; ho, coming; sha, part of kosha, flock.

wiki, a descriptive term indicating the manner of flight; the birds do not move in a straight line or course; they waver from one side to the other, now higher, now lower.

rira, coming.

898   See line 897.
899   Kosha hosha wiki rira.   See line 897.
900   See line 897.

Explanation by the Ku'rahus

In the early spring the birds lay their eggs in their nests, in the summer they rear their young, in the fall all the young ones are grown, the nests are deserted and the birds fly in flocks over the country. One can hear the fluttering of a startled flock, the birds suddenly rise and their wings make a noise like distant thunder. Everywhere the flocks are flying. In the fall it seems as though new life were put into the people as well as into the birds; there is much activity in coming and going.

This song tells of the flocking of birds. We do not use the drum as we sing it, but we blow the whistle. The whistle is made from the wing bone of an eagle. In this song we are singing of the eagle and the other birds, so we use the whistle.

When the eggs are hatched and the young are grown, the birds flock; the promise of young has been fulfilled. In this song, which we sing toward the close of the ceremony, we are thinking of the fulfilling of the promise given by the Hako, that children will be granted to the people, so that they may be many and strong, and we sing that the great flocks are coming.

Translation of Second Stanza

901   Ho-o-o-o! An introductory exclamation.
902   Wera kosha hoshta wiki rira.
　　　wera, they yonder; ra gives the idea that the flock is at a
　　　　　distance.
　　　kosha, flock.
　　　hoshta, the noise made by the birds in flying and in alighting;
　　　　　hosh, the noise; ta, to alight.
　　　wiki, descriptive of the manner of flight. See translation of
　　　　　the word in the first stanza, line 897.
　　　rira, coming.
903   See line 902.
904   Kosha hoshta wiki rira. See line 902.
905   See line 902.

Explanation by the Ku'rahus

As we sing the second stanza we are thinking of the great flocks of birds. The noise of their wings is a mighty noise. As they fly from one tree to another they shake the branches as they alight, and the tree quivers as they rise. The flocks are many and powerful; so, through the promises of the Hako, the people will become many and powerful.

Translation of Third Stanza

906   Ho-o-o-o!   An introductory exclamation.
907   Wera kishpa hosha wiki rira.
 wera, they yonder.
 kishpa, scream (singular number).
 hosha; on account of the singular number of the verb kishpa,
  the word as here used indicates that a bird out of the
  flock is flying toward the people.
 wiki, descriptive of the manner of flight.   See line 897.
 rira, coming.
908   See line 907.
909   Kishpa hosha wiki rira.   See line 907.
910   See line 907.

Explanation by the Ku'rahus

In this stanza we sing that a single bird, an eagle, comes out of the
flock and flies toward the people.   It is Kawas that comes flying
toward us, the messenger of the powers, the bringer of the promises
of the Hako.   Kawas comes to us as the eagle leaving the flock goes
to her young.

Translation of Fourth Stanza

911   Ho-o-o-o!   An introductory exclamation.
912   Wetu kishpa hoshta wiki rira.
 wetu, it has.
 kishpa, screaming noise made by the eagle.   As the eagle has
  come near its cry is likened to a scream.
 hoshta, a composite word; hosh, the sound made by the wings
  of a bird when flying; ta, to alight.
 wiki, a word descriptive of the manner of flight.   See line 897.
 rira, coming.
913   See line 912.
914   Kishpa hoshta wiki rira.   See line 912.
915   See line 912.

Explanation by the Ku'rahus

As the mother eagle comes near, flying to her nest, her cries are
like screams, so we sing this stanza with the whistle, for now Kawas
is coming to us as to her nest.   The lodge of the Son is her nest;
there she will alight; there she will bring the gift of children.   Our
hearts are glad and strong as we sing.

Translation of Fifth Stanza

916   Ho-o-o-o!   An introductory exclamation.
917   Were kaksha hosha wiki rira.
 were, they.
 kaksha, a tumultuous noise.
 kosha, flock.
 wiki, a word descriptive of the manner of approach.   See line 897.
 rira, coming.

918　See line 917.
919　Kaksha hosha wiki rira.　See line 917.
920　See line 917.

Explanation by the Ku'rahus

This stanza tells us that the noise made by the people as they gather together on the morning of the fifth day for the presentation of gifts to the Fathers is like the coming of a great flock of birds. The people move like the birds; they do not come in a straight line to the lodge of the Son, but they come from this side and from that just as the birds gather together in a flock.

Translation of Sixth Stanza

921　Ho-o-o-o!　An introductory exclamation.
922　Wetu kaksha hosha wiki rira.
　　　wetu, it has.
　　　kaksha, a tumultuous noise.
　　　hosha, flock.
　　　wiki, manner of approach.　See line 897.
　　　rira, coming.
923　See line 922.
924　Kaksha hosha wiki rira.　See line 922.
925　See line 922.

Explanation by the Ku'rahus

As the people approach the lodge they make a great noise. All is bustle; the neighing ponies to be given to the Fathers are brought forward, and the people are calling to one another; there is the singing of songs and the shouts of pleasure; all these sounds mingling make a noise like distant thunder. This stanza refers to this joyous tumult.

Just before I came on to Washington I performed this ceremony, and now as I sit here and tell you about the meaning of this song, I can hear the happy shouts of the people as I heard them some weeks ago. Their voices seemed to come from everywhere! Their hearts were joyful. I am glad, as I remember that day. We are always happy when we are with the Hako.

PART II. THE SIXTEEN CIRCUITS OF THE LODGE

Explanation by the Ku'rahus

The last act of the last night is the making of four times four circuits of the lodge.

I have told you that the four circuits of the lodge which we have been making are in recognition of the four paths down which the lesser powers descend to man. We have been asking for help from these powers and so we have remembered the paths down which they travel to reach us with the gifts we desire. In the four tim s four circuits we remember all the powers represented in the Hako.

We must begin with the Corn, which comes from our Mother Earth, for she has been the leader ever since the time when she sought the Son and opened the path for us to travel safely to him. She led on our journey to his village; she led as we entered his lodge and during its consecration, and she has led us through all the days and nights of the ceremony. So when we take up the feathered stems and turn to the north to begin the first circuit of this series we sing the following song:

FIRST SONG

Words and Music

M. M. ♩=116.

• = Pulsation of the voice.   Transcribed by Edwin S. Tracy.

I

926   Ha-a-a-a!
927   Ha! Atira! Ha! Atira! Ha! Atira! Ha! Atira!
928   Ha! Atira! Ha! Atira! Ha! Atira! Ha! Atira!
929   Ha! Atira! Ha! Atira! Ha! Atira! Ha! Atira.

II

930   Ha-a-a-a!
931   Nawahiri! Nawahiri! Nawahiri! Nawahiri!
932   Nawahiri! Nawahiri! Nawahiri! Nawahiri!
933   Nawahiri! Nawahiri! Nawahiri! Nawahiri!

Translation of First Stanza

926   Ha-a-a-a! An introduction exclamatory.
927   Ha! Atira! Ha! Atira! Ha! Atira! Ha! Atira!
        ha! look on! behold!
        atira, mother. The term is applied to the ear of corn.
928, 929 See line 927.

Explanation by the Ku'rahus

"Behold Mother Corn!" we sing; and we think and the Children think, as they sing with us, of all that Mother Corn has done, how she sought the Son, led us to him, and now is here with the power of life and plenty.

Four times we sing this first stanza as we make the first circuit of the lodge, moving by the north, east, and south back to the west. After a pause we start upon the second circuit and sing the second stanza.

Translation of Second Stanza

930   Ha-a-a-a!   An introductory exclamation.
931   Nawahiri! Nawahiri! Nawahiri! Nawahiri!
      nawahiri, a ceremonial term signifying thanks; a recogni-
      tion that all is well. The usual form is nawairi, but an
      h is prefixed to the third syllable to give greater ease and
      euphony in singing.
932, 933   See line 931.

Explanation by the Ku'-rahus

Mother Corn is leading toward the fulfilment of the promises made through the Hako, and as the Children behold her they sing with thankful hearts, "All is well!"

SECOND SONG

Words and Music

M. M. ♪ = 116.
• = Pulsation of the voice.   Transcribed by Edwin S. Tracy.

                    I
    934   Ho-o-o-o!
    535   Eru! H'Atira! Eru! H'Atira! He! Iri!
    936   Eru! H'Atira! Eru! H'Atira! He! Iri!
    937   Eru! H'Atira! Eru! H'Atira! He!

                    II
    938   Ho-o-o-o!
    939   Nawa! H'Atira! Nawa! H'Atira! He! Iri!
    940   Nawa! H'Atira! Nawa! H'Atira! He! Iri!
    941   Nawa! H'Atira! Nawa! H'Atira! He!

Translation of First Stanza

934 Ho-o-o-o! An introductory exclamation.
935 Eru! H'Atira! Eru! H'Atira! He! Iri!
  eru! an exclamation of reverence.
  h', the symbol of breath, the life-giving power.
  atira, mother. The term refers to the ear of corn.
  he! a part of i'hare, an exclamation calling on one to reflect
    upon a subject now brought to mind. See line 1.
  iri! a part of nawairi! an exclamation of thanks and of
    trustfulness.
936 See line 935.
937 Eru! H'Atira! Eru! H'Atira! He! See line 935.

Explanation by the Ku'rahus

The life of man depends upon the earth (h'Atira). Tira'wa atius
works through it. The kernel is planted within Mother Earth and
she brings forth the ear of corn, even as children are begotten and
born of women.

We sing the first stanza as we make the third circuit of the lodge.
We give the cry of reverence (Eru!) to Mother Corn, she who brings
the promise of children, of strength, of life, of plenty, and of peace.
As we reflect upon her gifts we sing our thanks and bid the Children
join us.

When the circuit is complete we pause at the west. Then we turn
toward the north and begin the fourth circuit, singing the second
stanza.

Translation of Second Stanza

938 Ho-o-o-o! An introductory exclamation.
939 Nawa! H'Atira! Nawa! H'Atira! He! Iri!
  nawa, a part of nawairi, a ceremonial word for expressing
    thanks, confidence, trust.
  h', the symbol of breath, life, bringing forth or into.
  atira, mother. The term is applied to the ear of corn, repre-
    sentative of Mother Earth.
  he! a part of i'hare, an exclamation calling upon one to
    reflect upon that which is now brought to mind. See
    line 1.
  iri! a part of nawairi! thanks! all is well!
940 See line 939.
941 Nawa! H'Atira! Nawa! H'Atira! He! See line 939.

Explanation of the Ku'rahus

"Nawa! H'Atira!" It is Tira'wa atius who causes Mother Earth
to bring forth the corn, who gives fruitfulness to man, who sends the
gifts which Mother Corn breathes upon us. As we reflect upon this

we give thanks to Tira'wa, and with the Children sing "Nawa! H'Atira! Nawa! H'Atira! He! Iri!" over and over until we complete the fourth circuit.

In these first four circuits we have remembered the power of Tira'wa atius with Mother Earth; in the next four circuits we shall sing of the eagles.

THIRD SONG

Words and Music

M. M. ♪ = 138.
= Pulsation of the voice.

Transcribed by Edwin S. Tracy.

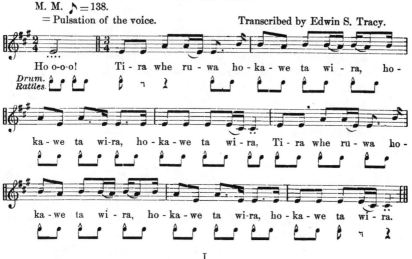

I

942 Ho-o-o-o!
943 Tira whe ruwa hokawe ta wira, hokawe ta wira, hokawe ta wira.
944 Tira whe ruwa hokawe   wira, hokawe ta wira, hokawe ta wira.

II

945 Ho-o-o-o!
946 Tias we ria kishpa ka wia, kishpa ka wia, kishpa ka wia.
947 Tias we ria kishpa ka wia, kishpa ka wia, kishpa ka wia.

Translation

I

942 Ho-o-o-o! An introductory exclamation.
943 Tira whe ruwa hokawe ta wira, hokawe ta wira, hokawe ta wira.
    tira, a part of atira, mother. The term refers to Kawas.
    whe, it.
    ruwa, flying toward the speaker.
    hokawe, shadow.
    ta, a part of wita, coming.
    wira, it is coming.
944 See line 943.

II

945 Ho-o-o-o! An introductory exclamation.
946 Tias we ria kishpa ka wia, kishpa ka wia, kishpa ka wia.

> tias, a part of atius, father. The term refers to the white
> eagle, the male feathered stem.
> we, it.
> ria, hovering.
> kishpa, the loud cry of the eagle.
> ka, a part of akaro, lodge, dwelling place.
> wia, coming, moving.
> kishpa, the scream of the eagle.
> ka, the word has here a double reference, to the lodge, and to
> the nest. The lodge represents the nest.
> wia, moving about, coming.
> kishpa, the scream of the eagle.
> ka, a part of akaro, lodge. Refers to the nest.
> wia, coming.

947 See line 946.

Explanation by the Ku'rahus

This song has very few words, but a story goes with it to explain
its meaning.

One day a man was walking on the prairie; he was thinking, and his
eyes were upon the ground. Suddenly he became aware of a shadow
flitting over the grass, moving in circles that inclosed his feet. He
stood still, wondering what this could mean; then he looked up and
beheld a brown eagle flying round and round over his head. As he
gazed the bird paused, looked down upon him, then flapped its wings
and flew away (first stanza).

Again the man was walking and thinking, when he caught sight of
a tall tree about which a great white eagle was flying, around and
around as if it were watching over something. As it flew it screamed,
making a great noise. It was the father bird guarding its nest (second stanza).

The brown eagle which the man saw was Kawas; where she went
when she flew away is told in the next song. The blue-feathered
stem, with the brown eagle feathers upon it, is carried next to the
Children and waved over their heads, for she is the mother and cares
for the young.

The white eagle is the male; the green-feathered stem, with his
feathers upon it, is carried upon the outside, for he guards the nest.

The lodge where the Children are (the lodge where the ceremony is
being performed) is the nest.

The white eagle which the man saw protecting the nest teaches all
men to be brave and vigilant, to guard their children and make safe
their home. In token of this duty, the warrior father wears the white
eagle feather.

The whistle is used when we sing the second stanza, because the white eagle whistled when he flew around his nest.

FOURTH SONG

Words and Music

M. M. ♪ = 144.
• = Pulsation of the voice.   Transcribed by Edwin S. Tracy.

Ha-a-a-a! Ka-was ru-a, Ka-was ru-a, Ka-was ru-a, Ka-was ru-a whe-e ru-a
e; Ka-was ru-a, Ka-was ru-a whe-e ru-a e; He! Ka-was whe-e ru-a
e; He! Ka-was whe-e ru-a e; Ka-was ru-a, Ka-was ru-a whe-e ru-a e.

Drum.
Rattles.
Whistle.

I

948 Ha-a-a-a!
949 Kawas rua, Kawas rua, Kawas rua, Kawas rua whe-e rua e;
950 Kawas rua, Kawas rua whe-e rua e;
951 He! Kawas whe-e rua e; He! Kawas whe-e rua e:
952 Kawas rua, Kawas rua whe-e rua e

II

953 Ha-a-a-a!
954 Kawas tia, Kawas tia, Kawas tia, Kawas tia wheri ria e;
955 Kawas tia, Kawas tia wheri ria e;
956 He! Kawas wheri ria e; He! Kawas wheri ria e;
957 Kawas tia, Kawas tia wheri ria e.

Translation

I

948 Ha-a-a-a! An introductory exclamation.
949 Kawas rua, Kawas rua, Kawas rua, Kawas rua whe-e rua e.
  Kawas, the brown eagle, symbol of the feminine powers.
  rua, flying toward an object.
  whe, it.
  e, vowel prolongation.
  rua, flying toward.
  e, vocable.
950 Kawas rua, Kawas rua whe-e rua e.   See line 949.

951   He! Kawas whe-e rua e;   He! Kawas whe-e rua e.
          he! a part of i'hare, an exclamation calling one to reflect.
              See line 1.
          Kawas whe-e rua e.   See line 949.
952   See line 950.

II

953   Ha-a-a-a!   An introductory exclamation.
954   Kawas tia, Kawas tia, Kawas tia, Kawas tia wheri ria e.
          Kawas, the brown eagle, the feminine power.
          tia, flying overhead.
          wheri, it here.
          ria, above and very near.
          e, vocable.
955   Kawas tia, Kawas tia wheri ria e.   See line 954.
956   He! Kawas wheri ria e;   Kawas wheri ria e.
          he! a part of i'hare, an exclamation calling one to reflect
              upon a subject.   See line 1.
          Kawas wheri ria e.   See line 954.
957   See line 955.

Explanation by the Ku'rahus

The story of this song which has come down to us is that when
the man saw the shadow on the grass and beheld the brown eagle
flying over him, the eagle, recognizing the man, flapped its wings
and flew away.   The brown eagle was Kawas, the mother bird, and
she flew straight to her nest, to her young, who cried out with joy as
she came near.   We use the whistle when we sing this song because
the young eagles scream as the mother returns to them.

When we sing the second stanza we remember that the lodge of
the Son is the nest of Kawas, that she is here flying over the heads
of the Children, bringing near to them the fulfilment of the promises
of the Hako.

The whistle which accompanies this stanza represents the cry of
the Children in recognition of the fulfilment which Kawas is bringing.   With this song we complete the fourth circuit of the eagles
and the eighth circuit of the lodge.

The songs of the next four circuits refer to the rites.

Words and Music

M. M. Melody. ♩.=69.
M. M. Drum. ♪=138.
• = Pulsation of the voice.   Transcribed by Edwin S. Tracy.

Ho-o-o-o-o! H'A-ti-ra, ru! H'A-ti-ra, ru! Ka   hi - sha; H'A-ti - ra,   ru! Ka
hi - sha - a; H'A - ti - ra, ru! H'A - ti - ra, ru! Ka...... hi - sha - a;   H'A -
ti - ra, ru! H'A-ti-ra, ru! Ka   hi-sha; H'A-ti-ra, ru! Ka........ hi - sha.

958   Ho-o-o-o-o!
959   H'Atira, ru! H'Atira, ru! Ka hisha;   H'Atira, ru! Ka hisha-a;
960   H'Atira, ru! H'Atira, ru! Ka hisha-a;
961   H'Atira, ru! H'Atira, ru! Ka hisha;   H'Atira, ru! Ka hisha.

II

962   Ho-o-o-o-o!
963   Hra shira ko; hra shira ko, ka hisha: hra shira ko, ka hisha-a;
964   Hra shira ko; hra shira ko, ka hisha-a;
965   Hra shira ko; hra shira ko, ka hisha; hra shira ko, ka hisha.

Translation

I

958   Ho-o-o-o-o!   An exclamation introductory to the song.
959   H'Atira, ru! H'Atira, ru! Ka hisha;   H'Atira, ru! Ka hisha-a.
        h', the symbol of breath; life-giving.
        atira, mother.   The term refers to all the feminine powers
            represented with the Hako.
        ru! an exclamation of joy.
        ka, a part of akaro, lodge, dwelling place.
        hisha, reached, entered.
        h'Atira, ru! Translated above.
        ka hisha-a.   Translated above.   The final a is a vowel pro-
            longation.
960   H'Atira, ru! H'Atira, ru! Ka hisha-a.   See line 959.
961   See line 959.

LI

962 Ho-o-o-o-o! An exclamation introductory to the song.
963 Hra shira ko; hra shira ko; ka hisha; hra shira ko, ka hisha-a.
       hra, an abbreviation of haras, you, plural.
       shira, came bringing.
       ko, a part of Hako.
       ka, a part of akaro, lodge, dwelling.
       hisha, reached, entered.
964 Hra shira ko; hra shira ko, ka hisha-a.   See line 963.
965 See line 963.

Explanation by the Ku'rahus

In the first stanza of this song, the Fathers give the cry of joy that they have entered the lodge of the Son with the Mother breathing forth life.

In the second stanza the Children respond: "Truly you have come, bringing the Hako with its gifts and its promises of joy."

SIXTH SONG

Words and Music

M. M. ♪ = 144.
• = Pulsation of the voice.   Transcribed by Edwin S. Tracy.

966 Ho-o-o!
967 Kakati chiri wakari pirau Tira'a;
968 Kakati chiri wakari pirau Tira'a;
969 Kakati chiri wakari pirau Tira'a;
970 Kakati chiri wakari pirau Tira'a;
971 Kakati chiri wakari pirau Tira'a;
972 Kakati chiri wakari pirau Tira'a.

II

973   Wetati chiri wakari pirau ta hao;
974   Wetati chiri wakari pirau ta hao;
975   Wetati chiri wakari pirau ta hao;
976   Wetati chiri wakari pirau ta hao;
977   Wetati chiri wakari pirau ta hao;
978   Wetati chiri wakari pirau ta hao.

Translation

I

966   Ho-o-o!   An introductory exclamation.
967   Kakati chiri wakari pirau Tiraa.

     kakati, I do not.

     chiri, a part of titichiri, to know.

     wakari, a modified form of wakow, voice, with the plural sign,
        ri; the word wakari refers to chanted prayers.

     pirau, children; a general term.

     Tira'a, a modification of Tira'wa, the mighty power.

968–972   See line 967.

II

973   Wetati chiri wakari pirau ta hao.

     wetati, I now.

     chiri, know.   See line 967.

     wakari, chanted prayers.   See line 967.

     pirau, children.

     ta, my.

     hao, offspring; my own son or child.

974–978   See line 973.

Explanation by the Ku'rahus.

The old men who made these songs so long ago thought much upon Tira'wa atius and they prayed to him out on the hills nights and days at a time. They observed all the sacred ceremonies, for they knew that the rites were given to help the people. This Hako ceremony was given by the great power. The old men were careful in teaching its songs to those who were to come after them, and they explained their meaning. I am singing these songs and explaining them just as they were taught me, and as they had been handed down to the Ku'rahus who gave them to me. I did not make them.[a]

This song is very old and this is the story that came with it:

---

[a] The recording of this ceremony occupied several weeks in each of four years, and the reiterations of the Ku'rahus as to the fidelity of his communications were not apparent to him. They were natural expressions of his earnestness and his desire to be faithful. I have deemed it best to follow my original notes, giving these reiterations just as they were made.

Long ago a Ku′rahus went with a Hako party to a distant tribe to make a Son. On the last night of the ceremony he said to the people: "Children, there is a power above which knows all things, all that is coming to pass. I do not know what will happen, but I hope good will come to you. I have prayed that long life and children and plenty may be given to you, but I know not if my prayers are heard or if they will be answered."

He went with the Hako a second time to the same tribe, but he said nothing. He went a third time, but he said nothing. He went the fourth time, and he was then a very old man. On the last night of the ceremony he spoke and said: "Children, I look over you and see the little boys whom I held in my arms when they were painted [a] now grown to manhood. I see that many children have been given to them; I see that your people have prospered and now I know that my prayers for you when I first came with the Hako have been answered. I know and am sure that the great power to which I prayed hears and answers the prayers of a man."

The first stanza refers to the prayer of the Ku′rahus when he first carried the Hako to the Children.

The second stanza speaks of the offspring that had been given to the Children, that he saw when he went the fourth time with the Hako.

We sing these stanzas on the last night of the ceremony, because it was on the last night that the Ku′rahus spoke to the Children. As we sing we remember what he said he had been taught, that Tira′wa atius hears us pray for the Children and will answer our prayers.

We now begin the last four circuits of the lodge. The first song refers to Tira′wa atius, the father of all. The second speaks of the lesser powers, those which can be seen or heard or felt by man.

We have sung these two songs before; the first time was on the first day, when we made the first circuit of the lodge, in the presence of all the Children, before they partook of the food prepared for them (eighth ritual). We sang them a second time on the third day, after the sacred feast of corn, and before we sang to Mother Earth and made the offering of smoke (thirteenth ritual). Now we sing them for the third time, at the close of the fourth and last night. They are our appeal before we begin the secret ceremonies pertaining to the little child.

---

[a] This is a reference to the ceremonies with the little child which take place on the fifth morning.

SEVENTH SONG

Words and Music

M. M. ♩= 126.

• = Pulsation of the voice.　　　Transcribed by Edwin S. Tracy.

Ha - a - a - a! H'A-ars Ti - ra-wa ha - ki; H'A-ars Ti - ra - wa ha - ki;

Drum.
Rattles.

H'A-ars Ti - ra-wa ha - ki; H'A-ars Ti - ra-wa ha - ki; H'A-ars Ti - ra-wa ha - ki.

979　Ha-a-a-a!	982　H'Aars Tira'wa haki;
980　H'Aars Tira'wa haki;	983　H'Aars Tira'wa haki;
981　H'Aars Tira'wa haki;	984　H'Aars Tira'wa haki.

For translation, see eighth ritual, lines 437–442.

EIGHTH SONG

Words and Music

M. M. ♩=126.

• = Pulsation of the voice.　　　Transcribed by Edwin S. Tracy.

Ha - a - a - a! H'A - ars e he! Ti - ra-wa ha - ki; H'A-ars e he!

Drum.
Rattles.

Ti - ra-wa ha-ki; Hi-dhi! Ti-ra-wa ha-ki; H'A - ars Ti-ra-wa ha-ki.

985　Ha-a-a-a!	988　Hidhi! Tira'wa haki;
986　H'Aars e he! Tira'wa haki;	989　H'Aars Tira'wa haki.
987　H'Aars e he! Tira'wa haki;	

For translation, see eighth ritual, lines 443–447.

Explanation by the Ku'rahus

The songs we sing during the last two circuits are the same that we sang when we prepared the Hako (first ritual). The first was when we painted the stem blue, the color of the sky, representing the abode of the powers above. The other was when we painted the stem green, the color of the covering of the fruitful earth. When we sang these songs we called upon the powers to come and give life and potency to the stems, and now we call upon them again asking for the fulfilment of the promises of the Hako.

NINTH SONG

Words and Music

M. M. ♪ = 126.
• = Pulsation of the voice.   Transcribed by Edwin S. Tracy.

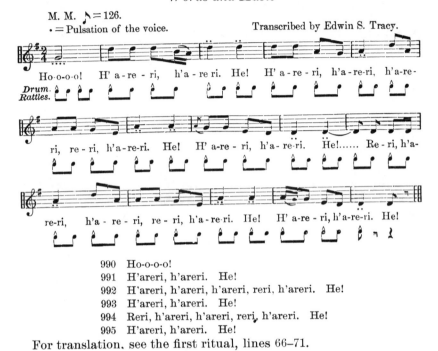

990   Ho-o-o-o!
991   H'areri, h'areri. He!
992   H'areri, h'areri, h'areri, reri, h'areri.   He!
993   H'areri, h'areri.   He!
994   Reri, h'areri, h'areri, reri, h'areri.   He!
995   H'areri, h'areri.   He!

For translation, see the first ritual, lines 66–71.

TENTH SONG

Words and Music

M. M. ♪ = 126.
• = Pulsation of the voice.   Transcribed by Edwin S. Tracy.

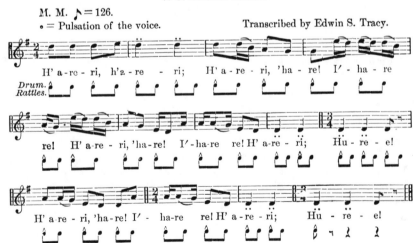

996 H'areri, h'areri;
997 H'areri, 'hare! I'hare re!
998 H'areri, 'hare! I'hare re! H'areri;
999 Hure-e!
1000 H'areri, 'hare, I'hare re! H'areri;
1001 Hure-e!

For translation, see the first ritual, lines 72-77.

Explanation ky the Ku'rahus

We have now made four times four circuits of the lodge. In the first four we remembered Mother Earth through the corn. In the second four we sang of the eagles, which are the messengers of the powers above. In the third four we spoke of the prayers we send to Tira'wa through this ceremony. In the last four we lifted our voices to the powers themselves, the mighty power above and all those which are with the Hako.

Four times four means completeness. Now all the forces above and below, male and female, have been remembered and called upon to be with us in the sacred ceremonies which will take place at the dawn.

The night is nearly over when the last circuit is completed; then the Children rise and go home.

SIXTEENTH RITUAL (FIFTH DAY, DAWN)

PART I. SEEKING THE CHILD

Explanation by the Ku'rahus

After the Children have gone, the Fathers lie down and wait for the first sign of dawn. They have eaten nothing since they last fed the Children shortly after noon, and they must fast until the close of the ceremony.

At the first sign of dawn the Fathers rise and, preceded by the Ku'rahus with the feathered stems, the chief with the corn and wildcat skin, the doctors with their eagle wings, and the singers with the drum, go forth to the lodge where the family of the Son is living. As they march they sing the following song; the words mean that the Father is now seeking his child.

The child referred to is usually a little son or daughter of the Son, the man who has received the Hako party. Upon this little child we are to put the signs of the promises which Mother Corn and Kawas bring, the promise of children, of increase, of long life, of plenty. The signs of these promises are put upon this little child, but they are not merely for that particular child but for its generation, that the children already born may live, grow in strength, and in their turn increase so that the family and the tribe may continue.

In the absence of a little child of the Son an older person or a mother and her baby may be substituted.

FIRST SONG

Words and Music

M. M. ♪ = 126.
• = Pulsation of the voice.   Transcribed by Edwin S. Tracy.

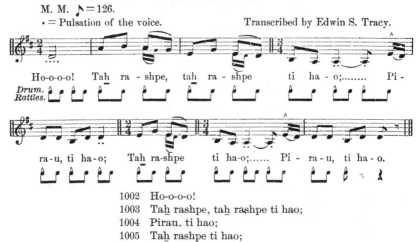

Ho-o-o-o! Tah ra - shpe, tah ra - shpe ti ha - o;........ Pi -
ra - u, ti ha - o; Tah ra-shpe ti ha-o;...... Pi - ra - u, ti ha - o.

    1002   Ho-o-o-o!
    1003   Tah rashpe, tah rashpe ti hao;
    1004   Pirau, ti hao;
    1005   Tah rashpe ti hao;
    1006   Pirau, ti hao.

Translation

1002   Ho-o-o-o!   An introductory exclamation.
1003   Tah rashpe, tah rashpe ti hao.
         tah, I.
         rashpe, am seeking.
         tah rashpe, I am seeking.
         ti, my.
         hao, child, offspring.
1004   Pirau, ti hao.
         pirau, children, a general term.
         ti, my.
         hao, child, offspring.
1005   Tah rashpe ti hao.   See line 1003.
1006   See line 1004.

Explanation by the Ku'rahus

As we approach the lodge of the Son we pause and sing the following song. It is the same that we sang when we halted on the border of
the village at the end of our journey (sixth ritual, part II).   Then we
were about to enter the village and go to the lodge which the Son had
prepared for us.   Now we have been four days and nights in that lodge,
singing the songs and performing the rites of the ceremony and at
the dawn of this the fifth day we once more seek the lodge where the
Son and his family are dwelling, that we may carry these sacred
objects to his own fireplace and there touch with them one of his
children, that the promises we have brought may be fulfilled.   So we
sing the first stanza as we halt.

SECOND SONG

Words and Music

M. M. ♪ = 116.

• = Pulsation of the voice.   Transcribed by Edwin S. Tracy.

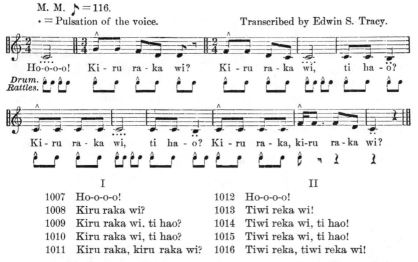

Ho-o-o-o! Ki - ru ra - ka wi?   Ki - ru ra - ka wi,   ti ha - o?

Drum.
Rattles.

Ki - ru ra - ka wi,   ti ha - o? Ki - ru ra - ka, ki - ru   ra - ka wi?

	I		II
1007	Ho-o-o-o!	1012	Ho-o-o-o!
1008	Kiru raka wi?	1013	Tiwi reka wi!
1009	Kiru raka wi, ti hao?	1014	Tiwi reka wi, ti hao!
1010	Kiru raka wi, ti hao?	1015	Tiwi reka wi, ti hao!
1011	Kiru raka, kiru raka wi?	1016	Tiwi reka, tiwi reka wi!

For translation, see the sixth ritual, lines 365-374.

Explanation by the Ku'rahus

After singing the first stanza we move on, and when we are near the lodge we pause and sing the second stanza, "Here is the lodge of my Son wherein he sits waiting for me!"

When we are close to the lodge of the Son we halt, and all the party of the Fathers who can not count war honors remain with the two Ku'rahus, the chief, and the singers who carry the drum, for the Hako can not take part in anything that refers to strife or war; its mission is to unite the people in peace.

The Ku'rahus chooses two men, a chief representing the brown eagle and a warrior representing the white eagle, to accompany the warriors as they step stealthily around the lodge, as if to surprise an enemy, and rush in through the entrance way.

The two chosen men go at once to the child and stand beside it, the chief on the right, the warrior on the left, while the warriors gather around the child and count their honors over it, all talking at once. When they have finished, the warrior touches the child on the left shoulder, then turns and faces it and speaks of the good gifts he has received from Tira'wa. His touch means the imparting to the child of that which he has received from Tira'wa. Then the chief touches the child on the right shoulder, turns and faces it and tells of the honor and favor Tira'wa has granted him. His touch means imparting to the child of that granted him by Tira'wa.

The touch of the warrior and the chief, representatives of the white and the brown eagle, signify the approach of the Hako.

Part II. Symbolic Inception

Explanation by the Ku'rahus

Now the Ku'rahus with the feathered stems, the chief with the corn and the wildcat skin, and the singers with the drum, advance to the door of the lodge, enter, and walk down the long passageway into the dwelling. They go around the fire to the west, where the Son and his little child await them.

As we stand before the little child we sing this song (first stanza). We have sung it once before (sixth ritual, part I), at the time when the messenger representing the Son came to us outside the village. We sing it now as we look on the little child who represents the continuation of the life of the Son.

FIRST SONG

Words and Music

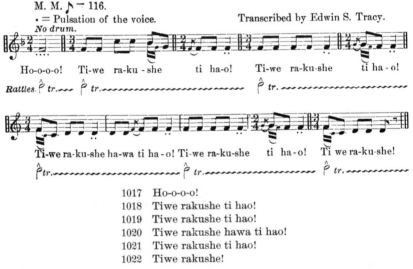

```
1017   Ho-o-o-o!
1018   Tiwe rakushe ti hao!
1019   Tiwe rakushe ti hao!
1020   Tiwe rakushe hawa ti hao!
1021   Tiwe rakushe ti hao!
1022   Tiwe rakushe!
```

For translation, see the sixth ritual, lines 353–358.

Explanation by the Ku'rahus

The Ku'rahus takes from the hands of the chief the wildcat skin, in which the ear of corn and the crotched plum tree stick are wrapped, and while he holds the ear toward the little child, we sing the song.

We have sung this song once before, at the time the ear of corn was painted (first ritual, part III). The ear of corn represents h'Uraru, Mother Earth who brings forth; the power which causes her to bring forth is from above, and the blue paint represents that power.

We hold the painted ear of corn toward the little child that the powers from above and from below may come near it.

SECOND SONG

Words and Music

M. M. ♪ = 138.
• = Pulsation of the voice.   Transcribed by Edwin S. Tracy.

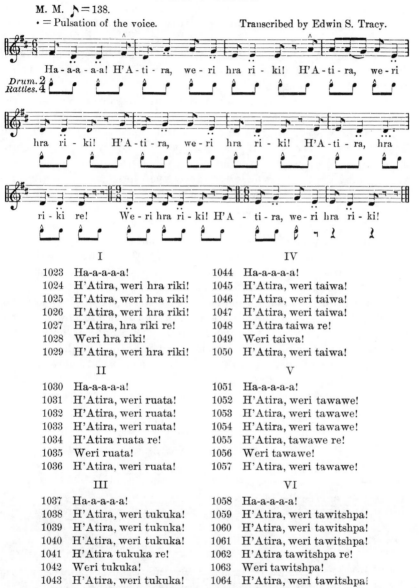

I		IV	
1023	Ha-a-a-a-a!	1044	Ha-a-a-a-a!
1024	H'Atira, weri hra riki!	1045	H'Atira, weri taiwa!
1025	H'Atira, weri hra riki!	1046	H'Atira, weri taiwa!
1026	H'Atira, weri hra riki!	1047	H'Atira, weri taiwa!
1027	H'Atira, hra riki re!	1048	H'Atira taiwa re!
1028	Weri hra riki!	1049	Weri taiwa!
1029	H'Atira, weri hra riki!	1050	H'Atira, weri taiwa!

II		V	
1030	Ha-a-a-a-a!	1051	Ha-a-a-a-a!
1031	H'Atira, weri ruata!	1052	H'Atira, weri tawawe!
1032	H'Atira, weri ruata!	1053	H'Atira, weri tawawe!
1033	H'Atira, weri ruata!	1054	H'Atira, weri tawawe!
1034	H'Atira ruata re!	1055	H'Atira, tawawe re!
1035	Weri ruata!	1056	Weri tawawe!
1036	H'Atira, weri ruata!	1057	H'Atira, weri tawawe!

III		VI	
1037	Ha-a-a-a-a!	1058	Ha-a-a-a-a!
1038	H'Atira, weri tukuka!	1059	H'Atira, weri tawitshpa!
1039	H'Atira, weri tukuka!	1060	H'Atira, weri tawitshpa!
1040	H'Atira, weri tukuka!	1061	H'Atira, weri tawitshpa!
1041	H'Atira tukuka re!	1062	H'Atira tawitshpa re!
1042	Weri tukuka!	1063	Weri tawitshpa!
1043	H'Atira, weri tukuka!	1064	H'Atira, weri tawitshpa!

For translation, see the first ritual, lines 82–123.

Explanation by the Ku'rahus

As we sing the second stanza, the Ku'rahus moves the ear of corn, as if it were flying toward the child. I explained this movement when I told you about the painting of the corn (see the first ritual, part III, explanation of second stanza of the song by the Ku'rahus).

While we sing the third stanza, the Ku'rahus touches the little child
on the forehead with the ear of corn.   The spirit of Mother Corn, with
the power of Mother Earth, granted from above, has touched the child.

The touch means the promise of fruitfulness to the child and its
generation.

As we sing the fourth stanza, the Ku'rahus strokes the child with
the ear of corn, down the front, down the right side, down the back,
and then down the left side.

These motions, corresponding to the four lines on the ear of corn,
represent the four paths down which the powers descend to man.
The four lines stroked upon the little child make the paths and open
the way for the descent of the powers upon it.   Every side of the child
is now open to receive the powers, and as he goes through life, where-
ever he may be, on every side the powers can have access to him.

As we sing the fifth stanza, the Ku'rahus touches the child here
and there with the ear of corn.

This movement signifies that Mother Corn with the powers are
spreading over the child and descending upon it.

The sixth stanza tells that it is accomplished; the child is now
encompassed by the spirit of Mother Corn and the powers and has
received the promise of fruitfulness.

The Ku'rahus hands back to the chief the wildcat skin, inclosing the
crotched stick and the ear of corn, and takes the two feathered stems.
He wraps the white-eagle feathered stem within the feathers of the
brown-eagle stem and, holding with both hands the bundle, he stands
before the little child, and, while the first stanza of the following song
is sung, he points the stems toward it.

This movement means that the breath of life is turned toward the
child.   The breath passes through the stem.

THIRD SONG

Words and Music

M. M. ♪ = 126.
• = Pulsation of the voice.   Transcribed by Edwin S. Tracy.

Ha-a-a-a-a! Ka - was we - ri hra ri - ki, re hra ri - ki! Ka - was we - ri

Drum.
Rattles.

hra ri - ki, re hra ri - ki! Ka - was we - ri hra ri - ki, re hra ri - ki!

I

Ha-a-a-a-a!
1065   Kawas weri hra riki, re hra riki!
1066   Kawas weri hra riki, re hra riki!
1067   Kawas weri hra riki, re hra riki!

II

1068   Ha-a-a-a-a!
1069   Kawas weri ruata, re ruata!
1070   Kawas weri ruata, re ruata!
1071   Kawas weri ruata, re ruata!

III

1072   Ha-a-a-a-a!
1073   Kawas weri tukuka, re tukuka!
1074   Kawas weri tukuka, re tukuka!
1075   Kawas weri tukuka, re tukuka!

IV

1076   Ha-a-a-a-a!
1077   Kawas weri taiwa, re taiwa!
1078   Kawas weri taiwa, re taiwa!
1079   Kawas weri taiwa, re taiwa!

V

1080   Ha-a-a-a-a!
1081   Kawas weri tawawe, re tawawe!
1082   Kawas weri tawawe, re tawawe!
1083   Kawas weri tawawe, re tawawe!

VI

1084   Ha-a-a-a-a!
1085   Kawas weri tawitshpa, re tawitshpa!
1086   Kawas weri tawitshpa, re tawitshpa!
1087   Kawas weri tawitshpa, re tawitshpa!

Translation of First Stanza

1064   Ha-a-a-a-a!   An introductory exclamation.
1065   Kawas weri hra riki, re hra riki.

> Kawas, the brown eagle, representing the female forces.
> weri, I am.   The singular pronoun refers to Hako party, not
>   merely to the Ku'rahus.
> hra, a modification of rararit, to hold.
> riki, standing, present time.
> re, plural sign, indicating the two feathered stems which have
>   been folded together, the united male and female.
> hra, holding.
> riki, standing, the present time.

1066, 1067   See line 1065.

Translation of Second Stanza

1068 Ha-a-a-a-a! An introductory exclamation.
1069 Kawas weri ruata, re ruata.
       Kawas, the brown eagle, the female.
       weri, I am.
       ruata, flying. See line 90.
       re, plural sign; the two feathered stems.
       ruata, flying.
1070, 1071 See line 1069.

Explanation by the Ku'rahus

As we sing the second stanza the Ku'rahus moves the feathered
stems as if they were flying through space toward the child; the
united male and female stems are drawing near.

Translation of Third Stanza

1072 Ha-a-a-a-a! An introductory exclamation.
1073 Kawas weri tukuka, re tukuka.
       Kawas, the brown eagle; the female.
       were, I am.
       tukuka, touching, now touches.
       re, plural sign; refers to the two feathered stems.
       tukuka, now touches, are now touching.
1074, 1075 See line 1073.

Explanation by the Ku'rahus

While we sing the third stanza the Ku'rahus touches the little child
on the forehead with the united feathered stems. The breath of
promised life has now touched the child. That is the meaning of the
touch of the feathered stems.

Translation of Fourth Stanza

1076 Ha-a-a-a-a! An introductory exclamation.
1077 Kawas weri taiwa, re taiwa.
       Kawas, the brown eagle; the female.
       weri, I am.
       taiwa, to rub downward, making a mark.
       re, plural; the two feathered stems.
       taiwa, making a mark with a downward motion.
1078, 1079 See line 1077.

Explanation by the Ku'rahus

As we sing the fourth stanza the Ku'rahus makes with the united
feathered stems the four paths by downward strokes upon the child,

as was done with the ear of corn.　These movements mean that all the powers which bring life have access to the child, so that the promise of fruitfulness may be fulfilled.

Translation of Fifth Stanza

1080　Ha-a-a-a-a!　An introductory exclamation.
1081　Kawas weri tawawe, re tawawe.
　　　　Kawas, the brown eagle.
　　　　weri, I am.
　　　　tawawe, to spread.
　　　　re, plural; refers to the two feathered stems.
　　　　tawawe, to spread.
1082, 1083　See line 1081.

Explanation by the Ku'rahus

While we sing the fifth stanza the Ku'rahus touches the child here and there with the united feathered stems; this means the spreading over it of the powers represented by the male and female stems.

Translation of Sixth Stanza

1084　Ha-a-a-a-a!　An introductory exclamation.
1085　Kawas weri tawitshpa, re tawitshpa.
　　　　Kawas, the brown eagle.
　　　　weri, I am.
　　　　tawitshpa, a word denoting the accomplishment of a purpose,
　　　　　　the attainment of an end.
　　　　re, plural; refers to the two united feathered stems.
　　　　tawitshpa.　Translated above.
1086, 1087　See line 1085.

Explanation by the Ku'rahus

This stanza means that it is accomplished, that the child has been encompassed by the powers represented by the united stems.　It is a promise of procreation.

PART III. ACTION SYMBOLIZING LIFE

Explanation by the Ku'rahus

At the close of the song the Ku'rahus, separating the two stems, hands the white-eagle feathered stem to his assistant and retains the brown-eagle stem.　The father of the child makes it sit upon the ground.　The chief chooses a man to carry the child from the lodge of its father, the Son, back to the lodge where the ceremony of the preceding four days has been performed.

22 ETH—PT 2—04——14

The chosen man takes his position a little distance in front of the child, the Ku'rahus and his assistant stand on each side of the man, facing the child, and the chief, carrying the cat skin and the corn, stands in front, facing the child (figure 177).

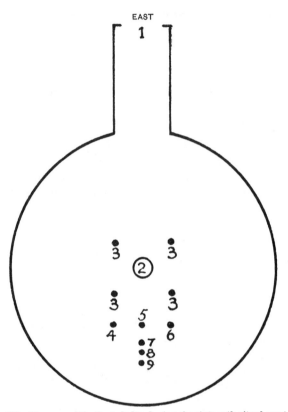

Fig. 177. Diagram of the Son's lodge during the sixteenth ritual, part III.

1, the entrance to the lodge; 2, the fireplace; 3, inner posts supporting the dome-shaped roof; 4, the Ku'rahus; 5, the Father (a chief); 6, the Ku'rahus's assistant; 7, the one chosen to carry the child; 8, the child; 9, the father of the child, the Son.

The following song is then sung in a gentle tone, that the child may be willing to be taken up and carried by a stranger. The words are: "Come and fear not, my child; all is well."

FIRST SONG

Words and Music

M. M. ♩.=58.
· = Pulsation of the voice.

Transcribed by Edwin S. Tracy.

Ho-o-o-o-o-o!   I - hi - si - ra,   i - hi - si - ra,   i - hi - si - ra,

Drum.
Rattles.

i - ra ta ha - o;   I - hi-si - ra, i - hi - si - ra,   i - ra ta ha - o.

1088   Ho-o-o-o-o-o!
1089   Ihisira, ihisira, ihisira, ira ta hao;
1090   Ihisira, ihisira, ira ta hao.

Translation

1088   Ho-o-o-o-o-o!   An introductory exclamation.
1089   Ihisira, ihisira, ihisira, ira ta hao.

    ihisira; isira, come; an invitation to advance.   The syllable
    hi, which follows i, is used to fill out the rhythm of the
    music and to give a coaxing effect.

    ira, a part of the word nawairi, a word implying confidence,
    among its other meanings; it means here, it is all right,
    fear not.

    ta, a part of the word kutati, my.

    hao, child, offspring.
1090   Ihisira, ihisira, ira ta hao.   See line 1089.

Explanation by the Ku'rahus

The man who is to carry the child turns his back toward it and
drops upon one knee.   The child, lifted to its feet by its father, takes
four steps forward, while we, still facing the child, sing this song:
"I am ready; come, my child; have no fear!"
The four steps taken by the child represent the progress of life.

SECOND SONG

Words and Music

M. M. ♩=58.
• = Pulsation of the voice.   Transcribed by Edwin S. Tracy.

Ho-o-o-o!   E-he-si - ra,   e-he-si - ra,   e-he- si - ra,   e-he- si - ra,

Drum.
Rattles. tr........ tr........ tr........ tr........ tr........

i - ra ta ha - o;   E-he-si - ra,   e - he- si - ra,   i - ra ta ha - o.

tr........   tr........   tr........

1091   Ho-o-o-o!
1092   Ehesira, ehesira, ehesira, ehesira, ira ta hao;
1093   Ehesira, ehesira, ira ta hao.

Translation

1091   Ho-o-o-o!   An introductory explanation.
1092   Ehesira, ehesira, ehesira, ehesira, ira ta hao.
      ehesira; esira, come, I am ready for you or to receive you.
      The syllable he, which follows e, is to fill out the rhythm
      and the movement of the song.
1093   Ehesira, ehesira, ira ta hao.   See line 1092.

Explanation by the Ku'rahus

The man takes the child upon his back and rises to his feet.   The
chief steps aside and the man bearing the child moves forward
toward the door of the lodge.   The Ku'rahus and his assistant and
the chief walk behind him, and the rest of the company follow.

As we walk back to the lodge in the early daylight we sing this
song: "Behold your father walking with the child!"

THIRD SONG

Words and Music

M. M. ♩=56.
• = Pulsation of the voice.   Transcribed by Edwin S. Tracy.

Ho-o-o-o!   I - ha - ri.   ha!   H'ars si - re ra - ta;   I - ha-ri,

Drum.
Rattles. tr........

ha!   H'ars si - re   ra - ta;   I - ha-ri,   ha!   H'ars si - re ra - ta.

1094   Ho-o-o-o!
1095   Ihari, ha!   H'ars sire rata;
1096   Ihari, ha!   H'ars sire rata;
1097   Ihari, ha!   H'ars sire rata.

Translation

1094   Ho-o-o-o!   An exclamation introductory to the song.
1095   Ihari, ha!   H'ars sire rata.
    ihari, a term for young; it here refers to the little child.
    ha! an exclamation, calling attention.
    h', an abbreviation of ha, your.
    ars, a modification of atius, father.
    sire, carrying, refers to the child.
    rata, walking with.
1096, 1097.   See line 1095.

SEVENTEENTH RITUAL

PART I.   TOUCHING THE CHILD

Explanation by the Ku'rahus

When the Hako party, led by the man carrying the child, arrived at the lodge, the child was taken to the west, behind the holy place, and set upon the ground, facing the east, and clad in gala dress.

The warriors ranged themselves in a curved line, both ends of which touched the walls of the lodge, thus inclosing a space within which was the holy place, the child, the singers and the drum, the Ku'rahus and his assistant, the chief, the doctors, and an old man selected by the Ku'rahus. The warriors stood close together, letting their robes drop until the lower edge touched the ground, making a screen over which no one could look to see what was taking place within the inclosure.

On the preceding evening, before the Children had gathered within the lodge, the Ku'rahus had sent a young man to fill a vessel from a running stream. The vessel was at once covered closely and put beside the holy place and no one was permitted to even touch it. (In old times pottery vessels made by our women were used. They were shaped small at the bottom, larger in the middle, and smaller again at the neck. The handles on the sides had holes through which sticks could be thrust to lift the vessel from the fire. They were ornamented by lines drawn by a stick in the soft clay.)

The chief now approached the vessel, lifted the cover and poured some of the water into a wooden bowl set aside for this purpose, and put it down before the old man. This man had been chosen because of his long life, and his having received many favors from the powers above, in order that similar gifts might be imparted to the child.

The preparation of the child, which took place within the line of warriors, was concealed from their view by an inner group closely surrounding it. The old man sat before the child, a little to the south, the chief (the Father) directly behind it with the cat skin and ear of corn, the doctor with the left eagle wing toward the north, the doctor with the right eagle wing toward the south, and the

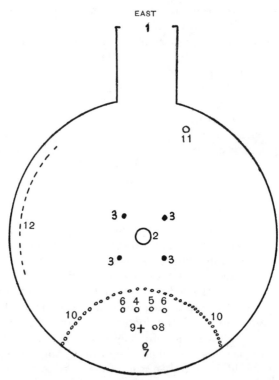

FIG. 178. Diagram of the Son's lodge during the seventeenth ritual, part I.

1, the entrance to the lodge; 2, the fireplace; 3, inner posts supporting the dome-shaped roof; 4, the Ku'rahus; 5, his assistant; 6, the bearers of the eagle wings; 7, the Father (a chief); 8, the old man who prepares the child; 9, the little child; 10, the line of warriors; 11, the Son, father of the little child; 12, members of the Hako party.

Ku'rahus with his assistant in front, all facing the child (figure 178).

During the singing of the following songs the cat skin with the crotched stick and the ear of corn, the feathered stems, and the eagle wings are waved to its rhythm.

FIRST SONG

Words and Music

M. M. ♪ = 126.

• = Pulsation of the voice.   Transcribed by Edwin S. Tracy.

I

1098 Ho-o-o!
1099 Hiri! 'Hari; Hiri! Kitzu we re hre kusi hi!
1100 Hiri! 'Hari; Hiri! Kitzu we re hre kusi hi!
1101 Hiri! 'Hari; Hiri! Kitzu we re hre kusi hi!

II

1102 Ho-o-o!
1103 Hiri! 'Hari; Hiri! Kitzu we re ru ata ha!
1104 Hiri! 'Hari; Hiri! Kitzu we re ru ata ha!
1105 Hiri! 'Hari; Hiri! Kitzu we re ru ata ha!

III

1106 Ho-o-o!
1107 Hiri! 'Hari; Hiri! Kitzu we ri tukuka ha!
1108 Hiri! 'Hari; Hiri! Kitzu we ri tukuka ha!
1109 Hiri! 'Hari; Hiri! Kitzu we ri tukuka ha!

IV

1110 Ho-o-o!
1111 Hiri! 'Hari; Hiri! Kitzu we ri ta iwa ha!
1112 Hiri! 'Hari; Hiri! Kitzu we ri ta iwa ha!
1113 Hiri! 'Hari; Hiri! Kitzu we ri ta iwa ha!

V

1114 Ho-o-o!
1115 Hiri! 'Hari; Hiri! Kitzu we ri ta wawe he!
1116 Hiri! 'Hari; Hiri! Kitzu we ri ta wawe he!
1117 Hiri! 'Hari; Hiri! Kitzu we ri ta wawe he!

VI

1118 Ho-o-o!
1119 Hiri! 'Hari; Hiri! Kitzu we ri ta witshpa ha!
1120 Hiri! 'Hari; Hiri! Kitzu we ri ta witshpa ha!
1121 Hiri! 'Hari; Hiri! Kitzu we ri ta witshpa ha!

Translation of First Stanza

1098 Ho-o-o!   An introductory exclamation.
1099 Hiri! 'Hari; Hiri! Kitzu we re hre kusi hi!
         hiri! give heed!
         'hari, a part of iha'ri, child, young.
         hiri! an exclamation calling to give heed.
         kitzu, a modified form of kiitzu, water.
         we, now.
         re, am.
         hre, holding.
         kusi, sitting.
         hi! part of hiri! give heed! harken!
1100, 1101.   See line 1099.

Explanation by the Ku'rahus

As we sing the first stanza the old man takes up the bowl and holds
it in both hands.

Water is for sustenance and the maintenance of health; it is one of
the great gifts of Tira'wa atius.

The white man speaks of a heavenly Father; we say Tira'wa atius,
the Father above, but we do not think of Tira'wa as a person.   We
think of Tira'wa as in everything, as the power which has arranged
and thrown down from above everything that man needs.   What the
power above, Tira'wa atius, is like, no one knows; no one has been
there.

The water is in a bowl shaped like the dome of the sky, because
water comes from Tira'wa atius.   The little child is to be cleansed
and prepared for its future life by the water—sustained and made
strong by the water.

Translation of Second Stanza

1102 Ho-o-o!   An introductory exclamation.
1103 Hiri! 'Hari; Hiri! Kitzu we re ɪu ata ha!
         hiri! give heed!
         'hari, a part in iha'ri, child.
         hiri! give heed!
         kitzu, water.
         we, now.
         re, am, or is.
         ru, it.
         ata, flying.
         ha! behold!
1104, 1105   See line 1103.

Explanation by the Ku'rahus

When we sing the second stanza the old man sets the bowl down and dips the finger of his right hand in the water and moves it toward the child.

This means that the water is moving through the air, coming from above toward the child with its gifts.

Translation of Third Stanza

1106 Ho-o-o! An introductory exclamation.
1107 Hiri! 'Hari; Hiri! Kitzu we ri tukuka ha!
      hiri! give heed!
      'hari, a part of iha'ri, child.
      hiri! give heed!
      kitzu, water.
      we, now.
      ri, it.
      tukuka, touching.
      ha! behold!
1108, 1109   See line 1107.

Explanation by the Ku'rahus

As we sing the third stanza the old man touches the forehead of the child with the water.

The power of the water has now reached the child.

Translation of Fourth Stanza

1110 Ho-o-o! An introductory exclamation.
1111 Hiri! 'Hari; Hiri! Kitzu we ri ta iwa ha!
      hiri! give heed!
      'hari, a part of iha'ri, child.
      hiri! give heed!
      kitzu, water.
      we, now.
      ri, it.
      ta, a part of taokut, to touch.
      iwa, running down.
      ha! behold!
1112, 1113   See line 1111.

Explanation by the Ku'rahus

While we sing the fourth stanza the old man makes certain wet lines on the face of the child. These signify that the sustaining of life through the power of water comes from Tira'wa atius.

Translation of Fifth Stanza

1114 Ho-o-o!   An introductory exclamation.
1115 Hiri! 'Hari; Hiri! Kitzu we ri ta wawe he!
  hiri! give heed!
  'hari, a part of iha'ri, child.
  hiri! give heed!
  kitzu, water.
  we, now.
  ri, it.
  ta, a part of taokut, to touch.
  wawe, spreading over.
  he! from hiri! give heed!
1116, 1117   See line 1115.

Explanation by the Ku'rahus

During the singing of the fifth stanza the old man touches the face of the child with water here and there so as to make it wet.

This is to signify that the cleansing power of water, which brings health, is from Tira'wa.

Translation of Sixth Stanza

1118 Ho-o-o!   An introductory exclamation.
1119 Hiri! 'Hari; Hiri! Kitzu we ri ta witshpa ha!
  hiri! give heed!
  'hari, a part of iha'ri, child.
  hiri! give heed!
  kitzu, water.
  we, now.
  ri, it.
  ta, a part of taokut, to touch.
  witshpa, accomplished, completed.
  ha! behold!
1120, 1121   See line 1119.

Explanation by the Ku'rahus

In the sixth stanza we sing that it is accomplished, that water has come with all its power from Tira'wa atius to the child.

The old man takes up a brush of stiff grass and holds it while we sing the first stanza of the following song.

SECOND SONG

Words and Music

(a) M. M. ♪ = 126.

• = Pulsation of the voice.

Transcribed by Edwin S. Tracy.

I

1122 Ho-o-o!
1123 Hiri! 'Hari; Hiri! Pichŭts we re hre kusi hi!
1124 Hiri! 'Hari; Hiri! Pichŭts we re hre kusi hi!
1125 Hiri! 'Hari; Hiri! Pichŭts we re hre kusi hi!

II

1126 Ho-o-o!
1127 Hiri! 'Hari; Hiri! Pichŭts we re ru ata ha!
1128 Hiri! 'Hari; Hiri! Pichŭts we re ru ata ha!
1129 Hiri! 'Hari; Hiri! Pichŭts we re ru ata ha!

III

1130 Ho-o-o!
1131 Hiri! 'Hari; Hiri! Pichŭts we ri tukuka ha!
1132 Hiri! 'Hari; Hiri! Pichŭts we ri tukuka ha!
1133 Hiri! 'Hari; Hiri! Pichŭts we ri tukuka ha!

IV

1134 Ho-o-o!
1135 Hiri! 'Hari; Hiri! Pichŭts we ri ta iwa ha!
1136 Hiri! 'Hari; Hiri! Pichŭts we ri ta iwa ha!
1137 Hiri! 'Hari: Hiri! Pichŭts we ri ta iwa ha!

V

1138 Ho-o-o!
1139 Hiri! 'Hari; Hiri! Pichŭts we ri ta wawe he!
1140 Hiri! 'Hari; Hiri! Pichŭts we ri ta wawe he!
1141 Hiri! 'Hari; Hiri! Pichŭts we ri ta wawe he!

VI

1142 Ho-o-o!
1143 Hiri! 'Hari; Hiri! Pichŭts we ri ta witshpa ha!
1144 Hiri! 'Hari; Hiri! Pichŭts we ri ta witshpa ha!
1145 Hiri! 'Hari; Hiri! Pichŭts we ri ta witshɪa ha!

Translation of First Stanza

1122 Ho-o-o! An introductory exclamation.
1123 Hiri! 'Hari; Hiri! Pichŭts we re hre kusi hi!
    hiri! give heed!
    'hari, a part of iha'ri, child.
    hiri! give heed.
    pichŭts, a brush made of stiff grass.
    we, now.
    re, am.
    hre, holding.
    kusi, sitting.
    hi! part of hiri! give heed! harken!
1124, 1125 See line 1123.

Explanation by the Ku'rahus

The grass of which the brush is made is gathered during a ceremony belonging to the Rain shrine. It represents Toharu, the living
covering of Mother Earth. The power which is in Toharu gives food
to man and the animals so that they can live and become strong and
able to perform the duties of life. This power represented by the
brush of grass is now standing before the little child.

Translation of Second Stanza

1126 Ho-o-o! An introductory exclamation.
1127 Hari! 'Hari; Hiri! Pichŭts we re ru ata ha!
    hiri! give heed!
    'hari, a part of iha'ri, child.
    hiri! give heed!
    pichŭts, a brush of grass.
    we, now.
    re, am or is.
    ru, it.
    ata, flying.
    ha! behold!
1128, 1129 See line 1127.

Explanation by the Ku'rahus

As we sing the second stanza, the old man moves the brush toward
the child. This means that the power of Toharu is flying through the
air toward the child.

Translation of Third Stanza

1130 Ho-o-o!   An introductory exclamation.
1131 Hiri! 'Hari; Hiri! Pichŭts we ri tukuka ha!
      hiri! give heed!
      'hari, a part of iha'ri, child.
      hiri! give heed!
      pichŭts, a brush of grass.
      we, now.
      ri, it.
      tukuka, touching.
      ha! behold!
1132, 1133   See line 1131.

Explanation by the Ku'rahus

While we sing the third stanza the old man touches the forehead
of the child with the brush of grass. The power of Toharu has
reached the child, has come in contact with it to impart the strength
that comes from food.

Translation of Fourth Stanza

1134 Ho-o-o!   An introductory exclamation.
1135 Hiri! 'Hari; Hiri! Pichŭts we ri ta iwa ha!
      hiri! give heed!
      'hari, a part of iha'ri, child.
      hiri! give heed!
      pichŭts, a brush of grass.
      we, now.
      ri, it.
      ta, a part of taokut, to touch.
      iwa, a downward movement.
      ha! behold!
1136, 1137   See line 1135.

Explanation by the Ku'rahus

During the singing of the fourth stanza the old man makes certain
lines upon the face of the child with the brush of grass. These lines
mean that the power by which Toharu gives strength through food
comes from above, and that man should always remember that when
he eats.

Translation of Fifth Stanza

1138 Ho-o-o! An introductory exclamation.
1139 Hiri! 'Hari; Hiri! Pichŭts we ri ta ware he!
 hiri! give heed!
 'hari, a part of iha'ri, child.
 hiri! give heed!
 pichŭts, a brush made of grass.
 we, now.
 ri, it.
 ta, a part of taokut, to touch.
 ware, spreading over.
 he! from hiri! give heed!
1140, 1141 See line 1139.

Explanation by the Ku'rahus

As we sing this stanza, the old man touches the head of the child and smooths its hair with the brush of grass. In this act the brush prepares the hair for the sacred symbols which are to be put upon it.

In this act we are thinking only of the brush and its usefulness, and not of Toharu, as represented by the grass.

Translation of Sixth Stanza

1142 Ho-o-o! An introductory exclamation.
1143 Hiri! 'Hari, Hiri! Pichŭts we ri ta witshpa ha!
 hiri! give heed!
 'hari, a part of iha'ri, child.
 hiri! give heed!
 pichŭts, a brush made of grass.
 we, now.
 ri, it.
 ta, a part of taokut, to touch.
 witshpa, accomplished; completed.
 ha! behold!
1144, 1145 See line 1143.

Explanation by the Ku'rahus

In this stanza we sing that it is accomplished, the power of Toharu has nourished and prepared the child for the ceremonial acts which are now to take place.

PART II. ANOINTING THE CHILD

Explanation by the Ku'rahus

The ointment used in this act of anointing the child is red clay mixed with fat from a deer or buffalo which has been consecrated or set apart at the time it was killed as a sacrifice to Tira'wa. The first animal killed on a hunt belongs to Tira'wa.

The ointment is kept in a kind of bag made of the covering of the animal's heart, dried and prepared for this purpose. (It is said that insects do not attack this skin covering.)

Before anyone can take part in a religious ceremony he must be anointed with this sacred ointment.

SONG

Words and Music

(b) M. M. ♪ = 126.

• = Pulsation of the voice.

Transcribed by Edwin S. Tracy.

Ho-o-o! Hi - ri! 'Ha-ri; Hi-ri! Ki-cha-wa re hre ku - si..... hi!... Hi -

Drum.
Rattles.

ri! 'Ha - ri; Hi - ri! Ki-cha-wa re hre ku - si hi!... Hi -

ri! 'Ha - ri; Hi-ri! Ki-cha-wa re hre ku - si..... hi!.....

I

1146 Ho-o-o!
1147 Hiri! 'Hari; Hiri! Kichawa re hre kusi hi!
1148 Hiri! 'Hari; Hiri! Kichawa re hre kusi hi!
1149 Hiri! 'Hari; Hiri! Kichawa re hre kusi hi!

II

1150 Ho-o-o!
1151 Hiri! 'Hari; Hiri! Kichawa re ru ata ha!
1152 Hiri! 'Hari; Hiri! Kichawa re ru ata ha!
1153 Hiri! 'Hari; Hiri! Kichawa re ru ata ha!

III

1154 Ho-o-o!
1155 Hiri! 'Hari; Hiri! Kichawa ri tukuka ha!
1156 Hiri!' Hari; Hiri! Kichawa ri tukuka ha!
1157 Hiri! 'Hari; Hiri! Kichawa ri tukuka ha!

IV

1158 Ho-o-o!
1159 Hiri!' Hari; Hiri! Kichawa ri ta iwa ha!
1160 Hiri! 'Hari; Hiri! Kichawa ri ta iwa ha!
1161 Hiri! 'Hari; Hiri! Kichawa ri ta iwa ha!

V

1162 Ho-o-o!
1163 Hiri! 'Hari; Hiri! Kichawa ri ta wawe he!
1164 Hiri! 'Hari; Hiri! Kichawa ri ta wawe he!
1165 Hiri! 'Hari; Hiri! Kichawa ri ta wawe he!

VI

1166   Ho-o-o!
1167   Hiri! 'Hari; Hiri! Kichawa ri ta witshpa ha!
1168   Hiri! 'Hari; Hiri! Kichawa ri ta witshpa ha!
1169   Hiri! 'Hari; Hiri! Kichawa ri ta witshpa ha!

Translation of First Stanza

1146   Ho-o-o!   An introductory exclamation.
1147   Hiri! 'Hari; Hiri! Kichawa re hre kusi hi!
    hiri! give heed!
    'hari, a part of iha'ri, child.
    hiri! give heed!
    kichawa; ki, from kitzu, water; chawa, bubbles of fat; the
        term is applied to the ointment made from the fat of an
        animal which has been consecrated to Tira'wa. This
        ointment is used for anointing preparatory to a sacred
        ceremony.
    re, am.
    hre, holding.
    kusi, sitting.
    hi! from hiri! give heed!
1148, 1149   See line 1147.

Explanation by the Ku'rahus.

While we sing the first stanza the old man takes and holds in his
hand some of the sacred ointment.   The consecrating power which is
in the ointment now stands before the child.

Translation of Second Stanza

1150   Ho-o-o!   An introductory exclamation.
1151   Hiri! 'Hari; Hiri! Kichawa re ru ata ha!
    hiri! give heed!
    'hare, a part of iha're, child.
    hiri! give heed!
    kichawa, ointment.
    re, is.
    ru, it.
    ata, flying.
    ha! behold!
1152, 1153.   See line 1151.

Explanation by the Ku'rahus

While we sing the second stanza the old man moves the sacred
ointment toward the child.   This means that the power which is in
the ointment is drawing near.

Translation of Third Stanza

1154　Ho-o-o!　An introductory exclamation.
1155　Hiri! 'Hari; Hiri! Kichawa ri tukuka ha!
　　　　hiri! give heed!
　　　　'hari, a part of iha'ri, child.
　　　　hiri! give heed!
　　　　kichawa, ointment.
　　　　ri, it.
　　　　tukuka, touching.
　　　　ha! behold!
1156, 1157.　See line 1155.

Explanation by the Ku'rahus

As we sing the third stanza the old man touches the forehead of the child with the ointment.　This act signifies that the child is singled out from among his fellows and touched for consecration.

Translation of Fourth Stanza

1158　Ho-o-o!　An introductory exclamation.
1159　Hiri! 'Hari; Hiri! Kichawa ri ta iwa ha!
　　　　hiri! give heed!
　　　　'hari, a part of iha'ri, child.
　　　　hiri! give heed!
　　　　kichawa, ointment.
　　　　ri, it.
　　　　ta, a part of taokut, to touch.
　　　　iwa, downward movement.
　　　　ha! behold!
1160, 1161.　See line 1159.

Explanation by the Ku'rahus

As we sing this fourth stanza the old man makes the same lines upon the face of the child as he made with the water and the brush of grass.　This is in recognition that the life which has been sustained and nourished is now consecrated to Tira'wa atius, the father above, who gives life to all things.

Translation of Fifth Stanza

1162 Ho-o-o! An introductory exclamation.
1163 Hiri! 'Hari; Hiri! Kichawa ri ta wawe he!
      hiri! give heed!
      'hari, a part of iha′ri, child.
      hiri! give heed!
      kichawa, ointment.
      ri, it.
      ta, a part of taokut, to touch.
      wawa, spreading over.
      he! from hiri! give heed!
1164, 1165 See line 1162.

Explanation by the Ku′rahus

While we sing the fifth stanza, the old man touches the child here and there with the sacred ointment. This means that the strength that is in every part of a man and all that belongs to him must be consecrated to Tira′wa.

Translation of Sixth Stanza

1166 Ho-o-o! An introductory exclamation.
1167 Hiri! 'Hari; Hiri! Kichawa ri ta witshpa ha!
      hiri! give heed!
      'hari, a part of iha′ri, child.
      hiri! give heed!
      kichawa, ointment.
      ri, it.
      ta, a part of taokut, to touch.
      witshpa, accomplished, completed.
      ha! behold!
1168, 1169 See line 1167.

Explanation by the Ku′rahus

In this stanza we sing that it is accomplished, that the child has been consecrated and made ready for the holy rites, and that we have recognized that all things come from Tira′wa atius, the father above.

PART III. PAINTING THE CHILD

Explanation by the Ku'rahus

While we sing the first stanza of the following song, the old man
takes a shell containing red paint and holds it before the consecrated
child.

FIRST SONG

Words and Music

(c) M. M. ♪ = 126.
• = Pulsation of the voice.   Transcribed by Edwin S. Tracy.

Ho-o-o! Hi - ri! 'Ha-ri; Hi-ri! Kits-pa-hat we re ku - si..... hi!.... Hiri! 'Ha - ri; Hi - ri! Kits-pa-hat we re ku - si hi!.... Hiri! 'Ha - ri; Hi-ri! Kits-pa - hat we re ku - si..... hi!.....

I

1170 Ho-o-o!
1171 Hiri! 'Hari; Hiri! Kitspahat we re kusi hi!
1172 Hiri! 'Hari; Hiri! Kitspahat we re kusi hi!
1173 Hiri! 'Hari; Hiri! Kitspahat we re kusi hi!

II

1174 Ho-o-o!
1175 Hiri! 'Hari; Hiri! Kitspahat re ru ata ha!
1176 Hiri! 'Hari; Hiri! Kitspahat re ru ata ha!
1177 Hiri! 'Hari; Hiri! Kitspahat re ru ata ha!

III

1178 Ho-o-o!
1179 Hiri! 'Hari; Hiri! Kitspahat ri tukuka ha!
1180 Hiri! 'Hari; Hiri! Kitspahat ri tukuka ha!
1181 Hiri! 'Hari; Hiri! Kitspahat ri tukuka ha!

IV

1182 Ho-o-o!
1183 Hiri! 'Hari; Hiri! Kitspahat ri ta iwa ha!
1184 Hiri! 'Hari; Hiri! Kitspahat ri ta iwa ha!
1185 Hiri! 'Hari; Hiri! Kitspahat ri ta iwa ha!

V

1186 Ho-o-o!
1187 Hiri! 'Hari; Hiri! Kitspahat ri ta wawe he!
1188 Hiri! 'Hari; Hiri! Kitspahat ri ta wawe he!
1189 Hiri! 'Hari; Hiri! Kitspahat ri ta wawe he!

VI

1190   Ho-o-o!
1191   Hiri! 'Hari; Hiri! Kitspahat ri ta witshpa ha!
1192   Hiri! 'Hari; Hiri! Kitspahat ri ta witshpa ha!
1193   Hiri! 'Hari; Hiri! Kitspahat ri ta witshpa ha.

Translation of First Stanza

1170   Ho-o-o!   An introductory exclamation.
1171   Hiri! 'Hari; Hiri! Kitspahat we re kusi hi!
          hiri! give heed!
          'hari, a part of iha'ri, child.
          hiri! give heed!
          kitspahat; kits, from kitzu, water; pahat, red.   The term
            means red paint.
          we, now.
          re, am.
          kusi, sitting.
          hi! from hiri! give heed!
1172, 1173   See line 1171.

Explanation by the Ku'rahus

The Ku'rahus had prepared the paint by mixing red clay with running water.   He mixes it rather dry so that what is left can remain in
the shell.   Only the right half of a shell can be used to hold the paint.
You remember what I told you of the shell and why we use it (first
ritual, part II).   The red clay we use for paint was made by Tira'wa
for this purpose.

The paint symbolizes the red clouds of the dawn, the coming of the
new day, the rising sun, the vigor of life.   The power of the new day,
the new life, is now standing before the child.

Translation of Second Stanza

1174   Ho-o-o!   An introductory exclamation.
1175   Hiri! 'Hari; Hiri! Kitspahat re ru ata ha!
          hiri! give heed!
          'hari, a part of iha'ri, child.
          hiri! give heed!
          kitspahat, red paint.
          re, is.
          ru, it.
          ata, flying.
          ha! behold!
1176, 1177   See line 1175.

Explanation by the Ku'rahus

During the singing of the second stanza the old man moves the shell containing the paint toward the child. The vigor of life is coming to the child, flying toward it as through the air, like the coming of dawn.

Translation of Third Stanza

1178   Ho-o-o! An introductory exclamation.
1179   Hiri, 'Hari; Hiri! Kitspahat ri tukuka ha!
       hiri! give heed! harken!
       'hari, a part of iha'ri, child.
       hiri! harken! give heed!
       kitspahat, red paint.
       ri, it.
       tukuka, touching.
       ha! behold!
1180, 1181   See line 1179.

Explanation by the Ku'rahus

As we sing this third stanza the old man touches the forehead with the red paint. The vigor of life, the power of the touch of the sun, is now on the child.

Translation of Fourth Stanza

1182   Ho-o-o! An introductory exclamation.
1183   Hiri! 'Hari; Hiri! Kitspahat ri ta iwa ha!
       hiri! give heed! harken!
       'hari, a part of iha'ri, child.
       hiri! harken!
       kitspahat, red paint.
       ri, it.
       ta, a part of taokut, to touch.
       iwa, downward movement.
       ha! behold!
1184, 1185   See line 1183.

Explanation by the Ku'rahus

While we sing the fourth stanza the old man makes the same lines on the face of the child as those made with the water, the brush of grass, and the ointment. This means that the vigor of life, the power of the touch of the sun, the new life of the dawn, are all from Tira'wa atius.

Translation of Fifth Stanza

1186 Ho-o-o! An introductory exclamation.
1187 Hiri! 'Hari; Hiri! Kitspahat ri ta wawe he!
    hiri! harken! give heed!
    'hari, a part of of iha'ri, child.
    hiri! harken!
    kitspahat, red paint.
    ri, it.
    ta, a part of taokut, to touch.
    wawe, spreading over.
    he! from hiri! give heed!
1188, 1189 See line 1187.

Explanation by the Ku'rahus

As we sing the fifth stanza the old man touches the child's face here and there, and then spreads the red paint entirely over it. This symbolizes the full radiance of the sun with all its power, giving to the child its vigor of life.

Translation of Sixth Stanza

1190 Ho-o-o! An introductory exclamation.
1191 Hiri! 'Hari; Hiri! Kitspahat ri ta witshpa ha!
    hiri! harken!
    'hari, a part of iha'ri, child.
    hiri! give heed!
    kitspahat, red paint.
    ri, it.
    ta, a part of taokut, to touch.
    witshpa, accomplished; completed.
    ha! behold!
1192, 1193 See line 1191.

Explanation by the Ku'rahus

We sing in this stanza that it is accomplished, that the child is encompassed by the power which Tira'wa atius has given to the sun and the vigor imparted to its day.

The old man now takes a shell containing blue paint which had been prepared by the Ku'rahus from blue clay and running water, and while we sing the first stanza of the following song he holds it before the child. This is a very sacred act.

SECOND SONG

Words and Music

(d) M. M. ♩ = 126.

• = Pulsation of the voice.   Transcribed by Edwin S. Tracy.

I

1194   Ho-o-o!
1195   Hiri! 'Hari; Hiri! Awi kots we re hre kusi hi!
1196   Hiri! 'Hari; Hiri! Awi kots we re hre kusi hi!
1197   Hiri! 'Hari; Hiri! Awi kots we re hre kusi hi!

II

1198   Ho-o-o!
1199   Hiri! 'Hari; Hiri! Awi kots we re ru ata ha!
1200   Hiri! 'Hari; Hiri! Awi kots we re ru ata ha!
1201   Hiri! 'Hari; Hiri! Awi kots we re ru ata ha!

III

1202   Ho-o-o!
1203   Hiri! 'Hari; Hiri! Awi kots we ri tukuka ha!
1204   Hiri! 'Hari; Hiri! Awi kots we ri tukuka ha!
1205   Hiri! 'Hari; Hiri! Awi kots we ri tukuka ha!

IV

1206   Ho-o-o!
1207   Hiri! 'Hari; Hiri! Awi kots we ri ta iwa ha!
1208   Hiri! 'Hari; Hiri! Awi kots we ri ta iwa ha!
1209   Hiri! 'Hari; Hiri! Awi kots we ri ta iwa ha!

V

1210   Ho-o-o!
1211   Hiri! 'Hari; Hiri! Awi kots we ri ta wawe he!
1212   Hiri! 'Hari; Hiri! Awi kots we ri ta wawe he!
1213   Hiri! 'Hari; Hiri! Awi kots we ri ta wawe he!

VI

1214   Ho-o-o!
1215   Hiri! 'Hari; Hiri! Awi kots we ri ta witshpa ha!
1216   Hiri! 'Hari; Hiri! Awi kots we ri ta witshpa ha!
1217   Hiri! 'Hari; Hiri! Awi kots we ri ta witshpa ha!

Translation of First Stanza

1194   Ho-o-o!   An introductory exclamation.
1195   Hiri! 'Hari; Hiri! Awi kots we re hre kusi hi!
   hiri! give heed!
   'hari, a part of iha'ri, child.
   hiri! harken!
   awi, a part of awiu, a picture.
   kots, a part of rekots, whitish; as a thin cloud through which
     one can see a tinge of the blue sky beyond.   Light blue.
   we, now.
   re, am.
   hre, holding.
   kusi, sitting.
   hi! from hiri! give heed!
1196, 1197   See line 1195.

Explanation by the Ku'rahus

Blue represents the sky, the place where Tira'wa atius dwells, and with this blue paint we are to make upon the child a picture of the face of Tira'wa atius.   It is a mark of Tira'wa atius' acceptance of the consecrated child and a sign of his presence.   The symbol of the dwelling place of Tira'wa atius stands before the child.

Translation of Second Stanza

1198   Ho-o-o!   An introductory exclamation.
1199   Hiri! 'Hari; Hiri! Awi kots we re ru ata ha!
   hiri! harken!
   'hari, a part of iha'ri, child.
   hiri! give heed!
   awi, a part of awiu, a picture.
   kots, light blue (paint).
   we, now.
   re, is.
   ru, it.
   ata, flying.
   ha! behold!
1200, 1201   See line 1199.

Explanation by the Ku'rahus

While we sing the second stanza the old man moves the shell containing the blue paint toward the child.   The blue of the sky where Tira'wa atius dwells is coming near, descending through the air.

Translation of Third Stanza

1202   Ho-o-o!   An introductory exclamation.
1203   Hiri! 'Hari; Hiri! Awi kots we ri tukuka ha!
      hiri! harken!
      'hari, a part of iha'ri, child.
      hiri! give heed!
      awi, a part of awiu, a picture.
      kots, light blue (paint).
      we, now.
      ri, it.
      tukuka, touching.
      ha! behold!
1204, 1205   See line 1203.

Explanation by the Ku'rahus

As we sing the third stanza the old man touches the forehead with the blue paint. The blue sky has reached the child; its forehead has been touched by the abode of Tira'wa atius.

Translation of Fourth Stanza

1206   Ho-o-o!   An introductory exclamation.
1207   Hiri! 'Hari; Hiri! Awi kots we ri ta iwa ha!
      hiri! give heed!
      'hari, a part of iha'ri, child.
      hiri! give heed!
      awi, a part of awiu, a picture.
      kots, light blue (paint).
      we, now.
      ri, it.
      ta, a part of taokut, to touch.
      iwa, downward movement.
      ha! behold!
1208, 1209   See line 1207.

Explanation by the Ku'rahus

While we sing the fourth stanza the old man traces with the blue paint the lines he has made with the water, the brush of grass, the sacred ointment, and the red paint. In these lines we see the face of Tira'wa atius, the giver of life and power to all things (see figure 179).

The lines forming an arch across the forehead and down each cheek of the child represents the dome of the sky, the abode of Tira'wa atius. The line from the middle of the forehead, the center of the arch, down the ridge of the nose is the breath of Tira'wa atius. It descends from the zenith, passing down the nose to the heart, giving life to the child.

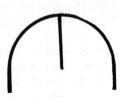

FIG. 179. The symbol of Tira'wa.

The picture of the face of Tira'wa atius is put upon the face of the consecrated child.

Translation of Fifth Stanza

1210 Ho-o-o! An introductory exclamation.
1211 Hi-ri! 'Hari; Hiri! Awi kots we ri ta wawe he!
    hiri! give heed!
    'hari, a part of iha'ri, child.
    hari! harken!
    awi, a part of awiu, a picture.
    kots, light blue (paint).
    we, now.
    ri, it.
    ta, a part of taokut, to touch.
    wawe, to spread.
    he! from hiri! give heed!
1212, 1213 See line 1211.

Explanation by the Ku'rahus

As we sing the fifth stanza the old man touches the lines here and there to make them clear; he can not spread the paint, for he is making a picture.

Translation of Sixth Stanza

1214 Ho-o-o! An introductory exclamation
1215 Hiri! 'Hari; Hiri! Awi kots weri ta witshpa ha!
    hiri! harken! give heed!
    'hari, a part of iha'ri, child.
    hari! give heed!
    awi, a part of awiu, a picture.
    kots, light blue (paint).
    we, now.
    ri, it.
    ta, a part of taokut, to touch.
    witshpa, accomplished; completed.
    ha! behold!
1216, 1217 See line 1215.

Explanation by the Ku'rahus

In the sixth stanza we sing that it is done, that the face of Tira'wa atius is upon the face of the consecrated child.

There is a group of stars overhead which forms a circle (Corona Borealis). This is a circle of chiefs. Tira'wa atius placed them there and directed them to paint their faces with the same lines we have put upon the child, and all who are to be leaders must be so painted.

From this circle of stars came a society called Raristesharu. All dances (societies) given by Tira'wa atius are called raris; tesharu means chief (the te is a modification of le, in the word lesharu, chief). The members of the society Raristesharu are chiefs, and these men are permitted by the star chiefs to paint their faces with the blue lines and to wear the downy feather on the head. The members of this society do not dance and sing; they talk quietly and try to be like the stars.

I was told that it was from this society that permission was given to paint the child with the blue lines and to put the downy feather upon it.

PART IV. PUTTING ON THE SYMBOLS

Explanation by the Ku'rahus

The old man now takes a bunch of eagle down, and as we sing the first stanza of the following song he holds it before the child.

FIRST SONG

Words and Music

(e) M. M. ♪ = 126.

• = Pulsation of the voice.   Transcribed by Edwin S. Tracy.

I

1218 Ho-o-o!
1219 Hiri! 'Hari; Hiri! Kaokto we re hre kusi hi!
1220 Hiri! 'Hari; Hiri! Kaokto we re hre kusi hi!
1221 Hiri! 'Hari; Hiri! Kaokto we re hre kusi hi!

II

1222 Ho-o-o!
1223 Hiri! 'Hari; Hiri! Kaokto we re ru ata ha!
1224 Hiri! 'Hari; Hiri! Kaokto we re ru ata ha!
1225 Hiri! 'Hari; Hiri! Kaokto we re ru ata ha!

III

1226 Ho-o-o!
1227 Hiri! 'Hari; Hiri! Kaokto we ri tukuka ha!
1228 Hiri! 'Hari; Hiri! Kaokto we ri tukuka ha!
1229 Hiri! 'Hari; Hiri! Kaokto we ri tukuka ha!

IV

1230   Ho-o-o!
1231   Hiri! 'Hari; Hiri! Kaokto we ri kittawe he!
1232   Hiri! 'Hari; Hiri! Kaokto we ri kittawe he!
1233   Hiri! 'Hari; Hiri! Kaokto we ri kittawe he!

V

1234   Ho-o-o!
1235   Hiri! 'Hari; Hiri! Kaokto we ri ta witshpa ha!
1236   Hiri! 'Hari; Hiri! Kaokto we ri ta witshpa ha!
1237   Hiri! 'Hari; Hiri! Kaokto we ri ta witshpa ha!

Translation of First Stanza

1218   Ho-o-o!   An introductory exclamation.
1219   Hiri! 'Hari; Hiri! Kaokto we re hre kusi hi!
        hiri! harken.
        'hari, a part of iha'ri, child.
        hiri! give heed!
        kaokto, down from the eagle.
        we, now.
        re, am.
        hre, holding.
        kusi, sitting.
        hi! from hiri! give heed!
1220, 1221   See line 1219.

Explanation by the Ku'rahus.

The down represents the high, light clouds (cirrus) in the blue of the sky; they are near the abode of Tira'wa atius.

The down is taken from under the wings of the white eagle. The white eagle is the mate of the brown eagle, and the child is the child of Kawas, the brown eagle. The down grew close to the heart of the eagle and moved as the eagle breathed. It represents the breath and life of the white eagle, the father of the child.

Translation of Second Stanza

1222   Ho-o-o!   An introductory exclamation.
1223   Hiri! 'Hari; Hiri! Kaokto we re ru ata ha!
        hiri! harken!
        'hari, a part of iha'ri, child.
        hiri! give heed!
        kaokto, eagle's down.
        we, now.
        re, is.
        ru, it.
        ata, flying.
        ha! behold!
1224, 1225   See line 1223.

Explanation by the Ku'rahus

As we sing the second stanza, the old man moves the down near the child. The soft, white clouds that are near the abode of Tira'wa atius are coming near the head of the child.

Translation of Third Stanza

1226 Hc-o-o! An introductory exclamation.
1227 Hiri! 'Hari; Hiri! Kaokto we ri tukuka ha!
  hiri! harken!
  'hari, a part of iha'ri, child.
  hiri! give heed!
  kaokto, the down of the eagle.
  we, now.
  ri, it
  tukuka, touching.
  ha! behold!
1228, 1229 See line 1227.

Explanation by the Ku'rahus

As we sing this stanza, the old man touches the head of the child with the down. The light clouds have reached the child.

Translation of Fourth Stanza

1230 Ho-o-o! An introductory exclamation.
1231 Hiri! 'Hari; Hiri! Kaokto we ri kittawe he!
  hiri! give heed.
  'hari, a part of iha'ri, child.
  hiri! give heed.
  kaokto, eagle's down.
  we, now.
  ri, it.
  kittawe; kit, top; ta, from taokut, to touch; we, a part of
   tawe, standing; the word means standing on the top of
   the child's head.
  he! from hiri! give heed!
1232, 1233 See line 1231.

Explanation by the Ku'rahus

While we sing the fourth stanza the old man opens his hand and lets the down fall upon the hair. The soft, white clouds near the abode of Tira'wa atius have dropped and covered the head of the child.

Translation of Fifth Stanza

1234 Ho-o-o!   An introductory exclamation.
1235 Hiri! 'Hari; Hiri! Kaokto we ri ta witshpa ha!
      hiri! give heed!
      'hari, a part of iha'ri, child.
      hiri! give heed!
      kaokto, eagle's down.
      we, now.
      ri, it.
      ta, a part of taokut, to touch.
      witshpa, accomplished.
      ha! behold!
1236, 1237 See line 1235.

Explanation by the Ku'rahus

We sing in the fifth stanza that it is accomplished, the head of the consecrated child now rests in the soft, white clouds which float near the dwelling place of Tira'wa atius.

The Ku'rahus takes from the brown-eagle feathered stem a downy feather and gives it to the old man, who, while we sing the first stanza, holds it before the child.

SECOND SONG

Words and Music

(f) M. M. ♪ = 126.
  • = Pulsation of the voice.   Transcribed by Edwin S. Tracy.

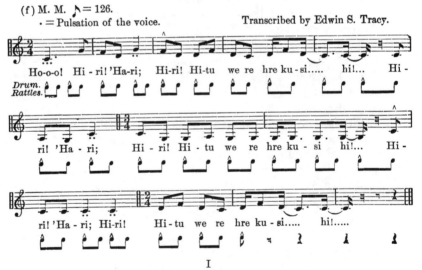

I

1238 Ho-o-o!
1239 Hiri! 'Hari; Hiri! Hitu we re hre kusi hi!
1240 Hiri! 'Hari; Hiri! Hitu we re hre kusi hi!
1241 Hiri! 'Hari; Hiri! Hitu we re hre kusi hi!

II

1242 Ho-o-o!
1243 Hiri! 'Hari; Hiri! Hitu we re ru ata ha!
1244 Hiri! 'Hari; Hiri! Hitu we re ru ata ha!
1245 Hiri! 'Hari; Hiri! Hitu we re ru ata ha!

III

1246 Ho-o-o!
1247 Hiri! 'Hari; Hiri! Hitu we ri tukuka ha!
1248 Hiri! 'Hari; Hiri! Hitu we ri tukuka ha!
1249 Hiri! 'Hari; Hiri! Hitu we ri tukuka ha!

IV

1250 Ho-o-o!
1251 Hiri! 'Hari; Hiri! Hitu we ri kittawe he!
1252 Hiri! 'Hari; Hiri! Hitu we ri kittawe he!
1253 Hiri! 'Hari; Hiri! Hitu we ri kittawe he!

V

1254 Ho-o-o!
1255 Hiri! 'Hari; Hiri! Hitu we ri ta witshpa ha!
1256 Hiri! 'Hari; Hiri! Hitu we ri ta witshpa ha!
1257 Hiri! 'Hari; Hiri! Hitu we ri ta witshpa ha!

Translation of First Stanza

1238 Ho-o-o! An introductory exclamation.
1239 Hiri! 'Hari; Hiri! Hitu we re hre kusi hi!
  hiri! give heed!
  'hari, a part of iha'ri, child.
  hiri! give heed!
  hitu, feather; a downy, soft feather.
  we, now.
  re, am.
  hre, holding.
  kusi, sitting.
  hi! from hiri! give heed!
1240, 1241 See line 1239.

Explanation by the Ku'rahus

The downy, white feather came from the white eagle, the father of the child. Soft, blue feathers were bound around its stem, to which a small buckskin thong was attached, so that the feather could be tied upon the hair of the child. The soft, blue feathers represent the blue sky above the clouds; the white, downy feather itself, which is ever moving, as if it were breathing, represents Tira'wa atius, who dwells beyond the blue sky, which is above the soft, white clouds.

All during the ceremony this feather has been tied upon the brown-eagle feathered stem, close to the owl feathers. It is different from the downy feather worn by the Ku'rahus and his assistant, for at its stem there is a little one, like a small branch, that is to show that the little child is the child of Tira'wa atius.

This double feather now stands before the child.

Translation of Second Stanza

1242 Ho-o-o! An introductory exclamation.
1243 Hiri! 'Hari; Hiri! Hitu we re ru ata ha!
    hiri! give heed!
    'hari, a part of iha'ri, child.
    hiri! give heed!
    hitu, a downy feather.
    we, now.
    re, is.
    ru, it.
    ata, flying.
    ha! behold!
1244, 1245 See line 1243.

Explanation by the Ku'rahus

As we sing the second stanza the old man moves the feather toward the child's head. The feather representing Tira'wa atius is now flying through the air, coming near the head of the little child.

Translation of Third Stanza

1246 Ho-o-o! An introductory exclamation.
1247 Hiri! 'Hari; Hiri! Hitu we ri tukuka ha!
    hiri! give heed!
    'hari, a part of iha'ri, child.
    hiri! give heed!
    hitu, downy feather.
    we, now.
    ri, it.
    tukuka, touching.
    ha! behold!
1248, 1249 See line 1247.

Explanation by the Ku'rahus

During the singing of this stanza the old man touches the head of the child with the downy white feather. The symbol of Tira'wa atius has reached the child and rests above the white, downy clouds.

Translation of Fourth Stanza

1250 Ho-o-o! An introductory exclamation.
1251 Hiri! 'Hari; Hiri! Hitu we ri kittawe he!
  hiri! give heed!
  'hari, child.
  hiri! give heed!
  hitu, downy feather.
  we, now.
  ri, it.
  kittawe, standing on top (of the child's head).
  he! from hiri! give heed!
1252, 1253 See line 1251.

Explanation by the Ku'rahus

While we sing this fourth stanza, the old man ties the downy feather on the child's hair. Tira'wa atius is now with the little child as the double feather waves over its head.

Translation of Fifth Stanza

1254 Ho-o-o! An introductory exclamation.
1255 Hiri! 'Hari; Hiri! Hitu we ri ta witshpa ha!
  hiri! harken!
  'hari, child.
  hiri! harken! give heed!
  hitu, downy feather.
  we, now.
  ri, it.
  ta, a part of taokut, to touch.
  witshpa, accomplished, completed.
  ha! behold!
1256, 1257 See line 1255.

Explanation by the Ku'rahus

Now we sing that all is accomplished. The child has been fully prepared, the sacred symbols put upon it, the powers from above have come, and Tira'wa atius breathes over it.

The child is now told to look into the bowl of water and behold its face. The running water symbolizes the passing on of generations, one following another. The little child looks on the water and sees its own likeness, as it will see that likeness in its children and children's children. The face of Tira'wa atius is there also, giving promise that the life of the child shall go on, as the waters flow over the land.

A black covering is now put over the child's head by the Ku'rahus, that no one may look on the holy symbols. Only Tira'wa looks on them and knows all that they mean. We do not look on them, for they are holy.[a]

The Ku'rahus, handing the bowl of water to the young man who brought it into the lodge, tells him what to do before he throws it away.

The young man with the bowl passes through the circle of warriors and goes by the south to the east, then to the northeast, where he lifts a few drops to that direction and lets them fall on the rim of the fireplace. Then he passes to the northwest and repeats his action. At the west he lifts a few drops to the zenith and lets them fall on the rim of the fireplace. Then he passes on to the southwest, offering the water as before, and then to the southeast, where he repeats his offering. Thence he goes to the inner door of the lodge, where he pauses, then passes through the entrance way, and when he is out under the early morning sky he throws the water toward the east.

This is done because all the rivers flow toward the east.

EIGHTEENTH RITUAL. FULFILMENT PREFIGURED

PART I. MAKING THE NEST

Explanation by the Ku'rahus

The old man who has been preparing the child now rises from his position and, stepping to one side, leaves the Ku'rahus and his assistant standing directly in front of the little child.

These two lift the feathered stems and the rattles and wave their arms like the wings of a bird as the following song is sung three times. No drum is used, but the rattles and the whistle accompany the song.

SONG

Words and Music

M. M. ♪ = 192.
• = Pulsation of the voice.   Transcribed by Edwin S. Tracy.
No drum.

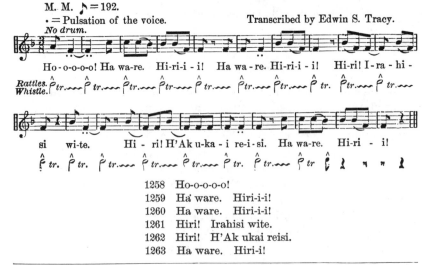

Ho-o-o-o-o! Ha wa-re. Hi-ri-i - i! Ha wa-re. Hi-ri-i - i! Hi-ri! I-ra - hi -

si wi-te. Hi - ri! H'Ak u-ka- i re-i-si. Ha wa-re. Hi-ri - i!

```
1258   Ho-o-o-o-o!
1259   Ha' ware.   Hiri-i-i!
1260   Ha ware.    Hiri-i-i!
1261   Hiri!   Irahisi wite.
1262   Hiri!   H'Ak ukai reisi.
1263   Ha ware.   Hiri-i!
```

---

[a] The Ku'rahus did not remember what was formerly used as a covering for the head of the child; latterly it has been a black silk handkerchief.

Translation

1258 Ho-o-o-o-o! An introductory exclamation.
1259 Ha ware. Hiri-i-i!
       ha, yonder.
       ware, a part of teware, flying, circling about.
       hiri! give heed! harken!
       i-i, vowel prolongations.
1260 See line 1259.
1261 Hiri! Irahisi wite.
       hiri! give heed! harken!
       irahisi, irasi, it is you.   The syllable hi is introduced to
          modify the word so as to conform to the music.
       wite, conjecture, surmise.
1262 Hiri! H'Ak ukai reisi.
       hiri! give heed! harken!
       h'Ak; h', the sign of breath, life; ak, a part of akaro, a
          dwelling: h'Ak, the stretch of the earth under the dome
          of the heavens.
       ukai, to put in.
       reisi, a modification of irasi, it is you.
1263 See line 1259.

Explanation by the Ku'rahus

After the third repeat, the Ku'rahus calls out, "Open a way!" and
the warriors who form the line separate at the north and at the south,
and the brown-eagle feathered stem is carried through the north opening and the white-eagle feathered stem through the south opening.
The white eagle then flies back and forth before the line of warriors
guarding the brown eagle as she circles the fireplace.

When the Ku'rahus, carrying the brown-eagle feathered stem,
reaches the west he pauses, and then goes to the northwest, near the
rim of the fireplace, where he makes a circle with the big toe of his
left foot and covers the outline with down.   Then he passes to the
northeast and makes another circle, marking it also with down; then
to the southeast, where he makes a third circle, then to the southwest,
where he makes the fourth circle.   Meanwhile the song is being sung
for the fourth time, and the white eagle is still flying back and forth
in front of the line of warriors.

The circle represents a nest, and is drawn by the toe because the
eagle builds its nest with its claws.   Although we are imitating the
bird making its nest, there is another meaning to the action; we are
thinking of Tira'wa making the world for the people to live in.   If you
go on a high hill and look around, you will see the sky touching
the earth on every side, and within this circular inclosure the people
live.   So the circles we have made are not only nests, but they also

represent the circle Tira'wa atius has made for the dwelling place of all the people. The circles also stand for the kinship group, the clan, and the tribe.

The down represents the light clouds near the dwelling place of Tira'wa—the dome of the sky over the dwelling place of the people—and it stands for the protection of Tira'wa. When there is no down to be had, white ashes can be used. I do not know what the ashes mean, but I think they are to make the outline distinct and to represent the white down.

The nests are four, because at the four directions are the paths down which the powers from above descend. The four winds guard these paths and protect the life of man.

After the four nests are made, the feathered stems are laid at rest.

The Ku'rahus then takes bits of fat which have been preserved from an animal consecrated to Tira'wa and puts them with some native tobacco into an oriole's nest and hands the nest to the chief, who conceals it in his hands.

The bits of fat represent the droppings that mark the trail made by the hunters as they carry the meat home from the field. This trail is called the path dropping fatness, and means plenty. Fat, therefore, stands for the promise of abundant food.

The oriole's nest is used because Tira'wa made this bird build its nest so that no harm could come to it. It hangs high, is skillfully made, and is secure. An eagle's nest may be torn away by a storm, but the oriole's nest sways in the wind and is not hurt.

PART II. SYMBOLIC FULFILMENT

Explanation by the Ku'rahus

Now a robe is spread on the ground and the child is placed on it with his feet and legs projecting beyond the edge. Four men are appointed to carry the child. One goes on each side and takes hold of the robe and lifts it; a man at the back of the child steadies it as it is raised and carried, while the fourth man holds another robe over its feet and legs.

The chief and the Ku'rahus precede the child to the circle at the northwest, where it is held over the nest so that its feet rest within the circle. The chief puts his hands under the robe held over the child's legs and drops the oriole's nest within the circle so that the child's feet rest on it. No one but the chief and the Ku'rahus know what is being done beneath the robe. The chief takes up the nest, concealing it from view, and goes to the circle at the northeast, to which the child has also been carried, and in the same way places its feet on it. The same act is repeated at the circles in the southeast and the southwest.

The child represents the young generation, the continuation of life, and when it is put in the circle it typifies the bird laying its eggs. The child is covered up, for no one knows when a bird lays its eggs or when a new birth takes place; only Tira′wa can know when life is given. The putting of the child's feet in the circle means the giving of new life, the resting of its feet upon the oriole's nest means promised security to the new life, the fat is a promise of plenty of food, and the tobacco is an offering in recognition that all things come from Tira′wa. The entire act means that the clan or tribe of the Son shall increase, that there shall be peace and security, and that the land shall be covered with fatness. This is the promise of Tira′wa through the Hako.

Four times the child is taken around the fire and its feet are placed within the four circles during the singing of the following song, but the nest is used only on the first round.

SONG

Words and Music

M. M. ♪ = 126.
• = Pulsation of the voice.
No drum.   Transcribed by Edwin S. Tracy.

Ho-o-o! We ra ti ka ri - ki ra ri - ki hi! Pi - ra-o ka ri - kï
ra ri - ki hi! Pi - ra - o ka ri - ki ra ri - ki hi!

1264   Ho-o-o!
1265   We ra ti ka riki ra riki hi!
1266   Pirao ka riki ra riki hi!
1267   Pirao ka riki ra riki hi!

Translation

1264   Ho-o-o!   An introductory exclamation.
1265   We ra ti ka riki ra riki hi!
     we, now.
     ra, is.
     ti, he.
     ka, from akaro, an inclosure; the space or room within.
     riki, standing.
     ra, is.
     riki, standing.
     hi, vowel prolongation.

1266   Pirao ka riki ra riki hi!
    pirao, child.
    ka, within.
    riki, standing.
    ra, is.
    riki, standing.
    hi, vowel prolongation.
1267   See line 1266.

Explanation by the Ku'rahus

At the close of this song and ceremony the child is carried back
and seated behind the holy place. The chief stands behind the child,
and a feathered stem is laid on each side of it, the brown eagle to the
north.

PART III. THANK OFFERING

Explanation by the Ku'rahus

Live coals are brought and put on the holy place before the child,
and the Ku'rahus cuts bits of consecrated fat and sweet grass and
lays them on the coals. All the people silently watch the sweet-
smelling smoke as it curls upward. When the smoke is well on its
way to Tira'wa, the Ku'rahus, standing at the west, lifts the feathered
stems, the wildcat skin, and all the other sacred objects of the Hako
and waves them four times through the smoke toward the east, and
then lays them down as they were before. When the chief and his
assistant have raised the child to its feet, the chief puts his hands in
the sweet smoke and passes them over its head, then puts his hands
back into the smoke and rubs the child from its shoulders down its
arms. Again he puts his hands in the smoke and passes them down
the body of the child. For the fourth time he puts his hands in the
smoke and strokes the legs of the child to its feet and presses them
upon the earth. Then the child is again seated.

Now the Ku'rahus says, "My Children, the offering of sweet smoke
is for you." After that the chief and the assistant will put smoke
on any of the Children who so desire. This takes some time, for
every one of the Children present wishes to have the blessing of the
smoke. At length the chief puts the smoke upon himself, and the
Ku'rahus and his assistant on themselves, and last of all the two
young men who are to perform the final dance bless themselves with
the smoke.

The Ku'rahus returns the coals to the fireplace and spreads the
ashes over the ground so that nothing will show where they have
been. Next he goes to the first circle in the northwest and with his
right foot rubs away the outline. He then proceeds to the nest-circle
at the northeast and rubs that away, and so on with the other two.
The doctors follow, the one with the left wing sweeping away all signs
of the nests on the north side of the fireplace, while the doctor with
the right wing does the same to those on the south side.

The chief, the Father of the Hako party, now takes the little child in his arms and, going outside of the lodge, sits down near the door, where he remains during the final dance and the presentation of gifts by the children.

THIRD DIVISION. THE DANCE OF THANKS

NINETEENTH RITUAL

PART I. THE CALL TO THE CHILDREN

Explanation by the Ku'rahus

Before the entrance to the lodge mats are spread, on which sit those who are to take part in the coming ceremony.

The Ku'rahus and his assistant are directly before the door. At the left of them are two doctors who have not heretofore taken part. They carry their large rattles, and have lent two similar ones to the Ku'rahus and his assistant. They have also lent for this occasion their peculiar drums to the singers. These drums are made of the section of a tree hollowed out by fire, over the open end of which a skin has been stretched and securely tied. The singers are seated in a semicircle about each of the two drums (see figure 180). In front of the Ku'rahus and the singers sits the chief, and before him is the little child. The doctors with the eagle wings are on either side, the one with the left wing toward the north, the one with the right wing toward the south. In front of them are the two dancers. The space within which they are to dance is inclosed on the south by a line of prominent men from the Son's party, and on the north by a line from the Father's. These lines beginning at the lodge end each with a warrior selected by the Ku'rahus for his valorous record. These warriors wear buffalo robes with the hair side out and are girded about the waist with a hair lariat, which is to be used in leading the horses brought as gifts to the Fathers. Beyond these lines of prominent men, who are seated, are gathered the people, those belonging to the tribe of the Son on the south and those of the Hako party on the north.

The Ku'rahus gives a small tuft of white down to a man whose hands have not been painted with sacred ointment, and directs him where to place it on the head of the chief. The place is on the spot where a baby's skull is open, and you can see it breathe. The white down represents the white clouds which lie near the abode of Tira'wa atius, whence he sends down the breath of life to man. Chiefs were appointed by Tira'wa through the North Star. The tuft of down also signifies that the chief's office is from above.

The two feathered stems, the rattles, the wildcat skin, and the ear of corn are given to the chief to hold.

The two young men who have been selected to dance are stripped to the breechcloth, and red circles are made with the sacred paint on their backs and breasts. The circles are outlined faintly, so as not to

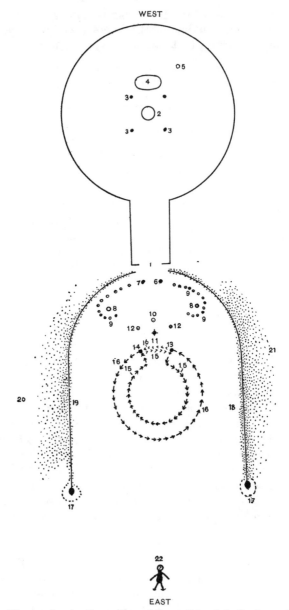

FIG. 180. Diagram showing the positions of the participants in the dance of thanks.

1, the entrance to the lodge; 2, the fireplace; 3, inner posts supporting the roof; 4, the holy place; 5, the drum; 6, the Ku'rahus; 7, his assistant; 8, the drums of the doctors; 9, singers; 10, the Father (a chief); 11, the little child; 12, the bearers of the eagle wings; 13, the dancer with the brown-eagle feathered stem; 14, the dancer with the white-eagle feathered stem; 15, the line of the brown-eagle dancer; 16, the line of the white-eagle dancer; 17, warriors who take the ponies off; 18, prominent men of the Hako party; 19, prominent men of the Son's party; 20, members of the Son's tribe, the Children; 21, members of the Hako party; 22, effigy on which war honors are enacted.

attract attention, for they represent the nest and are a part of the secret ceremony. The downy eagle feather which until now has been worn by the Ku'rahus is fastened to the scalp lock of the dancer who is to bear the brown-eagle feathered stem, and the downy feather worn by the assistant is tied to the hair of the dancer who will hold the white-eagle feathered stem.

A man, previously chosen by the Ku'rahus, steps up to the chief and receives from him the two feathered stems and the rattles. He makes the sign of thanks for the honor by passing his hands down the arms of the chief.   Then, holding the brown-eagle feathered stem in his right hand, he recounts a successful capture of booty, then tells of a war adventure in which he struck an enemy without receiving any harm.   After this he hands the brown-eagle feathered stem and a rattle to the dancer sitting at the north.   Holding up the white-eagle feathered stem, he tells of a successful foray, in which he captured ponies, and then of a victory in war, after which he hands the white-eagle feathered stem and a rattle to the dancer sitting at the south and takes his own place in the line of prominent men belonging to the Father's party.

The first song is now sung, to the accompaniment of the large rattles, the doctors' drums, and the whistle.

FIRST SONG

Words and Music

M. M. ♪ = 152.
• = Pulsation of the voice.   Transcribed by Edwin S. Tracy.

1268 Hiri! Hura-a i, hura i;   1271 Hiri! Hura;
1269 Hiri! Hura i, hura i, hura i;   1272 Hiri! Hura; Hiri! Hura iha!
1270 Hiri! Hura i, hura i;

Translation

1268 Hiri! Hura-a i, hura i.

   hiri! an exclamation calling attention and demanding that
      heed be given; harken!

   hura, let come.

   a, vowel prolongation.

   i, a part of the word iha're, young, or children.

   hura i, let the children come.

1269 Hiri! Hura i, hura i, hura i. See line 1268.

1270 Hiri! Hura i, hura i. See line 1268.

1271 Hiri! Hura. See line 1268.

1272 Hiri! Hura; Hiri! Hura iha!

   Hiri! Hura; Hiri! Hura. See line 1268.

   iha, a part of the word iha're, children, young.

Explanation by the Ku'rahus

This song is addressed to the Children that they may know that all
is now ready for the reception of their gifts.

The words of the song mean: "Harken! Give attention! Let the
Children come!"

The song is sung twice and then we pause; this is to give the Children time to come together.

After a little while we sing the second song.

SECOND SONG

Words and Music

M. M. ♪ = 152.
• = Pulsation of the voice.   Transcribed by Edwin S. Tracy.

1273 I ra, i ra, hira-a hira ha-a;
1274 I ra, i ra, hira-a hira ha-a;
1275 Iri ra!
1276 I ra, i ra, hira-a;
1277 I ra, hira ha-a!

Translation

1273 I ra, i ra, hira-a hira ha-a.

    i, a part of the word iha're, children, young.

    ra, come.

    hira, when come, when they do come.

    a, vowel prolongation.

    hira, translated above.

    ha, yonder.

    a, vowel prolongation.

1274 See line 1273.

1275 Iri ra!

    iri, there.

    ra, coming.

1276 I ra, i ra, hira-a.   See line 1273.

1277 I ra, hira ha-a!   See line 1273.

Explanation by the Ku'rahus

The Children are now gathering; they are moving about on their side (see figure 180), men, women, and children.

The words mean: "When the Children come, they will come from yonder."

Although there is much noise and bustle where the Children are busily preparing, yet this song can be heard by them and they hasten with their preparations.

We sing the song twice.

As the people are seen moving toward the place where we are sitting, we sing the next song.

THIRD SONG

Words and Music

M. M. ♩.=56.

• = Pulsation of the voice.

Transcribed by Edwin S. Tracy.

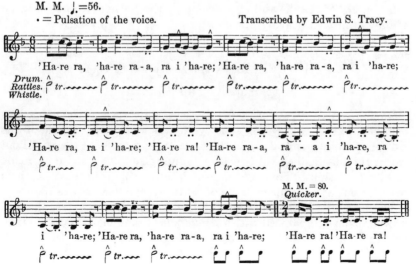

'Ha-re ra, 'ha-re ra-a, ra i 'ha-re; 'Ha-re ra, 'ha-re ra-a, ra i 'ha-re;

Drum.
Rattles.
Whistle.

'Ha-re ra, ra i 'ha-re; 'Ha-re ra! 'Ha-re ra-a, ra - a i 'ha-re, ra

M. M. = 80.
Quicker.

i 'ha-re; 'Ha-re ra, 'ha-re ra-a, ra i 'ha-re; 'Ha-re ra! 'Ha-re ra!

1278   'Hare ra, 'hare ra-a, ra i 'hare;
1279   'Hare ra, 'hare ra-a, ra i 'hare;
1280   'Hare ra, ra i 'hare;
1281   'Hare ra!
1282   'Hare ra-a, ra-a i 'hare, ra i 'hare;
1283   'Hare ra, 'hare ra-a, ra i 'hare;
1284   'Hare ra!   'Hare ra!

Translation

1278   'Hare ra, 'hare ra-a, ra i 'hare.
       'hare, a part of the word iha're, children, young.
       ra, coming.
       'hare ra.   Translated above.
       a, vowel prolongation.
       ra, come, or coming.
       i, a part of the word titako, here, where I am.
       'hare, children.
1279   See line 1278.
1280   'Hare ra, ra i hare.   See line 1278.
1281   'Hare ra!   See line 1278.
1282   'Hare ra-a, ra-a i 'hare, ra i 'hare.   See line 1278.
1283   See line 1278.
1284   'Hare ra!   'Hare ra!   See line 1278.

Explanation by the Ku'rahus

The words of this song mean: "The Children are coming, coming here where I am sitting."

At the close of this song a man selected by the Ku'rahus utters a long, loud cry: "Ho-o-o-o-o-o-o!" It is answered by all the Hako party; their shout is broken by the hands beating on the mouth: "Ha-a-a-a-a-a!" The drums and rattles sound at the same time.

It is a cry of thanks and of welcome by the Fathers to the Children as they approach bearing gifts.

As soon as the cries cease the Ku'rahus begins one of the dance songs.

PART II.   THE DANCE AND RECEPTION OF GIFTS

Explanation by the Ku'rahus

On the fourth night (of the Hako ceremony), while the lodge was being circled sixteen times, some young men, at the direction of the Ku'rahus, went out and made the figure of a man from grass and old garments and fastened it to a small sapling so that it could be made to stand upright. This figure, which has been concealed, is now brought out and set up in front of all the people (see figure 180).

The men of the tribe of the Children, dressed in their regalia and war bonnets, and painted with the symbols of the society to which they belong, come up with their horses, which are led by one of the owner's little children.   Each man stops at the effigy and there, treating the figure as he did his enemy, he acts out a deed of valor and then recounts its story.   He does this to honor his child, who is taking the gift of a horse to the Fathers.

As the child approaches, the chief goes toward him with the wild-cat skin and the ear of corn; he strokes the child's head with the ear of corn.   This movement means thanks for the gift and the invoking of a blessing upon the child.

Meanwhile one of the warriors at the end of the line (see figure 180) comes forward, and with his hair rope leads the horse away and gives it in charge of some one, and the man appointed to keep count makes a record of it.

These things are all going on at once while the young men are dancing.   When the dance song begins the two young men rise, each holding in his left hand, high up over his head, a feathered stem and in his right a rattle.   Both start at the same time and as they leap and dance they wave the feathered stems to simulate the flight of the eagle.   The dancer with the brown-eagle feathered stem goes from the north around by the south and pauses when he reaches the place where the dancer with the white-eagle feathered stem started, while the latter goes outside the path of the former by the south and pauses when he reaches the place at the north where the dancer bearing the brown-eagle feathered stem had stood.   There the two dancers stand until the song is finished, when they cross over and take their own proper places, the brown eagle at the north and the white eagle at the south.   Whenever the song is repeated, they rise and dance again in the same manner.

The circle of the white eagle is always outside that of the brown eagle, for the white eagle is the male and its place is outside to defend the female.   The brown eagle always moves from the north around to the south and the white eagle goes from the south to the north; the two move in opposite directions so that they may come together; the male and female must conjoin.

There are two dance songs; they both mean the same and there is no order in which they must be sung.

The words mean "Now fly, you eagles, as we give thanks to the Children."

DANCE SONG

Words and Music

M. M. ♪ = 200.

• = Pulsation of the voice.   Transcribed by Edwin S. Tracy.

Ho-o-o-o! Ra-wa sa wa-ri! I-ri i-ha-re! I-ri i-ha-re-e!

Ra-wa sa wa-ri, ra-wa sa wa-ri! I-ri i-ha-re!

I-ri i-ha-re-e! Ra-wa sa wa-ri, ra-wa sa wa-ri!

I-ri i-ha-re! I-ri i-ha-re-e! Ra-wa sa wa-ri!

```
1285  Ho-o-o-o!
1286  Rawa sa wari!  Iri ihare!  Iri ihare-e!
1287  Rawa sa wari, rawa sa wari!  Iri ihare!  Iri ihare-e!
1288  Rawa sa wari, rawa sa wari!  Iri ihare!  Iri ihare-e!
1289  Rawa sa wari!
```

Translation of Fourth Song

1285 Ho-o-o-o! An introductory exclamation.
1286 Rawa sa wari! Iri ihare! Iri ihare-e!
  rawa, now; a signal to start.
  sa, you; refers to the eagles personated by the dancers.
  wari, fly.
  iri, a part of nawairi, an expression of thankfulness.
  ihare, children, young; refers to the Children.
  iri, translated above.
  ihare, translated above.
  e, vowel prolongation.
1287 Rawa sa wari, rawa sa wari! Iri ihare! Iri ihare-e! See line
  1286.
1288 See line 1287.
1289 Rawa sa wari! See line 1286.

DANCE SONG

Words and Music

M. M. ♪ = 200.
· = Pulsation of the voice.   Transcribed by Edwin S. Tracy.

Ho-o-o-o! Ha! I-ra hi-ru-ra! Ha! I-ra hi-ru-ra! Ha! I-ra hi-ru-ra!

Drum.
Rattles.

Ha! I - ra...... hi-ru-ra! Ha! I - ra...... hi-ru-ra! Ha! I - ra...... hi-ru-ra!

Spoken.

Ha! I-ra hi-ru-ra! A! Hi ra-a! Ha! I-ra hi-ru-ra! Ha! I-ra...... hi-ru-ra!

1290 Ho-o-o-o!
1291 Ha! Ira hirura!
1292 Ha! Ira hirura! Ha! Ira hirura!
1293 Ha! Ira hirura! Ha! Ira hirura!
1294 Ha! Ira hirura! Ha! Ira hirura!
1295 A! Hi ra-a!
1296 Ha! Ira hirura! Ha! Ira hirura!

Translation of Fifth Song

1290 Ho-o-o-o! An introductory exclamation.
1291 Ha! Ira hirura!
  ha! behold!
  ira, coming.
  hirura, yonder he is coming (refers to the child bringing a
   gift).
1292–1294 See line 1291.
1295 A! Hi ra-a!
  a! the same as ha! behold!
  hi, a part of hirura, yonder he is coming.
  ra-a; ra, coming; a, vowel prolongation.
1296 See line 1291.

Explanation by the Ku'rahus

If a man of the Father's party desires to count his war honors he steps out in front of the dancers. The men stop and go to their proper places; the song stops and the man tells his deed of valor. At its close the responsive cry is given by the people; then the song begins again and the dance is resumed.

Sometimes one of the Children has not been able to catch the horse he intends to give away. He comes forward with his little child, who carries a small stick and hands it to the chief, who turns it over to the assistant chief, who passes it on to the record keeper. The child is blessed with the corn.

At any time during this dance of thanks a poor person can come up to the consecrated child who is sitting in front of the chief and take away the robe that is on it, for the robe has been put on the child as a gift to the poor. When one robe is taken, the assistant chief places another robe on the child, and it often happens that several robes or blankets are given away to the poor in this manner.

After a time one of the chiefs of the tribe of the Son rises and asks if all have made their gifts. This is a signal that the end is near. Finally, some one of the party of the Son rises and says, " Father, you must be tired; end this!" and he makes the sign with his hands which signifies cutting off, and the dance stops. Sometimes only the sign is made, but generally the words are spoken.

Then the prominent men of the Fathers and of the Children enter the lodge for the final ceremony.

FOURTH DIVISION. PRESENTATION OF THE HAKO

TWENTIETH RITUAL

PART I. BLESSING THE CHILD

Explanation by the Ku'rahus

At the close of the dance of thanks the Children scatter in every direction, but the leading men enter the lodge and sit down at the south side. The Son sits either in the middle of the line on the south, or in his proper place just south of the entrance, near the door.

The consecrated child is taken by the chief behind the holy place. The two dancers advance to lay down the feathered stems, one at each side of the little child, the brown-eagle feathered stem toward the north, the white feathered stem toward the south. Then they remove the downy feathers from their hair and give them to the Ku'rahus, who ties them on the feathered stems.

The Ku'rahus then girds the robe about his waist with the hair rope and lifts tne brown-eagle feathered stem. His assistant takes up the white-eagle feathered stem, the chief, with the cat skin and the ear of corn, steps between the Ku'rahus and his assistant, and the doctors with the eagle wings take their places at either side. The five men stand before the child and sing the following song (see figure 181).

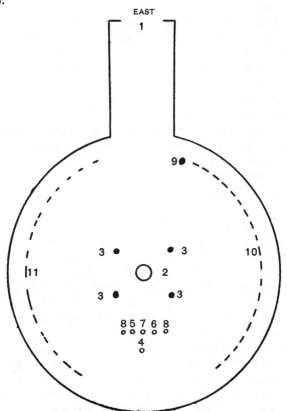

FIG. 181. Diagram of the Son's lodge during the presentation of the Hako.

1, the entrance to the lodge; 2, the fireplace; 3, inner posts supporting the dome-shaped roof; 4, the little child; 5, the Ku'rahus; 6, his assistant; 7, the Father (a chief); 8, the bearers of the eagle wings; 9, the Son, father of the little child; 10, leading men of the Son's party; 11, leading men of the Father's party.

SONG

Words and Music

M. M. ♩=56.

• = Pulsation of the voice.   Transcribed by Edwin S. Tracy.

No drum.

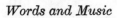

Ho-o-o-o! H'I re ra! H'I re ra!   Pi-ra u-ta ha - o!   Pi-ra u-ta, u - ta ha - o!

Rattles.

1297 Ho-o-o-o!
1298 H'I re ra!
1299 H'I re ra!
1300 Pira uta hao!
1301 Pira uta, uta hao!

Translation

1297 Ho-o-o-o! An introductory exclamation to the song.
1298 H'I re ra!
   h', the symbol of breath; breathing forth life.
   I, a part of the word Tira'wa, the mighty power above.
   re, is.
   ra, coming. The word as here used conveys the idea of coming
    from a great distance.
1299 See line 1298.
1300 Pira uta hao!
   pira, a part of the word pirao, child, a general term.
   uta, a part of the word kuta, possessed by or belonging to
    some one other than the speaker.
   hao, offspring.
1301 Pira uta, uta hao! See line 1300.

Explanation by the Ku'rahus

When I sing this song I pray to Tira'wa to come down and touch
with his breath the symbol of his face and all the other symbols on
the little child. I pray with all my spirit that Tira'wa atius will let
the child grow up and become strong and find favor in its life.

This is a very solemn act, because we believe that Tira'wa atius,
although not seen by us, sends down his breath as we pray, calling
on him to come.

As I sing this song here with you I can not help shedding tears. I
have never sung it before except as I stood looking upon the little
child and praying for it in my heart. There is no little child here,
but you are here writing all these things down that they may not be
lost and that our children may know what their fathers believed and
practiced in this ceremony. So, as I sing, I am calling to Tira'wa
atius to send down his breath upon you, to give you strength and
long life. I am praying for you with all my spirit.

This song is sung eight times.

As we sing it first we bow above the little child, and make a movement as if to touch it with the feathered stems and the ear of corn.
The second time we sing it we again bow low over the child and the
chief touches it on the forehead with the ear of corn, while the Ku'rahus and his assistant stroke it on each side with the feathered
stems. We then pass to the south, to the right side of the child, and
sing for the third and the fourth time. The first time we make the
motion of touching the child, the second time the chief touches its
head with the ear of corn, and the feathered stems are passed down
its sides. Then we go west to the back of the child and there sing for
the fifth and sixth times, making the same motions and again touching it. Then we go north, to the left of the child, and sing for the

seventh and eighth times, making the same movements and touches; and then we return to the front of the child. These movements are all descending movements; they are following the breath line drawn on the face of the child.

The rattles which belong to the feathered stems are used alone with this song.

The purport of this song is hidden from the people, but this is what it means: All that I have been doing to you, little child, has been a prayer to call down the breath of Tira'wa atius to give you long life and strength and to teach you that you belong to him—that you are his child and not mine.

When we have finished singing the chief steps back, and the Ku'rahus, taking the two feathered stems, folds the white-eagle within the feathers of the brown-eagle feathered stem and, without singing, goes through the same two movements, the feint and the touch, first on the front of the child, then on its right side, then on the back and then on the left side, after which he spreads the feathered stems, laying the brown-eagle stem to the left and the white-eagle feathered stem to the right of the child.

The chief goes in front of the child and kneels before it. He takes the right leg of the wildcat skin and with the soft hair near its thigh he lightly wipes the blue lines from the child's face, and then the red paint.

He spreads the wildcat skin between the two stems, lays the ear of corn upon it, places the two feathered stems beside the ear of corn, with the crotched stick, the two rattles, the two eagle wings, and the pipe which has been used by the Children. He removes the black covering from the head of the child, takes off the white down and the downy feather, wraps them in the covering, and lays them also on the wildcat skin. He rolls the skin into a bundle, holding it in his arms while he stands before the child and talks to it of the good which will come through this ceremony.

PART II.　PRESENTING THE HAKO TO THE SON AND THANKS TO THE CHILDREN

Explanation by the Kinahus

When the chief has finished speaking he puts the bundle in the arms of the little child and leads it to its father, the Son, who receives it, and the child runs off to play.

Another bundle, containing the bowl which held the water into which the child looked and other things that have been used, and all the mats on which the people have been sitting, are brought to the Son and presented to him.

The chief, the leader of the Father's party, stands at the doorway with the Son, making the movements of thanks. He strokes the Son's head and arms, and, holding his hands, talks to him. The Ku'rahus follows and does the same, then the assistant comes, then the two doctors and the prominent men of the Father's party. After thanking the Son they all pass round the south side of the lodge to thank the prominent men of the Son's party; then they return to the north side of the lodge and sit down.

After they are seated, the Children express the wish that the distribution of the ponies, waiting without, may be happily accomplished, to which the Fathers reply, "Nawairi!" "Thanks!" The Children now rise and go out of the lodge and leave the Fathers alone during the distribution of the gifts.

The Ku'rahus appoints two influential men to go out and divide the gift of ponies, setting apart a number for the chiefs and the leading men who do not wish to do this for themselves, lest the people think them selfish. Two ponies are for the Ku'rahus; that is his portion ordinarily. If there are a great number of horses he is given more. The chiefs and leading men select from the ponies set apart for them, each man taking one until all the ponies are apportioned. The rest of the party choose from the other ponies, one at a time, the men first and then the women. After this the sticks representing ponies are divided.

All the saddles, bridles, feathers, that may have been on the horses given away are piled on the north side of the lodge. These belong to the Ku'rahus. He keeps what he wants and divides the rest between his assistant, the server, and other members of the party.

When the distribution has been made the Fathers leave the lodge and go to their camp, where they break their long fast and seek some rest. The next day all the party start for home except the chief. He remains to collect the ponies which have not been brought in.

The Son, to whom the Hako has been presented, can give the eagle wings to a doctor or the pipe to a friend, but he must keep for himself the sacred objects of the ceremony. They have brought to him the promise of long life and children, and have established peace and security through a tie as strong as that of kinship.

INCIDENTAL RITUALS

The following four rituals can be sung during the public ceremony whenever they are called for by the Children.

COMFORTING THE CHILD

Explanation by the Ku'rahus

I have told you before that in order to be instructed in this ceremony, to be taught its songs and their meaning, one must make many gifts, pay a great deal to the Ku'rahus who teaches him. This is our custom, for a man must make sacrifices, must give large presents in payment for what he receives, in order to show that he places a value upon the knowledge he wishes to acquire. I have paid a great deal to the Ku'rahus who taught me.　Besides I had to promise him that I would not give the teachings away, but would hold them as they had been held, teaching them only to those who would pay me.　I give these (incidental rituals) to you, so that they may be preserved and kept with all the other songs that belong to the Hako.

Long ago there lived a holy man who knew all the songs and the rites of this ceremony, and to him came a vision wherein he was taught how to bring comfort to a little child when, during the ceremony, it cried and could not be pacified.　In this vision he was shown what he must do to bring comfort to the little child, and he heard the songs that he must sing.　The songs which he heard have been handed down through many generations.

When during the ceremony a child cries and can not be comforted, the mother, or some one sent by her, can approach the Ku'rahus who carries the brown-eagle stem and ask him to come and quiet the child. The Ku'rahus must comply with this request, so he rises and stands before the holy place, takes up the feathered stem and sings this song, which tells the brown eagle, Kawas, that its baby is crying.

All the people hear the song and know that help for the child is being asked.

FIRST SONG

Words and Music

M. M.　♩ = 60.

• = Pulsation of the voice.　　　　Transcribed by Edwin S. Tracy.

No drum.

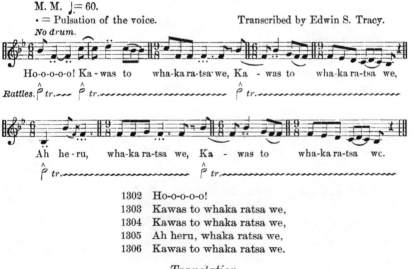

Ho-o-o-o-o! Ka - was to   wha-ka ra-tsa· we, Ka - was to   wha-ka ra-tsa we,

Rattles. ^ tr.⁀⁀ ^ tr.⁀⁀⁀⁀⁀⁀⁀⁀⁀⁀⁀⁀⁀⁀ ^ tr.⁀⁀⁀⁀⁀⁀⁀⁀⁀⁀⁀⁀⁀⁀

Ah he - ru,   wha-ka ra-tsa we, Ka - was to   wha-ka ra-tsa we.

^ tr.⁀⁀⁀⁀⁀⁀⁀⁀⁀⁀⁀⁀⁀⁀ ^ tr.⁀⁀⁀⁀⁀⁀⁀⁀⁀⁀⁀⁀⁀⁀

1302	Ho-o-o-o-o!
1303	Kawas to whaka ratsa we,
1304	Kawas to whaka ratsa we,
1305	Ah heru, whaka ratsa we,
1306	Kawas to whaka ratsa we.

Translation

1302　Ho-o-o-c-o!　An introductory exclamation.

1303　Kawas to whaka ratsa we.

　　　　Kawas, the brown eagle, representing the feminine principle.

　　　　to, its, denoting ownership of the child that is crying.

　　　　whaka, voice, noise from the mouth.

　　　　ratsa, a high pitch, screaming.

　　　　we, personal pronoun; refers to the child.

1304   See line 1303.
1305   Ah heru, whaka ratsa we.
     ah, yes.
     heru, truly, verily.
     whaka, voice.
     ratsa, screaming.
     we, refers to child.
1306   See line 1303.

Explanation by the Ku'rahus

The assistant takes up the white-eagle feathered stem, and then he and the Ku'rahus move toward the child, singing this song and waving the feathered stems. They are speaking to the child; they are bidding it cry no more, for its father is coming.

The father is Tira'wa atius, the father of all, the father of all the powers represented with the Hako, of all living things, of all the people. And now this mighty power, the Father, is coming to the little child to bring it comfort. That is why the child is told not to cry, since its father is coming.

These songs are very wonderful.

SECOND SONG

Words and Music

M. M. ♪ = 60.
• = Pulsation of the voice.   Transcribed by Edwin S. Tracy.

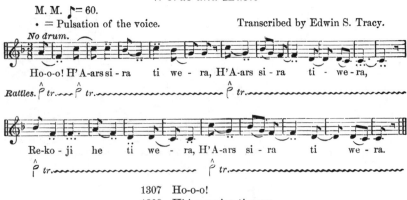

Ho-o-o! H'A-ars si - ra   ti we - ra, H'A-ars si - ra   ti - we-ra,

Re-ko - ji he   ti we - ra, H'A-ars si - ra   ti   we - ra.

1307   Ho-o-o!
1308   H'A-ars sira ti wera,
1309   H'A-ars sira ti wera,
1310   Rekoji he ti wera,
1311   H'A-ars sira ti wera.

Translation

1307   Ho-o-o! An introductory exclamation.
1308   H'Aars sira ti wera.
     h'A-ars; h', an aspiration, the sign of breath; aars, from atius, father: h'Aars, Father breathing forth (life).
     sira, is coming.
     ti, here.
     wera, now coming.

1309 See line 1308.

1310 Rekoji he ti wera.

> rekoji, stop crying.
>
> he, part of the word h'Aars, Father breathing forth (life).
>
> ti, here.
>
> wera, now coming.

1311 See line 1308.

Explanation by the Ku'rahus

When the Ku'rahus and his assistant have reached the child they stand before it and sing the first stanza. The white-eagle feathered stem is on the outside; there it is waved to guard the child from all harm. The brown-eagle stem is waved over the little one, and the mother, or whoever is holding it, must place it so that it can see the feathered stem, for the song bids the child look up and see that the mighty power Tira'wa has come, has acknowledged it as the child of the permanent heavens, that place far above even the light fleecy clouds, which is always the same.

THIRD SONG

Words and Music

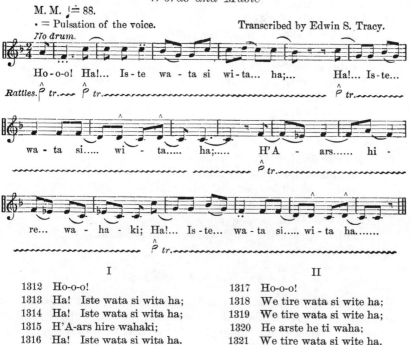

M. M. ♩= 88.

• = Pulsation of the voice.   Transcribed by Edwin S. Tracy.

	I		II
1312	Ho-o-o!	1317	Ho-o-o!
1313	Ha! Iste wata si wita ha;	1318	We tire wata si wite ha;
1314	Ha! Iste wata si wita ha;	1319	We tire wata si wite ha;
1315	H'A-ars hire wahaki;	1320	He arste he ti waha;
1316	Ha! Iste wata si wita ha.	1321	We tire wata si wite ha.

Translation

I

1312 Ho-o-o! An exclamation introductory to the song.

1313 Ha! Iste wata si wita ha.

    ha! an exclamation; behold!

    iste, you (referring to the child).

    wata, look upward.

    si, they, refers to the powers above.

    wita, owner, refers to the child belonging to the power above.

    ha, part of the word meaning young, or child.

1314 See line 1313.

1315 H'A-ars, hire wahaki.

    h'A-ars, Father breathing forth life.

    hire, there, above, meaning Tira′wa.

    wahaki, heavens; "the heavens that are always there above the reach of the clouds."

1316 See line 1313.

II

1317 Ho-o-o! An exclamation introductory to the song.

1318 We tire wata si wite ha.

    we, he or she, meaning the child.

    tire, has, an action performed.

    wata, looked.

    si, they, refers to the powers above.

    wite, the true owner; refers to Tira′wa as the true owner of the child.

    ha, part of the word meaning young, child.

1319 See line 1318.

1320 He arste he ti waha.

    he, his or her, refers to the child.

    arste, a modified form of atius, father.

    he, his; refers to Tira′wa.

    ti, here, at the present time.

    waha, part of the word wahaki, the permanent heavens.

1221 See line 1318.

Explanation by the Ku'rahus

When the second stanza is sung the little child always stops crying and looks up. It responds to the presence of the mighty power. The song tells the child that it belongs to Tira′wa atius, the father of all, the giver of life, whose dwelling place is far above the clouds in the permanent heavens that never change.

The child smiles and is comforted.

PRAYER TO AVERT STORMS

Explanation by the Ku'rahus

We like to have the sky clear during the time this ceremony is taking place. We do not like to have clouds come between us and the abode of Tira'wa atius, particularly storm clouds. We feel this way because we do not want anything to intercept the prayers of the Fathers or to hinder the descent of the help that we ask for the Children. If, however, clouds arise and a storm threatens, the Children may request this song to be sung, but the Fathers may not volunteer to sing it.

After the request for the song has been made, the following ceremony takes place: The Ku'rahus, with the Kawas feathered stem, his assistant with the white-eagle feathered stem, and the chief with the wildcat skin, in which are the crotched stick, the ear of corn, and the sacred pipe, rise from their seats at the west and pass out of the lodge. When they are outside under the open sky, they face the gathering clouds and sing the first stanza four times. While they sing the song and wave the eagle stems to the rhythm of the music, the chief holds the cat skin up toward the storm clouds. He holds it the same way while we sing the second stanza four times.

The words of these stanzas are few, but their meaning has come down to us with the story of the song.

Long, long ago the woodpecker was told by Tira'wa that the lightning would never strike the tree upon which it had built its nest. The four beings at the west who have control of the thunder and lightning would protect the bird, so that it need never fear the storm.

The woodpecker which came to the man to whom this ceremony was revealed taught him this song and told him when to sing it. He was to sing it only when the storm threatened; if he sang it at any other time he would bring rain and storm upon the people.

SONG

Words and Music

M. M. ♩ = 63.

• = Pulsation of the voice.   Transcribed by Edwin S. Tracy.

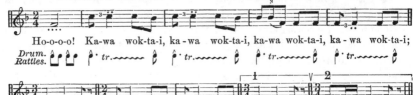

Ho-o-o-o! Ka-wa wok-ta-i, ka-wa wok-ta-i, ka-wa wok-ta-i, ka-wa wok-ta-i;

Drum. Rattles.

H'A-ars si-i; Ka-wa wok-ta-i, ka-wa wok-ta-i; H'A-ars si-i. H'A ti-us si - i.

I

1322 Ho-o-o-o!
1323 Kawa woktai, kawa woktai, kawa woktai, kawa woktai;
1324 H'A-ars si-i;
1325 Kawa woktai, kawa woktai;
1326 H'A-ars si-i.

II

1327 Ho-o-o-o!
1328 Ti wawaki-i, ti wawaki-i, ti wawaki-i, ti wawaki-i;
1329 H'A-ars si-i;
1330 Ti wawaki-i, ti wawaki-i;
1331 H'Atius si-i.

Translation

I

1322 Ho-o-o-o! An introductory exclamation.
1323 Kawa woktai, kawa woktai, kawa woktai, kawa woktai.
    kawa; ka, part of katuharu, trees; wa, plural sign; kawa
        means thick or heavy timber.
    woktai; wok, sound or noise; tai, on trees. Woktai, a sound
        made on the trees. The word refers to the tapping of
        the woodpecker upon the trees.
1324 H'Aars si-i.
    ḥ', contraction of ha, behold.
    aars, a modified form of atius, father.
    si-i; si, your; i, vowel prolongation.
1325 Kawa woktai, kawa woktai. See line 1323.
1326 See line 1324.

II

1327 Ho-o-o-o! An introductory exclamation.
1328 Ti wawaki-i, ti wawaki-i, ti wawaki-i, ti wawaki-i.
    ti, they; refers to the powers.
    wawaki-i; waki, speak; wa, plural sign; final i, vowel pro-
        longation. Wawaki-i, many are speaking.
1329 See line 1324.
1330 Ti wawkai-i, ti wawaki-i. See line 1328.
1331 H'Atius si-i. See line 1324.

Explanation by the Ku'rahus

In the first stanza we call upon the woodpecker, who is busy making a noise, tapping upon the trees in the thick woods, and we ask him to remind his father of the promise that the storm should not come near his nest.

The woodpecker is with us on the stem, and the storm is now threatening our nest, the lodge where we are holding the ceremony, so we call on him, the woodpecker, and ask him to remind his father of the promise given.

The second stanza tells us that the four beings at the west speak, for when the thunders sound they all speak. These now answer the woodpecker, who has reminded them of their promise when Tira'wa atius, the father of all things, placed the bird and its nest under their protection.

If, after we have sung these stanzas, the clouds part, we know that our prayers have been heard. We all return to the lodge, and the wildcat skin is spread upon the holy place at the west, the crotched stick is put in position, the eagle stems and all the other articles are laid at ceremonial rest. When this has been done the chief takes the sacred pipe and, accompanied by the priest of the shrine containing the objects sacred to the powers of the rain, goes out and makes an offering of smoke. The priest directs the chief where to point the pipestem. By this act of offering smoke we give thanks to the powers, who have heard our prayers and averted the storm.

PRAYER FOR THE GIFT OF CHILDREN

Explanation by the Ku'rahus

This ceremony is very old and has now become obsolete. It is a prayer for the power of procreation. It was never performed except at the request of the Son, and was only in the interest of a man to whom children had not been born. It took place either in the early morning or at night, never during the day.

When the request for the ceremony had been made, the Ku'rahus selected a man from among the Fathers whose duty it became to carry the Son and to care for him as a father would care for a little child.

A white buffalo robe was kept for this particular ceremony. After the Son had been lifted on the back of the Father, this white robe was thrown over the two and was held together in front by the Father, as a person would hold his robe if he were carrying a child on his back. As the Father, carrying the Son, moved toward the entrance of the lodge, he was followed by the Ku'rahus and his assistant bearing the feathered stems and the chief with the cat skin and the ear of corn, while the following song was sung.

The words are: "Behold! Your father is walking with his child!"

FIRST SONG

Words and Music

M. M. ♩= 56.
• = Pulsation of the voice.
Transcribed by Edwin S. Tracy.

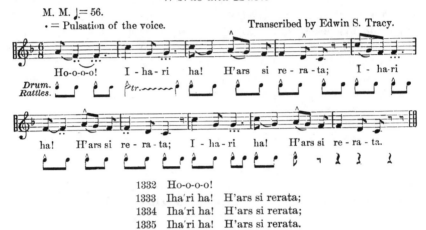

Ho-o-o-o! I - ha- ri ha! H'ars si re - ra - ta; I - ha-ri

Drum.
Rattles.

ha! H'ars si re - ra - ta; I - ha-ri ha! H'ars si re - ra - ta.

```
1332   Ho-o-o-o!
1333   Iha'ri ha!   H'ars si rerata;
1334   Iha'ri ha!   H'ars si rerata;
1335   Iha'ri ha!   H'ars si rerata.
```

Translation

1332   Ho-o-o-o!   An introductory exclamation.
1333   Iha'ri ha!   H'ars si rerata.
    iha'ri, a term for offspring or young; refers here to the Son.
    ha! behold!
    h', an abbreviation of ha, your.
    ars, an abbreviation of atius, father.
    si, refers to iha'ri, in this instance the Son.
    rerata, walking with.
1334, 1335   See line 1333.

Explanation by the Ku'rahus

When the Father, with the Son on his back, and the Ku'rahus and his associates had reached the open air and had gone a little distance from the lodge, the Son was taken from the back of the Father. All were now standing under the sky where they could be seen by the powers. The Son represented a little helpless child—the child that he desired the powers to give to him.

As the following song was sung the Father undressed the Son as he would a little child, and while he did so the Son prayed for the gift of children.

SECOND SONG

Words and Music

M. M. ♩= 66.
● = Pulsation of the voice.   Transcribed by Edwin S. Tracy.
No drum.

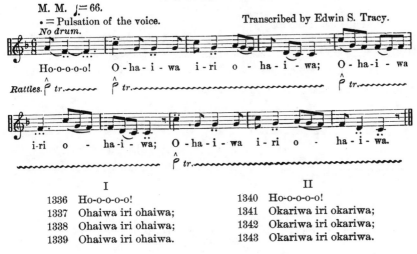

Ho-o-o-o-o!   O - ha - i - wa   i - ri   o - ha - i - wa;   O - ha - i - wa

Rattles. ᵖ tr.   ᵖ tr.   ᵖ tr.

i-ri   o - ha - i - wa;   O - ha - i - wa   i - ri   o - ha - i - wa.

ᵖ tr.

I		II	
1336	Ho-o-o-o-o!	1340	Ho-o-o-o-o!
1337	Ohaiwa iri ohaiwa;	1341	Okariwa iri okariwa;
1338	Ohaiwa iri ohaiwa;	1342	Okariwa iri okariwa;
1339	Ohaiwa iri ohaiwa.	1343	Okariwa iri okariwa.

Translation

I

1336   Ho-o-o-o-o!   An exclamation introductory to the song.
1337   Ohaiwa iri ohaiwa.
　　　　ohaiwa, a composite word; the o is taken from okiwausu,
　　　　　foam; hai is from haiwa, floating; wa is a part of nawa,
　　　　　now.
　　　　iri, an expression of thankfulness.
　　　　ohaiwa, translated above.
1338, 1339   See line 1337.

I₁

1340   Ho-o-o-o-o!   An exclamation introductory to the song.
1341   Okariwa iri okariwa.
　　　　okariwa, a composite word; oka, breechcloth; kari, male
　　　　　organ (the syllable ka is common to the first and second
　　　　　word); wa, from rakura, to take off.
　　　　iri, an expression of thankfulness.
　　　　okariwa, translated above.
1342, 1343   See line 1341.

THIRD SONG

Words and Music

M. M. ♩=126.
• = Pulsation of the voice.   Transcribed by Edwin S. Tracy.
No drum.

Ho-o-o-o!   O - ha - i - wa, c - ha - i - wa, na - wa ho - ha -

Rattles. *tr.* ~~~~~ *tr.* ~~~~~~~~~~~~~~~~~~~~~~~~

i - wa;   O - ha - i - wa   na - wa   ho - ha - i - wa.

~~~~~~~~~ *tr.* ~~~~~~~~~~~~~~~~~~~~~~

I		II	
1344	Ho-o-o-o!	1347	Ho-o-o-o!
1345	Ohaiwa, ohaiwa, nawa hohaiwa;	1348	Okariwa iri okariwa okariwa;
1346	Ohaiwa nawa hohaiwa.	1349	Okariwa iri okariwa.

Translation

I

1344 Ho-o-o-o! An exclamation introductory to the song.
1345 Ohaiwa, ohaiwa, nawa hohaiwa.
    ohaiwa, floating foam. See line 1337.
    nawa, now.
    hohaiwa, to urinate.
1346 Ohaiwa nawa hohaiwa. See line 1345.

II

1347 Ho-o-o-o! An introductory exclamation
1348 Okariwa iri okariwa okariwa.
    okariwa, a composite word, translated in line 1341.
    iri, an expression of thankfulness.
    okariwa. See line 1341.
1349 Okariwa iri okariwa. See line 1341.

Explanation by the Ku'rahus

During the singing of the first stanza (third song) the Son obeyed, as a child would do, the directions given him by the Father.

As the second stanza was sung the Father reclothed the Son as he would a little child. The Son was then taken again on the back of the Father to be carried to the lodge.

FOURTH SONG

Words and Music

M. M. ♪ = 132.
• = Pulsation of the voice.　　　　　　　Transcribed by Edwin S. Tracy.
No drum.

Ho-o-o-o! Ha - a! Ra - i　ha! ha! ra - i　　ha! ra - a;　　Hi - ra　ra - i

Rattles.

ha! ra - a;　　Ha - a! Ra - i　ha! ha! ra - i　　ha! ra - a.

I		II	
1350	Ho-o-o-o!	1354	Ho-o-o-o!
1351	Ha-a! Rai ha! ha! rai ha! ra-a;	1355	Ho-okai ha! hokai ha. ka-a;
1352	Hira rai ha! ra-a;	1356	Werawane ha! ka-a;
1353	Ha-a! Rai ha! ha! rai ha! ra-a.	1357	Ho-okai ha! hokai ha! ka-a.

Translation

I

1350　Ho-o-o-o!　An exclamation introductory to the song.
1351　Ha-a! Rai ha! ha! rai ha! ra-a.
　　　　ha-a! ha! behold! a, a vowel prolongation to carry the voice.
　　　　rai, coming.
　　　　ha! ha! behold!
　　　　rai, coming.
　　　　ha! behold!
　　　　ra-a; ra, a part of the word rai, coming; a, vowel prolonga-
　　　　　tion.
1352　Hira rai ha! ra-a;
　　　　hira, he coming.
　　　　rai, coming.
　　　　ha! behold!
　　　　ra-a, a part of the word meaning coming.
1353　See line 1351.

II

1354　Ho-o-o-o!　An introductory exclamation.
1355　Ho-okai ha! hokai ha! ka-a.
　　　　ho-okai; hokai, to enter; the vowel o is prolonged to carry
　　　　　the voice while singing.
　　　　ha! behold!
　　　　hokai, to enter, or entering.
　　　　ha! behold!
　　　　ka-a, a part of the word hokai, entering.

1356   Werawane ha! ka-a.
       werawane, spreading out the arms.
       ha! behold!
       ka-a, part of the word hokai, entering.
1357   See line 1355.

Explanation by the Ku'rahus

As the Father and the Son, wrapped in the white robe, turned toward the lodge, the Ku'rahus and his associates followed, and as they walked they sang the first stanza.

The words are, "Behold! He is coming! The Son is coming!"

At the door of the lodge they sang (second stanza), "Behold! He is entering!" With the word "werawane," the Father spread out his arms, loosening the white robe, but still holding it by the edges, while the Son slipped to the ground and returned to his place in the lodge, the place he had left at the beginning of the ceremony.

CHANGING A MAN'S NAME

Explanation by the Ku'rahus

If any man of the Son's party had achieved success in war, and his achievements had been acknowledged by the people, he could request the Son to have the ceremony of changing his name performed.

This act could take place in the afternoon of the fourth day. The Son would make the request known to the Father, the chief, who passed it on to the Ku'rahus.

If the Hako ceremony was held in an earth lodge, the Ku'rahus, accompanied by the Father and the Son, went outside and ascended the roof; there, standing before the people gathered below, the Ku'rahus recited in a loud voice the ritual used when changing a man's name.

If the Hako ceremony had been held in a tent, a semicircular inclosure was made with saplings and there, under the open sky, in the presence of all the people. the ritual was given and the name was changed.

Pawnee Text

1358   Hiri! Waku'raruta sharu witi rarawa-a kiru sharu reru ki ,awi rahwi'-
       rahriso tira kahho ri'wiri.
1359   Hiri! Raru ki'tawi rahwi'rahriso rao ti shira rutu'rahwitz pari usa'ru
       i re.
1360   Hiri! Ra'ru ki'tawi rahwi'rahriso rao ti shire'ra ki'tawa usa'ru.

1361   Hiri! Riru'tziraru; rasa rŭxsa pakara'ra witz pari; hiri! ti'ruta; hiri!
       ti'rakŭse tararawa'hut, tiri.
1362   Hiri! Riru'tziraru; rasa rŭxsa pakara'ra witz pari; hiri! ti'ruta; hiri!
       Tira'wa, ha! tiri.
1363   Hiri! Riru'tziraru; sira waku ri'kata iwa'hut; hiri! ti'ruta; hiri! ti'ra ŭse
       tirarawa'hut, tiri.

1364   Hiri!   Riru'tziraru; sira waku rari'sut: hiri! ti'ruta; hiri!   Tira'wa, ha! tiri.
1365   Hiri!   Riru'tziraru; Rarari'tu, kata wi'tixsutta.
       Raki'ris taka'ta wi'tixsutta.
       Raki'ris tarukŭx'pa, raru'tura tuka'wiut tari.
1366   Hiri!   Riru'tziraru; ruri Papapi'chus taka wi'tixsutta.
       Ruri Papapi'chus tarukŭx'pa raru'tura tuka'wiut tari.
1367   Hiri!   Riru'tziraru; ruchix kuso'ho riraka'ta kŭx'sata.   Kaha'riwisiri, ku
       katit tiki; kaha'riwisiri, ku paha'ti tiki; kaha'riwisiri, ku raka'ta tiki;
       kaha'riwisiri, ku taka tiki.
1368   Hiri!   Riru'tziraru; sira sura waurux' para, raru'tura tuka'wiut tari.

1369   Rawa!   Hawa urasharu we tatki'wati.
1370   Hiri!   Tatux tapakiaho, hawa, Rarutska'tit!   Hiri!   Raro rikcha ro re.
1371   Hiri!   Wakoru ratora pake'ŭsto.
1372   Hiri!   Akitaro hiwa werataweko.
1373   Hiri!   Shaku'ru Wa'rukste.   Hiriwa witi rakawa'karu ko re.

Translation

1358   hiri! an exclamation, harken! give heed!
       waku'raruta, it came to pass a long time ago.
       sharu, part of u'rasha'ru, name.
       witi, they.
       rarawa-a, discarded, had done with, threw away.
       kiru, ancient.
       sharu, from kŭssharu, a certain place known only by tradition.
       reru, it came about, or it was.
       ki'tawi, from ki, through, and ta'wi, them.
       rahwi'rahriso, a title. This title was bestowed through certain
         ceremonies connected with one of the shrines. The man
         who had received this title was qualified to act as a leader,
         to have charge of a war expedition.
       tira, they.
       kahho, a wide expanse; kah conveys the picture that this expanse
         is spanned, as by a roof; ho suggests an inclosed space, as a
         dwelling; kahho calls up the idea that the earth is a vast
         abode, roofed by the heavens, where dwell the powers.
       ri'wiri, walking; the persons spoken of as walking are not pres-
         ent. Rara'wari is to travel, walking, like warriors, and the
         word in the text refers to such walking, to the rahwi'rah-
         riso and the men under his leadership walking the wide
         earth beneath the arching sky.
1359   hiri! harken! give heed!
       raru, a company, or a number of persons.
       ki'tawi, through them. See same word in line 1358.
       rahwi'rahriso, the leader. See translation in line 1358.
       ra'o, a victory song. This class of songs could be composed
         and sung for the first time by a leader. They might
         afterward be sung by his followers and by other persons.
       ti, part of tira, they.

shira, from shire'ra, brought. The re is eliminated for euphony.

rutu'rahwitz, overtake.

pari, walking; singular number, present tense.

usa'ru, a place wherein an event took place or something occurred. Both the locality and the occurrence are known only by tradition and the tradition is preserved in song.

i re, singing vocables.

1360 hiri! harken.

ra'ru, a number of persons. The word as here used refers both to the leader and his men and to the people of their village.

ki'tawi, through them. The word has here a double reference similar to the preceding one.

rahwi'rahriso, the leader.

rao, victory song.

ti, they. An abbreviated form of tira, they.

shire'ra, brought.

ki'tawa, from kit, the top; ta, coming; wa, part of waku, hill. Ki'tawa conveys the picture of the returning men singing their victory song as they reach the top of the hill near their village.

usa'ru; the word here means that the victory song commemorated the event at the time when the leader instituted the custom of changing the name.

1361 hiri! harken!

riru'tziraru, by reason of, by means of, because of. The word has a wide significance and force throughout the ritual.

rasa, the man stood.

rŭxsa, he said or did.

pakara'ra, a loud call or chant, sending the voice to a great distance.

witz, from tawitz'sa, to reach or arrive.

pari, traveling. These five words tell of a religious rite performed by the leader. The first two refer to his going to a solitary place to fast and pray, seeking help and favor from the powers above; the last three describe his voice, bearing his petition, traveling on and on, striving to reach the abode of Tira'wa.

hiri! harken! a call for reverent attention.

ti'ruta, special or assigned places, referring to the places where the lesser powers dwell, these having been assigned by Tira'wa atius, the father of all.

hiri! harken! a call for reverent attention.

ti'rakŭse, sitting; present tense, plural number.

tararawa'hut, the sky or heavens. It implies a circle, a great distance, and the dwelling place of the lesser powers, those which can come near to man and be seen or heard or felt by him.

tiri, above, up there, as if the locality were designated by
    pointing upward.

1362 hiri! harken!

riru'tziraru, by reason of, because of.

rasa, the man stood.

rŭxsa, did.

pakara'ra, send voice to a distance.

witz, reached.

pari, traveling.

hiri! harken! a call for reverent attention.

ti'ruta, the abodes of the lesser powers.

hiri! harken! a call for reverent attention.

Tira'wa, Tira'wa atius, the father of all.

ha! an exclamation of awe.

tiri, above all; refers to Tira'wa atius being above all the powers.

1363 hiri! harken!

riru'tziraru, by reason of.

sira, they took.

waku, they said.

ri'kata, received.

iwa'hut, from iwa, to hand over or pass on to the one next,
    and tira'wahut, the circle above where the lesser powers
    are. Iwa'hut means handed or passed around the circle.

hiri! harken! a call for reverent attention.

ti'ruta, abodes of the lesser powers.

hiri! harken! a call for reverent attention.

ti'rakŭse, sitting.

tirarawa'hut, the circle above of the lesser powers.

tiri, up above.

1364 hiri! harken!

riru'tziraru, because of, by reason of.

sira, they took.

waku, they said.

rari'sut, gave consent, granted.

hiri! harken! a call for reverent attention.

ti'ruta, abodes of the lesser powers.

hiri! harken! a call for reverent attention.

Tira'wa, Tira'wa atius, the father of all.

ha! an exclamation of awe.

tiri, above all.

1365 hiri! harken!

riru'tziraru, by reason of, in consequence of.

Rarari'tu, an old term for Winds. It also means heavy storm
    clouds. Rari'tu, a cyclone. The word in the text has a
    double significance. It stands for the Winds, the lesser
    power, and for the summoning by this lesser power, the
    Winds, of the storm clouds, their messengers in the west.

kata, rising up, climbing up.

wi'tixsutta, reached there (whence the summons came).

Raki'ris, Thunders, plural form.

taka'ta, ascending, advancing.

wi'tixsutta, reached a given place.

Raki'ris, Thunders.

tarukŭx'pa, an action concluded.

raru'tura, from raru, at that, and tura, ground.   The word
means that at the conclusion of the action (here understood) they, the Thunders, descended to the earth.

tuka'wiut, slantwise.

tari, the end of a mission or an action.

1366   hiri! harken!

riru'tziraru, by means of, or by the agency of.

ruri, at that time.

Papapi'chus, Lightning; papa, zigzag; pichus, darting, flashing.

taka, within, inclosed.

wi'tixsutta, reached there.

ruri, at that time.

Papapi'chus, Lightning.

tarukŭx'pa, an action concluded.

raru'tura, and then they descended to earth.   See translation
of this word in line 1365.

tuka'wiut, slantwise.

tari, the end of their mission.

1367   hiri! harken!

riru'tziraru, by means of, by reason of.

ruchix, they did.

kuso'ho, flock.

riraka'ta, in front of.

kŭx'sata, from side to side, as when ranging a path.

kaha'riwisiri, swallows.

ku, breast.

katit, black.

tiki, they were.

kaha'riwisiri, swallows.

ku, breast.

paha'ti, red.

tiki, they were.

kaha'riwisiri, swallows.

ku, breast.

raka'ta, yellow.

tiki, they were.

kaha'riwisiri, swallows.

ku, breast.

taka, white.

tiki, they were.

1368   hiri! harken.

riru'tziraru, by reason of, because of.

sira, they took; refers to the leader and to the men who
      followed and depended on him.

sura, possess; to become one's own.

waurux', grasped, as a staff.

para, walked.

raru'tura, refers to that which descended to earth.

tuka'wiut, slantwise.

tari, end, or accomplished mission.

1369   rawa! attend! a call for attention at the moment.

hawa, once more.

urasharu, name.

we, I.

tatki'wati, change.

1370   hiri! harken!

tatux, we used to.

tapakiaho, speak of him.

hawa, once more.

Rarutska'tit, the former name, meaning black-feathered arrow.

hiri! harken!

raro, owner.

rikcha, lying.   These words refer to the achievement com-
      memorated by the name about to be thrown away.

ro re, vocables used for euphony and measure.

1371   hiri! harken!

wakoru, now we are.

ratora, all people.

pake'ŭsto, speak out and say.

1372   hiri! harken!

akitaro, tribe.

hiwa, in the.

werataweko, prominent.

1373   hiri! harken!

Shaku'ru Wa'rukste, the new name now announced ("Sacred
      Sun").

hiriwa, in the process of making.

witi, himself.

rakawa'karu, what he is.

ko re, vocables used for euphony and measure.

Closing Remarks of the Ku'rahus

During the days I have been talking with you (the writer) I have
been carried back in thought to the time when Estamaza (the father
of Francis LaFlesche) came to the Chaui.   I met him in this ceremony; he was the Father, and as I have worked here day and night,

my heart has gone out to you. I have done what has never been done before, I have given you all the songs of this ceremony and explained them to you. I never thought that I, of all my people, should be the one to give this ancient ceremony to be preserved, and I wonder over it as I sit here.

I think over my long life with its many experiences; of the great number of Pawnees who have been with me in war, nearly all of whom have been killed in battle. I have been severely wounded many times—see this scar over my eye. I was with those who went to the Rocky Mountains to the Cheyennes, when so many soldiers were slain that their dead bodies lying there looked like a great blue blanket spread over the ground. When I think of all the people of my own tribe who have died during my lifetime and then of those in other tribes that have fallen by our hands, they are so many they make a vast cover over Mother Earth. I once walked with these prostrate forms. I did not fall but I passed on, wounded sometimes but not to death, until I am here to-day doing this thing, singing these sacred songs into that great pipe (the graphophone) and telling you of these ancient rites of my people. It must be that I have been preserved for this purpose, otherwise I should be lying back there among the dead.

ANALYTICAL RECAPITULATION

ORIGIN AND GEOGRAPHIC DISTRIBUTION OF THE CEREMONY

Where the Hako ceremony originated and through how many generations it has come down to the present time it may be impossible ever to determine. Even a partial knowledge of its geographic distribution upon our continent would demand an archeologic and historical research too extended to be attempted at this time. However, a few facts may be stated.

From the Journal of Marquette, giving an account of his voyage of discovery in 1672, it is learned that the sacred symbols, the feathered stems, were held in honor by tribes belonging to the Algonquian, Siouan, and Caddoan linguistic stocks dwelling in the Mississippi valley from the Wisconsin to the Arkansas.

Marquette calls the feathered stem a "calumet" and his description of its ceremony, which he saw among the Illinois, due allowance being made for his lack of intimate acquaintance with native religious customs, indicates that the ceremony as he saw it over two hundred years ago in a tribe that no longer exists differs little from the same ceremony as observed within the last twenty years in the Omaha tribe. He says of this "calumet" that it is "the most mysterious thing in the world. The scepters of our kings are not so much respected, for the Indians have such a reverence for it that one may call it the god of peace and war, and the arbiter of life and death. . . . One with this calumet may venture among his enemies, and in the hottest battles they lay down their arms before the sacred pipe. The Illinois presented me with one of them which was very useful to us in our voyage."

That the feathered stem was recognized over so large a part of the great Mississippi valley and among so many tribes differing in language and customs indicates considerable antiquity for its rites, as much time would have been required for so wide an acceptance and practice of the ceremony.

As observed among the Pawnees, there is evidence not only that the ceremony is old, but that it has been built upon still older foundations, and has been modified in the process of time to adapt it to changed conditions of environment. For example, the substitution of the buffalo for the deer and the transference of songs, as that formally sung to the mesa while on the journey, which is now sung within the lodge.

279

The leadership accorded to the corn indicates that an earlier form of the ceremony is to be sought among a people dependent upon agriculture, and the peculiar treatment of water would seem to have arisen in a semi-arid region.   Again, the development in the purpose of the ceremony from the simple longing for offspring to the larger desire of establishing intertribal relationships was most likely to have taken place among peoples whose settled mode of life had fostered an appreciation of the benefits to be derived from peace and security.

Efforts to spread this ceremony among tribes less sedentary than those of the Mexican plateau and the Southwest may, on the one hand, have been prompted by prudential reasons, while on the other hand its adoption and promulgation over the wide territory occupied by the so-called hunting tribes marks the growth of political ideas and gives a higher place to these tribes in the line of social development than has usually been accorded them.

PURPOSE OF THE CEREMONY

The purpose of this ceremony was twofold: first, to benefit certain individuals by bringing to them the promise of children, long life, and plenty; second, to affect the social relations of those who took part in it, by establishing a bond between two distinct groups of persons, belonging to different clans, gentes, or tribes, which was to insure between them friendship and peace.

In every tribe where the ceremony was known this twofold purpose was recognized, and by no tribal variation in the details of the rite was it lost sight of or obscured.

From a study of this ceremony it seems probable that its original instigation was a desire for offspring, that the clan or kinship group might increase in number and strength and be perpetuated through the continuous birth of children.

The ceremonial forms here used to express this desire were undoubtedly borrowed from earlier ceremonies through which the people had been familiarized with certain symbols and rites representing the creative powers.   Thus, the male and female cosmic forces, symbolized in greater or less detail by day and night, sun and moon, the heavens and the earth, are found in the Hako ceremony.

The eagle and the ear of corn also represent in general the male and female forces, but each is specialized in a manner peculiar to these rites.   There are two eagles; the white, representing the male, the father, the defender; and the brown, representing the female, the mother, the nestmaker (see pages 288, 289).   In the treatment of these eagles the dual forces are still further represented.   The feathers of the white or male eagle are hung upon a stem painted green to symbolize the earth, the female principle; while those of the brown or female eagle are hung upon the stem painted blue to symbolize the heavens, the male principle. The same treatment of the corn is observed. The ear of corn, which is born of Mother Earth, is symbolically painted to represent a living contact with the heavens.

These symbolic articles thus treated are peculiar to this ceremony and essential to its rites. They express with unmistakable clearness the original instigating desire for children.

The second purpose of this ceremony, that of establishing a bond between two distinct groups of persons belonging to different clans, gentes, or tribes, which should insure between them friendship and peace, was probably an outgrowth of the first purpose and may have been based upon tribal experience in the practice of exogamy.

In a tribe composed of clans or gentes, where exogamy prevailed, two factors tended to promote peace and security among the people, namely, children born to parents representing two distinct political groups, and rites which recognized a common dependence upon the supernatural and were obligatory upon all.

With the growth of social ideas the thought seems to have arisen that ties might be made between two tribes differing from and even competing with each other, through a device which should simulate those influences which had proved so effective within the tribe. The Father, representing one tribe, was the incentive force; he inaugurated the Hako party. The tie was made by a ceremony in which the feminine principle, represented by the corn and Kawas, was the dominant factor. Through this mother element life was given and a bond was established between the Father and a Son of another tribe. It is remarkable how close to the model this device of an artificial tie has been made to correspond.

Apart from the social and religious significance of the ceremony, it became a means of exchange of commodities between tribes. The garments, regalia, and other presents brought by the Fathers to the Children were taken by the latter to some other tribe, when they in turn became the Fathers. Thus manufactures peculiar to one tribe were often spread over a wide territory, and the handicraft of one region became known to different sections of the country.

STRUCTURE OF THE CEREMONY

The perpetuation and distribution of a ceremony is dependent upon its structure, its symbolism, and its purpose. Its parts must be so coordinated as to make it possible to keep the rite intact during oral transmission, while its symbolism must appeal to common beliefs and its purpose to common desires.

Examining the ceremony of the Hako, we find it to possess these requisites. Its purpose awoke a response in every human heart, its symbolism appealed to the people wherever corn ripened and eagles flew; and though its structure was elaborate, it was built upon a simple plan. It is made up of many rituals, each complete in itself, but all so related to each other as to form an unbroken sequence from the beginning of the rites to their end. Each ritual contains one general thought, which is elaborated by songs and attendant acts. These songs and acts are so closely related to the central thought that one helps to keep the other in mind; moreover, the thought embodied in one ritual leads so directly to the thought contained in the next that they form a sequence that, in the mind of the Pawnee, can not logically be broken, and thus the preservation of the entirety of the ceremony is insured.

The compact structure of the Hako ceremony bears testimony to the mental grasp of the people who formulated it. As we note the balancing of the various parts, and the steady progression from the opening song of the first ritual to the closing prayer in the twentieth, and recall the fact that the ceremony was constructed without the steadying force of the written record, we are impressed, on the one hand, by the intellectual power displayed in the construction, and, on the other, by the sharply defined beliefs fundamental to the ceremony.

RHYTHMIC EXPRESSION IN THE CEREMONY

When we examine the songs which accompany every ceremonial act we find that the thought to be expressed has determined the rhythm, which, in its turn, has controlled both words and music and fixed as well the time or duration of the notes. The unit of time is marked by pulsations of the voice or by drum beats, and the words are found bent by elisions or stretched by added vocables to make them conform to the musical measure.

Rhythm dominates the rendition, which is always exact, no liberties being taken for the purpose of musical expression, in our sense of the term. Any such treatment would so blur the song to the native ear as to destroy its character. A further use of rhythm is manifest in the number of the musical phrases and stanzas. These are found to correspond to the number of ceremonial motions used to indicate the powers which are being addressed. By close examination this peculiarity will be apparent, but in order to facilitate an understanding the words of each musical phrase have been printed as a separate line, so that the eye can easily catch the rhythmic form. As a further help, a diagram has been prepared to show the relative time values of notes, the exceptional accents, and the voice pulsations of each musical phrase. To illustrate, take the first song:

The unit of time is an eighth note, represented by a short dash, –; a quarter note is represented by a longer dash, two beats, —; a three-eighths note by a still longer dash, three beats, ——, and so on. The dots indicate the number of voice pulsations given to a tone while it is held. Where there is emphasis it is marked on the diagram by the accent sign ′.

A rhythmic rendition, which aims not only to convey the literal meaning but to embody the elucidations of the Ku′rahus as well, has been made. Its words have been so chosen that the lines shall conform to the rhythm of the corresponding phrases of the song. This rendition is for the purpose of presenting to the eye and the ear of the English reader the song as it appeals to the Pawnee who has been instructed in the rite.

The variety of rhythmic forms in the songs of the rituals offers interesting material for the study of the relation of the musical phrase to the development of metrical language. The movements which accompany each song and act of the ceremony give further testimony to the fundamental character of rhythm.

In the following analysis the scheme of the ceremony will be closely observed.

THE PREPARATION

FIRST DIVISION. INITIAL RITES

FIRST RITUAL. MAKING THE HAKO

PART I. INVOKING THE POWERS

The ceremony of the Hako, we are told by the Ku′rahus, is a prayer for offspring. It opens with a song which recalls the creation of man, the gifts bestowed on him by Tira′wa atius through the powers, and the establishment of rites by which he can appeal to the powers. The content of the song prefigures the fulfilment of man's desire for the reproduction of his life, and the orderly approach by which he should make his desire known. Such a prefiguring seems to be essential at the opening of a ceremony to give it a supernatural warrant.

The preparation of the Hako constitutes the opening ritual, the first song of which is an appeal to the lesser powers in the order of their coming near to man from the holy place, Awahokshu (first song, line 4). They are said to descend by the four paths at the four cardinal points (line 9), and the ceremonial motions indicating these quarters are an indirect way of mentioning the powers. Each stanza of the appeal, falling into four musical phrases, suggests this four-fold symbol.

The appeal is in the form of a litany, each stanza beginning with a call to "give heed," and closing with the response that heed has been given. The climax in both words and music is reached in the third phrase, which is a direct invocation of one of the powers.

In this song we meet exclamations characteristic of many others of the ceremony. These exclamations express the emotions evoked in the progress of the appeal. Few words are used, their iteration making the memorizing of the song easier than if the emotion had been fully elaborated in many different words. This apparent poverty of expression, which may in part be accounted for by the necessity of oral transmission, has not prevented metrical forms throughout the ceremony; with one exception, the songs are rhythmic. In the present instance the repetition of the exclamation I'hare! extended through the musical phrase by the echoing of its syllables, conveys even to the eye of a stranger the meaning as given by the Ku'rahus in his explanation of line 2. "The repetition of the word as we sing I'hare, 'hare, 'aheo indicates that our minds are dwelling upon the subject brought to our attention."

This opening song is in two parts. One refers to the powers, the other to the inauguration of rites through which man can turn toward these powers.

Six stanzas belong to the first part, suggesting the six symbolic motions, indicating the four directions, the above, and the below. The first stanza is an appeal to Tira'wa; its form is noteworthy when viewed in connection with the opening stanza of the second part. Tira'wa is not addressed directly, but the mind is turned to his place of abode, Awahokshu, as to a definite locality where prayer should be sent, whence help may come. The fixing of the mind upon a holy place serves as a precedent for the establishment of a holy place, Kusharu (stanza VII), where man is to think of Tira'wa, and where rites in accordance with his thought are to be performed. The order in which the powers are addressed in these first six stanzas reveals something of the Pawnee's idea of man's relation to the supernatural. First, the holy place, the abode of Tira'wa, the father of all, is addressed; second, Hoturu, the invisible Wind, the bearer or giver of breath; third, Chakaru, the Sun, the father of strength; fourth, H'Uraru, the Earth, the mother, the conserver of life; fifth, Toharu, Vegetation, the giver of food; sixth, Chaharu, Water, the giver of drink.

Starting from the abode of the central power, Tira'wa, designated in the first stanza, the lesser powers bring to man first breath, next vitality or strength, then the ability to conserve and use that strength, and, finally, they give him food and drink to sustain his life. The physical man stands forth in these first six stanzas as the result of the gifts of the powers.

The second part of the song is in seven stanzas. The number suggests the seven symbolic motions, indicating the four directions, the above, the below, and the center, the ego.

The first stanza of the second part (VII) calls the people to "give heed" to Kusharu, the place set apart for sacred purposes. Concern-

ing this the Ku'rahus says: "The first act of a man must be to set
apart a place that can be made holy and consecrated to Tira'wa, a
place where a man can be quiet and think about the mighty power."
As the first part opens with the mention of Awahokshu, the holy
place, the abode of Tira'wa, whence life is given to men by the intermediary powers, so the second part begins by indicating that man
should set apart a holy place whence his thoughts can ascend to the
powers which gave him life.   The fixing of the sacred place made
a center from which man's daily life could be set in order, and made
the inauguration of rites possible—rites which served as a common
bond to hold the community together.   In the next stanza (VIII) the
term h'Akaru is used.   H' is the sign of breath, of the giving of life;
akaru is a modification of akaro, a dwelling place.   The change
from ro to ru indicates that the word is typical rather than special.
h'Akaru conveys the idea of an abode of life, a place where life (h',
breath) can be received.   The progression noted in the first part
is here recalled; the power first mentioned after the holy place,
Awahokshu, was Hotoru, the Wind, the giver of breath.   The next
stanza (IX) speaks of Keharu, an inclosure, the actual dwelling to be
erected for the protection of life.   Keharu seems to correspond to the
male element which, in the first part, is represented by the Sun, the
father, the giver of strength, and we find that throughout this ceremony the position of the feathered stem, representing the male, is
upon the outside, where it acts as guard and protector, a wall of
defense to the interior of the lodge, with its fireplace, which represents
the nest (see line 44).   The fireplace, Kataharu, is next mentioned
(X).   This is the center, where the life within the lodge is conserved;
it represents the female principle.   This stanza corresponds to the
fourth of the first part, where h'Uraru, Mother Earth, is invoked.   In
the two following stanzas, Keharu, the glowing coals (XI), and Koritu,
the flames, the word of the fire (XII), refer directly to the act of
making fire by friction, a ceremony which seems to underlie most, if
not all, aboriginal rites through which man appeals to the powers for
the means of sustaining life, food, and drink (stanzas V and VI).

   The first six stanzas of the second part seem to be a reflex of the
six composing the first part.   In the first part physical life is created,
in the second part psychical life is recognized.   By the institution of
rites a way is opened through which man turns toward the powers
which created him.   In the seventh stanza of the second part (XIII),
the passageway is spoken of.   This passageway represents the ego,
the path wherein man passes to and fro as he lives his individual and
communal life.

   The structure of this song is notable when taken by itself, but it
becomes more remarkable when the scope of the ceremony is considered.   It will then be seen that this opening song foreshadows the
movement and purpose of the entire ceremony.

SONG *a*

Diagram of Time

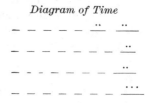

Rhythmic Rendition

I

We heed as unto thee we call;
Oh, send to us thy potent aid!
Help us, Oh, holy place above!
We heed as unto thee we call.

II

We heed as unto thee we call;
Oh, send to us thy potent aid!
Help us, Hotoru, giver of breath!
We heed as unto thee we call.

III

We heed as unto thee we call;
Oh, send to us thy potent aid!
Help us, Shakuru, father of strength!
We heed as unto thee we call.

IV

We heed as unto thee we call;
Oh, send to us thy potent aid!
Help us, h'Uraru, mother of all!
We heed as unto thee we call.

V

We heed as unto thee we call;
Oh, send to us thy potent aid!
Help us, Toharu, giver of food!
We heed as unto thee we call.

VI

We heed as unto thee we call;
Oh, send to us thy potent aid!
Help us, Chaharu, giver of drink!
We heed as unto thee we call.

VII

We heed as unto thee we call;
Oh, send to us thy potent aid!
Help us, Kusharu, sacred to rites!
We heed as unto thee we call.

---

a See the music on page 27.

VIII

We heed as unto thee we call;
Oh, send to us thy potent aid!
Help us, h'Akaru, abode of life!
We heed as unto thee we call.

IX

We heed as unto thee we call;
Oh, send to us thy potent aid!
Help us, Keharu, wall of defense!
We heed as unto thee we call.

X

We heed as unto thee we call;
Oh, send to us thy potent aid!
Help us, Kataharu, center within!
We heed as unto thee we call.

XI

We heed as unto thee we call,
Oh, send to us thy potent aid!
Help us, Kekaru, promise of fire!
We heed as unto thee we call.

XII

We heed as unto thee we call;
Oh, send to us thy potent aid!
Help us, Koritu, word of the fire!
We heed as unto thee we call.

XIII

We heed as unto thee we call;
Oh, send to us thy potent aid!
Help us, Hiwaturu, emblem of days!
We heed as unto thee we call.

PART II. PREPARING THE FEATHERED STEMS

The first thing to be made is the feathered stem carried by the Ku'rahus. It represents the female element; it leads in the ceremony. Other sacred rites among the Pawnees explain this leadership as based upon the belief that life first took form through the female; "She was the first and the leader."

The stem is painted blue with blue clay mixed with running water. The running water, we are told, represents the continuation of life by generation following generation. The color is the symbol of the sky, the dwelling place of the powers.

The song which accompanies the act of painting is in five musical phrases, suggesting the five motions symbolic of the four directions and the above. The exclamation he! (a part of i'hare! give heed!), at the close of each phrase, bears out this interpretation.

The iterated words h'areri (h', breath; areri, a particular place) tell that the thoughts of the singers are fixed on the giving of life by the powers above, whose presence is symbolized by the blue paint now put upon the stem.

Each stanza of all the songs throughout this ceremony is sung four times. The Ku'rahus tells us that this is in recognition of the four paths at the four cardinal points, down which the powers descend, and that it is also an indirect recognition of the powers themselves.

FIRST SONG[a]

Diagram of Time

Rhythmic Rendition

Take we now the blue paint,
Touch with it the stem, putting on the sacred symbol,
Emblem of the clear sky,
Where dwell the gods, who, descending, bring us good gifts,
Gifts of life and plenty.

The feathered stem carried by the Ku'rahus's assistant represents the male element. It is painted green, the color symbolizing Toharu, the living covering of Mother Earth. The key to the symbolism lies in the abbreviated word hure-e, "coming from above." It conveys the idea that the power by which Mother Earth brings forth her green covering, Toharu, comes from the power above, Tira'wa atius.

The fan-shaped pendant hung upon the green stem is made of seven feathers from the young brown eagle, spoken of by the Ku'rahus as the white eagle. These are the feathers worn by warriors, and the bird is the war eagle, the fighter, the defender, the protector.

The combining of the male and female forces on each of the leading requisites of the ceremony, the feathered stems and the ear of corn, has already been noticed.

The song which is sung as the stem is painted green is in six musical phrases, corresponding to the six ceremonial motions: the four directions, the above, and the below.

SECOND SONG[b]

Diagram of Time

Rhythmic Rendition

Take we now the green paint,
Touch with it the stem, the mated stem,
Putting on the emblem, the sacred and living symbol,
Mother earth.
From above descending, bountiful blessings on thee,
Mother earth.

The fan-like appendage of ten brown mottled feathers from the mature brown eagle are here tied upon the blue stem. This eagle is called Kawas; it represents the mother. She is the bearer of life from above and shares with the corn the leadership throughout the ceremony.

It is noticeable that the eagle receives the gifts it bears to man through the lesser powers and not directly from Tira'wa atius. Birds are not powers, but messengers, intermediaries between the lesser powers and man. A glimpse is here obtained of the order which natural forces and objects take in the mind of the Pawnee.

The song of this act is in three phrases. The number three is not symbolized by ceremonial motions; throughout the ceremony songs accompanying acts which do not imply a direct appeal to the powers above fall into three musical phrases.

THIRD SONG[a]

Diagram of Time

Rhythmic Rendition

Oh, Kawas, come, with wings outspread in sunny skies!
Oh, Kawas, come, and bring us peace, thy gentle peace!
Oh, Kawas, come, and give new life to us who pray!

PART III. PAINTING THE EAR OF CORN AND PREPARING THE OTHER SACRED OBJECTS.

The putting of a peculiar design in blue paint on the ear of corn is replete with symbolism. The ear of corn not only represents a life-sustaining product of the earth, but the omniscience which the earth is believed to possess. This omniscience, predicated of the ear of corn, constituted one of its qualifications to act as leader. The Ku'rahus says (line 118): "Mother Earth knows all places and all that happens among men; therefore the corn which comes from her must lead, must direct us where to go."

The painting of the ear of corn represents the securing of its credentials as leader. The blue paint used on this occasion is not put into a shell, as it was when the stems were colored, but into a wooden bowl. The shape of the bowl, an inverted dome, typifies the arching sky, the blue paint its color (see the explanation of line 83). The design put on the ear of corn signifies its journey to the abode of the powers and its return, with their sanction, as leader.

---

[a] Music on page 41.

It is difficult to follow the Pawnee's thought in the words and accompanying act of this song unless it is remembered that he regards the spirit of man, animals, and all other things as able to travel about independent of the body. Moreover, that he conceives it possible for a number of persons so to unite as to think and act as one spirit.

In the song Mother, Atira, is the term applied to the ear of corn as the representative of Mother Earth. This word is preceded by the aspirate, h', significant of the breath, the giving forth of life. h'Atira not only refers to the sustaining of life by food, but also carries the idea that, as leader, the corn bears life-giving power.

The word weri, I am, does not mean the man who paints the corn, but the concerted spirits of the Hako party, which are spoken of in the singular, as though they were one spirit. The use of the plural sign re a little later on in the stanza (line 86) implies the personification of the ear of corn; its spirit is standing with the spirit of the Hako party. These two spirits move together throughout this drama of the consecration of the ear of corn as leader.

In the next stanza the two spirits are flying through the air. There is no incongruity in this procedure; the already mentioned belief relative to spirits makes it rational. In like manner, the color of the paint can hold within it the spirit of the abode of the powers.

The different stages in the progress of the ear of corn on its journey to the abode of the powers are depicted in the different stanzas of the song. In the first, she stands; in the second, she flies; in the third, she touches the boundary of the sky, "where it begins"; in the fourth, she ascends; in the fifth, she reaches the dome, her destination; in the sixth, she descends, the purpose of the journey having been accomplished.

The music is divided into six phrases; six stanzas record the stages of the journey; the number suggests the six ceremonial motions typifying the four directions, the above, and the below.

It would seem from the acts accompanying this song that the ear of corn went up to the abode of the powers by the four paths at the four cardinal points, down which we are told the powers descend, as the lines representing these paths were drawn on the ear before the blue paint was spread over its tip to represent the dome of the sky.

SONG[a]

Diagram of Time

a Music on page 43.

Rhythmic Rendition

I

Tira'wa, harken! Mighty one,
Above us in blue, silent sky!
We standing wait thy bidding here.
The Mother Corn standing waits,
Waits to serve thee here;
The Mother Corn stands waiting here.

II

Tira'wa, harken! Mighty one,
Above us in blue, silent sky!
We flying seek thy dwelling there.
The Mother Corn flying goes
Up to seek thee there;
The Mother Corn goes flying up.

III

Tira'wa, harken! Mighty one,
Above us in blue, silent sky!
We touch upon thy country now.
The Mother Corn touches there,
On the border land;
The Mother Corn is touching there.

IV

Tira'wa, harken! Mighty one,
Above us in blue, silent sky!
The path we reach leads up to thee.
The Mother Corn enters there,
Upward takes her way;
The Mother Corn ascends to thee.

V

Tira'wa, harken! Mighty one,
Above us in blue, silent sky!
Behold! We in thy dwelling stand.
The Mother Corn, standing there,
Leader she is made;
The Mother Corn is leader made.

VI

Tira'wa, harken! Mighty one,
Above us in blue, silent sky!
The downward path we take again.
The Mother Corn, leading us,
Doth thy symbol bear;
The Mother Corn with power leads.

SECOND RITUAL. PREFIGURING THE JOURNEY TO THE SON

The ceremony of offering the Hako was believed to bring great benefits. As the tie to be formed was a close one and likely to have a bearing on the welfare of two tribes, the selection of the man who was to be the Son was not left exclusively to the Father. His choice had to be submitted to the chiefs of his tribe for their approval. Nor did the matter end here, for the chiefs, seemingly unwilling to assume the entire responsibility of a final decision, threw the confirmation of the selection of the Son upon the supernatural, represented by the ear of corn.

To be able to follow the Pawnee's thought one should keep well in mind the native belief in the reality of an invisible world accessible to man. The Ku'rahus explained that in this rite the spirit of the corn and the spirits of the assembled company must meditate together upon the proposed candidate for the Son, must consider his qualifications and his ability to meet the requirements for a successful issue of the ceremony. He said: "As we meditate we sit with bowed heads, and Mother Corn sits with bowed head." When the decision is reached "Mother Corn lifts her head and stands erect, then she moves through the air on her journey to the Son, and we follow."

In this mystical journey Mother Corn "opens the way" between the land of the Fathers and that of the Children. She does more. She enters the village and passes around among the lodges of the people to that of the selected man. She goes in and touches him while he sleeps. It is the spirit of Mother Corn that touches the spirit of the man in a dream. He does not see her who has touched him, but he sees one of the birds which belong to the feathered stem, the eagle, the owl, the duck, or the woodpecker, for the spirits of these birds are there with the spirit of Mother Corn in the lodge of the sleeping man. If, when he awakes, he is able to recall his dream, it is because Mother Corn has "opened his mind." Therefore when the messengers of the Father's party arrive with the tidings, "Your Father is coming," the dreamer is not taken by surprise, but is ready to respond without unnecessary delay.

The old man narrated this symbolic procedure of the ear of corn and its attendant spirits without consciousness that he was saying anything unusual or contrary to ordinary experience. His only comment was, that it was very difficult for the men of the party of the Father so to fix their minds upon the desired end as to secure its accomplishment. He referred to this difficulty several times while explaining the words and meaning of the song. When questioned as to whether the attempt was always successful, he said that when it failed the failure was always due to a lack of earnestness or sincerity on the part of the persons so fixing their minds. By this he did not mean that the men failed because they did not try hard enough to keep their attention upon the desired object, but that there was in their character something which prevented them from .effectually exerting their will power.　He evidently had no doubt as to the reasonableness of the procedure.　To him it was entirely logical.

The journey prefigured by this flight of Mother Corn, afterward actually taken by the party of the Father, has its special songs. Several of them refer directly to this traveling of the spirit of Mother Corn.

The song of this ritual is in two parts, each with four stanzas. The first part relates to finding the Son, "opening the way" to him. The second deals with the Son, preparing him to receive the Father, "opening his mind."

The stanzas are in four musical phrases corresponding to the four paths down which the lesser powers descend to man.　Each closes with the exclamation ha! calling attention, as to an invisible presence.

SONG *a*

Diagram of Time

```
        ..  /  _  ..  ..
_ _ _
/           ..  /  _  ..  _ _
_ _ _ _ _  _  _
/  _  ..  ..
_
        ..  /  _  ..
_ _ _
```

Rhythmic Rendition

I

Mother Corn, Oh hear!　Open our way!
Lo!　As we draw near, let our souls touch thine
While we pray thee:
Children give to us!　Mother Corn, hear!

II

Mother Corn, Oh hear!　Open our way!
Lo!　Our heads we bow, while our souls touch thine;
Then as one mind
Make the choice of Son.　Mother Corn, hear!

III

Mother Corn, Oh hear!　Open our way!
Lo!　With head erect Mother stands, and then
Moves she through air
On her mission bent.　Mother Corn, hear!

IV

Mother Corn, Oh hear!　Open our way!
Lo!　Now over hills, over streams. we go
Taking our way
Toward the Children's land.　Mother Corn, hear!

a Music on page 50.

V

Mother Corn, Oh hear! Open our way!
Lo! Our journey's end now is near, we look
O'er the strange land,
Seeking Children there! Mother Corn, hear!

VI

Mother Corn, Oh hear! Open our way!
Lo! Our eyes behold where they dwell. In their
Village we walk,
Seeking there the Son. Mother Corn, hear!

VII

Mother Corn, Oh hear! Open our way!
Lo! His lodge we find, through the door we pass.
Sleeping he lies,
Knows not we are there. Mother Corn, hear!

VIII

Mother Corn, Oh hear! Open our way!
Lo! Now at her touch comes a dream; then a
Bird calls, "My Son!"
While his soul responds. Mother Corn, hear!

THIRD RITUAL. SENDING THE MESSENGERS

The four messengers were selected informally by the Father from among his near relatives. They were generally young men, lithe and strong of limb, and able to make a long journey quickly. The distance to be traveled varied from a few miles to a hundred or more, and as they must carry all their provisions, it became necessary for them to get over the ground as rapidly as possible.

The formal appointment of these messengers took place in the lodge of the Father, in the presence of the sacred objects spread at ceremonial rest.

When the messengers arrived at the lodge of the Son, he sent for his kindred and consulted with them. Only a recent death in his family or some catastrophe which deprived him of his property would be accepted as sufficient excuse for his not receiving the Hako party. If he accepted the tobacco he would bid the messengers return to the Father and say, "I am ready." In either case he must make gifts to the messengers in recognition of the proffered honor.

The homeward journey was made as quickly as possible, for during the absence of the messengers nothing could be done. As soon, however, as the returning young men were discerned on the prairie the village was astir, and the men of the Father's party, with the Ku'rahus, assembled at his lodge to receive them ceremonially and to hear their tidings.

The messenger dispatched on such errands was called Rawiska'-rarahoru, One who walks carrying the tobacco.

The music of the song of this ritual is in three phrases. Like other songs in this ceremony having the same number, it accompanies acts which do not directly appeal to the supernatural.   The first stanza is addressed to the messengers; the second to the Father's party within the lodge.

SONG a

Diagram of Time

Rhythmic Rendition

I

I bid you travel o'er the land to the Son,
And with you take these words of mine unto him:
"Behold!. Your Father comes to you speedily."

II

We wait their journey o'er the land to the Son,
When they will give these words of mine unto him:
'Behold! Your Father comes to you speedily."

FOURTH RITUAL

PART I.   VIVIFYING THE SACRED OBJECTS

These first four rituals are in sequence and deal with the peculiar preparations required for the ceremony.   In the first ritual the sacred articles are prepared; in the second ritual the Son is selected; in the third ritual the Father notifies the Son, who responds; and in the fourth ritual the sacred articles are vivified and assume leadership.   In these preparations the supernatural powers bear a leading part.   At the very beginning, in the first song of the first ritual, their presence is invoked, and in the fourth ritual, after man's preparations for the ceremony are completed, they accept his work.

The first, second, and third rituals took place in the lodge of the Father, where the sacred objects were guarded day and night by the Ku'rahus, his assistant, and the chief, or by persons appointed to act as their substitutes.   In the fourth ritual the objects were for the first time taken outside the lodge, under the open sky, where the final act of their preparation took place.   They were tied upon a pole and elevated in the early dawn, that they might be vivified by the powers and acknowledged as their representatives.

The order in which these sacred objects were tied upon the pole indicates their relative significance in this ceremony.   The two feathered stems were placed near the top, because they typify the powers of the upper world.   But they also represent the male and female elements, therefore the male stem was placed toward the south—the light, the day, the sun; and the female stem toward the north—the darkness, the night, the moon.   Beneath the feathered stems were the rattles and the ear of corn, representing the living covering of

---

a Music on page 56.

the earth, and below these was the wildcat skin. These typify the powers of the lower world.

All these articles were tied on the pole so as to face the east. We are told in the song of the ninth ritual that down the path at the east came the powers that are potent in this rite.

Behind these objects, toward the west, where dwell the powers which influence the life of man and control disaster and death, were bound the right and left wing of an eagle. These wings were spread as though supporting the sacred objects, as the wings sustain the body of a bird in the air. Throughout the ceremony the position of the two eagle wings, both when on the pole and when borne at each end of the line of men, serves to unify the different sacred objects into the similitude of a winged body. This unification does not, however, interfere with the separate functions of each article or with the character of its symbols.

The dawn ritual throws light on the significance of the elevation of the sacred objects under the open sky before the break of day. Before this act, these objects had lain at rest; but after it, when they had been vivified by the wind and the sun, they at once became active and thenceforth they led the people throughout the ceremony.

PART II. MOTHER CORN ASSUMES LEADERSHIP

This activity is manifest in the song of part II, where the ear of corn passes to the front and assumes the position of leader. The ceremonial steps taken by the chief, as he carries this representative of Mother Earth with her life-sustaining force, dramatically represent the corn as advancing out of the past (from behind the Ku'rahus with his symbolic feathered stem), coming into the present (beside him), and then going on before, moving along the unbroken path that stretches out of the past into the future. The four steps taken by the chief bearing the ear of corn refer to the four paths down which the powers descend to man, and the four steps taken by the six men following Mother Corn as the second stanza is sung indicate the dependence of man upon these supernatural powers.

This song falls into six phrases. The number suggests the recognition of all the powers which come near to man, which are represented by the four directions, the above, and the below, thus bearing out the full significance of the symbolic steppings.

SONG <i>a</i>

Diagram of Time

— — — — — — — — — — —
— — — — — — — — — — —
— — — — — — — — — — —
— — — — — — — — — — —
— — — — — — — — — — —
— — — — — — — — — — —

---

a Music on page 60.

Rhythmic Rendition

I

Mother with the life-giving power now comes,
Stepping out of far distant days she comes,
Days wherein to our fathers gave she food;
As to them, so now unto us she gives,
Thus she will to our children faithful be.
Mother with the life-giving power now comes!

II

Mother with the life-giving power is here.
Stepping out of far distant days she comes.
Now she forward moves, leading as we walk
Toward the future, where blessings she will give,
Gifts for which we have prayed granting to us.
Mother with the life-giving power is here!

PART III. THE HAKO PARTY PRESENTED TO THE POWERS

The recognition of man's dependence on the supernatural is still
further emphasized by the peculiar dramatic movements which
accompany the songs after the Hako party for the first time as a body
passes outside of the lodge, within which all the preceding ceremonies
have taken place.

The sacred objects, which under the open sky had been vivified and
acknowledged by the supernatural powers, now lead the party along
certain lines defined by their symbolically numbered steps to face the
localities where these powers were believed to dwell. First the east
was faced and the powers there were addressed; then the west; next the
south; and then the north. At each of these points the sacred objects
were elevated, while the people invoked the powers to "behold" (to
recognize and accept) those who were about to perform the ceremony.
When each of the four cardinal points had been addressed and the
leader had completed the ceremonial steps, the outline of a man had
been traced upon the ground. Concerning this outline the Ku'rahus
explained that it "is the image from Tira'wa." "Its feet are where
we now stand, its feet are with our feet."

This figure would seem to represent a visible answer to the ceremonial appeal of the people and to indicate a willingness of the supernatural powers to grant their presence throughout the coming
ceremony. This interpretation of the tracing is borne out by the
words of the Ku'rahus when he says that "it will move with our feet
as we now, bearing the sacred objects, take four steps in the presence
of all the powers, and begin our journey to the land of the Son."

The song addressed to the east is in four musical phrases, while
the songs to the west, south, and north are in six musical phrases. The
four-phrase song is sung to Tira'wa atius, the father of all things,
and it is noticeable that all the songs throughout the ceremony which
specially address this power are in a four-phrase rhythm. When all

the other powers are addressed, those at the four directions, the above, and the below, a six-phrase rhythm is used.

The number of the repeats and phrases of the songs seems also to be connected with the ceremonial steps, which are in groups of four, eight, and sixteen. The number sixteen is said by the Ku'rahus to represent completeness.

According to native measurement, the height of a man is equal to the stretch of his arms. Looking at the diagram of the figure stepped upon the ground, we note that sixteen steps give the spread of the arms and the same number of steps marks the length of the man. This bears out the statement of the Ku'rahus that sixteen, or four times four, represents completeness.

FIRST SONG a

Diagram of Time

Rhythmic Rendition

Look on us as here we are standing, raising our voices!
Look on us as here we, presenting, lift now these emblems that are so holy up to
thy gaze!
Swift, a flash from out of the heavens
Falls on us as here we are standing, looking at thee.

SECOND SONG b

Diagram of Time

Rhythmic Rendition

I

Look down, West gods,c look upon us! We gaze afar on your dwelling.
Look down while here we are standing, look down upon us, ye mighty!
Ye thunder gods, now behold us!
Ye lightning gods, now behold us!
Ye that bring life, now behold us!
Ye that bring death, now behold us!

---

a Music on page 63.
b Music on page 65.
c Gods, meaning powers, is used solely on account of the rhythm.

II

Look down, South gods, look upon us!   We gaze afar on your dwelling.
Look down while here we are standing, look down upon us, ye mighty!
Ye daylight gods, now behold us!
Ye sunshine gods, now behold us!
Ye increase gods, now behold us!
Ye plenty gods, now behold us!

III

Look down, North gods, look upon us!   We gaze afar on your dwelling.
Look down while here we are standing, look down upon us, ye mighty!
Ye darkness gods, now behold us!
Ye moonlight gods, now behold us!
Ye that direct, now behold us!
Ye that discern, now behold us!

The structure of the first division of the Preparation, initial rites, is worthy of notice.   Each of its four rituals is complete in itself, but the symbols, rhythms, and movements of all are closely connected, forming a drama of two worlds.   The four rituals are a compact whole, from the opening appeal in the first song of the first ritual to the culmination in the fourth ritual, from the appeal to the powers in the order of creation for their presence to the answer of this appeal made visible by the rhythmic ceremonial steps, in the form of the symbolic presence whose "feet will move with" the feet of the suppliants as they journey to the land of the Son.

SECOND DIVISION.   THE JOURNEY

FIFTH RITUAL

PART I.   MOTHER CORN ASSERTS AUTHORITY

The three songs of the first part of the fifth ritual have a fixed sequence, and relate to the supernatural leadership of the ear of corn.

The first refers to the second ritual, where the spirits of those assembled in the lodge became as one spirit and joined the spirit of Mother Corn in her search for the Son (see explanation by the Ku'rahus, fifth ritual, first song).   The journey then prefigured is now about to begin.   The Father's party are again enjoined to become as one spirit, and as one spirit to follow Mother Corn over "the devious way."

FIRST SONG a

The first song, like that of the second ritual, is in four musical phrases.   Both refer to the four paths down which the lesser powers descend.

Diagram of Time

<hr>

a Music on page 68.

Rhythmic Rendition

I

The Mother leads and we follow on,
Her devious pathway before us lies.
She leads us as were our fathers led
Down through the ages.

II

The Mother leads and we follow on,
Her pathway straight, where a stage each day
We forward walk, as our fathers walked
Down through the ages.

When the familiar landmarks about the village had disappeared in the distance and the people looked over the wide stretch of country, the dangers of the journey were naturally suggested, so that the first stanza of the second song is an appeal to Mother Corn, asking her whether a safe path lies before them.   The second stanza gives her assuring answer, that the path does lie straight before them.

This song, being one of procedure only, is in three phrases.

SECOND SONG*a*

Diagram of Time

Rythmic Rendition

I

Looking o'er the prairie, naught our eyes discern there,
Wide the land stretches out before us;
Then we cry aloud to Mother Corn: "Doth thy pathway lie here?"

II

Heeding now our crying, while our eyes she opens,
Mother Corn moveth out before us
On the lonely prairie, where we see straight the pathway lies there!

In the third song, Mother Corn reminds the people of the supernatural leadership bestowed on her by the powers above in the distant past, and now renewed in the ceremonies which have just taken place.

This song, referring directly to the powers above, is in five musical phrases, suggesting the motions toward the four directions and the above.

---

a Music on page 70.

THIRD SONG[a]

Diagram of Time

Rythmic Rendition

I

Hark! She speaks, and quickly we turn to her,
Looking toward the west to the spot where we
Passed 'neath the eyes of gods; and now do we heed her words:
" Yonder is the place in the distant west
Whence I have come out of the past to you."

II

" Born of the earth and touched by the deep blue sky,
Have I chosen been by the gods to lead.
You are to hear my voice and follow my strict commands,
As your fathers did in the days gone by.
Thence come I to open your pathway here."

These three songs, the first part of the fifth ritual, seem to have been disciplinary in their influence. They tended to restrain the individual from self-seeking by placing over the party a supernatural leader, on whom all minds must be fixed and to whom all must give obedience. Thus, from the very outset, an authority was established against which none dared rebel.

PART II. SONGS AND CEREMONIES OF THE WAY

The Hako party was an impressive sight as it journeyed over the country. It could never be mistaken for an ordinary group of hunters, warriors, or travelers. At the head of the long procession, sufficiently in advance to be distinguished from the others, walked three men—the Ku'rahus, holding before him the brown-eagle feathered stem, on his right the chief, grasping with both hands the wildcat skin and Mother Corn, and at his left the assistant Ku'rahus, bearing the white-eagle feathered stem. These three men wore buffalo robes with the hair outside. On their heads was the white downy feather of their office and their faces were anointed with the sacred ointment and red paint. They bore the sacred objects forward steadily and silently, looking neither to the right nor left, believing that they were under supernatural guidance. Behind them walked the doctors with their insignia, the eagle wings; then the singers with the drum, and behind them the

---

[a] Music on page 71.

men and women of the party with the ponies laden with gifts and needed supplies of food.

Over the wide prairie for miles and miles this order was preserved day after day until the journey came to an end. If from some distant vantage point a war party should descry the procession, the leader would silently turn his men that they might not meet the Hako party, for the feathered stems are mightier than the warrior; before them he must lay down his weapon, forget his anger, and be at peace.

No object met on the journey to the Son presented its ordinary aspect to the Hako party. Everything seen was regarded as a manifestation of the supernatural powers under whose favor this ceremony was to take place; hence the trees, the streams, the mountains, the buffalo were each addressed in song. This attitude toward nature is strikingly brought out in the two songs, which are in sequence, sung at the crossing of a stream.

Throughout this ceremony water is treated as one of the lesser powers. It is employed only for sacred purposes, and is never used in the ordinary way. To profane water would bring punishment upon the whole party (see the first ritual, line 29), and consequently when a stream ran across a line of travel no person could step into it as he commonly would do. A halt was called and the Ku'rahus led in the singing of the song in which Kawas is asked to grant the party permission to ford the stream. According to Pawnee rituals, water at the creation was given to the woman, so Kawas, representing the mother, could grant permission. The request is embodied in four stanzas. In the first the water touches the feet; in the second the feet stand in the water; in the third the feet move in the water; in the fourth the water covers the feet (note the resemblance of entering the stream to entering the lodge, seventh ritual, part I).

After the stream was crossed the people halted on the bank to sing the song to the wind, led by the Ku'rahus. It also is in four stanzas. The wind is called upon to come and dry the water which the people may not irreverently touch. In the first stanza the wind touches the people; in the second it lightly brushes their bodies; in the third it circles about them; in the fourth it envelops them. Thus the wind, one of the lesser powers, comes between the people and the penalty incurred by profanely touching water.

In these ceremonies the people were constantly reminded that they were in the presence of the unseen powers manifested to them in the natural objects met upon the journey. To those initiated into the inner meaning of the rite, the appeal at the crossing of the stream to Kawas (the feminine element) and to the wind (typical of the breath of life) was connected with the symbolism of running water, explained in the seventh ritual as representing the giving of life from generation to generation.

The seventh, eighth, ninth, and tenth songs originally belonged to the journey, but we are told the buffalo are no longer seen; neither are the mountains or the mesas; so these songs are now sung in the lodge and only that the objects seen by past generations may be remembered.

There are no present means of ascertaining whether the songs here given comprise all that were used by the Pawnees on the journey; they are all that had been taught the Ku′rahus who is the authority for this record of the Hako ceremony.

SONG TO THE TREES AND STREAMS a

Diagram of Time

Rhythmic Rendition

I

Dark against the sky yonder distant line
Lies before us.   Trees we see, long the line of trees,
Bending, swaying in the breeze.

II

Bright with flashing light yonder distant line
Runs before us, swiftly runs, swift the river runs,
Winding, flowing o'er the land.

III

Hark! Oh hark!   A sound, yonder distant sound
Comes to greet us, singing comes, soft the river's song,
Rippling gently 'neath the trees.

SONG WHEN CROSSING THE STREAMS b

Diagram of Time

Rhythmic Rendition

I

Behold, upon the river's brink we stand!
River we must cross;
Oh Kawas, come!   To thee we call.   Oh come, and thy permission give
Into the stream to wade and forward go.

---

a Music on page 73.   b Music on page 75.

II

Behold, the water touches now our feet!
River we must cross;
Oh Kawas, hear! To thee we call. Oh come, and thy permission give
On through the stream to pass and forward go.

III

Behold, our feet now in the water move!
River we must cross;
Oh Kawas, heed! To thee we call. Oh come, and thy permission give
On through the stream to pass and forward go.

IV

Behold, the water covers now our feet!
River we must cross;
Oh Kawas, hear! To thee we call. Oh come, and thy permission give
On through the stream to pass and forward go.

SONG TO THE WIND [a]

Diagram of Time

Rhythmic Rendition

I

Hither, Winds, come to us, touch where water
O'er us flowed when we waded;
Come, Oh Winds, come!

II

Now the Winds come to us, touch where water
O'er us flowed when we waded;
Now the Winds come.

III

Here and there touch the Winds where the water
O'er us flowed when we waded;
Now the Winds touch.

IV

Lo! The Winds round us sweep where water
O'er us flowed. Safe now are we,
By the Winds safe.

SONG TO THE BUFFALO [b]

Diagram of Time

---

[a] Music on page 77.   [b] Music on page 79.

Rhythmic Rendition

I

When to prepare us a pathway Mother Corn sped
Far in her search for the Son, passing this place,
Lo! She beheld buffalo in many herds here.

II

Now, as we walk in the pathway Mother Corn made,
Looking on all that she saw, passing this place,
Lo! We behold buffalo and many trails here.

SONG OF THE PROMISE OF THE BUFFALO *a*

Diagram of Time

```
 /           ..            ..
— — — — — — — — — — — — — —
 /            ..
— — — — — — — —
 /         ..
— — — — —
          /      ..
— — — — — — — —
```

Rhythmic Rendition

I

Clouds of dust arise, rolling up from earth,
Spreading onward; herds are there,
Speeding on before,
Going straight where we must journey.

II

What are those we see moving in the dust?
This way coming from the herd;
Buffalo and calf!
Food they promise for the Children.

SONG TO THE MOUNTAINS *b*

Diagram of Time

```
 ./.      ..          ..    ..        ...
— — — — — — — — — — — — — —
 /        ..          ..              ...
— — — — — — — — — —
         ..                    ..
— — — — — — — — —
 /        ..    ..               ..
— — — — — — — — —
```

Rhythmic Rendition

I

Mountains loom upon the path we take;
Yonder peak now rises sharp and clear;
Behold! It stands with its head uplifted,
Thither go we, since our way lies there.

---

a Music on page 80.　　　　　*b* Music on page 82.

II

Mountains loom upon the path we take;
Yonder peak now rises sharp and clear;
Behold! We climb, drawing near its summit;
Steeper grows the way and slow our steps.

III

Mountains loom upon the path we take;
Yonder peak that rises sharp and clear,
Behold us now on its head uplifted;
Planting there our feet, we stand secure.

IV

Mountains loom upon the path we take;
Yonder peak that rose so sharp and clear,
Behold us now on its head uplifted;
Resting there at last, we sing our song.

SONG TO THE MESA [a]

Diagram of Time

Rhythmic Rendition

I

The mesa see; its flat top like a straight line cuts across the sky;
It blocks our path, and we must climb, the mesa climb.

II

More mesas see; their flat tops rise against the sky, they bar our path;
We reach their base, and we must climb, the mesas climb.

III

The mesa's side we now ascend, the sharp ridge pass, its flat top reach;
There lies our path that we must take, and forward go.

IV

The mesas rise around us still, their flat tops cut across the sky;
They block our way, yet still we climb, the mesas climb.

PART III. MOTHER CORN REASSERTS LEADERSHIP

The next two songs are in sequence and refer to the mystical journey and leadership of Mother Corn. They return to the theme of part I of this ritual.

Upon the journey the people had been led to appeal to different objects as manifestations of the supernatural powers, but now that the journey was nearing its end the maintenance of discipline required that the people should be reminded that Mother Corn was leading and that to her they were still to render undivided obedience.

The first song was sung at the border of the land of the Son.

---

[a] Music on page 84.

FIRST SONG *a*

Diagram of Time

Rhythmic Rendition

I

Here we give our thanks, led by Mother Corn,
As our eyes dwell upon the borders of the land
Where dwell the Children we are seeking.

II

Now we travel on, led by Mother Corn,
Soon our eyes catch the print of footsteps on the ground,
Made by the Children we are seeking.

III

Still we travel on, led by Mother Corn,
Now our eyes look on people walking to and fro;
They the Children are we are seeking.

When the village where the ceremony was to take place was clearly in sight the second song was sung.

At the close of the song the sacred objects were laid at rest. This was the first time during daylight, since the journey began, that they had been so placed. They had always been in the hands of the Ku′rahus and his assistants, who walked at the head of the long procession as it moved over the country.

SECOND SONG *b*

Diagram of Time

Rhythmic Rendition

I

Here is the place where I came, seeking to find the Son;
Here have I led you again, here is our journey's end.
Thanks we give unto the Mother Corn!
Here is the place where she came, seeking to find the Son;
Here she has led us again, here is our journey's end.

---

a Music on page 86.　　　　　　*b* Music on page 88.

II

Here to this place have we come, bringing the Son our gifts,
All of the gifts that go forth bearing the promised help.
Thanks he'll give as he sees, Mother Corn,
All of the gifts that we bring, bring to his village here;
Here, where you led, Mother Corn; here, where our journey ends.

THIRD DIVISION. ENTERING THE VILLAGE OF THE SON AND CON-
SECRATING HIS LODGE

SIXTH RITUAL

PART I. THE SON'S MESSENGER RECEIVED

The messenger dispatched by the Son to the Hako party, which was
now camped outside the village, was received as a son. He was met,
conducted to the tent of the Father, where food was offered him, and
he was clad in gala garments. The first song accompanied these acts,
which, the K 'rahus explained, represented "the care of a father for
his child."

SONG *a*

Diagram of Time

Rhythmic Rendition

I

Now our eyes look on him who is here;
He is as the Son we have sought;
He brings again tidings from the Son:
"Father, come to me, here I sit,
Waiting here for thee."

II

Now our·eyes look on him who is clad
As befits the Son we have sought;
He, arising, walks; follow we his steps,
Moving slowly on toward the Son,
Where he waiting sits.

PART II. THE HAKO PARTY ENTER THE VILLAGE

Led by the Son's messenger, the party moved to the edge of the
village, where a halt was made, in order to conform to the movements
of Mother Corn in her mystical journey (second ritual). "We must
do as she did," says the Ku'rahus.

---

a Music on page 90.

After singing the first stanza, the party entered the village and passed on to the lodge pointed out to them by the messenger, where they again halted and sang the second stanza.

These songs are repeated in the sixteenth ritual, when the child is sought.

SONG a

Diagram of Time

Rhythmic Rendition

I

Where is he, the Son?
Where his dwelling place that I seek?
Which can be his lodge, where he sits
Silent, waiting, waiting there for me?

II

Here is he, the Son,
Here is his dwelling place that I seek;
This is here his lodge, where he sits
Silent, waiting, waiting here for me.

SEVENTH RITUAL THE CONSECRATION OF THE LODGE

PART I. TOUCHING AND CROSSING THE THRESHOLD

The ceremony at the door of the lodge is another instance of the prefiguration of an act. The chief, with the cat skin and the ear of corn, advanced, and during the singing of the first stanza of the following song stepped on the threshold and touched but did not cross it.

The stanzas, which are in five musical phrases, were sung four times in remembrance of the path at the four directions, down which Tira'wa atius sends, by the lesser powers, the gifts promised through this ceremony.

While the second stanza was being sung, the chief crossed the threshold, and, in recognition of the powers and to represent the progression of a long life, took the four ceremonial steps, which are sometimes spoken of as reaching and crossing the four hills.

Thus the way into the lodge was opened by Mother Corn, assisted by the tact of the wild cat carried by the chief (see page 23), so that the direct representatives of the powers above, the feathered stems, might enter.

The chief retired two steps behind the Ku'rahus, outside the lodge door. The Ku'rahus and his assistant, carrying the feathered stems,

---

a Music on page 92.

advanced and repeated in the same order the movements made by the chief. Meanwhile the third and fourth stanzas were sung. At the close the two men retired and took their places beside the chief.

SONG*a*

Diagram of Time.

Rhythmic Rendition

I

Sent down by powers on high,
She bears a promise most sure;
The Mother Corn breathes forth life,
On threshold She stands
Of my Son's dwelling.　All's well!

II

Sent down by powers on high,
She bears a promise most sure;
The Mother Corn breathes forth life,
The threshold crosses
Of my Son's dwelling.　All's well!

III

Sent down by powers on high,
She bears a promise most sure;
Now Kawas brings new life,
On threshold She stands here
Of my Son's dwelling.　All's well!

IV

Sent down by powers on high,
She bears a promise most sure—
Now Kawas, bringing new life,
The threshold crosses
Of my Son's dwelling.　All's well!

PART II.　CONSECRATING THE LODGE

When the Hako entered the long passageway the wildcat skin and the ear of corn were carried a few steps in advance of the feathered stems, thus being the first to enter the large circular room. This relative position of the corn was maintained during the first two circuits around the lodge, Mother Corn "opening the way."

The stanzas of the song are in four musical phrases, and each

----

a Music on page 94.

stanza is sung four times in recognition of the four directions, for Mother Corn is breathing forth within the lodge the gift of life brought down from Tira'wa atius by the lesser powers.

FIRST SONG a

Diagram of Time

Rhythmic Rendition

I

The Mother Corn, with breath of life,
Now enters into my Son's lodge;
There she walks within;
With breath of life walks Mother Corn.

II

The Mother Corn, with breath of life,
Now circles she within the lodge,
Walking round within;
With breath of life walks Mother Corn.

Now the wildcat skin and the ear of corn are taken back into line with the feathered stems, and Kawas becomes the leader. The first stanza of the song accompanying the third and fourth circuits of the lodge speaks of her hovering as over a nest. In the second she flies about, cleansing her nest of all impurities by the flapping of her wings. Meanwhile the two doctors with their eagle wings also simulate the cleansing of the nest, sweeping out of the lodge all harmful influences.

SECOND SONG b

Diagram of Time

Rhythmic Rendition

I

Kawas, bearing new life, entereth this dwelling,
Comes as to her own nest, on her spread pinions;
There so gently she hovers over these her Children.

II

Kawas, bearing new life, flieth through this dwelling,
All the lodge she cleanses, with her wings sweeping,
Making clear the place, sweeping out the harm and danger.

---

a Music on page 97.　　　　　　　　　b Music on page 98.

PART III. CLOTHING THE SON AND OFFERING SMOKE

The lodge having been made ready as a nest within which life might be given and made secure, the Father performed his first act of recognition and responsibility. He put upon the Son the garments he had previously prepared for the purpose. When clad in the finely embroidered clothing, the Son was told to make the offering of smoke to Tira'wa atius, as a prayer for the consecration of the new-born relationship.

FIRST SONG[a]

Diagram of Time

Rhythmic Rendition

I

My son, now heed, attend to the command I give to you:
Oh, speak to the gods list'ning [b] above us!
Oh, let your prayers ascend to the mighty ones on high!

II

My son obeys. His voice is now trav'ling far, speeding on;
It goes to the list'ning gods above us;
There will his prayer be heard by the mighty ones on high.

The ceremony of offering smoke was conducted by a priest, who instructed the Son as to the order in which the stem of the pipe and the smoke must be offered to the various directions. Meanwhile the Fathers with the Hako stood before the Son singing this song, which voiced their participation in the offering.

SECOND SONG[b]

Diagram of Time

Rhythmic Rendition

See the smoke pass by!
Rising high above, follows where his voice
Sped, intent to reach
Where the gods[c] abide in the deep blue sky.
See the smoke pass by!

---

[a] Music on page 101.
[b] Music on page 103.

[c] The word gods, meaning powers, is used because of the rhythm.

See the smoke ascend!
Now the odor mounts, follows where his voice
Sped, intent to reach
Where the gods *a* abide.   There the odor pleads,
Pleads to gain us help.

In the first ritual of the Preparation, when the making of the Hako had been completed, the Father had offered smoke to Tira'wa atius, the father of all, the giver of life.   It was a prayer for the fulfilment of the ceremony about to be inaugurated.   Now when the lodge had been made ready as a nest, smoke was offered by the Son, who was to be the recipient of the gifts promised by Tira'wa through the ceremony. This act of the Son, performed at the request of the Father, bringing the two together before Tira'wa atius, closed the first division of the Hako ceremony.

THE CEREMONY

FIRST DIVISION. THE PUBLIC CEREMONY

EIGTHTH RITUAL (FIRST DAY).   THE FATHERS FEED THE CHILDREN

Heretofore the rites of preparation had been in the presence of the Hako party, the Son, and his immediate kindred, but after the offering of smoke the heralds were commanded to summon the people to the lodge.   Anyone could now come in and join the party of the Son in the making of gifts, and share in the general benefits of the ceremony.

When the messenger of the Son had come to the Fathers, outside the village, he had been fed, as a paternal act, and now, when the people, representing the Children, were gathered within the lodge, the Father's first act was to place food before them.   While it was yet standing beside the fire, the sacred objects were taken up from their place at the west and carried four times around the lodge. The songs which accompanied these circuits were for the instruction of the people, teaching them to remember the powers before partaking of their gifts.   The first, an appeal to Tira'wa atius, is in five musical phrases, suggesting the five motions symbolic of the four directions and the above.   It was sung four times.

FIRST SONG *b*

Diagram of Time

/ __ __ ___ / ..
_ __ __ ___ _ __

/ __ __ ___ / ..
_ __ __ ___ _ __

/ __ __ ___ / ..
_ __ __ ___ _ __

/ __ __ ___ / ..
_ __ __ ___ _ __

/ __ __ ___ / ..
_ __ __ ___ _ __

---

a Gods, meaning powers, is used because of the rhythm.   *b* Music on page 107.

Rhythmic Rendition

Father, unto thee we cry!
Father thou of gods *a* and men;
Father thou of all we hear;
Father thou of all we see—
Father, unto thee we cry!

The second song refers to the lesser powers only, they who can approach man, bringing him help derived from Tira'wa atius. Their symbols are the four motions, indicating the four paths at the cardinal points down which they descend. The song is in four musical phrases; it was given four times.

SECOND SONG *b*

Diagram of Time

Rhythmic Rendition

Father, thou above, father of the gods, *a*
They who can come near and touch us,
Do thou bid them bring us help.
Help we need. Father, hear us!

The third song refers to Mother Corn, who leads in all the opening ceremonies. She is an intermediary between the lesser powers and man, and as she now walks before the Children, bearing the promise of peace and plenty, they give her thanks.

THIRD SONG *c*

Diagram of Time

Rhythmic Rendition

I

See! The Mother Corn comes hither, making all hearts glad!
Making all hearts glad!
Give her thanks, she brings a blessing; now, behold! she is here!

II

Yonder Mother Corn is coming, coming unto us!
Coming unto us!
Peace and plenty she is bringing; now, behold! she is here!

---

a The word gods, meaning powers, is used solely on account of the rhythm.
b Music on page 108.
c Music on page 109.

The purpose of the ceremony, in the carrying out of which the male and female elements were so fully symbolized, was kept continually before the people.

The lodge was divided, the north half was female, the south was male; the north was night and the south was day. The brown-eagle feathered stem, Kawas, when at rest in the holy place, lay toward the north, and the white-eagle feathered stem, the male, was toward the south.

When the feathered stems were waved over the heads of the people to the rhythm of the songs, as they moved from the west by the north, east, and south, to the west again, Kawas, the mother, was carried next to the Children, and the white-eagle feathered stem was borne on the outside, as the defender.

Each time the sacred objects were taken up four circuits were made. These, we are told, were in recognition of the four paths; they also signified the four powers which were active at the creation of man, and they represented the two eagles, the ear of corn, and the wildcat. This multiplication of symbols is not uncommon. In this instance they all refer to the gift of life, the birth of children. Down the four paths came the lesser powers; four of these were instrumental in placing man upon the earth; and the four ceremonial articles are the bearers of the promise of unfailing generations.

During each circuit a stanza was sung four times. At the end of the fourth circuit "the symbol of completion," four times four, had been given in song.

While the lodge in general referred to the nest, the holy place at the west, back of the fire, was its special representative. There the Hako were laid at ceremonial rest after each four circuits of the lodge. From the beginning of the public ceremony this act was always accompanied by songs and movements expressive of its meaning.

The songs are in groups of two. The first in each group relates to the eagle flying toward her nest, the young birds crying out at her approach. Their welcoming cry is signified by the song, and the flying of the eagle by the movements of the feathered stems. The second song refers to the alighting of the bird upon its nest. At the close of the second stanza the stems were leaned upon the crotched stick, their feather pendants resting upon the cat skin, thus symbolizing the mother bird settled down upon her nest.

The songs of these two groups are repeated a great many times during the progress of the ceremony, for after every fourth circuit of the lodge the feathered stems must be laid at rest and the act accompanied by one group of these songs, according to the choice of the Ku'rahus.

SONGS FOR LAYING DOWN THE FEATHERED STEMS

SONG a

Diagram of Time

Rhythmic Rendition

I

See where she comes to her little ones lying so snugly and safely the nest in!
Hark! She is calling; hear her,
List as her nestlings make answer;
See how she gently hovers.
Happy our hearts as we look on her hovering over her nestlings so gently.

II

See where she comes to her little ones lying so snugly and safely the nest in!
Hark! She is calling; hear her,
List as her nestlings answer;
See her alighting gently.
Happy our hearts as we see her alighting there over her nestlings so gently.

SONG b

Diagram of Time

Rhythmic Rendition

I

Loud, loud the young eagles cry, cry, seeing their mother come;
Flies she to them slantwise, flies;
Then over the nest she hangs, there hovering, stays her flight;
Thanks, thanks as we look we give.

II

Thanks, thanks, from our hearts we give, thanks give as we watch the bird
As she to them slantwise flies:
Then over her nest she drops; there, folding her wings, she rests,
Rests safely within her nest.

---

a Music on page 111.   *b* Music on page 113.

SONG *a*

Diagram of Time

_ _ _ _ _ _ _ _ ´ _ _ _ ´ _ _ . . ´ _ _ _ _ _ _ _ _ _
_ _ ´ _ _ _ . . ´ _ _ _ _ _ _ _ . . .
_ _ _ _ _ _ _ ´ _ _ . . ´ _ _ _ _ _ _

Rhythmic Rendition

I

Behold! An eagle now approaches; sedately flying, her course straight winging to
　us she is coming;
'Tis Kawas we are watching, 'tis Kawas coming to seek here her nest.
Behold her ever nearer flying, still nearer coming, her young ones calling her.
　Will she alight?

II

Behold! An eagle now is circling, is widely circling above us, winging her way to
　her nestlings;
'Tis Kawas we are watching, 'tis Kawas coming to seek here her nest.
Behold her ever nearer circling, still nearer circling, her young ones calling her
　there to alight.

SONG *b*

Diagram of Time

_ .. _ _ _ .. _ _ _ _ _ _ _ _ _ .. _ _ _ _ .. _ _ _ _ .. _
_ .. _ _ _ _ .. _ _ _ _ .. _ _ _ _ .. _ _ _ _ _

Rhythmic Rendition

I

Now she soareth, Kawas soareth, leaves her nestlings, flies above them; will she
　leave them, leave her young?
Far she gazes, sees no danger, then contented she descends.

II

Slow she falleth, Kawas falleth, wings outspreading, hovers o'er them, o'er her
　nestlings, o'er her young;
Long she hovers, then, descending, on her nestlings she alights.

When the Hako had been laid at rest the Fathers served the food,
which had been waiting by the fire, to the children. At the conclusion of the meal the Children dispersed to their homes, and the first
day's ceremony came to an end.

NINTH RITUAL (FIRST NIGHT). INVOKING THE VISIONS

The gathering of the Children, the four circuits of the lodge by the
Hako, and the partaking of food provided by the Fathers were introductory to the opening of the ceremony proper, which took place on
the first night.

---

a Music on page 114.　　　　　*b* Music on page 116.

The stars were shining when the Children were again seated in the lodge. The wood was piled upon the fire, and as the flames leaped high, the Ku'rahus, his assistant, and the chief arose from behind the holy place and took up the Hako. Among the Omahas this act was accompanied by a song referring to the eagle rising from its nest, which the movements of the feathered stems vividly pictured. The Pawnees had no such songs, and the Hako were taken up without any symbolic movements.

In the song belonging to this first night, the visions that "attend the Hako" were invoked.

According to the explanations of the Ku'rahus, these visions resembled dreams, inasmuch as they often came during sleep, but they also appeared when the dreamer was awake. They might be called revelations, which served either to strengthen a purpose or to suggest means by which a plan could be carried out to insure success to some cherished project. Through such visions, we are told, the manner of procedure of the ceremony had been taught and its details prefigured, details which were afterward carefully followed so as to conform to what was regarded as a supernaturally given model.

The birds, the animals, and the products of the earth represented on the Hako communicated with man by visions. In the song of invocation these visions are personified. They hear the summons in their dwelling place above; they descend and pass over the quiet earth, making their way to the door of the lodge, where they pause; they cross the threshold and "walk within"; they move around and fill the space, touching all the people; this accomplished, they "walk away" and ascend to their abode on high.

We note that the visions follow the same sequence of movements that the Hako party followed in entering the lodge; they pause at the door, then enter and "walk within"; they move about and touch the people in prefiguration of the bestowal of gifts promised through the ceremony.

This song was quite impressive, sung as the writer heard it by a hundred or more voices. The Ku'rahus and his assistants, as they moved around the lodge, were followed by the choir, singers bearing the drum, and the song was taken up by all the people—men, women, and children—until the lodge vibrated with the sonorous melody. At the close of the fourth stanza the Hako were laid at rest with the songs belonging to that act; the eagle had gone to her nest, leaving the space clear for the mystic visitors, the visions, who now walked within the lodge. After a time the Hako were again taken up and the last four stanzas were sung; then the eagle once more alighted upon her nest, the visions had departed, they had "touched" the Children, and, as the Ku'rahus said, "the people could now go home to have pleasant dreams."

The face of the old man was radiant as he explained this song and dwelt upon the happiness brought to all by the touch of the visions which attend the Hako. This song and all others which belong to the night season he would sing and talk about only in the evening, never during the day.

SONG *a*

Diagram of Time

Rhythmic Rendition

I

Holy visions!
Hither come, we pray you, come unto us,
Bringing with you joy;
Come, Oh come to us, holy visions,
Bringing with you joy.

II

Holy visions!
Near are they approaching, near to us here,
Bringing with them joy;
Nearer still they come—holy visions—
Bringing with them joy.

III

Holy visions!
Lo! Before the doorway pause they, waiting,
Bearing gifts of joy;
Pausing there they wait—holy visions—
Bearing gifts of joy.

IV

Holy visions!
Now they cross the threshold, gliding softly
Toward the space within;
Softly gliding on—holy visions—
Toward the space within.

V

Holy visions!
They the lodge are filling with their presence,
Fraught with hope and peace;
Filling all the lodge—holy visions
Fraught with hope and peace.

VI

Holy visions!
Now they touch the children, gently touch them,
Giving dreams of joy;
Gently touch each one—holy visions—
Giving dreams of joy.

a Music on page 118.

VII

Holy visions!
Ended now their mission, pass they outward,
Yet they leave us joy;
Pass they all from us—holy visions—
Yet they leave us joy.

VIII

Holy visions!
They, the sky ascending, reach their dwelling;
There they rest above;
They their dwelling reach—holy visions—
There they rest above.

TENTH RITUAL.   THE DAWN

PART I.   THE BIRTH OF DAWN

The opening ceremonies began after dark and continued until past
midnight.   At their close the Children and the Fathers retired to their
tents, but the Son remained at his post near the inner door of the
lodge, while the Ku'rahus and his assistants watched from behind
the holy place, where the Hako lay at rest.   The fire burned to
embers, the noise of the camp died slowly away, and darkness and
silence settled down within the lodge.

It was a long watch, but at length the Ku'rahus bade his server lift
the skins, hanging at the inner and the outer door of the long passageway, and stand outside to report when the gray hue was seen in the
east.   When the voice of the server was heard proclaiming the sign
of dawn, the Ku'rahus and his assistants rose, and as they stood
behind the holy place, facing the open door, they sang the first song
in this drama of the mystic birth of Day.   It was sung "slowly and
with reverent feeling, for it speaks of the mysterious act of Tira'wa
atius in the birth of dawn," said the Ku'rahus; "it is something very
sacred, although it happens every day."

In the first stanza, the Earth, h'Atira (h', breath; atira, mother),
Mother breathing forth life, is called on to awake, that she may
receive fresh power of life to be given with the new day.   In the
second, h'Atira responds, she wakens from the sleep of night.

In the next stanza, h'Kawas (h', breath; Kawas, as the representative of the upper powers), the life-breathing powers above, are called
to awake and receive fresh life through the new-born Day.   In the
fourth stanza, h'Kawas, awakening from sleep, responds.   All the
forces below and above have now been called, they are awake and
ready to receive the gift of the new life.

In the fifth stanza, Kawas, the mother, the leader in this ceremony,
stands up and speaks from her nest.   She explains to the Ku'rahus
that day is born of night by the power of Tira'wa, that it is the breath
of this new-born child, the Dawn, which gives fresh life to all things

below and to all things above. The Ku'rahus replies, in the sixth stanza, that now he understands the meaning of the signs of the east, where Tira'wa, moving on Darkness, causes her to bring forth the Day, whose breath, awakening man and all things, gives them new life.

In the seventh stanza the Ku'rahus turns to the Son, bidding him awake to receive the breath of the new day. In the eighth the Son awakes, and with the Ku'rahus watches the coming of Dawn.

This opening song of eight stanzas is in two parts; the first relates to the male and female forces, the above and below, awaking to receive a fresh influx of power from the breath of the new-born Day. In the second, the meaning of the signs in the east is revealed to the Ku'rahus by the mother, Kawas. With the assurance that new life is to be given, he awakes the Son, that he may receive the promise from the new-born child of Night.

The second song is in two parts. In the first the Morning Star, representative of Tira'wa atius, the father, is discerned slowly advancing from the far distance, the birthplace of Dawn. The light is dim, and as the people look it is gone; then they catch sight of it again, steadily approaching, growing brighter and brighter until, in the second stanza, it stands resplendent as a man girded with the strength of youth, the breath of life stirring the downy feather upon his head, symbol of Tira'wa atius, already rosy with the touch of the advancing sun. As they gaze, he slowly recedes and vanishes from their sight.

In the third stanza, along the path opened by the Morning Star, the representative of the Father, comes the new-born Dawn, dim at first and difficult to discern, but ever advancing, coming nearer and nearer, its breath stirring all things with life newly given from Tira'wa atius, the father of all. In the fourth stanza the sky is filled with the brightness of dawn; then the Dawn recedes and vanishes in the light of day.

The third song opens with the shout, "Day is here!" The light is everywhere and all things are clearly seen. The Son is called to lift his head and behold the light.

In the second stanza, the glad shout, "Day is here!" calls from their coverts the animals, led by the deer, bringing her young into the light of day. All creatures are now alert and moving about; the new Day has given new life.

In the fourth song the Ku'rahus bids the Son awaken the Children. In the second stanza the Children arise, and, as they step out under the glowing sky, they, too, are touched by the breath of the new-born Day.

The four songs represent four movements or parts of this ritual: (1) The awakening of the forces; (2) the approach of the new-born Dawn; (3) the stir of life among the creatures; (4) the touch of the breath of Dawn upon the Children. The sixteen stanzas make the symbol of completeness.

Such is the drama of the dawn as it appeared to the instructed
Pawnee. The explanation of the Ku'rahus has given us a view of its
imagery and meaning from the center of the circle, rather than from
the outer edge, which otherwise would have been our only point of
view. Seen as the Ku'rahus shows it to us, through its words and
music, its simplicity, beauty, and reverent feeling can not fail to
appeal to everyone who has watched the silent majesty of the dawn.

SONG a

Diagram of Time

Rhythmic Rendition

I

Awake, Oh Mother, from sleep!
Awake! The night is far spent;
The signs of dawn are now seen
In east, whence cometh new life.

II

The Mother wakens from sleep;
She wakes, for night is far spent;
The signs of dawn are now seen
In east, whence cometh new life.

III

Awake, Oh Kawas, from sleep!
Awake! The night is far spent;
The signs of dawn are now seen
In east, whence cometh new life.

IV

Now Kawas wakens from sleep,
Awakes, for night is far spent;
The signs of dawn are now seen
In east, whence cometh new life.

V

Then Kawas stands and speaks forth:
"A child from Night is now born;
Tira'wa, father on high,
On Darkness moving, brings Dawn."

VI

I understand now, I know
A child from Night has been born;
Tira'wa, father on high,
On Darkness moving, brings Dawn.

a Music on page 123.

VII

Oh Son, awaken from sleep!
Awake! The night is far spent;
The signs of dawn are now seen
In east, whence cometh new life.

VIII

The Son awakens from sleep;
He wakes, for night is far spent;
The signs of dawn are now seen
In east, whence cometh new life.

PART II.   THE MORNING STAR AND THE NEW-BORN DAWN

SONG a

Diagram of Time

```
···      ··                        ··
___ _ ___ ___ ___ ___ ___

··       ··  ··
___ _ ___ ___ _ ___ ___ ___

_ ···  ··              ··
_ ___ ___ _ _ ___ ___ ___

··     ··  ··
___ _ ___ ___ ___ ___ ___ _
```

Rhythmic Rendition

I

Oh Morning Star, for thee we watch!
Dimly comes thy light from distant skies;
We see thee, then lost art thou.
Morning Star, thou bringest life to us.

II

Oh Morning Star, thy form we see!
Clad in shining garments dost thou come,
Thy plume touched with rosy light.
Morning Star, thou now art vanishing.

III

Oh youthful Dawn, for thee we watch!
Dimly comes thy light from distant skies;
We see thee, then lost art thou.
Youthful Dawn, thou bringest life to us.

IV

Oh youthful Dawn, we see thee come!
Brighter grows thy glowing light
As near, nearer thou dost come.
Youthful Dawn, thou now art vanishing.

---

a Music on page 128.

Part III. Daylight

SONG *a*

Diagram of Time

Rhythmic Rendition

I

Day is here!   Day is here, is here!
Arise, my son, lift thine eyes.   Day is here!   Day is here, is here!
Day is here!   Day is here, is here!
Look up, my son, and see the day.   Day is here!   Day is here, is here!
Day is here!   Day is here, is here!

II

Lo, the deer!   Lo, the deer, the deer
Comes from her covert of the night!   Day is here!   Day is here, is here!
Lo, the deer!   Lo, the deer, the deer!
All creatures wake and see the light.   Day is here!   Day is here, is here!
Day is here!   Day is here, is here!

Part IV. The Children Behold the Day

SONG *b*

Diagram of Time

Rhythmic Rendition

I

Arise, my son, and follow my command;
Go to the Children, bid them all awake,
Bid them look where day now breaks;
Go, send them forth into the light of day.

II

The son arose and followed these commands;
He bade the Children all awake, arise;
He bade them look where day now breaks;
He sent them forth into the light of day.

---

a Music on page 131.   *b* Music on page 132.

ELEVENTH RITUAL (SECOND DAY). THE MALE ELEMENT INVOKED

PART I. CHANT TO THE SUN

The chant to the Sun, the recognition of the male principle, took place the second day. It was in two parts, the first sung during the morning hours, and the second in the late afternoon and at sunset.

The first ray of the morning sun comes, we are told, "direct from Tira'wa" and is "like a man" untouched by weakness or age. It is particularly powerful, and can impart strength to whomsoever it reaches, therefore the advent of the first ray of the sun was watched with eagerness.

In the chant the ray is spoken of as if it were a bird; it alights and climbs in and out of the lodge (akaro). This term is used with double significance, for the earthly abode, the wide stretch from horizon to horizon, and for the lodge, erected for the protection of the family— the nest.

In the first verse of the chant, the ray enters the door and goes through the long passageway into the lodge. The passageway typifies the individual life, the career of a man (first ritual, part I, stanza XIII). In the seventh ritual the Hako touches the threshold, crosses it, and takes within the passageway the four steps symbolic of length of days. In the ninth ritual, the Visions halt at the door and then go through the passageway to reach and touch the Children; and now the ray, coming directly from above, enters as did the Hako and the Visions, bringing vitality and strength to the Son.

The ray comes from h'Ars (h', breath; ars, a contraction of atius, father), the father of breath; it is the bearer of breath from the Sun, the intermediary which received this gift of vitality and strength from Tira'wa atius (first ritual, part I, stanzas I and II).

After the Son had been touched by the ray, which entered through the long passageway, the Fathers gave the Children their morning meal, which had been prepared outside the lodge and brought within during the first verse.

At the conclusion of the meal the chant was resumed. The second verse speaks of the ray alighting on the edge of the central opening in the roof of the lodge, over the fireplace. The fireplace was feminine, and represented the protected center where life was conserved (first ritual, stanza X). The alighting of the ray over that center refers to the coming of the father bird to its nest.

In the third verse the ray climbs down, and in the fourth verse reaches the floor of the lodge and walks within the open space to touch the Children, bringing them the gift of vitality.

At the close of this verse the Hako were laid at rest with ceremonial movements and song.

The last four verses of the chant were sung late in the afternoon. In the fifth verse the ray has walked around the lodge and touched all within; in the sixth it climbs up and out, and in the seventh it rests upon the top of the hills that stand as a wall and inclose as a lodge the abode of the people. In the eighth verse the ray returns to the sun, having accomplished its task.

This is the only song in the ceremony which is in the form of a chant.

CHANT*a*

PART II. DAY SONGS

Diagram of Time

_ __ _ _ _ _ ¨ _ _ _ _ _ -. _ _ _ _ _ _ _ _ _ _ _ _ _
__ _ _ _ -. _ _ _ _ _.

Rhythmic Rendition

I

Now behold; hither comes the ray of our father Sun; it cometh over all the land, passeth in the lodge, us to touch, and give us strength.

II

Now behold, where alights the ray of our father Sun; it touches lightly on the rim, the place above the fire, whence the smoke ascends on high.

III

Now behold; softly creeps the ray of our father Sun; now o'er the rim it creeps to us, climbs down within the lodge; climbing down, it comes to us.

IV

Now behold; nearer comes the ray of our father Sun; it reaches now the floor and moves within the open space, walking there, the lodge about.*b*

V

Now behold where has passed the ray of our father Sun; around the lodge the ray has passed and left its blessing there, touching us, each one of us.

VI

Now behold; softly climbs the ray of our father Sun; it upward climbs, and o'er the rim it passes from the place whence the smoke ascends on high.

VII

Now behold on the hills the ray of our father Sun; it lingers there as loath to go, while all the plain is dark. Now has gone the ray from us.

VIII

Now behold; lost to us the ray of our father Sun; beyond our sight the ray has gone, returning to the place whence it came to bring us strength.

Between the fifth and sixth verses of the chant two songs had place. The first compares the noise and bustle of the coming of the Hako party to the alighting of a flock of birds. The significance of a flock is given in the fifteenth ritual.

In the first stanza of the second song the Father expresses his thank-

---

a Music on page 135.   *b* Here the Hako are laid at rest.

fulness for the good he is permitted to bear.　In the second stanza the Son responds with thanks for the coming of the Hako.

These are the only songs belonging to the ritual of the second day, but, if the Children desire, they can ask for one of the extra songs which can be sung in the daytime only.　Such a request must be accompanied by a gift.

The first extra song is a request to Mother Corn that she will lead the Father to the Son.　The song is in four stanzas.　In the first Mother Corn is asked to lead; in the second she consents; in the third the Father asks if they are near; in the fourth the end of the journey is discerned.

The second extra song refers to a young man who mounts his horse and makes his way toward the lodge to offer the animal as a gift to the Fathers.　Such an act gives to a man honor and recognition among his people.

FIRST SONG *a*

Diagram of Time

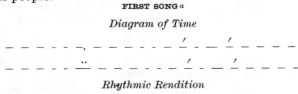

Rhythmic Rendition

I

Hark, the sound of their wings!　Mighty birds are here now alighting, bearing
　　　　　promised good.
Hark, the sound of their wings!　Surely the Hako is coming.　·Children, forward
　　　　　bring your gifts.

II

Hark, the sound of their wings!　Mighty birds are here now alighting, bearing
　　　　　promised good.
Hark, the sound of their wings!　See! The Hako has come.　We children forward
　　　　　bring our gifts.

SECOND SONG *b*

Diagram of Time

Rhythmic Rendition

I

We are thankful, thankful that now we are here
With the Hako, bearing its bountiful gifts.　As a son you will be,
By the Hako bound unto us as a Son.

II

I am thankful, thankful that now you are here
With the Hako, bearing its bountiful gifts.　As a son I will be,
By the Hako bound unto you as a Son.

---

a Music on page 140.　　　　　*b* Music on page 142.

EXTRA DAY SONG[a]

Diagram of Time

─ ── ─── ── ─── ─── ── ─── ── ── ─── ── ─── ── ──

── ── ─── ── ─── ─── ── ── ─── ── ── ─── ── ─── ── ─

Rhythmic Rendition

I

Let us seek him, led by her who breathes forth life. Seeking the Son
With the Mother, Mother Corn, seeking the Son let us go.

II

Now we travel, led by her who breathes forth life. Seeking the Son
With the Mother, Mother Corn, seeking the Son now we go.

III

May we find him, led by her who breathes forth life. Grant we find him,
Oh our Mother, Mother Corn, grant we may find, find the Son.

IV

We are near him, led by her who breathes forth life. Nearer we come;
Now our Mother, Mother Corn, answers our prayer. He is here.

EXTRA DAY SONG[b]

Diagram of Time

─ ── ─── ──

── ── ── ─── ── ── ── ── ── ── ── ── ── ──

── ── ── ──

── ── ── ── ── ── ── ──

── ── ─── ──

Rhythmic Rendition

I

Look where yonder rides
One who swiftly speeding o'er the prairie takes his way!
Who may he be?
Whence has he come, riding on so fast,
He who yonder comes?

II

Look! He turns this way,
He who rides so swiftly o'er the prairie turns this way
Hither comes he;
With a purpose brave within his heart
Rides he straightway here.

TWELFTH RITUAL (SECOND NIGHT). THE RITES CAME BY A VISION.

In the ritual of this second night the supernatural origin of the
ceremony is asserted, that its promises may be more fully depended
upon.

---

[a] Music on page 144.   [b] Music on page 146.

In the first song of the ritual the question is asked if the rite by which a Father could bind to himself a Son was prefigured in a vision? The affirmative answer is given in the second stanza.

The second song has the same theme, and reiterates that, verily, all knowledge of the rite was given through the vision which, the Ku'rahus stated, came down by the east. The second stanza implies the promise that similar visions from the same direction will descend to the Children.

FIRST SONG [a]

Diagram of Time

Rhythmic Rendition

Was it, we ask, in dreams that the Fathers saw
Clearly the Hako, wherewith I make you now
As my son,
My own begotten?
Was it in dreams they learned how to make you thus
My offspring?

Truly, in dreams it was that the Fathers saw
Clearly the Hako, wherewith I make you now
As my son,
My own begotten.
Truly, in dreams they learned how to make you thus
My offspring.

SECOND SONG [b]

Diagram of Time

Rhythmic Rendition

This is the teaching, this is the word sent
Down to us from our fathers:
All of the wise words, all of the good gifts,
Brought unto you as a Son,
Verily, through a dream all of these things,
All, by the east descended.

[a] Music on page 147.   [b] Music on page 149.

> This is the teaching, this is the word sent
> Down to us from our fathers:
> All of the wise words, all of the good gifts,
> Now brought to you as my Son,
> Verily, as of old, all of these things,
> All, by the east descended.

The song addressed to the Pleiades held a peculiar place in the ceremony. It had to be substituted for the last stanza of any song which was being sung when the constellation was reported as rising above the horizon. This right to set aside the stanza of a regular song preceding the act of laying down the Hako seems to bear out the explanation of the Ku'rahus, that the song to the Pleiades belonged "to the time when the ceremony was being made," and would imply that it was part of a ceremony from which the Hako drew authority.

"Tira'wa," the Ku'rahus said, "appointed the stars to guide their steps." The Pleiades not only guided but taught the people, as by an object lesson, "to remain together." The song would seem to have been received in some locality to the south of the dwelling place of the Pawnees, since the man who obtained it "turned to the north and reached his country." This song is one among many indications that earlier forms of the Hako ceremony will probably be found among the people of the Mexican plateau.

SONG TO THE PLEIADES[a]

Diagram of Time

Rhythmic Rendition

Look as they rise, up rise
Over the line where sky meets the earth;
Pleiades!
Lo! They ascending, come to guide us,
Leading us safely, keeping us one;
Pleiades,
Us teach to be, like you, united.

The songs which belong to the rituals of the night did not fill up the entire time, and extra songs could therefore be requested by the Children, provided a gift was made when the song was called for. A man would step up to the holy place, lay there a small stick, representing the gift of a horse, and say, "Father, sing for us!"

---

a Music on page 151.

From the first extra song we learn that the visions had a dwelling place called "Katasha," located just below the abode of the lesser powers. The visions could be summoned by these powers from Katasha and dispatched upon a mission. After its accomplishment, the visions returned to their dwelling place to "lie at rest" until again summoned by the powers. According to the Ku'rahus, visions were not transitory, called into being for some special occasion and then ceasing to exist, but they were of an enduring nature, retaining an identity by which they could be recognized by one whom they had visited. This differentiates the vision from the dream, which would seem to be the memory of a vision which came while one slept. Waking visions are not spoken of as dreams.

The Pawnees locate more or less definitely the powers which can affect man. In the above, far beyond the light, fleecy clouds, where no man has been or can see, dwells Tira'wa atius, the father of all, the giver of life and breath; in a circle below are the lesser powers, like a great council; beneath them is Katasha, the abode of the visions. The birds, the animals, and plants are intermediaries between man and the powers above and the powers below in the earth; they bring him the life and strength which is drawn by the powers from Tira'wa atius. Such is the outline, but the details are complex, no one power or intermediary being fixed or unchangeable in function or character.

The second extra song, as explained by the Ku'rahus, seems to point out that disaster is sometimes disciplinary and necessary to the strengthening of a man's purpose.

The third extra song teaches that when one dreams of Mother Corn one should go to a shrine where the sacred corn is kept and there offer smoke to the power which sent the corn to him in his dream.

EXTRA NIGHT SONG [a]

Diagram of Time

Rhythmic Rendition

I

Give heed! We tell of Katasha holy,
Whence the dreams come down, when draweth the night time near:
Near the gods [b] is their dwelling,
They who watch o'er men; all silently come they down.

---

[a] Music on page 152.　　　[b] Gods, meaning powers, is used on account of the rhythm only.

II

Give heed! The bird of whom we are telling
Sends the dreams to us, when draweth the night time near;
Kawas, she that is sending
Holy visions, bringing, silently bringing peace.

III

Give heed! The birds of whom we are telling
Climb with dreams to us, when draweth the night time near;
Down the path they are climbing;
Where the gods to men are traveling come they down.

IV

They climb, these birds; a dream each is bearing;
Bear they dreams to us, when draweth the night time near;
Kawas—she that is sending
Down the birds with dreams; so faithful the Hako birds!

V

Then back they speed, the birds that were bringing
Down the dreams that come when draweth the night time near;
Birds and dreams are ascending
Where the gods are dwelling, watching there over men.

VI

Now this we know in truth—where are resting
Dreams that come to us when draweth the night time near;
True it is that he did see them;
In a vision saw he Katasha, where they dwell.

EXTRA NIGHT SONG[a]

Diagram of Time

Rhythmic Rendition

I

Mother Corn! Mother Corn! We pray thee,
Be our leader, foes entrapping!
Trusting in thee, we wander far, yet we see no foe;
Food is gone, hope is dead within us.

II

Then in dreams Mother Corn spoke to me:
" I will lead you, foes entrapping!
" Testing your courage, far have I let you go astray;
" Rise, my child, follow me to vict'ry!"

---

[a] Music on page 157.

EXTRA NIGHT SONG*a*

Diagram of Time

Rhythmic Rendition

I

As I lay sleeping, as I lay dreaming,
Out of the distance came one advancing
One whom I ne'er had seen before, but when her voice addressed me, straight-
way I knew her—
Lo! 'Twas our Mother, she whom we know.

II

I rose from sleeping, my dream rememb'ring
Her words I pondered, words of our mother,
Then I asked of each one I met, Tell me, how far may her shrine be? When
I found it
.Sweet smoke I offered unto our Mother.

THIRTEENTH RITUAL (THIRD DAY).   THE FEMALE ELEMENT INVOKED

PART I.   THE SACRED FEAST OF CORN

On the morning of the third day the ritual of the Dawn was repeated.
The Children gathered at the lodge before sunrise and their morning
meal was given them by the Fathers.

On the preceding day the masculine principle, the sun, had been
"remembered." On this day the feminine, the earth, was to be
honored.

The ceremonies began by the sacred feast of Corn. It followed
closely upon the morning meal and was wholly ceremonial and communal in form, the people taking a spoonful from bowls that were
passed around the lodge from one group to another.

The corn was provided and prepared by the Children, they who
were to be the recipients of the good promised by the Hako and prefigured by this act—the gift of plenty that they were to receive.

PART II.   SONG TO THE EARTH

The song to the Earth followed the rite. Its responsive liturgical
form calls to mind the song which opens the first ritual. Its theme
is similar. As the ceremony proceeds, its purpose, the perpetuation
of the clan or tribe by the gift of children, is brought more and more
clearly to light.

---

a Music on page 159.

The two songs which precede the song to the earth were sung at the opening of the public ceremony (eighth ritual); they fix the mind upon the teaching that all power is derived from the great unseen force, Tira'wa atius. The power of the fructifying ray of Father Sun and the power of Mother Earth to bring forth, the ability to generate life and to conserve it, come from Tira'wa atius, the father of all.

FIRST SONG a

Diagram of Time

Rhythmic Rendition

Father, unto thee we cry;
Father thou of gods b and men;
Father thou of all we hear;
Father thou of all we see;
Father, unto thee we cry.

SECOND SONG c

Diagram of Time

Rhythmic Rendition

Father!   Thou above, father of the gods, b
They who can come near and touch us,
Do thou bid them bring us help.
Help we need.   Father, hear us!

THIRD SONG c

Diagram of Time

---

a Music on page 162.
b The word gods, meaning powers, is used solely on account of the rhythm.
c Music on page 163.

Rhythmic Rendition

I

Behold! Our Mother Earth is lying here.
Behold! She giveth of her fruitfulness.
Truly, her power gives she us.
Give thanks to Mother Earth who lieth here.

II

We think of Mother Earth who lieth here;
We know she giveth of her fruitfulness.
Truly, her power gives she us.
Our thanks to Mother Earth who lieth here!

III

Behold on Mother Earth the growing fields!
Behold the promise of her fruitfulness!
Truly, her power gives she us.
Give thanks to Mother Earth who lieth here.

IV

We see on Mother Earth the growing fields;
We see the promise of their fruitfulness.
Truly, her power gives she us.
Our thanks to Mother Earth who lieth here!

V

Behold on Mother Earth the spreading trees!
Behold the promise of her fruitfulness!
Truly, her power gives she us.
Give thanks to Mother Earth who lieth here.

VI

We see on Mother Earth the spreading trees;
We see the promise of her fruitfulness.
Truly, her power gives she us.
Our thanks to Mother Earth who lieth here!

VII

Behold on Mother Earth the running streams!
Behold the promise of her fruitfulness!
Truly, her power gives she us.
Give thanks to Mother Earth who lieth here.

VIII

We see on Mother Earth the running streams;
We see the promise of her fruitfulness.
Truly, her power gives she us.
Our thanks to Mother Earth who lieth here!

PART III. OFFERING OF SMOKE

This teaching is further accentuated by the offering of smoke which follows the song. The feathered stem, Kawas, the mother, is used as the pipestem for this purpose. The offering of smoke is the closest and most sacred form of direct communication with the great unseen power.

PART IV. SONGS OF THE BIRDS

In the songs of the birds, which close the day, the people are instructed in their parental duties. They must take upon themselves the care of providing for their children, even before they are born; they are to be cheerful and thankful for all they receive; they are to guide and protect their families, to be watchful and faithful in storm and in sunshine, by day and by night. By following these teachings they will receive in full measure, in completeness, the gifts of the Hako.

The diagram of time of each of the six songs of the birds is here given in the order of the text, but no rhythmical rendition has been made, as the story elaborates the meaning of each song.

THE SONG OF THE BIRD'S NEST [a]

Diagram of Time

```
_  ··  _  ··  ··  _  _  _
_  ··  _  _  ··  _  _
_  ··  _  ··  _  _  ·· 
_  ··  _  ··  _  _  ···
_  ··  _  _  _  ·· _  _
```

THE SONG OF THE WREN [b]

Diagram of Time

```
/  _  _  _  _  _  _  _  _  __  __
/  _  _  _  _  _  _  _  _  __  __
/  _  _  _  _  _  _  _  _  __  ___
/  _  _  _  _  _  _  _  _  _  __
/  _  _  _  _  _  _  _  _  _  __
/  _  _  _  _  _  _  _  __  __  __
```

THE SONG OF THE TURKEY AND THE WOODPECKER [c]

Diagram of Time

```
_  _  _  _  ··  _  _  ··  _  _  _  ··  ··
_  _  _  ··  _  _  ··  ·· _
_  _  _  _  ··  _  _  ··  ·· _
```

---

[a] Music on page 169. [b] Music on page 171. [c] Music on page 172.

THE SONG OF THE DUCK[a]

Diagram of Time

```
_ _ _ _ _ _ _ _ _ _ .. ..
_ _ _ _ _ _ _ _ .. ..
_ _ .. ..
_ _ _ _ _ _ _ _ .. ..
_ _ _ _ _ _ .. ..
_ _ _ ..
```

THE SONG OF THE OWL[b]

Diagram of Time

```
_ _ _ _ _ _ _ _ .. _ _ _ _ _ ..
_ _ .. _ _ _ .. _ _ _ .. _ _ _ _
.. _ _ _ _
```

THE SONG OF THANKFULNESS[c]

Diagram of Time

```
_ _ _ _ _ _ / _ .. _
_ / _ _ _ _ _ / _ .. _
_ _ _ .. _ _ / _ ..
_ _ _ _ _ _ / _ ..
```

FOURTEENTH RITUAL (THIRD NIGHT).   INVOKING THE VISIONS OF THE ANCIENTS

On the third night the visions which in the distant past had taught this ceremony to the fathers were called upon and asked to come from their abode on high, to enter the lodge and recognize the man who was to be made a Son.

The song was an appeal for supernatural sanction of the rites which had taken place and of those which were to follow. With this song the public ceremony came to an end.

SONG[d]

Diagram of Time

```
_ .. .. 
_ .. _ _ _ .. ..
_ .. / _
/ _ _ _ .. / / .. ..
_ .. / _
```

---

[a] Music on page 174.   [b] Music on page 175.   [c] Music on page 177.   [d] Music on page 178.

Rythmic Rendition

I

Oh, come hither,
Holy dreams—Our fathers knew them—
Hither come to us!
Thanks we give unto them.   They our message will hear,
Calling them to come.

II

This way come they,
Holy dreams—Our fathers knew them—
Come they now this way.
Thanks we give unto them.   Coming now, they draw near,
Coming now this way.

III

They come nearer,
Holy dreams—Our fathers knew them—
Come they now this way.
Thanks we give unto them.   On the threshold stand they,
Holy visions stand.

IV

Now they enter,
Holy dreams—Our fathers knew them—
Enter now the lodge.
Thanks we give unto them.   Enter they the lodge now,
Enter now the lodge.

V

The Son they see,
Holy dreams—Our fathers knew them—
See him now within.
Thanks we give unto them.   Entered now, they see him,
See the Son within.

VI

Now they hover,
Holy dreams—Our fathers knew them—
Hover us above.
Thanks we give unto them.   Pausing here above us,
Hover they above.

VII

Now depart they,
Holy dreams—Our fathers knew them—
Now they go away.
Thanks we give unto them.   They are passing from us,
Going from the lodge.

VIII

Above rest they,
Holy dreams—Our fathers knew them—
Rest they now above.
Thanks we give unto them.   Where they rest we send thanks,
Thanks send far above.

SECOND DIVISION. THE SECRET CEREMONIES

FIFTEENTH RITUAL (FOURTH NIGHT)

PART I. THE FLOCKING OF THE BIRDS

The last meal given by the Fathers was eaten by the Children during the forenoon of the fourth day. Afterward gifts were presented to the Children and they went to their homes.

The afternoon was occupied in preparation for the approaching secret ceremonies, which began at sunset and at which no one could be present but the Fathers, the Son, and his near relatives—those primarily concerned in the promises of the Hako.

These ceremonies opened with a song suggesting the fulfilment of the promises and the joy of the people. Again we note the use of prefiguration at the beginning of a rite.

This song—the flocking of birds—is in three groups of two stanzas each.

The first group speaks of the flock, the old birds, with their young now grown, moving about with strength and power, shaking the trees by their numbers as they alight and rise; so shall the people increase and be powerful by their numbers.

The second group speaks of Kawas as bringing from the powers the gift of this increase. She comes as a special messenger. Leaving the flock she flies direct to the people, as the eagle flies straight to its nest. The lodge of the Son is her nest, and she is coming to fulfil the promise of increase.

The third group deals with the rejoicing of the people over the promise received through this ceremony. The joyful noise which they make as they bring their thank offerings to the Fathers is like that of a great flock of birds.

The song not only pictures the increased power which is to come to the people through the Hako; it also refers to the immediate joyous influence of the ceremony on the people, in the happiness and gratitude felt in the giving and receiving of the required gifts.

The realistic whistle, made from the wing bone of the eagle, used to accompany the songs of these secret ceremonies, emphasizes the prophetic assurances of Kawas.

SONG[a]

Diagram of Time

-- _ _ _ _ _ _ _ _
_ _ _ _ _ _ _ _ _
..._ _ _ _ _ _ _
_ _ _ _ _ _ _ _ _

---

[a] Music on page 184.

Rhythmic Rendition

I

All around the birds in flocks are flying;
Dipping, rising, circling, see them coming.
See, many birds are flocking here,
All about us now together coming.

II

Yonder see the birds in flocks come flying;
Dipping, rising, circling, see them gather.
Loud is the sound their winging makes,
Rushing come they on the trees alighting!

III

From the flock an eagle now comes flying;
Dipping, rising, circling, comes she hither.
Loud screams the eagle, flying swift,
As an eagle flies, her nestlings seeking.

IV

It is Kawas coming, Kawas flying;
Dipping, rising, circling, she advances.
See! Nearer comes she, nearer comes.
Now, alighted, she her nest is making.

V

Yonder people like the birds are flocking,
See them circling, this side, that side coming.
Loud is the sound their moving makes,
As together come they, onward come they.

VI

Toward the lodge where sits the Son they hasten,
Bringing forward gifts with joyful shouting.
Hark! Now they like the eagle scream,
Glad of heart, as when her nest she seeth.

PART II. THE SIXTEEN CIRCUITS OF THE LODGE

After the song the Hako were laid at rest with ceremonial song and
movement. When they were next taken up it was to make the final
circuits of the lodge, sixteen in number, symbolic of completion.

The songs which accompanied these circuits are in four groups, and
in them are summed up the teaching and the promises of the ceremony.

The two songs of the first group refer to Mother Corn, she who had
opened the way and led to the Son, breathing forth the power of
Mother Earth in life, food, and plenty. Thanks and reverence are
given to her.

In the two songs of the second group the eagle, Kawas, comes to
the Son. Her shadow, passing over him, attracts his attention and

he watches her and her mate as they guard and cherish their young in the nest. Then he learns that his lodge is the nest; that the powers above, through the eagle, are sending him the promise of life that shall fill his nest and make strong the people.

The two songs of the third group refer to the Hako with its promises. The second song records the prayer of an old Ku'rahus and its fulfilment, and gives the assurance that Tira'wa answers the prayer of man made through the Hako ceremony.

The four songs of the fourth group had all been previously sung. The first two were given at the opening of the public ceremony, and again at the close of the sacred feast of Corn. They were now repeated, that the thoughts of the people might be turned toward Tira'wa atius, the father of all things, the giver of life, and to his messengers to man, the lesser powers. The third and fourth songs had been sung in the first ritual, when the feathered stems were painted to symbolize the powers above and the powers below, the male and female forces, which make for the perpetuation of all living forms.

The secret ceremonies contain the heart of the rite, its vital center. In the sequence of songs through which this center was approached we note a reflex of the order of the ceremony itself, a turning back from the external leadership of the corn and of Kawas to the silent prayer of the Ku'rahus, the appeal to Tira'wa atius as symbolically present.

At the close of the last circuit of the lodge the Hako were laid at rest with ceremonial song and movement for the last time. Midnight had passed, and the Children went to their homes, leaving the Fathers alone in the lodge to watch for the dawn.

FIRST SONG a

Diagram of Time

Rythmic Rendition

I

Look on her! She who sought far and near for a Son!
Look on her! She who led from afar unto you!
Look on her, Mother Corn, breathing life on us all!

II

Thanks we give unto her who came here for a Son!
Thanks we give unto her who has led us to you!
Thanks we give, Mother Corn, breathing life on us all!

a Music on page 188.

SECOND SONG a

Diagram of Time

_ _ _ _ _ _ _ _ _ _ .. _ _
_ _ _ _ _ _ _ _ _ _ .. _ _
_ _ _ _ _ _ _ _ _ _

Rythmic Rendition

I

Rev'rent our hearts turn unto the one who brings to us
Long life and children, peace, and the gifts of strength and food.
Rev'rent our hearts turn unto our Mother Corn!

II

Rev'rent our hearts turn unto the source whence come to us
Long life and children, peace, and the gifts of strength and food,
Gifts from Tira′wa, sent through our Mother Corn.

THIRD SONG b

Diagram of Time

_ _ _ _ _ _ _ _ _ _ _ _ _ _ _ _ _ _ ..
_ _ _ _ _ _ _ _ _ _ _ _ _ _ _ _ _ _ ..

Rythmic Rendition

I

O'er the prairie flits in ever widening circles the shadow of a bird about me as I
walk;
Upward turn my eyes, Kawas looks upon me, she turns with flapping wings and
far away she flies.

II

Round about a tree in ever widening circles an eagle flies, alertly watching o'er
his nest;
Loudly whistles he, a challenge sending far, o'er the country wide it echoes, there
defying foes.

FOURTH SONG c

Diagram of Time

_ _ _ ′ _ _ ′ _ _ ′ _ _ _ _ _ _ _ _
_ _ ′ _ _ ′ _ _ _ _ _ _ _ _ _
_ _ ′ _ _ _ ′ _ _ _ _ _ _
_ _ ′ _ _ _ _ _ _ _

Rhythmic Rendition

1

Kawas flying where her nestlings now are crying; loudly cry they when they hear
her wings;
Kawas flying, cry her children, as they hear her come.
'Tis Kawas who now homeward comes! 'Tis Kawas who now homeward comes!
Quickly flying as she hears her young ones in the nest.

---

a Music on page 189.   b Music on page 191.   c Music on page 193.

II

Kawas flying, o'er us flying, we her nestlings cry for joy as now we see her come;
Kawas flying! Glad our hearts as now we see her come.
'Tis Kawas brings to us good gifts! 'Tis Kawas brings to us good gifts!
Kawas brings gifts to us; we, like her nestlings, cry.

FIFTH SONG a

Diagram of Time

Rhythmic Rendition

I

Atira comes, she brings you life, she gives you joy; to her give thanks as she
   draws near.
Now in the lodge before our eyes Atira moves;
Look upon her who brings you life, who gives you joy. Oh, offer thanks to
   Mother Corn!

II

The Hako comes within the lodge, it walks within; let us give thanks as it draws
   near.
Now in the lodge with Mother Corn the Hako moves;
Thanks do we give for all the joy it brings to us, the children here, from realms
   above.

SIXTH SONG b

Diagram of Time

Rhythmic Rendition

I

I know not if the voice of man can reach to the sky;
I know not if the mighty one will hear as I pray;
I know not if the gifts I ask will all granted be;
I know not if the word of old we truly can hear;
I know not what will come to pass in our future days;
I hope that only good will come, my children, to you.

---

a Music on page 195.   b Music on page 196.

II

I now know that the voice of man can reach to the sky;
I now know that the mighty one has heard as I prayed;
I now know that the gifts I asked have all granted been;
I now know that the word of old we truly have heard;
I now know that Tira'wa harkens unto man's prayer;
I know that only good has come, my children, to you.

SEVENTH SONG [a]

Diagram of Time

Rhythmic Rendition

Father, unto thee we cry!
Father thou of gods and men;
Father thou of all we hear;
Father thou of all we see.
Father, unto thee we cry!

EIGHTH SONG [a]

Diagram of Time

Rhythmic Rendition

Father! Thou above, father of the gods,
They who can come near and touch us;
Do thou bid them bring us help.
Help we need; Father, hear us!

NINTH SONG [b]

Diagram of Time

---

[a] Music on page 199.   [b] Music on page 200.

Rhythmic Rendition

Take we now the blue paint,
Touch with it the stem, putting on the sacred symbol,
Emblem of the clear sky,
Where dwell the gods, who, descending, bring us good gifts,
Gifts of life and plenty.

TENTH SONG[a]

Diagram of Time

Rhythmic Rendition

Take we now the green paint,
Touch with it the stem, the mated stem;
Putting on the emblem, the sacred and living symbol.
Mother Earth,
From above descending, bountiful blessing on thee,
Mother Earth!

SIXTEENTH RITUAL (FIFTH DAY, DAWN)

PART I. SEEKING THE CHILD

At the first sign of dawn the Ku′rahus and his assistants, with the principal men of the Hako party, started for the lodge of the Son, there to seek his child and perform certain rites symbolic of birth. It is to be noted that these rites took place at the same hour as the singing of the Dawn ritual, which celebrated the mysterious birth of day.

They sang the first song of the ritual as they started, but when they were nearing their destination they repeated the song they had sung when they were about to enter the village of the Son (sixth ritual, second song).

The repetition of songs sung in the earlier part of the ceremony had the effect of tying back the later acts to those which were preparatory in character, and tended to consolidate the entire ceremony. When this song was sung for the first time the Father was seeking the Son, to whom he was bringing promises of good; when it was sung the second time the Father was seeking the child of the Son, that on it the promises brought might be fulfilled.

Of this part of the ceremony not only every detail, with its special meaning, but the function of each article used had been prefigured.

---

[a] Music on page 200.

FIRST SONG *a*

Diagram of Time

Rhythmic Rendition

With the dawn will I seek, seek my child,
Among the Children seek
One the gods *b* shall here make;
My offspring, my own child.

SECOND SONG *c*

Diagram of Time

Rhythmic Rendition

I

Where is he, the Son?
Where his dwelling place that I seek?
Which can be his lodge, where he sits
Silent, waiting, waiting there for me?

II

Here is he, the Son,
Here his dwelling place that I seek;
This here is his lodge where he sits
Silent, waiting, waiting here for me.

PART II. SYMBOLIC INCEPTION

The warriors—the male element—were the first to enter the lodge, in warlike fashion, as if to capture and hold it securely. The child was first touched by the representative of Kawas, that it might be given endurance; then it was touched by the chief, that it might be wise. After the warriors had performed their part, the Ku'rahus entered singing the song which had been sung when the messenger representing the Son was received outside the village (sixth ritual, first song). At that time he looked upon one who was to lead him to the Son; now he is looking upon the child which represents the continuation of the life of the Son.

---

a Music on page 202.   *b* The word is used because of the rhythm.
c See sixth ritual; music on page 203.

FIRST SONG *a*

Diagram of Time

_ _ _ _ _ _ _ _ ..

_ _ _ _ _ .. _ _ _ ..

_ _ _ _ _ .. _ _ _ _ _ ..

_ _ _ _ .. _ _ _ ..

_ _ _ _ _

Rhythmic Rendition

I

Now our eyes look on him who is here;
He is as the Son we have sought;
He brings us again tidings of the Son:
" Father, come to me, here I sit
Waiting here for thee."

The Ku'rahus first touched the child with the ear of corn (second song), singing the same song as when the ear of corn made its mysterious journey to the sky and received its authority to lead in the ceremony (first ritual, fifth song). The power granted at that time was for this ultimate purpose, to make the paths and open the way for the child to receive the gift of fruitfulness.

SECOND SONG *b*

Diagram of Time

/ _ _ .. _ .. _ .. _

/ _ _ _ _ .. _ .. _

/ _ .. _ .. _ .. _ _

_ _ .. _ ... _ _ .. _

.. _ _ _ .. _ _

/ _ .. _ _ .. _ .. _

Rhythmic Rendition

I

Tira'wa, harken! Mighty one
Above us in blue, silent sky!
We standing wait thy bidding here;
The Mother Corn standing waits,
Waits to serve thee here;
The Mother Corn stands waiting here.

---

a See sixth ritual. Music on page 204.   *b* Music on page 205.

II

Tira'wa, harken! Mighty one
Above us in blue, silent sky!
We flying seek thy dwelling there;
The Mother Corn flying goes
Up to seek thee there;
The Mother Corn goes flying up.

III

Tira'wa, harken! Mighty one
Above us in blue, silent sky!
We touch upon thy country fair;
The Mother Corn touches there
Upon the border land;
The Mother Corn is touching there.

IV

Tira'wa, harken! Mighty one
Above us in blue, silent sky!
The path we reach leads up to thee;
The Mother Corn enters there,
Upward takes her way;
The Mother Corn to thee ascends.

V

Tira'wa, harken! Mighty one
Above us in blue, silent sky!
Behold! We in thy dwelling stand;
The Mother Corn, standing there,
Leader now is made;
The Mother Corn is leader made.

VI

Tira'wa, harken! Mighty one
Above us in blue, silent sky!
The downward path we take again;
The Mother Corn, leading us,
Doth thy symbol bear;
The Mother Corn with power leads.

Then the Ku'rahus united the two feathered stems, the male and
the female (third song), and with them touched the child, following
with the gift of procreation the paths opened by the corn.

THIRD SONG *a*

Diagram of Time

a Music on page 206.

Rhythmic Rendition

I

Here stand we while upon Tira'wa now we wait;
Here Kawas stands, her mate with her is standing here;
They both are standing, waiting, bringing gifts with them.

II

We flying are, as on Tira'wa now we wait;
Here Kawas flies, her mate with her is flying here;
They both are flying, flying with the gifts they bring.

III

We touching are, as on Tira'wa now we wait;
Now Kawas and her mate the child so gently touch;
Its forehead touch they, there they gently touch the child.

IV

We op'ning are, as on Tira'wa now we wait
The four straight paths upon the child we open here,
Where soon descending from on high shall flow new life.

V

We spreading are, as on Tira'wa now we wait;
Here Kawas spreads, her mate with her is spreading here;
New life and power, the gifts that they are bringing here.

VI

We finished are, as on Tira'wa now we wait;
The task of Kawas with her mate accomplished is,
And all the work they came to do is finished now.

PART III. ACTION SYMBOLIZING LIFE

The child, surrounded by the creative forces, is urged to move, to arise as the first song is sung.

FIRST SONG*a*

Diagram of Time

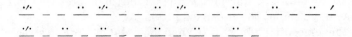

Rhythmic Rendition

I am ready; come to me now, fearing nothing; come now to me here!
Little one, come, come to me here; fearing nothing, come!

Then it was made to take four steps, symbolic of life, of long life, during the singing of the second song.

In the symbolizing, within the lodge of the Son, of the gift of birth by the power of the Hako, brought thither by the Father, we get a glimpse of the means by which the tie between the two unrelated men,

---

a Music on page 211.

the Father and the Son, was supposed to be formed; namely, the life of the Son was perpetuated through the gift of fruitfulness to his child, supernaturally bestowed by the Hako; consequently the Father who brought the Hako became symbolically the father of the future progeny of the Son.

SECOND SONG *a*

Diagram of Time

Rhythmic Rendition

Stepping forward is my child, he forward steps, the four steps takes and enters into life;
Forward stepping, four steps taking, enters into life.

The child was taken upon the back of one of the party and led the way to the ceremonial lodge, followed by the Ku'rahus and all the rest singing the third song.

THIRD SONG *a*

Diagram of Time

Rhythmic Rendition

Here we go singing, looking on the child
Borne in his father's arms, he leading us;
Follow we singing, looking on the child.

SEVENTEENTH RITUAL

PART I. TOUCHING THE CHILD

On reaching the lodge the child was seated at the holy place and surrounded by the Ku'rahus and his assistants with the Hako, and guarded by a wall of warriors, while an old man prepared it for the further reception of the promised gifts.

On the preceding night water had been taken from a stream; this water was now put into a bowl. Every detail of this act was symbolic. The time when the water was obtained was night, the mother of day; running water symbolized the continuity of life, one generation following another; the bowl which held the water resembled in its shape the dome of the sky, the abode of the powers which bestowed life.

The child was touched with the water upon the head and face, an invisible outline being made, which afterward was to become distinct. This first touching with water, one of the lesser powers, was to cleanse and give strength.

---

a Music on page 212.

The song (first) which accompanied this act is in three musical phrases and six stanzas. Again the symbolism of number, already noted, is suggested.

FIRST SONG *a*

Diagram of Time

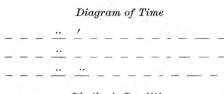

Rhythmic Rendition

I

Give heed, my child, lift your eyes, behold the one who is standing here;
Behold, my child! waiting here to bring the gift of strength to you.
Give heed, my child. Look! Water waits to bring to you gift of strength

II

Give heed, my child, lift your eyes, behold the one who is flying here;
Behold, my child! flying here to bring the gift of strength to you.
Give heed, my child. Look! Water flies to bring to you gift of strength.

III

Give heed, my child, lift your eyes, behold the one who is touching here;
Behold, my child! touching here your head, to bring the gift of strength.
Give heed, my child. Look! Water, touching, brings to you gift of strength.

IV

Give heed, my child, lift your eyes, behold the one who now follows here.
Behold, my child! Now the paths it follows, paths where the gods descend.
Give heed, my child. Look! Water down the four straight paths brings its gift.

V

Give heed, my child, lift your eyes, behold the one who is spreading here;
Behold my child! cleansing you, and spreading o'er you gift of strength.
Give heed, my child. Look! Water spreading over you gift of strength.

VI

Give heed, my child, lift your eyes, behold the one who has brought you strength.
Behold, my child! Strength you have and finished is the task.
Give heed, my child. Look! Water now has brought to you gift of strength.

Following the outline made by the water, the head and face of the child were next touched with grass, the representative of Toharu, the verdant covering of the earth.

The song (second) sung during this act is in the rhythm of the first.

In these two acts we note that "the order in which the powers come near to man," shown in the opening song of the first ritual, is observed in this rite. In that opening song, after the Winds, the Sun, and the Earth had brought life to man, food and drink were given that his

---

a Music on page 215.

life might be sustained. So, after the symbolic birth in the lodge of the Son, the child was touched by water and the product of the earth, that it might receive from them sustaining power.

SECOND SONG[a]

Diagram of Time

Rhythmic Rendition

I

Give heed, my child, lift your eyes, behold the one who is standing here;
Behold, my child! waiting here to bring the gift of food to you.
Give heed, my child. Look! Grass now waits to bring to you gift of food.

II

Give-heed, my child, lift your eyes, behold the one who is flying here;
Behold, my child! flying here to bring the gift of food to you.
Give heed, my child. Look! Grass now flies to bring to you gift of food.

III

Give heed, my child, lift your eyes, behold the one who is touching here;
Behold, my child! touching here your head to bring the gift of food.
Give heed, my child. Look! Grass now touching brings to you gift of food.

IV

Give heed, my child, lift your eyes, behold the one who now follows here.
Behold, my child! Now it follows the paths where the gods descend.
Give heed, my child. Look! Grass now down the four straight paths brings its
     gift.

V

Give heed, my child, lift your eyes, behold the one who is spreading here;
Behold, my child! spreading plenty o'er you, promised gift of food.
Give heed, my child. Look! Grass is spreading o'er you gift of food.

VI

Give heed, my child, lift your eyes, behold the one who has brought you food.
Behold, my child! Food you have received, and finished is the task.
Give heed, my child. Look! Grass has now here brought you the gift of food.

PART II. ANOINTING THE CHILD

The order of the opening song is followed still further in the anointing of the child.

The seventh stanza of the opening song speaks of Kusharu, the holy place, set apart for the observance of rites. The Ku'rahus explained that "the first act of a man" must be to set apart such a place, "where new life could be given." Following this order, the child was anointed and by this act of consecration set apart as the center of the rites which were to follow.

The song of this act follows the rhythm of the two preceding.

---

[a] Music on page 219.

Diagram of Time

Rhythmic Rendition

I

Give heed, my child, lift your eyes, behold the one who is standing here,
Behold, my child! waiting now to fit and set you here apart.
Give heed, my child.   Look!   Sacred ointment now is here come to you.

II

Give heed, my child, lift your eyes, behold the one who is flying here,
Behold, my child! flying here to make a consecrated child.
Give heed, my child.   Look!   Ointment flies to consecrate you, my child.

III

Give heed, my child, lift your eyes, behold the one who is touching here,
Behold, my child! touching here your head, as consecrating you.
Give heed, my child.   Look!   Sacred ointment touches upon your head.

IV

Give heed, my child, lift your eyes, behold the one who now follows here.
Behold, my child!   Now the paths it follows, paths where the gods descend.
Give heed, my child.   Look!   Ointment down the four straight paths comes to you.

V

Give heed, my child, lift your eyes, behold the one who is spreading here.
Behold, my child!   Sacred ointment, spreading, consecrates you.
Give heed, my child.   Look!   Sacred ointment over you spreads its power.

VI

Give heed, my child, lift your eyes, behold the one who has holy made.
Behold, my child!   You are set apart, and finished is the task.
Give heed, my child.   Look!   Sacred ointment now has set you apart.

PART III.   PAINTING THE CHILD

The red paint put on the child's head and face symbolized the
dawn, the rising sun.   The color was spread over the entire face to
represent "the full radiance of the sun," "giving to the child its
vigor of life."

The song and the rest of the songs of this ritual are in the same
rhythm as the preceding.

Diagram of Time

---

a Music on page 223.   b Music on page 227.

Rhythmic Rendition

I

Give heed, my child, lift your eyes, behold the one who is standing here,
Behold, my child! waiting here to bring the gift of life to you.
Give heed, my child.   Look!   Red paint waits, the vigor of life to bring.

II

Give heed, my child, lift your eyes, behold the one who is flying here,
Behold, my child! flying here to bring the gift of life to you.
Give heed, my child.   Look!   Red paint flies, the vigor of life to bring.

III

Give heed, my child, lift your eyes, behold the one who is touching here,
Behold, my child! touching here your head to bring the gift of life.
Give heed, my child.   Look!   Red paint touches, the vigor of life to bring.

IV

Give heed, my child, lift your eyes, behold the one who now follows here.
Behold, my child!   Now the path it follows, paths where gods descend.
Give heed, my child.   Look!   Red paint follows, vigor of life to bring.

V

Give heed, my child, lift your eyes, behold the one who is spreading here,
Behold, my child! over you is spread the glowing gift of life.
Give heed, my child.   See!   Red paint brings the vigor of life to you.

VI

Give heed, my child, lift your eyes, behold the one who has brought you life.
Behold, my child!   Life you have received and finished is the task.
Give heed, my child.   Look!   Red paint leaves the vigor of life with you.

The next act was the painting of the child's face with blue, the color of the sky, the abode of Tira'wa atius.

The design outlined by the water, the grass, the ointment, and the red paint was now clearly seen—an arch, crossing the forehead and resting on the cheeks, from the middle of which a line was drawn downward on the nose.   This design was said to "picture the face of Tira'wa."   The arch was the dome of the sky, his abode; the line, falling from the zenith, was the breath of Tira'wa descending on the child, meeting its breath.

We are told that this design came from the constellation Corona Borealis and was the insignia of a chief, as he who leads does so by the authority of Tira'wa and must bear his sign on the face.   In this ceremony this design, taken in connection with the symbols next placed on the child, seems to represent the presence of the power, "the father of all things."

SONG[a]

Diagram of Time

Rhythmic Rendition

I

Give heed, my child, lift your eyes, behold the one who is standing here,
Behold, my child! waiting here to make the sign of him above.
Give heed, my child.   Look!   Blue paint waits to bring to you sign of him

II

Give heed, my child, lift your eyes, behold the one who is flying here,
Behold, my child! flying here to make the sign of him above.
Give heed, my child.   Look!   Blue paint flies to bring to you sign of him.

III

Give heed, my child, lift your eyes, behold the one who is touching here,
Behold, my child! touching here to make the sign of him above.
Give heed, my child.   Look!   Blue paint touches, bringing you sign of him.

IV

Give heed, my child, lift your eyes, behold the one who now follows here.
Behold, my child! tracing here the arching dome, his dwelling place.
Give heed, my child.   Look!   Blue paint makes the line of the breath of life.

V

Give heed, my child, lift your eyes, behold the one who is spreading here,
Behold, my child! spreading on your face the sacred lines of blue.
Give heed, my child.   Look!   Sacred now the picture the blue paint makes.

VI

Give heed, my child, lift your eyes, behold the one who has brought the sign,
Behold, my child! brought to you the sign.   Accomplished now the task.
Give heed, my child.   Look!   Blue paint now has left with you sign of him.

PART IV.   PUTTING ON THE SYMBOLS

Eagle down was next put upon the head of the child.   The down
was taken from under the wing, "close to the heart" of "the white
eagle, the father of the child," so representing the eagle's "breath
and life."   It also typified the high, light clouds, and when the child's
head was covered with it the Ku'rahus said: "The head of the consecrated child now rests in the soft white clouds which float near the
dwelling place of Tira'wa atius."

It is noticeable that the song of this act has five stanzas, indicating
the five motions, the four directions and the above.

FIRST SONG[a]

Diagram of Time

_ _ _ _ .. / _ _ _ _ _ _ _ _ _
_ _ _ _ .. _ _ _ _ _ _ _ _ _ _
_ _ _ _ .. .. _ _ _ _ _ _ _ _ _

Rhythmic Rendition

I

Give heed, my child, lift your eyes, behold the one who is standing here,
Behold, my child! waiting here to bring the sign of clouds above.
Give heed, my child. Look! Down of eagle waits with the sign of clouds.

II

Give heed, my child, lift your eyes, behold the one who is flying here,
Behold, my child! flying here to bring the sign of clouds to you.
Give heed, my child. Look! Down of eagle flies with the sign of clouds.

III

Give heed, my child, lift your eyes, behold the one who is touching here,
Behold, my child! touching here your head to bring the sign of clouds.
Give heed, my child. Look! Down of eagle touches and brings the clouds.

IV

Give heed, my child, lift your eyes, behold the one who is dropping here,
Behold, my child! drops on you the sign of fleecy clouds above.
Give heed, my child. Look! Sacred symbol dropping upon your head.

V

Give heed, my child, lift your eyes, behold the one who has laid on you,
Behold, my child! sign of fleecy clouds that near Tira'wa float.
Give heed, my child. Look! Rests on you sign of the clouds above.

With the following song a white downy feather was tied on the head of the child. The Ku'rahus said: "This feather, which is ever moving, as if it were breathing, represents Tira'wa, who dwells beyond the blue sky which is above the soft white clouds."

This feather was double; it had a little plume like a branch, to stand for the child. The larger feather symbolized Tira'wa.

The song has five stanzas like the preceding.

SECOND SONG[b]

Diagram of Time

_ _ _ _ .. / _ _ _ _ _ _ _ _ _
_ _ _ _ .. _ _ _ _ _ _ _ _ _ _
_ _ _ _ .. .. _ _ _ _ _ _ _ _ _

Rhythmic Rendition

I

Give heed, my child, lift your eyes, behold the one who is standing here,
Behold, my child! waiting here to bring the last great gift to you.
Give heed, my child. Look! Waits to bring the emblem the Father sends.

---

[a] Music on page 235.   [b] Music on page 238.

II

Give heed, my child, lift your eyes, behold the one who is flying here,
Behold, my child! flying here to bring the last great gift to you.
Give heed, my child. Look! Flies to bring the emblem the Father sends.

III

Give heed, my child, lift your eyes, behold the one who is touching you,
Behold, my child! with the last great gift touching now your head;
Give heed, my child. Look! Touches with the emblem the Father sends.

IV

Give heed, my child, lift your eyes, behold the one who is placing here,
Behold, my child! on your head is placing now the sonship sign;
Give heed, my child. Look! Placing there the emblem the Father sends.

V

Give heed, my child, lift your eyes, behold the one who has left on you,
Behold, my child! left on you Tira'wa's breathing feather sign.
Give heed, my child. Look! On you rests the emblem the Father sent.

When the child was thus decorated, it was told to look at the reflection of its face in the bowl of water. To quote the words of the Ku'rahus: "The little child looks upon the water and sees its own likeness, as it will see that likeness in its children and children's children. The face of Tira'wa is there also, giving promise that the life of the child shall go on, as the water flows over the land."

After this prophetic view, a black covering was put over the child's head. The symbols were not for the people to see; they were holy and belonged only to the powers.

In the final disposition of the water remaining in the bowl there is a hint of other and older rites, fragments of which appear in the Hako ceremony.

EIGHTEENTH RITUAL. FULFILMENT PREFIGURED

PART I. MAKING THE NEST

During the singing of the next song the movements of the feathered stems simulated the flight of eagles. The white eagle passed through the line of warriors by the south, the masculine side of the lodge, and the brown eagle by the north, the feminine side. The white eagle flew back and forth in front of the warriors, enacting the protecting duty of the male, while the brown eagle flew to the fireplace and made a circle, a nest, at each of the four directions.

The location of these four nests, corresponding to the four paths, indicated a desire that the powers might descend on them. This desire was also manifested by the outlining of the circles with down, the symbol of the high clouds "which float near the abode of Tira'wa." The bits of fat dropped within the circles were not only a prayer for plenty, but also a promise that the prayer would be granted. The

oriole's nest represented security.   The four circles around the fire as
made by the Ku'rahus carrying the brown-feathered stem pictured to
the Pawnees the promise of children, the gifts of plenty and of peace
from the powers above.

SONG a

Diagram of Time

Rhythmic Rendition

Behold where two eagles come forth!
Now they soar high over head;
See where one flies, watching flies, guarding he
His mate who has gone to her nest, dropping there;
'Tis Kawas who brings there new life.

PART II.   SYMBOLIC FULFILMENT

The little child was put within each of these prophetic circles, its
feet touching the nest and the promised plenty.   Four times it was
taken around the fireplace and each time it touched the four circles.
The child was covered during the act of putting its feet in the nest.
This act symbolized the birth of children, a mystery to man, as "only
Tira'wa could know when generation would take place."

This simulated fulfilment of the promise of the Hako completed
the sequence of acts in the drama of birth.

SONG b

Diagram of Time

Rhythmic Rendition

Within the nest the child rests its little feet,
Awaiting there the gift sent by gods above;
Descending there to him comes the promised life.

PART III.   THANK OFFERING

The offering of sweet smoke followed immediately.   As the smoke
ascended all the articles of the Hako were waved through it, the child
was touched with it, and all the people passed their hands through it.
The sweet smoke offering was given that the powers above might

---

a Music on page 242.   b Music on page 245.

know that the ceremony had been carried out in accordance with the teachings given to the fathers in the visions.   Its odor reached the abode of Tira'wa, bearing the touch of all faithful participants in the rite.

After the offering of smoke all traces of the nests were obliterated, the coals used for the offering of smoke were returned to the fire, and the lodge once more was open to all the people.

THIRD DIVISION.   THE DANCE OF THANKS

NINETEENTH RITUAL

PART I.   THE CALL TO THE CHILDREN

The purpose of the rite was recognized by the important place given to children in this part of the ceremony.   The ponies presented to the Fathers were each lead up by a little child; the acting out of a man's warlike deeds was to honor his child, and the little child with the black covering upon its head and the picture of Tira'wa upon its face received, with the chief, the gifts as they were presented.

In every instance the child was the tie between the two groups, the Fathers and the Children.

FIRST SONG a

Diagram of Time

Rhythmic Rendition

Harken!   List!   We are calling you.   Come!   Come!   Children, come!
Come!   We're ready and waiting, your Father's waiting.   Come!   Children, come!
Hear us calling, calling you!   Children, come!
Children, come!   Come hither!
Harken!   List as we call you, call to the Children to come.

SECOND SONG b

Diagram of Time

---

a Music on page 249.   b Music on page 250.

Rhythmic Rendition

Ready and waiting, we call you, loud we call you, loudly call;
"Come to us, Children," call we loudly, call we long; Oh, come!
Come! Come! Come!
Hear us calling, calling, Children! Oh, come!
Hear us calling, come to us here! Come!

THIRD SONG a

Diagram of Time

```
_ __ .. _ .. _ .. _ / _ /
_ __ .. _ .. _ .. _ / _ _ _
_ __ .. _ / _ _ _
_ _ .. _ ..
.. _ .. _ .. _ ./. _ .. _ .. _ .. _ _
_ __ .. _ _ _ _ _ / _ _
_ _ .. _ _ _
```

Rhythmic Rendition

Look, where they come, see them, see them, young ones and old ones!
Look! Here they come, this way, that way flocking together.
Hither they come, shouting like eagles,
Shouting come.
Joyous, happy, gladly come they, gaily coming, coming hither.
See where they come, flocking like birds, shouting like eagles
As they come to the Fathers.

PART II. THE DANCE AND THE RECEPTION OF GIFTS

The two young men as they danced waved high above their heads
the feathered stems and simulated by their movements the flying and
sporting of birds. The lightness and beauty of this final dance can
never be forgotten by one who has been so fortunate as to see it well
executed.

DANCE SONG b

Diagram of Time

```
_. _ _ _ _, _ _ _ _ _, _ _ _ _ _ .. ..
_. _ _ _ _, _ _ _ _ _, _ _ _ _ _, _ _ _ _ .. ..
_ _ _ _ _, _ _ _ _ _, _ _ _ _ _, _ _ _ _ .. ..
_ _ _ _ _
```

DANCE SONG c

Diagram of Time

```
_ . ___ _ _ _ _
_ . ___ _ _ _ __ _ ___ _ _ _
_ . ___ _ _ _, _ ___ _ _ _
_ . ___ _ _ _, __ . ___ _ _ _
_ . ___ _ _ _ _ __ _ ___ _ _ _
```

FOURTH DIVISION.　PRESENTATION OF THE HAKO

TWENTIETH RITUAL

PART I.　BLESSING THE CHILD

At the close of the dance and the reception of gifts by the Fathers, the little child was again taken to the holy place and once more touched with the Hako upon all sides, from the east, the south, the west, and the north.

The song accompanying these movements was "a prayer to call down the breath of Tira'wa" upon the child that had been consecrated.

SONG *a*

Diagram of Time

Rythmic Rendition

Breathe on him!
Breathe on him!
Life thou alone canst give to him.
Long life, we pray, Oh Father, give unto him!

PART II.　PRESENTING THE HAKO TO THE SON AND THANKS TO THE CHILDREN

The Father (the chief) then removed the emblems from the face of the child, using for the purpose the fur of the wildcat, and took the covering and the symbols from its head.　These with the Hako he rolled together within the wildcat skin and placed the bundle in the arms of the child.

The Hako, which had been the medium of bringing the promises, was carried by the recipient of these promises, the little child, to its father, the Son, who received them from the hands of his offspring.

The tie had now been formed, and the little child was released from its symbolic duties and ran out into the sunlight to join its playmates. Within the lodge the Fathers thanked the Children, and the people departed to their daily avocations.

While the various articles of the Hako were generally scattered at the close of the ceremony, the two feathered stems were preserved intact and frequently passed from tribe to tribe as long as they held together.　Sometimes the Son was unwilling to part with those presented him, so, when he inaugurated a party, he had a new set made with the proper ceremony.　At all times and under all conditions the feathered stems were never handled carelessly, but were treated with respect and their sacred character was remembered.　During the entire time Tahi'rŭssawichi was engaged upon this ceremony he never allowed

---

a Music on p. 257.

the feathered stems to be placed on the floor or laid upon a chair;
they were always carefully deposited on the wildcat skin with a
decorum that was not once abated.

The Hako ceremony seems to have been peculiarly adapted to
impress the mind of the people and to win their confidence and affection.   It was picturesque, varied in movement, and communal in
feeling.   Its songs were rhythmic and attractive, and frequently
choral in form, particularly those belonging to the public ceremony,
where all, young and old, joined in the melody as the feathered stems
were swayed over their heads when the Ku'rahus and his assistants
made the circuits of the lodge.

The teachings of the public ceremony were general in character.
They emphasized, on the one hand, man's dependence on the supernatural for all the gifts of life, and on the other hand, his dependence
on the family tie for the gifts of peace and happiness.   The specific
teachings were reserved for the Son.   These began in the ritual to
the Dawn (tenth ritual) on the morning of the second and third days,
which prefigured the secret ceremonies of the fifth morning, when the
bond of the family relation was extended beyond blood kinship through
the symbolic rites which recognized the common source of life in
Tira'wa atius.

Looking over the entire ceremony, it is interesting to note how older
rites have had their share in the development of the Hako, and how
the trend of thought among the native seers has borne them toward a
conception of the brotherhood of man, a conception recognized as the
noblest known to the human family.

INCIDENTAL RITUALS

COMFORTING THE CHILD

The incidental rituals could be called for and given during the
public ceremony.

The three songs which belong to the first ritual have a common
musical motive, but this motive is treated differently in each song
so as to conform to the movement of the ceremony.

The appeal of the parents to the Ku'rahus is in the first song passed
on to Kawas.   It is sung by the Ku'rahus at the holy place as he
waves the brown-eagle feathered stem.   The words are in the nature
of a prayer, the music has the swing of a lullaby.

FIRST SONG a

Diagram of Time

Rhythmic Rendition

Kawas, harken; thy baby is crying!
It grieveth, wailing and weeping and crying so sore.
Ah! It cries, crieth so sorely;
Kawas, hasten, thy little one cryeth so sore.

The second song was sung as the Ku′rahus and his assistant walked toward the child. In the music one hears the coming of Tira′wa in the footsteps of his creatures, both great and small.

SECOND SONG*a*

Diagram of Time

```
__  ..    ..    ..   __  __  _
   ..   __   ..   __  __      .....
 _ __  ...  ..   ..  __  __    ..
   ..   __   ..   __  __  __  _
```

Rhythmic Rendition

Father cometh, now he cometh;
See him, little one; hark! his footsteps!
With him, see! coming are the eagles,
All are coming now to thee.

The third song is sung as the brown-eagle feathered stem is waved over the little child, who "looks up and smiles."

The caressing, almost playful, rhythm of the music twines about the religious feeling expressed in the words like the arms of an infant about the neck of its thougtful, reverent parent.

THIRD SONG*b*

Diagram of Time

```
__  _  ..  __  __  _  __  __  __
__  _  __  __  __  _  __  /  /  ____
__  __  __  __  _  __  __  __  _
__  _  __  ..  __  /  _  /  __  _
```

Rhythmic Rendition

I

Look, my child, who is coming unto you;
Look up, my little one, now your trouble goes away, away;
Look! Above you flies one who guards you,
Whose presence brings you joy. Now your sorrow has departed.

II

Ah, you look! See the eagles flying over you.
From up above they come, from the clear blue sky where Father dwells;
They to you this peace-bringing solace give.
A happy little child now is smiling here light-hearted.

---

a Music on page 262.　　　　*b* Music on page 263.

PRAYER TO AVERT STORMS

SONG a

Diagram of Time

PRAYER FOR THE GIFT OF CHILDREN

FIRST SONG b

Diagram of Time and Rhythm

SECOND SONG c

Diagram of Time

THIRD SONG d

Diagram of Time

FOURTH SONG e

Diagram of Time

CHANGING A MAN'S NAME

Before the graphophone record was taken the Ku'rahus engaged in silent prayer, after which he entoned the ritual. Rather a high pitch was taken for the recital, probably from habit, as the ritual was always given in the hearing of a multitude.

The words were separated into syllables. Sometimes an entire word or parts of two words were represented by a single syllable, and each syllable in the ritual was uttered as though it were a complete word.

Mr Murie spent three days in the translation and study of the ritual, assisted by the Ku'rahus, who explained many points that were somewhat obscure, owing to elisions, the employment of a single word as a mnemonic to call up the picture of a complicated action, and the forcing of words to a different application from that of ordinary speech—a not uncommon occurrence in rituals. The latter carefully watched the work lest mistakes should be made, remarking that the ritual "speaks of the powers above, of whom man should be careful what he says."

There is one aspect of the ritual, essential to its understanding, that was carefully explained by the Ku'rahus, and the substance of many conversations on the subject follows. A man's life is an onward movement. If one has within him a determined purpose and seeks the help of the powers his life will "climb up." Here the Ku'rahus made a gesture indicating a line slanting upward; then he arrested the movement and, still holding his hand where he had stopped, went on to say that as a man is climbing up he does something that marks a place in his life where the powers have given him the opportunity to express in acts his peculiar endowments, so this place, this act, forms a stage in his career, and he takes a new name to indicate that he is on a level different from that which he occupied previously. Some men, he said, can rise only a little way, others live on a dead level, and he illustrated his words by moving his hands horizontally. Men having power to advance, climb step by step, and here again he made his idea plain by a gesture picturing a slant, then a level, a slant, and a level. In this connection he called attention to the words, in line 1359, "rutu'rahwitz pari," "to overtake walking," saying that the people who desire to have a name, or to change their name, must strive to overtake in the walk of life an upper level, such a one as these ancient men spoken of in the ritual had reached, where they threw away the names by which they had been known before. "Rutu'rahwitz pari," is a call to the Pawnees, bidding them emulate these men and overtake them by the doing of like deeds.

Three facts connected with the Pawnee custom of taking a new name should be stated:

First. A man was permitted to take a name only after the performance of an act indicative of ability or strength of character.

Second. The name had to be assumed openly before the people to whom the act it commemorated was known.

Third. It was necessary that it should be announced in connection with such a ritual as that here given.

These facts indicate (1) that a man's name stood for what he had shown himself to be in the light of his actions; (2) that this was recognized by his tribesmen; and (3) that it was proclaimed by one having in charge the mediatory rites through which man could be approached by the supernatural.

The ritual is in three parts. The first gives a brief narration of the institution of the custom of changing the name in consequence of some new achievement. The second shows how the man was enabled to accomplish this act. It began with his lonely vigil and fast, when he cried to the powers for help. The scene then shifts to the circle of the lesser powers, who, in council, deliberate on the petition which makes its way to them and gains their consent. Then the Winds summon the messengers, and these, gathering at the lesser powers' command, are sent to earth to the man crying in lonely places, to grant his desire. This part closes with a few vivid words which set forth that only by the favor and help of the powers had the man been able to do the deed. The third deals with the man's names, the one to be discarded and the one now to be assumed.

This dramatic poem is in a rhythmic form impossible to reproduce in English; neither is a literal translation adequate to convey its meaning, since a single word sometimes represents a complex action, to the understanding of which a knowledge of the customs and beliefs of the tribe is essential. The terseness of expression was also intended to close the meaning to the uninitiated, keeping it sacred from the common people. Although the form of the following rhythmic rendition could not be determined as heretofore by musical phrases, the English version contains nothing which is not in the original text explained and amplified by the Ku'rahus.

Rhythmic Rendition of Pawnee Text

1358 Harken! 'Twas thus it came to pass:
     In ancient days, a Leader and his men
     Walked this wide earth, man's vast abode
     Roofed by the heavens, where dwell the gods.[a]
     They reached a place, the spot no man can tell,
     Faced dangers dread, and vanquished them:
     Then, standing as if born anew to life,
     Each warrior threw away the name
     That had been his ere yet these deeds were done.

1359 Harken! The Leader and his men
     Made there the Vict'ry Song, and set the mark
     Ye must o'ertake, if ye would be like them!

1360 Harken! The Leader and his men
     Turned then toward home. Their Vict'ry Song
     Proclaimed them near; the village rose,
     Looked toward the hill, where on the top
     Stood the brave men singing their Song,
     Heralding thus the favor of the gods
     By which they had surpassed all former deeds,
     Made new their claim to be accounted men.

---

[a] Gods, meaning powers, is used solely on account of the rhythm.

1361 Harken! And whence, think ye, was borne
      Unto these men courage to dare,
      Strength to endure hardship and war?
      Mark well my words, as I reveal
      How the gods help man's feebleness.
      The Leader of these warriors was a man
      Given to prayer.   Oft he went forth
      Seeking a place no one could find,
      There would he stand, and lift his voice
      Fraught with desire, that he might be
      Invincible, a bulwark 'gainst all foes
      Threat'ning his tribe, causing them fear.
      Nighttime and day this cry sped on,
      Traveling far, seeking to reach—
  Harken!   Those places far above—
  Harken!   Within the circle vast
      Where sit the gods, watching o'er men.

1362 Harken!   This poor man's prayer went on,
      Speeding afar into the blue
      Heavens above, reached there the place—
  Harken!   Where dwell the lesser gods—
  Harken!   And great Tira′wa, mightier than all!

1363 Harken!   It was because a god
      Received this prayer, considered it,
      Favored its plea, and passed it on
      To him whose place was next, in that grand ring,
      Who, in his turn received the prayer,
      Considered it, and sent it on—
  Harken!   Around that circle vast—
  Harken!   Where sit the gods above.

1364 Harken!   And thus it was the prayer
      Sent by this man won the consent
      Of all the gods.   For each god in his place
      Speaks out his thought, grants or rejects
      Man's suppliant cry, asking for help;
      But none can act until the Council grand
      Comes to accord, thinks as one mind,
      Has but one will, all must obey.
  Harken!   The Council gave consent—
  Harken!   And great Tira′wa, mightier than all.

1365 Harken!   To make their purpose known,
      Succor and aid freely to give,
      Heralds were called, called by the Winds;
      Then in the west uprose the Clouds
      Heavy and black, ladened with storm.
      Slowly they climbed, dark'ning the skies;
      While close on every side the Thunders marched
      On their dread way, 'till all were come
      To where the gods in stately Council sat
      Waiting for them.   Then, bade them go
      Back to the earth, carrying aid
      To him whose prayer had reached their circle vast.
      This mandate given, the Thunders turned toward earth,
      Taking their course slantwise the sky.

1366 Harken!   Another followed hard—
    Lightning broke forth out of the Cloud,
    Zizzag and dart, cleaving their way
    Slantwise to earth, their goal to reach.

1367 Harken!   For these two were not all
    That hastened to proclaim the gods' behest;
    Swift on their wings, Swallows in flocks
    Swept in advance, ranging the path,
    Black breasts and red, yellow, and white,
    Flying about, clearing the way
    For those who bore the message of the gods
    Granting the man courage to dare,
    Strength to endure, power to stand
    Invincible, a bulwark gainst all foes.

1368 Harken!   'Twas thus it came to pass:
    The Leader grasped the help sent by the gods;
    Henceforth he walked steadfast and strong,
    Leading his men through dangers drear,
    Knowing that naught could strike at him
    To whom the gods had promised victory.

1369 Attend!   Once more I change his name!

1370 Harken!   Riruts'katit, it was
    We used to call him by, a name he won
    Long days ago, marking an act
    Well done by him, but now passed by.

1371 Harken!   To-day all men shall say—

1372 Harken!   His act has lifted him
    Where all his tribe behold a man
1373 Clothed with new fame, strong in new strength,
    Gained by his deeds, blessed by the gods.

Harken!   Shaku'ru Wa'rukste shall he be called.

INDEX